THE WAY
of
ONE
and
The Fate of a World Divided

A Message from The Universal Source
` of Paul Solomon
For An Age on the Edge of Apocalypse

———

W. Alexander Wheeler

First published in 2018
By The Paul Solomon Foundation, Ireland.

ISBN-10: 1717009042
ISBN-13: 978-1717009043

Cover design by Adam Wheeler
adamfwheeler@gmail.com
Book production by BanbaDesign
www.banbadesign.com

To order additional copies, please contact:
The Paul Solomon Foundation Ltd.
www.paulsolomon.com
info@paulsolomon.com
Also available from Amazon
www.amazon.com

Disclaimer About Medical Information:

The medical information and reference materials contained in this book are intended solely for the general information of the reader. It is not to be used for treatment purposes, but rather for discussion with the patient's own physician.

The information presented here is not intended to diagnose health problems or to take the place of professional medical care. The information contained herein is neither intended to dictate what constitutes reasonable, appropriate or best care for any given health issue, nor is it intended to be used as a substitute for the independent judgment of a physician for any given health issue.

Contents

Part One

Theophany Of Love

Part Two

In The Image Of God

Part Three

Suspended Between Two Worlds

Part Four

Awakening: From The Beast To The Gods

Part Five

New Earth/New Eden

Acknowledgements

To Paul,

To your life,

To your Source.

———————————

I am indebted to Grace DeRond for allowing me to quote liberally from her professionally and superbly edited work *The Wisdom of Solomon*, a collection of Paul Solomon's public lectures and Source Readings.

Thanks are also due to Gerry Rice and Mary Siobhan McGibbon who are the very faithful curators, executive administrators, editors, and the very life's blood of The Paul Solomon Foundation, which can be found at: www.PaulSolomon.com.

A warm tribute as well to Al and Susan Miner for their generous permission to make use of the Lama Sing Readings (www.lamasing.org) in the context of this work.

And especial thanks to Nancy for your tireless long hours in preparing the draft of this text, and to both she and Squeek for all of their patient, longsuffering, and loving support.

Prologue

To some writers there falls the difficult task of bridging two worlds: one the world as seen from the ordinarily trance-like perspective of our consensually conditioned and fabricated reality; the other an intrinsic world that extends beyond the limitations of time, matter, and cultural agreement. The book here assembled invites the reader to step out of the mechanically habituated patterns of one's thinking to see the world and oneself from an unlimited perspective. It explores some very fundamental issues about the state of the world that has resulted from our mindlessness and irresponsibility along with the ominous direction toward which we and the world are currently headed because of it. And it gives revelations and understandings from the infinite and unlimited "Source" or Universal Mind of Paul Solomon as to why we are cut off from our own higher consciousness while at the same time providing methods and means of freeing ourselves and awakening from our collective pathological tendencies and the well-rationalized lunacies that threaten the very near future both of the planet and our human species.

Over twenty years ago I wrote a book based on the Paul Solomon Readings which addressed many of these issues. *The Prophetic Revelations of Paul Solomon: Earthward Toward a Heavenly Light* may have appeared twenty years too early. Its words fell upon deaf ears and upon minds too wedded to a life of unrequited consumerism, comfort, and pure self-indulgence to be capable of responding to its urgency in any committed or conscientious way. The book now before you has perhaps the opposite defect: it appears twenty years too late. Even for those who share its faith and effectively apply its truths in their own lives, the time for altering the currents of our consciousness on a much wider if not global scale may be too long overdue. Nevertheless, as many of the things imparted herein by the Source are to be grasped and tested in one's own personal experience, our aim will be achieved if at least a few of the readers of this book have found it to be a useful guide to their own conscious freedom and awakening to self-knowledge.

The prophetic import of the earlier book thus far has become apparent only by degrees, seeping into our consciousness piecemeal over a period of twenty-three years. Out of a concern at least for the degraded state of our planetary environment, remedial efforts are currently being made. This book, commissioned by the Source Itself, opens us to a whole new dimension not only of the spiritual and psychological climate which characterizes the modern world, but of our involvement for bringing it about and our responsibility for changing it. It is a singularly unique work. But in order to provide interpretive relevance and continuity to its thesis, certain extended excerpts from the earlier book have, where applicable, found their way into the body of its text. While some readers may find this to be a less than prudent approach, I can only assure you that it was not done casually, nor was it in any way intended merely as a recapitulation of earlier themes. It is absolutely necessary to the presentation of an entirely new message, one the Source regards as critical to the future of our world.

Divided into five main sections, the book works toward bringing to our aware-ness the unity of our being, both individually and as a race collectively, in the light of an all-pervasive, all-encompassing sacred substance or single Truth. Part one lays the foundation for a philosophical and scientifically theoretical understanding of the single omnipresent, eternal, boundless, and immutable principle or "Law" of which the Source speaks. Part Two brings this time-less principle to earth and applies it to our antediluvian past and our own planetary evolution. Part Three: it is only when we have assimilated all of this foreground experience that we can perhaps begin to approach an understand-ing of the spiritual malaise of a modern world grounded in violence, greed, and fear, and, consequently, the apocalyptic conditions that we now face. Part Four explores how we, out of our own best intentions, have contributed to the life-denying force of fear and how we might reach a higher transcendental san-ity to match the need of our time. In holding this Universal Law to be a model of sanity, Part Five indicates a path of revolutionary change that spreads not with arms or insurrection, but one that moves along the depth dimension of our innermost nature to re-establish our common ground of unity with each other and with the creative force of all Life, Love, and Truth.

The Readings of the Source are of such far-reaching relevance that they could change drastically our image of human nature, of culture and history, and of reality. But because a work of this nature, given its breadth and scope, can hardly hope to give "equal time" for all contending points of view, I did not want to burden it by lengthy justifications simply in order to make certain of the Source Readings appear more acceptable to those less willing to accept the truth. The credibility of the Source must stand on its own. Whatever errors and inadvertencies there are in this book are wholly the responsibility of the author.

W. Alexander Wheeler

Introduction

We are all fragmented and finite creatures, each of us isolated from the other, all subject to death --- a fact that would seem to render meaningless our lives individually and our experience collectively. Underneath the infinite flow of our being, however, beyond our perishable egos, gleams one fundamental truth, one creative principle or force that unites us all into one harmonious universe of a single piece. Every manifest thing owes its existence to this single creative force, and at the very seat of human reality, at our "Source", inheres the universe to which we all belong. Paul Solomon taught us that the universe involves us in the most extraordinarily magnificent way possible: the universe *is* us --- we *are* the universe. By consciously awakening to our source, we can in fact wed its wisdom of life to our knowledge of living and open ourselves to the world of spirit, the Logos, the Word of our very origin.

Paul Solomon rose to international fame through simple "word of mouth" from those who had been fortunate enough to hear the words spoken from the "I AM" Source of his own inner consciousness. The Source was *not* and is *not* an entity of any sort, but rather the expression of intelligent infinity as it is brought forth into intelligent energy from the universal Christ Presence Itself. For Solomon himself it was the Ark of the Covenant; it was the gate of Heaven through which one could pass beyond the space-time continuum in which the ego is trapped and into infinity and the unity of everything. In his trance state Solomon became "awakened" to all knowledge available to the whole of humanity and to eternal realities beyond in the way that one uses a library, but instantaneously. It is as if somewhere in eternity there is a kind of storehouse of all knowledge where the universe yields up its secrets --- of medicine, mathematics, physics, of every individual life and of all creation --- to those few super-intelligences able to climb up there and retrieve it. Solomon was one of these, and to those who were in the presence of the Source it was as if the voice of the universe itself was speaking. Once asked of the Source, "Does God speak through you?", the Source answered, **We would say to you, no. Understand this: we speak to you through God. The Source comes through you, through God to you, and becomes blessed of God** (Solomon Reading No. 9, 3/22/72).

Solomon's clairvoyance passed many rigorous pragmatic tests. His advice was sought eventually by major medical and educational institutions and universities and by world governments where findings from his "Readings", his teachings, and his lectures have been published in more than fifty journals and periodicals in many different languages. And although he had not fought in wars, explored mountains and jungles, battled in politics, or accumulated vast wealth, he was a man who fought nonetheless, to free the children, the orphans and teenage sex slaves of Thailand, and who for that reason was nominated for the Nobel Peace Prize in 1993.

While often misrepresented and misunderstood, Paul Solomon left the posthumous legacy of being a man of mysterious and extraordinary talents, of brilliant ability, of generous instincts, of kindliest nature, and one whose sincere desire it was to do his God-given (literally speaking) duty faithfully and stren-uously in behalf of all mankind. For he was first and foremost remembered as a prophet of the age now before us. Having appeared at the darkest hour of our sorest need, he came to sound a warning that the time for change in hu-man conduct is tenuously short, and to kindle in others the same enthusiasm for a one-world family that animated himself.

If our intended destination is the top of a mountain, then prophecy is like a topo-graphical map that form a 'bird's-eye view' indicates to us the path of least resist-ance. But it tells us that we must first pass through the abyss before we can begin our ascent. Paul Solomon was among the most precient and remarkable of all map makers of our day, both for his ability to chart the furthest horizons for our reality and from them to render infinite vistas of meaning. It was only upon reaching a delta state of deep sleep, in which awareness of all sensory perception totally van-ishes into the higher multidimensional field of the timeless and spaceless implicate, that the whole of the Source Mind poured through him, revealing to us from its 'God's-eye-view' the pattern and purpose of our forthcoming trials and illuminat-ing for us the path of our ascent. Through wave after wave of revelation it imparts with indubitable certainty not only that we are in the "last days of the earth," but like a kind of itinerary it maps for us the conditions governing every proph-esied step in our procession through the formidable and terrifying landscape of an immanent tribulation to the New Eden that lies beyond. Seeing that the possible courses of action are many and that our days for acting are numbered, the Source Readings inform us that the tragedy or triumph of our world lies in the power we possess to interact with the prophetic warnings that have been given, and in the extent to which we are able to embody rather than merely ritualistically mimic through doctrines and dogma the life-affirming power of One.

Through over twenty years of Readings or messages from his Source, Solomon taught us that the universe --- life and death, love and fear, God and humanity --- makes sense. In a period of history left mutilated by war and reduced to merely an objective reality shaped by a predominantly scientific culture, the twentieth century needed such an affirmation. Like Edgar Cayce before him, Paul Solomon believed that the best way to realize that affirmation is to real-ize oneself.

Just as Edgar Cayce himself was universally acknowledged to be among the great prophets of the world, so Cayce did not pass on before naming his suc-cessor. In a 1931 reading pertaining to the leadership of the Association for Research and Enlightenment (A.R.E.), the foundation established less than a year later in 1932 to preserve the Cayce readings, the sleeping Cayce stated: The leader will always be that one through whom the information comes, whether Edgar Cayce or others that may be chosen to carry on --- as Paul will enter in --- with the work." (Cayce Reading No. 254-53) The term "information" was nearly always used --- rarely the term "readings" --- both by Cayce himself and by Cayce's "Universal Mind". Thus, "that one through whom the information comes" clearly refers to that one through whom the "Greater Mind" or "Uni-versal Mind" delivers itself through the "readings". * Cayce's promise that "Paul

* Ursula Jahoda, "Should We Work With Psychics? A Return to the Readings," *The A.R.E. Journal*, XIX (July/Aug. 1984), p. 165.

will enter" to "carry on… with the work" bears with it the corollary assumption, therefore, that Paul would make himself known through the same channel of unconscious communication with the Universal Mind which served to distinguish Cayce as the "miracle man of Virginia Beach."

Who, then, if not Paul Solomon? After all, like Cayce before him, Paul Solomon never experienced his Source. Rather, Solomon was always the object of experience. It was Solomon, the individual character and personality, who was overwhelmed, taken over, called upon by his Source to deliver to mankind Its message of truth. Thus, it was not the Source which was an experience of Solomon, but Solomon who was an experience and an expression of the Source. As if to declare at the very outset the purpose of Its self-revelation, in only the third Reading ever delivered the Source stated:

> There is a veritable wealth of knowledge available for spiritual growth in the A.R.E. files. Since the death of [the] entity Edgar Cayce, there has been no satisfactory use of this knowledge. This entity [Paul Solomon] possesses [the] ability to understand and interpret records and knowledge in this file more thoroughly than anyone who would be able to advance this knowledge today. It is to your spiritual advantage that you cooperate together in seeking means to obtain knowledge from this file and to disseminate this knowledge to aid in spiritual growth of all other entities on your plane, and even future dwellers on your plane (Solomon Reading No. 3, 3/1/72).

It seems that even then, at that very earliest period of "awakening" to his Source, that Solomon was preeminently the man to carry on Cayce's work, to rekindle the living fire that went out with Cayce's death, and, in fact, to broaden the dimensions of Cayce's own accomplishments. But if there were any lingering doubts remaining as to who "Paul" might have been, the Source Itself laid them to rest in a 1991 Reading:

> Let those who have, whatever their doubts may be, let them know that there is a fulfilling of a prophecy here, that Edgar Cayce planted a seed and blazed a trail and said clearly, "Paul will enter the work." Paul *has* entered the work and for a specific purpose. Edgar Cayce introduced to the world in a magnificent way the possibility that man can set aside completely his own consciousness, his own mind and opinions, and can be a channel for the Divine. The next step in that work is that one should come, as Paul has come, to say to others, "You also have such access to the Source." It is not for one and not for all. It is not the case that every man can set aside his consciousness so completely as to be unconscious in trance. Only those who have overcome the fear of death can enter such a depth of trance, setting aside the mind. And yet anyone of you can learn through careful application of Inner Light Consciousness to set aside the mind sufficiently to communicate with the Source and to do that clearly. It does take discipline, and every step, every facet of the Inner Light Consciousness teaching is to facilitate the possibility that there might even be a time when the part of the brain that listens to the Source naturally, that method of learning which uses the subtler senses for communicating with the etheric world, this might be a part of the education of the whole mind, even in a secular sense.

But the way was shown. The trail was blazed. The seed was planted by the Prophet Edgar Cayce. And there has come another to take another step; not to repeat the same, but to apply and to fulfill even the prophecy of Edgar Cayce who said clearly, "There always will be a channel, and that channel should be the head of the work, the director, the leader, the inspirer of the work. Not a commander. Not a guru, nor dictator, but one who holds the message and the vision clearly." (Solomon Reading No. 1492, 7/30/91).

If Cayce's mission, indeed, his entire life, aimed at suggesting to us that the Greater Mind lives, then as the Solomon Source points out he achieved that goal. **For we say unto you, there hath not a greater one walked on the plane of earth than the channel Edgar Cayce. And that which he brought from this plane to yours and revealed might well become a measuring stick by which to know those who channel truth** (Solomon Reading No. 766, 2/14/76). Through Cayce's own embodiment of the universal, one came to recognize the transcendent possibilities of the transpersonal human mind. He proved that it could be done, but he himself didn't know how, nor could he explain to others how it was done. Why then simply repeat what Cayce had already accomplished?

Somewhere in the long metaphysical interlude between Cayce's death and Solomon's awakening to his Source it seems that the need and purpose had changed. The purpose of Solomon's "entering into the work" was to carry the work a step further and to show others the way to do it themselves. "The people who came to see me were the most desperate people in the world," recalls Paul Solomon. "Nobody ever came to me for a reading until they had tried everything else and found the other things didn't work. I had no idea that there were so many desperate people in the world. It was overwhelming. The responsibility of it was a whole new experience to me. I'd never had people depending on me before. I was a grill cook in a two bit hash house and to go from that to medical doctors and professors at Yale University Medical School, UCLA, Charing Cross teaching hospital in London, the University of Australia at Adelaide, the teaching hospital of the University of New Zealand, and elsewhere asking me questions was an enormous thing. I was overwhelmed by the responsibility. I didn't know how I could reach all those people. Then the voice in the readings said: 'Don't. That is not what you came to do.' Edgar Cayce reached all the people he could doing readings for them and the tragedy was that when it ended, there were still all those helpless people. The important thing to do is to teach people how to get their own information. That's where Inner Light Consciousness came from and the Source guided us through developing the techniques for relaxation, for diet and for exercise to get the mind and the body ready for the meditation experience --- how to develop the five subtler senses that are counterparts to the external senses --- to use those subtler senses for asking questions and getting feeling answers, audible answers or visual answers from subtler senses."

It was from the Source Readings themselves, then, that a collection of techniques, referred to as the Inner Light Consciousness, was formulated and specifically designed in order to awaken people to a full awareness of the highest capabilities of their own minds. This, for Paul Solomon, was the "new and greater work." For the final four years of his life, he traveled worldwide, seeding the aspirations of hundreds of thousands of people for the eternal heart of the God-Source within. He taught people from every religious background and every walk of life, in nations from every continent on earth, both to find what they did not possess and to rediscover what in essence they are. In so doing, he breathed life into the most ancient mystery of mankind's divinity. And through his Inner Light teachings, through the incarnation of the living Totality of his Being, he restored faith to its rightful place, above all doctrines and within the absolute dominion of the sacred mystery of life itself, where an expanding global community of people could find recourse and vision to the vast, seamless cosmology of Living Spirit within.

In the twenty-two years that Solomon delivered to us the wisdom and truth of his Source, there has been every reason to celebrate not only the perpetuation of Cayce's universal message to mankind but, in fact, the broadening and expanding of his mission. As prophesied by Cayce nine years before Paul Solomon was even born, Paul had indeed entered "the work". And guided by the dictates of his Source, Solomon resolutely continued to prophesy, to teach, to awaken others, and to affirm man's capacity for union with the Divine. Upon his passing from the physical in 1994, Paul Solomon wished that his legacy could awaken millions of people from around the world who are asleep to a life of love and personal commitment, both to others and to the living Earth itself.

That is the purpose of this book.

Part One

Theophany Of Love

Chapter 1

The Limitless Vision

"TURTLES ALL THE WAY DOWN"

For most of us the scale of the universe is utterly incomprehensible. While on a clear moonless night only a very small portion of our own galactic neighborhood --- about 2,000 stars --- is visible to the unaided eye, through a field binocular the number of stars visible increases to about 50,000. Mt. Wilson observatory's 100-inch telescope reveals nearly a half-billion stars which are but a fraction of the hundreds of billions whose continuous mists of light form the disc-shaped "island in space" known as the Milky Way galaxy. The earth is almost infinitely small within it. Even the eye of the imagination, however, can find no limits to the never-ebbing ocean of galaxies that, seen through the Hubble Telescope seem to stretch off to the edge of eternity. Looking back along the vistas of aeons, Hubble's eye on creation reveals layer upon layer of galaxies numbering over fifty billion, each composed of countless billions of suns whose light, traveling at 186,282 miles per second, has for some taken 12 billion years to reach earth. And as there is as yet no sign of any thinning out in any portion of deep space to which Hubble's lens is directed, the actual accumulation of island universes conjecturally is much greater. Lost in this boundless abyss, the earth becomes a microcosm of space/time, a mere windblown speck of sand drifting against the faint echo of cosmic radiation recorded from the prime instant of creation.

Now imagine all of this --- stars, planets, entire galaxies, billions in number, all the matter and energy in the universe --- packed into a space much much smaller than that occupied by the period at the end of this sentence. At one hundredth of a second after the most gigantic and catastrophic explosion of all time hurled forth the ingredients from which stars, planets, whole galaxies ultimately would coalesce, this was the grand proportional extent of the universe --- a mere point the size of a proton. And at time zero the density was infinite with no spatial dimension at all. These astonishing truths recall the words of astrophysicist Fred Hoyle at mid-century: "no literary imagination could have invented a story one-hundredth part as fantastic as the sober facts that have been unearthed."[1]

But that is not the end of the story --- far from it! For, in the 75 years since Hoyle's pronouncement scientific facts now give evidence of a universe far more fantastic than Hoyle himself could have imagined. For instance, some astronomers now talk candidly of leftover starlight from a future universe, its time flowing in the opposite direction from ours. Moreover, while we perceive only a single three-dimensional universe made up of ordinary objects and bound by concepts of causality and measurability, University of Texas physicist John A. Wheeler predicts on the basis of quantum mathematics not one but myriads of universes existing simultaneously across a gigantic platform of superspace whose dimensions are infinite. On this same plane of thought theoretical physicist David Bohm postulates that our entire physical cosmos and everything in it, from galaxies to grains of sand, is merely a shadowy abstraction or "pattern of excitation" from a much deeper order of existence. A boundless and more primary multidimensional ocean of energy surrounds us, maintains Bohm, and transcends all the spatial and temporal boundaries of our physical world. At the same time it creates, interpenetrates, sustains and transfigures our world moment by moment. Here too, the levels of manifestation are infinite. As Bohm adds, "beyond that ocean may be still a bigger ocean because, after all, our knowledge just simply fades out at that point... Eventually, perhaps, you might discover some further source of energy but you may surmise that that would in turn be floating in a still larger source and so on. It is implied that the ultimate source is immeasurable and cannot be captured within our knowledge... That really is rather what is implied by contemporary physics..."[2]

An Eastern parable tells of a sage who had discovered the secret of the universe. His followers, who were many, eagerly believed all they were told and always left satisfied with what couplets of wisdom the sage had to offer. All, that is, but one young disciple who one day presented himself before the sage and privately asked, "Master, what *is* the ultimate secret?" Drawing the young seeker aside, the sage whispered in his ear: "The world stands on the back of an enormous turtle." At which point the disciple bowed respectfully and, deeply absorbed in thought, took his leave. On the following day he returned as perplexed as before. "Master", he said, "what does the turtle stand on?" Glancing nervously about, the Master again drew the disciple near and, pressing his lips to his ear, whispered even more softly, "The turtle stands on the back of another turtle." On the following day, the disciple was back, pressing again for an answer to the cosmic riddle. Fearing an endless exchange, the Master drew him aside one final time and breathed these words into his ear: "It's turtles all the way down."

This conjuring of infinite regress, of worlds within worlds beyond worlds, is suggestive on a metaphorical level of the sheer unthinkable opacity of those dimensional realms proposed by Wheeler and Bohm. The implication being, therefore, that in this whole dizzying hierarchy of creations we find no vestige of an ultimate beginning --- no prospect of a final cosmic crunch. In the Beginning, there was no beginning. There will be no end. It's just "turtles all the way down."

The eighteenth-century French woman who called Copernicus's theory "a slander on mankind" might as well have been speaking of Wheeler and Bohm. Their calculations on the quantum universe have already begun to redefine us and, like Copernicus, they guide us through spaces that throw the mind wide open to new heresies, leaving us with nothing to say, nothing to feel but awe. Indeed, if quantum theory is in any real sense a window into phenomenal reality, then the entire physical universe that we inhabit is merely a bubble, multiplied endlessly, in the vast sea of the Absolute. Such thoughts as these stagger the mind. But for John Wheeler and David Bohm they are absolutely true.

A BREATHING COSMOS

Here, for Robert Jastrow, former director of NASA's Goddard Institute for Space Studies, the story comes finally to a bewildering climax. "For the scientist who has lived by his faith in the power of reason," he writes, "the story ends like a bad dream." Having scaled the mountains of ignorance, he stands facing the highest peak. As he struggles over the final precipice, he is greeted by a band of mystics who, in Jastrow's words, "have been sitting there for centuries." The great spiritual teachers --- Zarathustra, Buddha, Jesus, Eckhart --- likewise have ascended to the rim of these mountains. Although they have taken a countervailing path to the summit (faith defies proof, science demands it), they, too, have gazed upon the audacious spectacle of creation and what they have reported to us is something equally wonderful --- and equally incomprehensible.

While for all but a few of us the universe appears as a vast pattern of movement and structure, primordial light and impenetrable darkness, of boundless inanimate silence in which human consciousness alone is awake, to the supremely enlightened Self the entire universe is awake. Possessed of cosmical mind it is alive. It is what the ancient Hindus called a "breathing cosmos". Everything --- from camels to quasars, from sticks to stars --- is a part of a living symbiotic Whole, saturated by the rhythmic heartbeat of universal creation. And each level of existence contributes its own peculiar theme to the complex pattern of the whole. **You should think of an individual on this planet as a cell, a single microscopic cell within the earth, the planet itself being the smallest portion of a small gland in a great body,** declares the Solomon Source. **Even that you consider your solar system should be taken to relate to nothing more than a small organ within a much greater body. The planets in their orbits in relation to the sun might even be seen on such a small scale as the elements of an atom, a single atom, in a great body. From that perspective, see that the body itself is greater than what you know as the universe, the Universe of universes. [It] is a body which grows and which has initiations of its own. As there are initiations in the growth of each soul, so the planet [earth] itself, herself, has initiations...relative...to the growth of the entire Universe of universes** (Solomon Reading No. 1560 9/91). Each, we are told, from the level of the human to the single consciousness whose body is the entire galaxy of worlds, is at once an absolute awareness and a mere constituent of the Whole. And each, in its own way, is essential to the very existence of the Whole. The obvious inference, as Jacob Needleman points out, is that "A universe of merely unimaginable size excludes man and crushes him. But a universe that is a manifestation of great consciousness and order *places* man, and therefore calls to him. So much is obvious, for a conscious universe is the only reality that can include human consciousness. And only when I am completely included by something does the need arise for me to understand my relationship to it in all the aspects of my inner and outer life. Only a conscious universe is relevant to the whole of human life."[4]

Relevant, perhaps. But is it enough? Granted that there is a Oneness to the all, a Tao, a Dharmakaya, a Supreme Consciousness, a Universal Mind or First Cause, which brings perfect order and ultimate unity to the universe. Even if we are bound somehow to an eternal limitless Whole, even though there be a joining of our human energy with the energy of a living, conscious universe, are we not compelled to ask, "So what?" What does it avail us to accept that our minds belong to the infinite intelligence of a single Mind? Does it satisfy our desires, raise our hopes, strengthen our bond with humanity? Does it allow us to share sorrow when others grieve, feel disappointment with their frustration, joy when they are uplifted? If at the roots of our being, if at the foundation of everything is nothing more than a Universal Mind expressing through the living incarnation of the Whole, then all the world's supply of joy, happiness, and hope, and endless suffering, counts as nothing.

Here again, the story does not end. For these avataric messengers tell us something even more staggering, something inconceivable to any finite mind. They tell us that the entire universe with its myriads of worlds is permeated to the very depth of its existence with the living flame of divine love --- infinite, inexhaustible, unconditional love.   All things in Heaven and on earth are the eternal result of this one all-embracing energy or force, for it is the fundamental reality of the cosmos, the transcendental ground of existence. Love, they insist, is the formative power of life itself. Within it is contained the mystery of all genesis. Hence, the ancient text of the Rig Veda records that "In the beginning was love, which was the primal germ of the mind."[5] Or, as given by the Solomon Source, **In the beginning, before the world was, there lived only one power, one expression in all the universe. That power, that expression, is love. Then does it not follow, do you not see, that every cell, every atom of creation sprang, then, from this primal energy? Little ones, all there is is made from love. That is all there is. All things else are only caused that you might recognize [love]** (Solomon Reading No. 357, 5/12/74).

Hence, these God-filled men and women from every faith direct us with one voice beyond the hypnotic trance-like existence of our ordinary lives to the forgotten memory of life's highest imperative: Love. Not the finite love we have come to associate with emotion or sexual rapport, however intense, but love universal, infinite love, that with the power to move mountains and to shake the earth; that which enfolds all life in its radiance and that comprises in itself the fulfillment of all possible creations. **The power of the one energy, which may be called love,** declares the Source, **is called the light, the life, or the truth, all of these words used only to express the nature of the one and only singular force that is available in this life, this universe, and this experience.** (Solomon Reading No. 1709, 5/5/93).

Still there is more. These human incarnations of divine wisdom reveal to us an infinity within ourselves as well, comprising all the immensity and power of all worlds in all ages. They tell us that we are the very embodiment of the infinite and tumultuous spirit of creation itself. Tat tvam asi, "That art Thou." These avataric messengers tell us as much: we are not merely finite expressions of the whole, but deep down we are That which eternally IS --- the one all-comprehensive Reality containing within itself all realities. An old Tibetan scripture says "This little body holdeth all." Likewise, a verse from the Pali Canon reads --- "My friend, in this very body, six feet of it with its senses, thoughts, and feelings, is the world, the origin of the world, the ceasing of the world and the way of its cessation."[6]   Meister Eckhart affirms that the "space occupied by any soul is vastly greater than heaven and earth and God's entire creation. I say more: God might make heavens and earths galore yet these ... would be of less extent than a single needle-tip compared with the standpoint of a soul atoned in God."[7]   And just as this innermost Self is identical with the infinite all-inclusiveness in which things are free to live and move and have their being, so in accordance we and all others are intrinsically joined. In the mystical vision of Plotinus: "Each being contains in itself the whole intelligible world. Therefore All is everywhere. Each is there All, and All is each. Man as he now is has ceased to be the All. But when he ceases to be an individual, he raises himself again and penetrates the whole world."[8] Hence, in dying to self --- self-reasoning, self-will, self-possession --- we come at last to the awareness of a Self wholly inclusive of the full complexity of the All, being not *in* All but *of* the All. For "blessedness lieth not in much and many," instructs the late fourteenth-century *Theologia Germanica,* "but in One and oneness."[9] So therefore Jesus declares in the Gospel of St. Thomas: "I am the Light that is above them all, I am the All, the All came forth from Me and the All attained to Me. Cleave a piece of wood, I am there. Lift up the stone and you will find Me there."[10] To the Buddhist, there is a Buddha in every grain of sand.

"How can such a thing be," we ask? With one voice every Buddha, Christ, rishi and saint who ever scaled these mountains will answer, "It is absolutely true!" It is true when every enactment of mind and will becomes a mirror-image of that original creative impulse whose existence it affirms and toward which it reaches out with the only universal means we possess: Love.

THE ALL-EMBRACING VISION

To the scientific mind, in the hierarchy of universal existence we are of no conceivable consequence. The astronomical immensities that encompass us overwhelm us and in all their vastness reduce all the age-long striving of the human spirit to relative insignificance. In contrast, the great prophets and spiritual teachers, in bearing witness to the universality of the divine, tell us that the levels of conscious order that exist and that are written into the very structure of the cosmos are hidden within ourselves. Consequently, to become conscious of the unexplored, intrinsic regions of our own being is to become aware of and integrated with the purposes and energies of cosmic nature. Even a single moment of significant consciousness in the life of any of us can potentially transform us from a mere speck lost in a boundless universe into a boundless state of being capable of embracing and transcending that universe.

Which view is true? Which should be chosen, since in reason they are incommensurable? Struggling to make sense of our place in the cosmos, short of schizophrenia we are are simply unable to make the facts and theories of science fit with the universal truths of the Perennial tradition. Even our most salutary efforts seem as impossible as the mathematician's squaring of the circle. Could the truth itself be incompatible with scientific law? Or does the Perennial wisdom somehow stand on communicable terms with the now avant-garde of holistic science?

"Assuredly," writes Mircea Eliade, "all the disciplines of the mind and all the sciences of man are equally precious and their discoveries mutually so, but this solidarity does not mean confusion. What is important is to integrate the results of the diverse applications of the mind without confounding them."[11] But integrate them how? Simply fitting together the unevenly shaped fragments of two separate, incompatible and incommensurable world views --- the fact-based quantum view of science with the value oriented perspective of the mystics --- as if it were a jigsaw puzzle cannot yield us a single coherent picture unless, as Eliade insists, we "integrate the results into a wider perspective." The heightened Christ-like consciousness of the Source affords us just such a perspective. With the sheer aggregate wealth of Its limitless vision and understanding It perceives the whole of a living reality --- a reality that far exceeds what science can measure --- in terms of its intrinsic meaning, value and purpose. And it provides a true synthesis precisely because It apprehends life, convergently and independently, from every angle and dimension --- physical and spiritual, form and essence, transitory and eternal --- and weaves them into a more capacious unity than any single perspective, solely on its own merits, could visualize. In a sense, then, it is both the grand unified field of physics and the Mysterium Conjunctus wrought into a single whole, an all-embracing vision that resolves human experience into an order that is absolute.

Let us pause and consider....

Chapter 2

The Energy Of God

THE PARABLE OF THE FISH

An Eastern Parable tells of a fish who once lived in the great ocean:

> And because the water was transparent and always conveniently got out of the way of his nose when he moved along, he didn't know he was in the ocean. Well, one day the fish did a very dangerous thing, he began to *think*: "Surely, I am a most remarkable being, since I can move around like this in the middle of empty space." Then the fish became confused because of *thinking* about moving and swimming, and he suddenly had an anxiety paroxysm and thought he had forgotten how. At that moment he looked down and saw the yawning chasm of the ocean depths, and he was terrified he would drop. Then he thought: "If I could catch hold of my tail in my mouth, I could hold myself up." And so he curled himself up and snapped at his tail. Unfortunately, his spine wasn't quite supple enough, so he missed. As he went on trying to catch hold of his tail, the yawning black abyss below became ever more terrible, and he was brought to the edge of total nervous breakdown.
>
> The fish was about to give up, when the ocean, which had been watching with mixed feelings of pity and amusement, said, "What are you doing?' "Oh," said the fish, "I'm terrified of falling into the deep dark abyss, and I'm trying to catch hold of my tail in my mouth to hold myself up." So the ocean said, "Well, you've been trying that for a long time now, and still you haven't fallen down. How come?" "Oh, of course I haven't fallen down yet," said the fish, "because, because --- I'm swimming!" "Well," came the reply, "I am the Great Ocean, in which you live and move and are able to be a fish, and I have given all of myself to you in which to swim, and I support you all the time you swim. But here you, instead of exploring the length, breadth, depth, and height of my expanse, are wasting your time pursuing your own end." From then on, the fish put his own end behind him (where it belonged) and set out to explore the ocean.[12]

As it happens, the proverbial fish in the great ocean is us. Surrounding us and inseparably confluent with every atom of our being is a boundless and inexhaustible sea of cosmic energy from which flows in a continually unfolding-enfolding stream of endless creativity all forms of matter, all sequences of time, events and movement, all manifestations of reality. It is that energy by which synapses fire in the brain and stars pulsate in the heavens. Every electron in its orbit and every planet in its orb unfolds from it multidimensional depths. Just as within its infinite potentiality lay the seed of all creational activity, so in itself it represents a living form of universal calculus that makes matter visible from its primary elements right to the simultaneity of all its possible combinations. However mysterious and unfathomable, this energy is also us; nothing and no one is apart from it, for it is the etiological impulse of life itself. The molecules of oxygen and hydrogen, the air we breathe and water we drink, the chemical composition of our bodies and of everything --- stars, crystals, jellyfish, marigolds, humans --- all are forms of this single dynamic force of energy whose manifestations are limitless.

In the midst of this boundless ocean of energy we move and experience life as freely as the fish in the sea. There is no direction, declination, or spatio-temporal expanse which we are forbidden from exploring. But as soon as we emphasize our vicarious autonomy and isolation and resist the gravity that would bring us into a unity with every living expression of this energy, we separate ourselves not only from the entire stream of life but from the ground of our being as well. The wisdom of the body speaks in us as surely as the energy of life speaks through the unknowable deep within each of us, through measureless realms of living spirit utterly beyond our comprehension. But in our vain attempt to control the ocean rather than making ourselves one with it, we, like the fabled fish, lose touch with this energy of life and with its pre-conscious source within us. Thus, by pursuing our own ends to the exclusion of the Way of all life, we shrink back from that Great World into the embodiment of our tiny selves. The result is a suicidal loss of faith in anything but our own frail ego. Self and others, "I" and not-"I", man and cosmos, portray our fathomless fall from grace.

In truth, we are in no significant way isolated from this vast living energy of which we are a part. The fish exists because the ocean is there to support it. If, in a moment of unconditional acceptance, we were to experience with absolute certainty that we *are* a form of this energy and that we derive our finite being only from its infinite expanse, perhaps we would all at once know our Selves to be ineffably whole and, like an iceberg suddenly realizing itself as H_2O, perceive our identity with the ocean.

SWIMMING IN THE SAME OCEAN

At far deeper levels of our being, deeper levels, mathematically speaking, of quantum reality that lie beneath the atom and beyond the manifest world that surrounds us, the components of the universe --- space-time, mass, and energy --- are in fact a single universal unity. Everything is energy. Indeed, Einstein's famous equation $E=mc^2$ confirms that mass, even an object at rest, is nothing but a form of energy. Thus, to speak of substance at the subatomic level makes no sense since quantum particles are not made of "stuff", but are dynamic patterns of energy in an inseparable cosmic web. This ceaseless quantum activity is anthropomorphized in the Vedic deity of Shiva, the god of creation and destruction, who through his cosmic dance sustains the endless rhythm of the universe.

The theoretical physicist Fritjof Capra recounts an episode in which the spatio-temporal barriers of his ordinary reasoning consciousness suddenly dissolved, unveiling to his direct experience the underlying Reality of this cosmic dance. As he recalls:

I was sitting by the ocean one late summer afternoon, watching the waves rolling in and feeling the rhythm of my breathing, when I suddenly became aware of my whole environment as being engaged in a gigantic cosmic dance. Being a physicist, I knew that the sand, rocks, water and air around me were made of vibrating molecules and atoms, and that these consisted of particles which interacted with one another by creating and destroying other particles. I knew also that the Earth's atmosphere was continually bombarded by showers of 'cosmic rays', particles of high energy undergoing multiple collisions as they penetrated the air. All this was familiar to me from my research in high-energy physics, but until that moment I had only experienced it through graphs, diagrams, and mathematical theories. As I sat on that beach my former experiences came to life; I 'saw' cascades of energy coming down from outer space, in which particles were created and destroyed in rhythmic pulses; I 'saw' the atoms of the elements and those of my body participating in this cosmic dance of energy; I felt its rhythm and I 'heard' its sound, and at that moment I *knew* that this was the Dance of Shiva...[13]

The Dance of Shiva mythically represents what quantum theory has now confirmed: that discrete material entities have no independent existence apart from their character as temporal events abstracted from a single enduring field of energy. In other words, from the standpoint of quantum mechanics we are no different in kind from the earth beneath our feet and the stars above our heads. As Capra's experience illustrates, we are simply manifestations of this continuous and dynamic flow of energy as it gives form to a particular level of unfolding. The mystery is this: what is it that guides and organizes this field? What brings pattern and symmetry to the dance? Among the ordered elements of the universe there is a ghostly presence.

There are strong indications consistent with, and supported by, the current state of quantum research which suggest that quantum-mechanical phenomena generate and organize matter on a vast hierarchy of levels. In high-energy physics, for instance, the angular momentum, or rate of spin, of any subatomic particle is quantized just like energy and charge. It is fixed, definite, known. If the rate of spin of a particle (if one can conceive the idea of spin without something spinning) is altered, the particle is fundamentally changed such that it can no longer be regarded as an electron, or proton, or whatever it was before its spin altered. This suggests that subatomic particles are simply different states of motion or vibration of some greater unknown underlying field of energy or force, an "elsewhere" region transcending time, space, and matter. Furthermore, quantum electrodynamics reveals that subatomic particles occasionally emerge spontaneously from a perfect vacuum, then momentarily annihilate each other leaving no trace behind. "The spontaneous, temporary emergence of particles from a vacuum is called a vacuum fluctuation and is utterly commonplace in quantum field theory," points out Edward Tryon. "If it is true that our Universe has a zero net value for all conserved quantities, then it may simply be a fluctuation of the vacuum, the vacuum of some larger space in which our Universe is embedded."[14]

Professor Bohm refers to this larger hyperdimensional field as the "enfolded" or "implicate" order. Consciousness and matter, being and nonbeing, are all one in this common ground. It is from this oneness that forms "explicate" themselves into the finite world of physical reality and then "fold back in again," only to re-emerge again, in ceaseless succession. This ever-flowing activity of enfolding and unfolding, veiling and disclosing, dissolving and crystallizing, Bohm refers to as the "holomovement". So what we see at the visible level of the world, what Bohm calls the "explicate" or "unfolded" domain, are simply abstracted or precipitated forms of enfolded energy (shadows, as Plato would say, on the walls of the cave) which have emerged from a higher state of transcendental unity and wholeness and will return into it. "According to Hindu cosmology," writes Houston Smith, "during the nights of Brahma in which he sleeps, the terrestrial and intermediate planes vanish completely, the 'big bang' reverses --- matter vanishes into spreading black holes? --- leaving nothing for the (no longer existing) astronomers to detect. The lower realms, now reabsorbed into the celestial, are shown to have been but episodes in the divine expanse." [15] Thus, all manifestations --- ourselves, the earth, stars, the cosmos itself --- must ultimately roll back once more into the primordial energy stream from which they are unfolded.

Beyond this, Bohm postulates an incomprehensibly enormous "superquantum potential" or "super-implicate realm of inconceivable power which "represents information that 'guides' or organizes the self-active movement of the field."[16] Here we shift from the causal universe of the implicate to a teleological universe of total undifferentiated potential. "The point about the super-implicate order," advises Bohm, "is that though we have an implicate order, nothing organizes it. It is what's called 'linear', and it just passes through itself and diffuses around; special devices can unfold it but it does not have an intrinsic capacity to unfold an order. The super-implicate order, which is the so-called higher field (the implicate order would be a wave function), would be a function of the wave function, a higher order, a super-wave function. The super-implicate order makes the implicate order non-linear and organizes it into relatively stable forms with complex structures."[17]

Thus, the super-implicate is an incomprehensibly vast and all-encompassing universe of pure energy which organizes the wave-fields and form potentials of the implicate; the implicate is all-power manifesting; and the explicate, our physical universe (being but "a tiny ripple on this tremendous ocean of energy."[18]), is a relatively stable, although temporal, projection or manifestation of the unmanifest energy of the implicate. All three orders of reality are extensions of and animated by the same dynamic of energy expressing at varying levels of holonomic resonance and frequency within the quantum field. And given the n-dimensional properties of the field, each order interpenetrates every other in the same point of space, so that all points, not only in space but in time as well, are infinitely interconnected. Meaning that, the world and all its manifestations *is* ultimately indivisibly one. Given that consciousness, according to Bohm, is likewise a property of this field, it, too, is present everywhere at once. Therefore, the principle applies equally to ourselves: in form, consciousness, and superconscious potential we are *in fact* coextensive with all three orders of reality. We are indivisibly one with the world. Ultimately, we and the fish are swimming in the same ocean.

AN OCEAN OF LIGHT

" This ocean of energy could be thought of as an ocean of light," insists Bohm. For "light, by interactions of different rays, (as field theory in physics is investigating today), can produce particles and all the diverse structures of matter."[19] In fact, declares Bohm, "[light] is the potential for everything… Light is what enfolds all the universe."[20] The Solomon Source leaves us no doubt:

> Now, we would have you understand that in the expression, the sending forth of this energy which is light and which, as you have seen in the combination of the elements, through the simple conversion of light into electricity and thus into the building blocks of atomic structure, might then simply by changing [the] rate of vibration and varying combination of the positive, negative, and neutral charges, lay the groundwork for atomic structure. Having these, [then, we would] have the building blocks of the expression that you know of life. Life itself having preceded the expression of life which came through photosynthesis and the building blocks of life as you have discovered them to unfold (Solomon Reading No 1413, 5/29/90)

As given by the Source, light is not merely the dominant constituent of the universe, it is the primary condition of the rest of creation. It is the continuous, unbroken, and undivided background of all matter and all life.

The basic quantum unit of light is the tiny particle-wave called the photon. Its discrete, quantized character is fundamentally an abstraction from the unbroken continuum of electromagnetic radiations that saturates the cosmos. It is only when our eyes or instruments interact with this continuum that the field-properties of light become particalized in the form of photons. A photon has no mass but when, traveling at 186,000 miles per second, it collides with another particle it can create electrons and protons which do have mass. It has no charge, yet the secondary particles that result from its annihilation do. And for a pulse of light, time is absent. Clocks stop at the speed of light. Thus, mass, energy and time are created when a photon condenses into a particle. This is the initial activity in the generative process of all creation. All electromagnetic interactions from radio waves to light to cosmic rays --- in short, every subatomic constituent of mass and energy in the universe --- are mediated by photons. Thus, all the elements that now occupy the universe are, in finality, formed of light. "So matter, as it were, is condensed or frozen light," explains Bohm. "Light is not merely electromagnetic waves but in a sense other kinds of waves that go at that speed. Therefore all matter is a condensation of light into patterns moving back and forth at average speeds which are less than the speed of light… you could say that when we come to light we are coming to the fundamental activity in which existence has its ground, or at least coming close to it."[21]

Close, perhaps, but because every electron, neutron, and photon is predicated upon and guided ultimately by the quantum potential which informs its motion, then light itself must be seen as merely the proximate or secondary cause of all manifestation. The mathematical inference is that an "unknowable", nonlocal source of energy conceived all matter, time, space *and* light. From the limitless perspective of the Source we learn that light emanates from that sovereign Cause which far exceeds the plane of cosmology but which, in itself, intimately abides in *all* orders of reality --- the Creative Word or Logos --- that which in the beginning expressed Itself in the fiat, "let there be":

When the voice of God rang forth in the origin of what you know as creation, when the supreme primal voice that was the first stirring of vibration, sound and light manifest in the utter darkness and emptiness before the worlds were, this sound went out to create first light itself, which is units or quanta of potential energy expressing in darkness, darkness having no resistance to it whatsoever, no power over it in any manner.

So there went out one, and only one, original force. This force [was] a vibratory force which is best likened to the quanta of light called photons, having neither positive nor negative electrical charge, and yet having the potential to become charged negatively, positively and neutrally. So that if there were in the beginning of time nothing more than light, so yet you must understand from the point of view of your science of physics that that expression alone is sufficient. That all else that is created and manifest is possible from that one expression of the Divine.

But this expression, being a spectrum of vibration, allowed that creation be of light and of sound and within it contained the seeds of energies you know as electricity and finally magnetism. That which was sent out originally as light and sound has within it all potential to become gasses, liquids, solid matter. And the ability of the light responding to matter in the presence of water gives you an image of all that was necessary that life itself spring forth from this creative fiat.

...Now coming from that which we have referred to as creative fiat --- the sending forth light and vibration which came first as light and sound, then combine and recombine as positive and negative and neutral particles result[ing] from the travel of the photons --- there is the basis for all that is created. And the extent of creation might be understood as having come from this force which does not wholly disagree with your current theory, expressed as "Big Bang" (Solomon Reading No. 1423, 5/29/90).

THE VIBRATION OF GOD

From the standpoint of the Biblical Genesis, at the beginning of all there is a vision simply of unformed primordial chaos. Darkness covers the abyss. Then God utters the divine word: "Let there be light." And in the first act of creative fiat "there was light." What, then, is this formless activating principle which ceaselessly, moment by moment, gives birth to a living cosmos through the creative fiat of light? Like trying to nail a bead of mercury with one's thumb, it simply slips away. "The energy which is energetic is not the true Energy. The name that can be named is not the eternal name," writes Lao Tsu. "Stand before it and there is no beginning. Follow it and there is no end." The Chandogya Upanishad records that "an invisible and subtle essence is the Spirit of the whole universe. That is reality. That is Truth."[22] Quotations such as these could be multiplied indefinitely, from India, from China, from Sufi mystics of the Near East, from Christian mystics of the West, all relative to this eternal and nameless Force. What term should be applied to a totalizing principle of such infinite magnitude and potential but that melts away under the reflected light of our solicitude?

It would necessitate that we coin a new term, or use that closest, in describing the force which you have *not* isolated and for which you have no term in the present, but which has been variously described as consciousness. And this we will use as a preferable term, [although it] has as well been described as Love, or greater yet, the I AM force, and is the force referred to in the giving of the statement to the prophet Moses, "I AM LIFE." That force referred to as "Life" or "God-consciousness", then, is that adhering force that is the common energy, that is seen sometimes as vibration, motion of the particles, or the force that would suspend particles in motion. We've reference, then, to a force that pervades all things, an energy in which all things are suspended as if they were particles, yet not particles, but as might be described, slower vibrations or denser forms of that same force. It is the force responsible for healing and growth, the common force that is shared between the minds of men that can bridge the individual consciousness and bring thoughts, understandings, and transference of understanding from one to another (Solomon Reading No. 424, 9/74).

The Source points us, therefore, beyond the secondary cause of manifestation to the *First* Cause of the universal concrescence of all that exists from a common genesis. Being omnipresent, unlimited, In-finite in all directions that word can possibly point, the supreme energy enters and abides in all orders of creation as the "I AM" force which actualizes (engenders) and empowers all being in the mode of multiplicity and individuation. And in every seed of its creation it nourishes an insatiable appetite for life. Although it is far from God's totality, nevertheless it is, in the words of the Source, **the vibration of God: [For] all that exists is made of the vibration of God or God's vibration. Now your choice of the word 'vibration' does suggest binary code, for vibration is a movement in two directions repeatedly. Let us expand and say that all life is God expressing. The expression of God is life and all that is, all that exists, matter and its comparison, or light which exists [and] darkness which doesn't exist except as a point of comparison. All that is is the expression of God** (Solomon Reading No. 1733, 8/12/93). It is this that enables certain Sufis to affirm that "all is God," in compliance with the Quranic verse: "wheresoever ye turn, there is the Face of God."

This metaphorical "ocean" of energy from which we drive our existence is awash in wave patterns of varying frequency and amplitude, or wavelengths, which correspond with different levels of reality. These levels, all of which obtain within ourselves as micro-versions of the greater pattern, "are not separate layers," advises the Tibetan Buddhist Lama Govinda, "but rather in the nature of mutually penetrating forms of energy, from the finest 'all radiating,' all pervading, luminous consciousness down to the densest form of 'materialized consciousness,' which appears before us as our visible, physical body."[23] As the lower (material, corporeal, phenomenal) levels are subordinate to and derive from the higher, so the higher (subtle, celestial, numenal) levels contain all the qualities and attributes of the lower but are capable of generating appropriate forms of novelty surpassing the potential of each successive lower level.

Visualizing this ocean as a quantum field, the coarser, slower waves or vibrations on the surface correspond to the densest level of matter. If, in conjunction with Planck's Law, however, the photon's energy is directly proportional to the frequency of its vibration, then the smaller its light pulse, the more subtle and potentially powerful its energy. At the deepest levels of the sea, therefore, just above the level of the Absolute, are waves so minute and frequencies so exceedingly fine that they are undetectable by even the most sensitive of our instruments. Although at these levels the ocean appears calm, it contains tremendous energy and is filled with creative potential. When all motion comes finally to rest, that is, when the amplitude of a quantum wave becomes so small that the crests and valleys overlap, we have reached the unsurpassable depths of what the Buddhists refer to as "pure consciousness." Quantum physics confirms that consciousness *is* a form of energy, and Buddhism teaches that to be in touch with this consummate level is to be consciously identical with the energy of life itself. At this level of pure consciousness, the energy or "vibration of God" is an infinitely fine wavelength whose creative energy potential is correspondingly infinite, giving scientific credence to the soteriological notion of God's omnipotence.

How far does this speculation fit the facts? The answer is that on the whole it fits them very well. Consider again the example of Shiva. In the ancient tradition of the Hindus, the god Shiva manifests unlimited power and energy. Indeed, since July 16, 1945, when the first atomic bomb was detonated at the Trinity test site near Alamogordo, New Mexico, the powerful anatomy of the atom has been known. Unleashed into terrestrial nature was a basic energy of the cosmos never before active in any major way on earth, the energy latent in mass. J. Robert Oppenheimer, Manhattan project director and witness to the first atomic test, quoted the *Bhagavad Gita*: "I am become death, the shatterer of worlds." Shiva's entitlement as the destroyer of worlds would become ever more steadfastly assured in the cold war years ahead with the cumulative increase of global nuclear arsenals possessing the explosive yield of roughly one million six hundred thousand times the yield of the bomb that was dropped by the United States on the city of Hiroshima in Japan on August 6, 1945.

But Shiva's self-disclosure in what Einstein called the "tremendous energy" in mass was nothing by comparison to the infinite energy now believed to exist in a vacuum. For, in calculating the "zero-point energy" of space in which the number of possible subatomic waves is infinite, we are left with the mind boggling revelation that, as Walter Sullivan puts it, "in the thimbleful of vacuum there is more...energy than would be released by all atomic bomb fuel in the universe."[24] We now know that power stands in inverse ratio to size, and the shorter the wavelength of a particle, the greater the energy that is compressed into it. So that, in the words of Arthur Young, if "the energy necessary to create a proton is contained in a light pulse only about 10^{-13} centimeter in diameter, [then] the energy of a million protons would be contained in a light pulse a million times smaller."[25] The astonishing consequence, as David Bohm testifies, is that "If one computes the amount of energy that would be in one cubic centimeter of space, with [the] shortest possible wavelength, it turns out to be very far beyond the total energy of all matter in the known universe."[26] Extending the logic, philosopher of religion Huston Smith comments that "as the principle has 'no theoretical limit' speculation races toward the prospect that the energy of something that has no size at all --- God? --- might be infinite."[27]

But how is this possible? The obvious paradox that a mere fragment of empty space would be greater and would contain more energy than the universal spatio-temporal field that includes it stretches the ulterior limits of credibility. "What is implied by this proposal," explains Professor Bohm, "is what we call empty space contains an immense background of energy, and that matter as we know it is a small, 'quantized' wavelike excitation on top of this background, rather like a tiny ripple on a vast sea… The things that appear to our senses are derivative forms and their true meaning can be seen only when we consider the plenum, in which they are generated and sustained, and into which they must ultimately vanish. [Thus], what we perceive through the senses as empty space is actually the plenum [as opposed to vacuum], which is the ground for all existence of everything, including ourselves."[28] **Or see it in this manner,** states the Source, reversing the imagery: **All that is, is but a thought of God. Or seeing even further, all that might be manifest would begin at a central point, at an intensity of vibration that would produce no visible effect, nor an effect that could be sensed by any of your instruments, nor could it be measured, nor seen, nor weighed, nor detected in any manner, for so fine would be the vibration. Then further and further from the heart, from the mind of God, traveling further from the central purpose would the vibration become slower. [So] would the substance, then, that would be of that vibration, that quality, become denser [and] more apparent. Then ranging further and further from spirit, or from the finest of that which is God, would you find that that is denser on your plane. In such a manner might you understand that that is material** (Solomon Reading No. 148, 3/28/73). So conceived, the Hindus refer to God's dual character: Nirguna Brahman or God-without attributes (an ocean without wave or ripple), and Saguna Brahman or God-with attributes (the same ocean now billowing and turbulent, actualizing every grade of Its infinitude). Hence, from the rippling wave-like energy of dense matter at the surface to the infinitely subtle energy of pure consciousness that forms the unfathomable depths of the plenum, a striated order of dimensional levels emerges based on the frequency of the quantum wave.

Since it is from the unmanifest realm of the plenum, or pure consciousness, that all manifestation arises, it follows that the universe itself originates in consciousness --- Logoidal consciousness. **May we state it in this manner,** explains the Source:

> **"In the beginning was the Word, and the Word was with God and the Word was God."** Whereas it is written, in the beginning was the Logos and the Logos was with God and was God. There is, of course, a necessity for a word, an expression, a label for that existing in the beginning, and well you might see it as nought but peace. For what else could describe [the] absence of existence of energy? You have little ability to imagine or relate to the non-existence of energy, for your focusing upon such a beginning matter makes it energy, or it has energy to attract the attention by virtue of your focusing the attention, you see. Then labeling that you find as peace in the beginning, became a dynamic force through the awareness or consciousness of self or expression.

> Thus…the all-pervading energy of the universe, or the raw energy from which all others emanate, is consciousness. But let us state it on a higher

level for the limited nature of your term consciousness. For you associate
it with brain activity and such, but let it be seen rather in this manner: the
word Logos and its origin means expression, the expression of, or the Word
of, the definition of God. Then it would well be said that that raw material
from which all else was made is the expression, or definition of God, or is
simply God but stated in that term --- "Logos". Then Logos Itself, the raw
material from which all else is made, or was made, or awareness of self of
the Logos, or the consciousness --- Logoidal consciousness (Solomon Reading No. 642, 6/75).

The absolute and undifferentiated Cause from which all manifestation derives,
then, is Logoidal consciousness. It is, in the words of metapsychologist Ken
Wilber, "not one thing among many things, or the sum of many things or the
dynamic interaction of many things --- [It] is the condition, the nature, the
suchness of reality *of* each thing or event or process. It is not set apart *from*
any of them, yet neither is it in any way confined *to* them. It is identical *with*
the world, but not identical *to* it."[29]

In Itself, however, the Creative Word or Logoic consciousness is not the final
truth. God in His ultimate nature --- call it Nameless because It is beyond all
names that can be named --- is, for lack of a better term, infinite Mind. "The
quantum principle involves *mind* in an essential way," writes physicist Jack
Sarfatti: "mind creates matter."[30] Or, as the eminent physicist Max Planck
points out, "There is no matter as such! All matter originates and exists only
by virtue of a force which brings the particles of an atom to vibration and
holds this most minute solar system of the atom together... We must assume
behind this force the existence of a conscious and intelligent Mind. This Mind
is the matrix of all matter."[31] It is this infinite Mind that guides quantum
processes. Its form is meaning and energy. It is for the Upanishads the uncreated and absolutely ineffable Supreme, "nearer than the nearest"; it is That
in whose consciousness and being we live and move, and that expresses Itself
thus: "I am the Alpha and Omega, the Beginning and the End!" It is this *sine
qua nons* of all existence that constitutes for science the great unfathomable
question.

THE DIVINE MATRIX OF CREATION

If one accepts the idea that space, time, and matter all emerged from the initial
singularity, then at that point all our equations break down. There can be no
time without space, no *before* without time. Because science is axiomatically
closed to the suprasensory dimensions of the highest state of the Eternal, even
Bohm's notion of a timeless implicate or an infinite assemblage of superimpli-
cates yields us nothing in our quest for the ultimate Cause. Stretching our imagination beyond all forms of polarity, beyond dimension, beyond the event-
horizon of cosmogenesis itself, there in that emptiness of nothingness before
the Word spilled Itself forth into light, there remains the impenetrable mystery
of ... What? The mind is not made for grasping ultimates. What is "*It*" that
begins where all thought ends?

It is said that man mirrors the Infinite and that certain human divergences are providentially prefigured in the divine intelligence. But the Infinite is not related to the finite in the same way as, say, words are related to things; for, as St. Thomas said, "the divine essence by its immensity surpasses every form to which our intellect reaches; and thus we cannot apprehend it by knowing what it is."[32] Any understanding based on intellect alone is above all a restriction of perspective and a limitation from the point of view of totality and universality. What of "It", then, lies within our experiential reach but beyond our conceptual grasp? What of pre-cosmogenic entelechy repeats itself in some fashion in the human microcosm such that the Uncreated might yield to us something of the mystery of Its unknowable essence? What --- beyond all beyonds and *sine die* before all forms of existence --- dwelt within this unfathomable Nothingness?

As Paul Solomon sees it, "In that emptiness of nothingness there is peace and there is stillness. Even that is an energy. This energy of peace we would describe, perhaps, as a point without dimensions --- just a point in this stillness, this emptiness. But this point of peace we can also think of as potential. If this is emptiness it is potentially everything. It can be filled. This point, this focal point of peace, wants to fill this emptiness because it is and contains an energy we could call love. But if there is nothing, there is nothing to love. And so this point of peace that identifies itself as love, or as the energy of love, begins to expand itself to fill the dark and cold with light and warmth and the potential for life. This is its motivation. It loves and wants to fill the emptiness with the infinite potential for love."[33]

From the midst of this endless emptiness, from within the eternal womb of Darkness, there forms the bright spark of love, but only *in potentia*. It is the first step in transforming chaos into cosmos, in saturating the darkness with light. A Greek myth relates that from Chaos were born Night and also Erebus, the unfathomable depth that is the abode of Death. From Darkness and from Death (nothingness) Love was born, and from Love, Light. The Source tells us that the principle of Love, or Logos, being the first expression of God, was inherent in the Divine seed from the timeless beginning:

> [It] might be best said that the principle of the Mother God, or the Mother of all things, was that Divine pool of silence, [that] sea of silence or Prime Central Stillness in which the Father arose to action, acting upon the Mother. It might well be said that the Mother, or female principle of God, pre-existed the male to the extent of expression itself, for the male be not discernable as the masculine principle until it is active. But the female principle or potential existed even before creation or activity, The expression of the male was the action upon the potential, giving birth to manifestation.

> And what is the Son of God? The Son of God is manifest God. All things, then, that do exist were born out of Divine Mother through the action of Divine Father. Then, that that is the Father principle of God, or the active principle, [is] that of the Creator or [First] Cause; the Mother principle [is] the vehicle through which all things manifest.

> It is no accident that the ancients prayed only to the Father principle, never praying as is the manner of some in this day to the Father-Mother God, for

such a prayer shows ignorance of the principle. For that which is active is that which is called upon in prayer. That which is passive is the receptive within you. Then you become the womb to which you attract the Father principle, making of yourself the feminine or attractive principle by your very act of prayer. You become, then, the feminine principle wooing the masculine, asking It to act upon that receptive within you that you might give birth to that which is sought in the prayer. Then understand these principles in that manner (Solomon Reading No. 901, 10/21/76).

In a state pre-existing the initial stirring of the masculine principle, Ultimate Being consists of unity-totality. Within this unity-totality immanently abide all three aspects of the Godhead --- passive, active, and manifest --- as undifferentiatedly One. In order for the spark of Creation to be engendered, the force of activity must enact Itself upon the "Prime Central Stillness" or feminine principle of the Divine Unity, bringing forth from Its infinite potentiality the Son or "I AM" consciousness which is the active force of Love --- or in other words, manifest God. "Here we are not thinking of the designation in sexual terms at all," writes Jungian scholar June Singer, "but clearly as a description of a certain quality of energy flow."

It is Masculine in the sense that a fountain is Masculine. It has qualities of pushing out, thrusting, disseminating and dissipating itself. This Masculine flow of energy...is a process comparable to the Taoists' "circulation of light." The Masculine energy, Yang, as it begins to diminish, gradually flows over into its opposite. It is taken over by the Feminine energy, Yin, into which it flows. Where the Masculine energy spills over in its profligacy, the Feminine energy gathers up. The Feminine energy principle could be seen as the negative charge of the Masculine energy principle. Another way of conceptualizing it would be to say that the Feminine energy flows along the concave arc of the circle as the masculine energy flows along the convex. The Feminine is the internal flow of energy, complementing the external flow of energy of the Masculine. In microphysical terms, the Feminine energy would be represented by the electron and the Masculine energy by the nucleus of the atom.[34]

Extending this same analogy, physicist Fred Alan Wolf writes: "In quantum physics we deal with the universe as constructed from two movements. We call them wave and particle actions... Before there is any manifestation, there is only the female, ** the wave. In order for manifestation to occur, there must be particle action in which an object suddenly manifests, for a brief instant. That action is male --- a sudden penetration of the wave, producing manifestation. That ongoing manifestation, the dance between the wave and the particle, is the continual creation of the universe."[35]

As implied in the metaphor of union between the masculine and feminine prin-

---

* Echoing the Source, Wolf explains the "Mother" principle as the preceding state or condition of all primary creational activity: "The universe was created from three 'mother' letters, aleph, mem, and sheen, according to the Qabala. Aleph represented power, mem represented consciousness, and sheen was the wavelike action --- the flow from aleph into consciousness. The Hebrew letter, seen, another form of the letter sheen, was the particlelike action --- the flow from mem back to aleph, thus completing the circuit. The game was to achieve balance." Quoted in Fred Alan Wolf, *The Eagle's Quest* (New York: Simon and Schuster, 1991), p. 123.

ciple, the actuating force governing all primal and pre-cosmogenic activity was love, begetting the first manifestation of love --- the Logos. The Divine intent, therefore, was/is for the cosmic energy generated by the uniting of masculine transcendence and feminine immanence for the bringing forth the active principle of Love to be recapitulated in every successive re-creative act of manifestation.

IN THE BEGINNING...WAS PLASM

So it is written: "By the word [Logos] of the Lord the heavens were made...he spoke, and it [the earth] was made" (Psalms 33:6:9). From the creative potency of the initial archetypal event, there was *nothing* made that was not made as an expression of Divine Love. Consequently, the Logos or Logoidal consciousness, the as yet-to-be author of creation, objectifies from Its infinite potentiality the Logoidal plasm or raw material from which all else was made:

> Logoidal consciousness, then, that is, the Logos [Love] in consciousness of self, produced Logoidal plasma. As in your time, the desire for, the creation of, the attraction to self of the object of desire produces plasm that eventually will manifest in materialization. Logoidal consciousness, then, [is] the source of Logoidal plasm, [and] Logoidal plasm [is] the source of Logoidal energy. For the consciousness setting the plasm in motion produced energy that went forth and, as the next verse states from the Book of John, "Without Him was nothing made that was made." That is, all things, then, were made from Logoidal plasm through the action of Logoidal energy. Then if this be true, all that exists in your universe is created of the raw material of Logoidal plasm; that is, the final breakdown, the minutest form of all things that exist.
>
> All things, then, are created from Logoidal plasm, the energy of their manifestation, the energy of the plasm becoming form. "The Word became flesh and dwelt among us." That becoming form is Logoidal energy. Then Logoidal energy is the all-pervading force that may be equated to consciousness. Or see it in this manner: that energy will go as intent or purpose from one mind to another, whether in healing, whether in thought transference as you call it, or the field properties of thought. The vehicle is Logoidal plasm. The movement, or the energy itself [is] Logoidal energy. For all things, stepping beyond your terms of electricity or electromagnetic spectrum or any other spectrum, you see, all these things return to their source which is Logoidal plasm. It is a step beyond definitive terms in the sense of breaking it into any spectrum, for it is the source of all spectra. [This], then, [is] that all-pervading, pervasive energy and plasm in your universe and beyond. [It is] not limited to your universe, you understand, not limited to the universe. [It is] the plasm of all that is, Logoidal plasm, the expression of God, the expression of the Word, then (Solomon Reading No. 642, 6/75).

As indicated by the Source, fields of plasma are as apt to accommodate the human body as they are a celestial body, a galactic body, or the universe as a whole. In microcosmic terms, what is now referred to as the "bioplasmic" body was in ancient metaphysical traditions called the etheric body, the fluidic body, or pre-physical body because it exists *prior* to the formation of the physical body itself. William A. Tiller, former director of the Materials Science Department at Stanford University, believes it "may be another level of substance, producing a hologram, a coherent energy pattern...which is a force-field for organizing matter to building itself into this kind of a physical network."[36] The Solomon Source would agree: [it exists] **for the purposes of forming a pattern about the self for the integrity of the life form, that which gives form, shape, dimension, building and life force** (Solomon reading No. 906, 10/29/76). Whereas it is regarded in Peter Tompkins' view as "a magnetic area where immaterial or subatomic vortices of the cosmos are transformed into the individual, the channel through which life communicates with the physical body,"[37] nevertheless it seems to respond symptomatically to the activation of the life force within the individual as well. When, for example, through the experience of love, prayer, healing, or any form of creative activity the force of life is made conscious in every cell of our bodies and beings, therein, in the interaction between those electromagnetic energies being channeled by the bioplasma and the combinations of elements that make up our bodies, is produced a bio-energy which, to clairvoyant visualization, flares forth in luminous shafts or beams or crowns of light. Conversely, states of fear, anger, or hatred tend toward entropy, as a closed system does. The energies appear dimmed, darkened, distorted and withdrawn, indicating, as the Source points out, that plasmic substance is actually produced when inward reflectivity extends outward, beyond its own self-enclosed center and into the transpersonal dimensions that we refer to as "love."

Just as bioplasm is used by the higher consciousness of an organism for carrying the energies necessary for the formation of the physical body, so macrocosmically speaking, Logoidal consciousness produces that universal plasm from which the elements of a physical cosmos may emerge. From the all-embracing dimension of the Absolute, the ubiquitous plasm is set into resonant motion through the Logos, the all-compelling force of Love --- that is, the vibrational energy of God expressing as light --- thus precipitating the Logoic energy necessary to manifest form. The plasmic substance of the universe is a manifestation of this "Logoidal plasm", just as a cloud is, in a sense, a manifestation of atmospheric water vapor. Its protoplasmic form precedes its cosmogenic entelechy.

In the beginning, therefore, was plasm. The entire unformed universe was saturated with it. It is a vision of cosmic chaos, the formless and void state of the Torah, the Unknowable which could not be named of the Kabbalah, the *Massa Confusa* of Alchemic Lore, upon which order is prospectively imposed through that fiat expressing as photons of light. It is theorized that the radiation pressure of these photons may ultimately have forced the Big Bang itself. For, "at a certain stage," insists Bohm, "some of these light rays got together and made The Big Bang. And that unfolded into our universe..."[38] Then, following the cosmogenesis, gigantic plasma fields, ionized through the initial conditions of extreme heat and high levels of photonic radiation mainly in the form of high-energy X-rays and gamma rays, begin to condense into huge volumes of gas. All this while the universe is radiant with light, there being no darkness or night whatsoever.

Eventually, after 700,000 years, the time it takes for the universe to cool from 100 million degrees to 3,000 degrees K (the point at which the contents of the universe become transparent to radiation[39]), the density of the gas becomes greater than the mass density of radiant energy and electrons combining with nuclei form the first stable atoms of hydrogen, deuterium, then helium. With the formation of heavier elements, gravitation becomes a formative cosmic force. Under its influence, these immense clouds of gas gradually begin to contract forming stars which are then drawn together into galaxies.

Astrophysicists have now established through radio astronomy that just as there are solar winds, so there are galactic winds that sweep along magnetic fields enclosed in the plasma at a speed of 35 miles per second. Given that plasma comprises about 90 percent of all matter in the universe, it is estimated that the mass of ionized gas created by such movement is sufficient to form millions of new stars each year in the Milky Way galaxy alone. Furthermore, scientists now are able to observe plasma in a vacuum chamber forming itself into plasma vapors that assume the shape of a spiraling mist about 10 cm in diameter with a length of up to 50 cm. Thus, we can actually witness the formation of a universe in miniature.

Planets and solar systems now emerge, and on at least one of these worlds photosynthesis produces organic molecules, notably amino acids and nucleotides, which are the building-blocks of proteins, themselves an essential constituent of living cells. Through the evolution of energy forms, from Logoic energy through its subatomic expression as light, from plasma through complex molecular and cellular structures of DNA so small that a thimbleful would easily contain the regulating structures for the whole of humanity, there develops that physical expression of energy that is capable of knowing itself as energy --- *mankind*.

"GOD DOES NOT PLAY DICE..."

What are the chances, within the limits set by the uncertainty principle in physics, that from its explosive cosmic origins our present highly ordered and coherent cosmos would unfold? What are the odds that all these systems and processes and structures could have blindly sorted themselves into existence --- into *our* existence?

In 1964, bioevolutionists Malcolm Dixon and Edwin Webb calculated that, based on chance alone, the total volume of amino-acid solution required to get the needed amino acids close enough to form just one simple protein molecule would be equal to 10 to the power of 50 times the volume of the earth. In other words, in a solution saturated with amino acids the least quantity sufficient to produce the proper association of amino acids to form even a single protein molecule would be equal in capacity to one hundred quadrillion nonillion times the volume of our entire planet. Extending such calculations to the chance formation of a more complex protein such as hemoglobin, biochemists S.W. Fox and J.F. Foster came to the mind boggling conclusion that only after these simple protein molecules, packed solid, protein molecule to protein molecule, had been formed in such quantity that they filled a volume

10 to the power of 512 times the volume of the *entire known universe* could we reasonably expect that just one hemoglobin molecule might form itself by chance alone.

Then again, in the late 1970's, Fred Hoyle and Chandra Wickramasinghe recalculated the odds that life could have accidently arisen from an indiscriminate sloshing about of the legendary "primordial soup." Limiting the daunting task of an entire organism to a sequence of twenty or thirty key amino acids in the enzymes of some hypothetical cell, the number they came up with was one chance in $10^{40,000}$! "Odds like these become even more telling when we introduce the factor of time," observes cultural historian Theodore Roszak. "F.B. Salisbury has attempted to do just that. He undertook to calculate the probability for the haphazard assemblage of the thousand nucleotides necessary to synthesize even a small enzyme containing a mere three hundred amino acids. His conclusion was that there would be not even a fraction of the time needed in the entire history of the universe. This left Salisbury to observe that *chance* may be the factor that has to be eliminated if the evolutionary explanation of life is to retain its cogency. An ironic proposal. Chance, previously so powerful an explanatory device, now becomes the obstacle to coherent explanation."[40]

With each correct molecule occurring only once in an incomprehensible number of universes, and given the incalculable time factor involved, what, then, would be the odds that enough of them would be present within the miniscule space required for them to locate each other and link up to form a living cell? The answer, categorically and unequivocally, is none. None at all. And yet the scientific establishment would have us believe that it did happen in the relatively short period of our earth's history in the thin layer of moisture that forms but a portion of our planet's surface.

The inference, that all this resulted from one cosmic roll of the dice, is so freighted with astronomical improbability that, if true, it must in itself be considered nothing less than miraculous. Here, surely, is "blind faith!" The highly dubious resort to doctrinaire materialism, mechanical novelty, and random probability is more an excuse for salvaging scientific autonomy from the crumbling ruins of objectivity than it is for meeting the need for finding the truth. "The scientific attitude," declares Nobel prize winning biologist Jacques Monod, "implies what I call the postulate of objectivity --- that is to say, the fundamental postulate that there is no plan, that there is no intention in the universe." This, he maintains, is "the essential message of science" which has usurped "the ancient animist covenant between man and nature, leaving nothing in place of that precious bond but an anxious quest in a frozen universe of solitude."

> Modern societies accepted the treasures and the power that science laid in their laps. But they have not accepted --- they have scarcely even heard --- its profounder message: the defining of a new and unique source of truth, and the demand for a thorough revision of ethical premises... If he accepts this message --- accepts all it contains --- then man must at last wake out of his millenary dream and in doing so, wake to his total solitude, his fundamental isolation. Now does he at last realize that, like a gypsy, he lives on the boundary of an alien world. A world that is deaf to his music, just as indifferent to his hopes as it is to his suffering or his crimes.[41]

It seems incredible from the standpoint of the Source that human beings ever could have invented a way of knowing so devoid of significance, so completely immersed in clever-minded despair. For if truth be told, there is not the least quantum of probability in the design present in the structure of the cosmos. Put simply, all life, all universal existence, is a manifestation of Logoidal consciousness expressing Its intentionality through the divine energy of Love. This is not to say that we are bound by cosmological determinism. It is to say, as the eminent religious scholar Radhakrishnan observes, that "the Absolute has an infinite number of possibilities to choose from, which are all determined by its nature. It has the power of saying yes or no to any of them. While the possible is determined by the nature of the Absolute, the actual is selected from out of the total amount of the possible, by the free activity of the Absolute without any determination whatsoever. It could have created a world different in every detail from that which is actual. If one drama is enacted and other possible ones postponed, it is due to the freedom of the Absolute." God, after all, "does *not* play dice..." It is, therefore, "the abiding I AM," continues Radhakrishnan, "[that] is the creative mind of the world, with a consciousness of the general plan and direction of the cosmos, even before it is actualized in space and time. He holds the successive details in proper perspective and draws all things together in bonds of love...."[42]

By its very nature love is unitive, tendential, and ameliorative. One is "drawn up" by love. Moses was motivated and drawn on "by great love." Our hearts are "knit together in love" for "God *is* love." Indeed, the very elements of which we and the world are made, the thread of which nerves, stars, and atoms are woven, is the Logos, the one indivisible Source of life which draws all things onto Itself. It is love, then, that is the eternal energy of life, and life that is the inevitable expression of love. Within this infusion of life with love and the ecstatic desire of love for life lies the eternal dance of creation. If this were properly understood, says the Source, then our long and arduous search for the coveted unified field in physics would be over:

> We wish to say, then, that there is the one energy that is Life itself in expression. This, which we call Life, also has qualities which in an ancient time were referred to as agape (divine love). Life which, by its very nature seeks to expand and to share, life which desires to share, is known as love. And it was the desire to share --- from this original creative fiat that went out into light and sound and all those things, it was its desire to share itself that allowed life forms and other expressions to participate in its liveliness.

> Now, we wish to make the point clear that there was and is only one primal energy from which all other energies are components, results, expressions of this, the One. Here is the basis for your unified field, if it be understood that there is not at the ultimate point of expression [a] flowing forth of energy and vitality; there is not, as you have assumed, even in your theory of Big Bang, there is not a positive and a negative force and counterforce. At the beginning of, the origin of all that is created, there is more simply a pouring forth of light, which is something, which is living in fact, which is something which exists as evidenced by the fact that it can travel in units called photons, quanta of energy, as compared with its counterpart, darkness. Darkness, in truth, exists not. There are no quanta of units of darkness. There are not

such expressions of darkness which travel. It does not travel. It has neither substance nor reality in any form other than its appearance to be a point of reference for the existence of light. And so it exists only to that extent. That extent is the extent of nothing, which allows the fact that something exists to be known. That is its only purpose. And even as we speak of darkness as "it", we speak in improper terms, for it isn't "it". It rather simply isn't.

Then if this be so of light and darkness, it is as well so of life and death. For death, you can demonstrate for yourself, is not the annihilation, the disappearance of something which has expressed as life. You do not know some force or form which you can appropriately identify as death. For such does not exist. Experiment as you like and you will find that you can cause nothing to permanently cease its existence, whether of consciousness, of light, of plant, animal, or any other expression of life. Should you extinguish it quite totally, it simply will cease its expression for a time and then return to express itself again. There is no death. Thus, the word serves only the purpose of a point of reference to express a positive. Death is appropriately used only as an expression of the fact that there is something which is, which does exist, which is an opposite of that which doesn't exist, being called by a name: death --- but which is a name for something that isn't. Yet it serves a purpose for expressing that there is a counterpart which is, which does exist.

And may we offer then a third: that which we've referred to as agape --- the tendency, the need in that which lives to live more abundantly, to give its life, to share its life, to share and to share and to share in combination and recombination or expression. The force of agape, of love, is that force which causes all living things to wish to re-create. Re-creation is [the] ultimate expression of love. It is the desire in the soul of all that lives to give life and continue the living of life by spending the life force of itself for the purpose of giving that life force to something that will continue the expression of its existence.

Then love is so inherent in life that life itself might even attempt to quench itself for the purpose of giving new life to continue to live. Nor can life be caused to cease to exist. If you created of your planet a barren place, totally annihilating the expression of life upon it, you would find that for a time it would seem to be barren. And perhaps ice would form, and then begin to melt away. And with the melting a sprig of green would appear in photosynthesis and build the process of ever increasingly complex forms of life again to repopulate this place.

And may we further say to you: there is no sphere in all those spheres that you know in the universe that is without life. The life on these spheres does vary in its expression so that on many you would not encounter life with the limitation of your senses, for they [your senses] are peculiar to your planet. And you are not well equipped to enter, [to] interact with life from other spheres.

Then having said all of these things it is our intent to affirm that there is only one force which is in fact real. It is [the] original creative force. It is Logoic or Logoidal energy. It is, in the terms of the writer of the gospel of John, it is the

Word, the Living Word. It is the expression of God gone out to reveal itself in so many different forms that the broad spectrum of its expression might be known (Solomon Reading No. 1413, 5/29/90).

Hence, the entire design reveals a plan and purpose: nothing is left to accident or to fitful inspiration; all the infinitely diverse cosmos reflects the constant flowing and reflowing of the Logoic energy of Divine Love. Life, Love, Logos, the expression of Supreme Identity, that which from the harmonics and vibrations of sound and light to the vast hierarchy of synthetic, interlocking systems that make up the cosmos brings forth the whole enterprise of creation. All life, and thus all time, the great cycles of efformation, of birth and rebirth, the ancient forms of forgotten worlds, all the winding years of eternity and of universes yet unborn are exfoliated from this single radiant expression of the Eternal. And in the midst of this majestic and limitless theophany we live and move and have our being.

Chapter 3

The Energy That Gives Birth
To The Cosmos

THE WORD MADE FLESH

Anyone who has experienced a sudden and dramatic enlargement of vision
--- the breaking down of the dykes that separate us from the illimitable
ocean of our being and from the universal interconnectedness of things
and events --- is acutely aware of the immense primordial power of this
supersensual force of love. For many personally familiar with those spontaneous moments of so-called "mystical consciousness" when the flood-
gates of inner energy open onto a sea of transcendent meaning, eternal
life is found to be synonymous with all-encompassing and limitless love.
"Presently what seemed to be a swift, oncoming tidal wave of splendor
and glory ineffable came down upon me, and I felt myself being envel-
oped, swallowed up," writes one individual in a case in Richard Bucke's
celebrated study *Cosmic Consciousness*:

> I felt myself going, losing myself. Then I was terrified, but with a sweet
> terror. I was losing my consciousness, my identity, but was powerless to
> hold myself. Now came a period of rapture, so intense that the universe
> stood still, as if amazed at the unutterable majesty of the spectacle! Only
> one in all the infinite universe! The All-loving, the Perfect One! The
> Perfect Wisdom, truth, love and purity! And with the rapture came the
> insight. In that same wonderful moment of what might be called super-
> nal bliss, came illumination. I saw with intense inward vision the atoms
> or molecules, of which seemingly the universe is composed --- I knew
> not whether material or spiritual --- rearranging themselves, as the cos-
> mos (in its continuous, everlasting life) passes from order to order. What
> joy when I saw there was no break in the chain --- not a link left out
> --- everything in its place and time. Worlds, systems, all blended in one
> harmonious whole. Universal life, synonymous with universal love![43]

Worlds upon worlds, from the infinitesimal to the incomprehensibly vast,
from the subatomic constituents of matter and energy to stars and galaxies too numerous to count, all bodied forth from the immanent center of
all existence --- universal love.

Likewise, an account given by Richard Bucke of his own experience in
cosmic awareness recognizes in the universal life-force the same indivisible essence of love:

> All at once, without warning of any kind, I found myself wrapped
> in a flame-colored cloud. For an instant I thought of fire, an im-
> mense conflagration somewhere close by in that great city; the

next, I knew that the fire was within myself. Directly afterward there came upon me a sense of exultation, of immense joyousness accompanied or immediately followed by an intellectual illumination impossible to describe. Among other things, I did not merely come to believe, but I saw that the universe is not composed of dead matter, but is, on the contrary, a living Presence; I became conscious in myself of eternal life. It was not a conviction that I would have eternal life, but a consciousness that I possessed eternal life then; I saw that all men are immortal; that the cosmic order is such that without any peradventure all things work together for the good of each and all; that the foundation principle of the world, of all worlds, is what we call love....[44]

Again and again in the accounts given by people of visionary experiences, we find affirmation of the overpowering and inviolable force of divine light and universal love. Echoing the statements of mystics and those who have experienced ecstasies are the visionary accounts of those who are dying and of near-death survivors. Near-death researcher Dr. Kenneth Ring presents the case of forty-six-old author, publisher, and businessman Joseph F. Dippong:

...I became aware of the most powerful, radiant, brilliant white light. It totally absorbed my consciousness. It shone through this glorious scene like the sun rising on the horizon through a veil which had suddenly opened. This magnificent light seemed to be pouring through a brilliant crystal. It seemed to radiate from the very center of the consciousness I was in and to shine out in every direction through the infinite expanses of the universe. I became aware that it was part of all living things and that at the same time all living things were part of it. I knew it was omnipotent, that it represented infinite divine love. It was as if my heart wanted to leap out of my body towards it. It was almost as though I had met my Maker. Even though the light seemed thousands and thousands times stronger than the brightest sunlight, it did not bother my eyes. My only desire was to have more and more if it and bathe in it forever.[45]

Another of Ring's subjects reports that following her near-death occurrence: "I longed to understand, to find that feeling of love again. Some part of it remained in my heart, however, and that part continues. It is sometimes expanded and sometimes decreased, but it remains a sign to me of another dimension of Love, Life and Power. I think of the feeling as one of Love, although that word lacks its total import. It is certainly much more than that."[46] Additional testimony of the effects of near-death are recorded in the following words. "The most important thing that we have are our relationships with other people.... It all comes down to caring and compassion and love for your fellow man.... Love *is* the answer. It's the answer to everything."[47] As expressed so insistently to yet another visionary, love is the answer to the ultimate regeneration of the human race. The Light told her in these "exact words": "With the gift you have now received, go forth and tell the masses of people that life after death exists; that you shall all experience my PROFOUND LOVE! LOVE is the key to the universe; you must all learn to live in peace and harmony with one another on earth while you have the chance." [48]

*love
by*

Love is key because it is the one and only universal force that can offset the awful omniscience and omnipotence of our pathologically dehumanized technology, that can set free the earth and all its creatures from the insensate forces of hate and violence that threaten destruction, and that can aid us in our journey from multiplicity to unity. Any doctrine of indivisibility or wholeness that does not begin with love itself can hardly hope to produce either a unified self or a unified world.

More significantly, however, love is key to the entire physical, mental, and spiritual labyrinth of "life itself." As the Logos, it shows forth as the essence of all being, the only true reality, of which our sensory world and even our highest thoughts are but a pale, unsteady reflection. And as an effluence of the Logos, love is the force behind all social and personal integration, behind the very possibility of creative fulfillment through an ever-widening and ever more inclusive partnership with life. It is, in final analysis, the only energy through which the Suprapersonal Absolute can be experienced. Such is the metaphysics of love, that it draws each of us toward all of us by drawing us all toward the fundamental Source of life itself.

Towering above all the ethical superstructures of human creed and convention, beyond all limits or qualifications or right-minded convictions, however, is the universal Law of Love which commands of us that we open to the one force that reflects the eternal in human nature. For in connecting our lives with infinite life and in recognizing our highest welfare in the fulfillment of the laws of this infinite life, we become, thereby, the fulfillment of the Law. As we read in the Epistle of Paul, "love *is* the fulfilling of the law" (Romans 13:10). Hence, the Solomon Source emphatically enjoins us:

> Go beyond the reawakening of any single expression to bring again the Law of One or Law of Love, being the correct interpretation of those first words of the writing of John, which said: "In the beginning God expressed Himself, and the expression of God is God being expressed." That is to say, the Son of God is God expressing Himself. God the Father, the unmanifest; God the Son, the manifest of God, this Son being known as the Word or the Logos, the [term] Logos from the Greek being correctly interpreted as "expression". God expressed Himself and the expression of God is Love, living Love which is the Light, which is the enlightenment of every man who has come into the world. The ability to be enlightened ... to have light, to be *alive*, to know self and God, this is the Word made flesh who lives among us and is in every man. To those who know, who discover the life in them, the light, the ability to love, this is the Child of God. This is the very Christ. To those who come to know are given the gift of being the Sons and Daughters of God (Solomon Reading No. 1285, 3/6/88).

To acknowledge ourselves in this way, as children of God, is the final *desideratum* of the soul. Only love can so draw us, and in the fullest reciprocity of a love which infinitely exceeds our own we at last may be drawn, insofar as our recalcitrance permits, into an incandescent fusion with the very Being of love Itself, living love which is the Logos, which begat the entire wealth of cosmological existence as if it were but a cell in the life of Its infinite Mind. So that as with Eckhart we may declare: "The Father himself begets his Son, and what is more, he begets me as his son --- the self-same Son! Indeed, I assert that he begets me not only as his Son but himself as myself, begetting me in his own nature, his own being. At the inmost source I spring from the Holy Spirit, and there is one life, one being, and one action."[49] And as the Source would add, "one Law" in relation to which we as the "Children of God" are defined and in the fulfillment of which we are opened finally to the Infinite.

THE MEASURE OF THE SOUL

As self-reflective finite creatures, we cannot help but consider our position within the cosmos. Where do we stand in relationship to the All? Are we, as Sir Arthur Eddington calculates, almost precisely halfway in size between an atom and a star? Astrophysics points out that in magnitude we are all but equidistant between the size of the entire universe (10^{29}cm) and the smallest measureable size of the subatomic world (10^{-33}cm). Does this proportional distinction confer upon us any esoteric privilege? Like blind persons in a labyrinth we find ourselves struggling to maintain our point of equilibrium. Here, on our small planetary grain situated in the remote suburbs of a spiral galaxy that is but one among billions, we gaze out over the eternal landscape and reflect upon our identity with the infinite. Are we likewise midway between the beasts and the gods? How do our lives relate to the Source of all that we behold?

A thousand years ago we dwelled at the center of a medieval cosmical scheme that gave us a unique share in the attention of Heaven. The stars moved across the Empyrean in the paths which God had ordained, and in Dante's view this visible world was held together by an inscrutable force called "Love." By the 16th century, however, Copernicus had jolted us out of our privileged geocentricity along with our assumption that the universe might reasonably be supposed to have ourselves as its purpose and its explanation. If we were not at the center of the universe, we were no longer the single and unique focus of God's attention. It was this very denial of geocentric astronomy that later allowed Newton to imagine that the force that kept the moon in its orbit was the same that drew his apple to the ground. By substituting the technical word "gravity: for the frankly mysterious word "love," Newton inveighed against the old Christian cosmography and in so doing established the universality of the physical laws of science. Efficient causation replaced teleology as the accepted means of explanation, and God, who for the medievalists was immanent within earth's nature, became for the new science a wholly unknowable designer of a clockwork universe of which He was no longer an active part. The Newtonian God, now infinitely removed, no longer governed the world by direct intervention but rather by materialistic laws of force and motion. Once God had been secularized from the realm of physical nature, all that remained of the world

was what the hard facts and quantitative abstractions of scientific objectivity made it out to be: ponderously material, real in its own right,
and void of the transcendent symbolism and spiritual transparency that
once made us companionable with an omnipresent God. Moreover,
the mediocrity of our world among an infinite number of magnitudes
served, in our regard, only to emphasize and augment our diminished
sense of our place and consequence in the cosmic system.

Now once again we find ourselves living in the midst of a universe as mysterious as the heavens were ever thought to be. What was once ultimate (time,
space, matter, gravity) is ultimate no longer. Even the physical world is not at
all what it seems either to the senses or to common sense. Reality as we perceive it is as illusory as it was ever portrayed by the mystics, as incomprehensible as Dante's Love. What to the medievalists was conceived to be all spirit
is now said to be all energy. Might it not be, as the mystics have declared, that
all is Mind? Is it any more startling a breach of common sense or reason than,
say, the idea that instead of being qualitatively different matter and energy
are actually quantitatively convertible, or, as we are now told, that the entire
matter-space-time continuum is only the constructive interference of the inter-
penetrating universe? If, as science now affirms, the same laws and energies
that govern and constitute the world of physics also govern and constitute the
whole human world of consciousness, might it be that mind and energy are
likewise equivalent and, as the Source tells us, essentially commensurate in the
human and throughout the whole of a living universe? If we are to reaffirm
our place in the cosmos, then it seems that it must now be at a level at which
mind and energy coalesce, and perhaps at a point at which ancient thought
and modern physics converge.

The search for new, unifying concepts of the cosmos has compelled us to
reconsider our most fundamental assumptions about ourselves in the light of
which we are again as microcosms, distillations of form and consciousness,
of the structure, force and intelligence of the universe at large. Drawing upon
exiguous hypostatic associations that are beyond the reach of common logic
and human perception, science has now brought us to the completion of a perfect circle. Just as Plotinus could speak of "the whole in all, and in every part
the whole," so the new cosmology tells us that the information of the entire
universe is encoded in each of its parts which are relatively stable projections
of a primary reality of undivided wholeness intrinsic to the world. **Each body
or particle, even including subatomic expressions of energy, all of these are
holographic in nature,** affirms the Source. **For that reason, the smallest and
the largest imaginable structures of the universe carry within their very nature the hologram of the universe** (Solomon Reading No. 1739, 9/17/93). And
since each of us holographically contains the whole, theoretical physicists now
tell us that on a much deeper level we share, quite literally, one mind and one
consciousness. "Deep down the consciousness of mankind is one," points out
David Bohm. "This is a virtual certainty because even in the vacuum matter is
one; and if we don't see this it's because we are blinding ourselves to it."[50] Am-
plifying the point the eminent physicist Erwin Schrodinger writes, "Mind is by
its very nature a singulare tantum. I should say: the overall number of minds
is just one."[51] To speak of the multiplicity of consciousness[es] is meaningless.
Consciousness is one just as mind is one. We conceptually fractionalize and

localize it, in Schrodinger's words, "because of the spatio-temporal plurality of individuals, but it is a false construction."[52] The very same consciousness abides in all of us according to Schrodinger, and is identical on a higher level with Universal Mind which is equally undivided and that makes us all one. We are all of the One and in that deeper state of convergence each of us is all who have ever been and who forever again will be. So Schrodinger writes:

> A hundred years ago, perhaps, another man sat on this spot: like you, he gazed with awe and yearning in his heart at the dying light on the glaciers. Like you, he was begotten of man and born of woman. He felt pain and brief joy as you do. *Was* he someone else? Was it not you yourself? What is this Self of yours?... What clearly intelligible *scientific* meaning can this "someone else" really have?... Looking and thinking in [this] manner you may suddenly come to see, in a flash,...it is not possible that this unity of knowledge, feeling, and choice which you call *your own* should have sprung into being from nothingness at a given moment not so long ago; rather this knowledge, feeling, and choice are essentially eternal and un-changeable and numerically *one* in all men, nay in all sensitive beings. But not in *this* sense --- that *you* are a part, a piece, of an eternal infinite be-ing, an aspect or modification of it... No , but inconceivable as it seems to ordinary reason, you --- and all other conscious beings as such --- are all in all. Hence, this life of yours which you are living is not merely a piece of the entire existence, but is, in a certain sense, the *whole*; only this whole is not so constituted that it can be surveyed in one glance...Thus you can throw yourself flat on the ground, stretched out upon Mother Earth, with the certain conviction that you are one with her and she with you. You are firmly established, as invulnerable as she --- indeed, a thousand times firmer and more invulnerable. As surely as she will engulf you tomorrow, so surely will she bring you forth anew to new striving and suffering. And not merely, "someday"; now, today, every day she is bringing you forth, not *once,* but thousands upon thousands of times, just as every day she engulfs you a thousand times over. For eternally and always there is only *now,* one and the same now; the present is the only thing that has no end.[53]

Time is an eternal Now. Mind is One. And yet...our lives tick on, "uncon-nected with anything," as Rilke's young poet would say, "like a watch in an empty room." Or to put it another way, as Capra remarks we live our lives as if Newton, not Einstein, were right --- as if the world were frag-mented and mechanical and we were somehow separate from the reality that informs our senses.

In point of fact, the calculations of science, which have opened a path to other universes, have done little to substantially alter our own. It is true that by piecing together great masses of data science has been able to tell us plausible stories about the origins of the universe and, to a lesser extent, of our earthly selves. Furthermore, what may have come to the ancients by way of mystical insight and moral imperative has in some measure returned to us through the rigorous experimental and theoretical methods of value-free science and the painstakingly gradual process of disciplinary convergence. The laws of the universe are no longer regarded as absolute, while mind and nature have formed a necessary unity. Terms such as "symbiosis", "interrelatedness", "quantum connectedness", "holographic unity" have become *de rigueur*. But without any claim to reverence, with no sense of a nature alive and infused with purpose, concealing divinity never far below the surface of appearances, science can never regard us as anything more than creatures obtruded into a haphazard universe without continuity or kinship. It can never tell us how to realize our inherent intimacy with the unitive dimension of existence or with the intricate, moment-to-moment dance of creation. While it offers a theoretical understanding of consciousness, it neither discerns nor communicates the need for the development of consciousness. It can never regard truth as a multidimensional *experience*, an experience which resonates through the whole of a living cosmos. It can never give us a direct report of the Absolute and irreducible One.

Hence, even though we develop imposing systems of cosmological, ethical, and psychological thought in full intellectual accord with the idea of a higher unified field of consciousness, still we find difficulty in coming to grips with it on an existential level. Primarily so because no human language or concept can ever express such an experience. We simply cannot avoid the inherent dualism of words and thoughts which filter according to their measure the meaningful patterning of higher dimensional realms into conventional structures of time, space, subject-object, self-other. Experiential knowledge so grasped by thought alone is no more experienced than, say, water caught up from the stream is flowing. Physics may delineate for us an Absolute present, an eternal Now, a holomovement wherein time, space and consciousness are coalesced and not yet differentiated, but no matter how brilliant or impassioned it may be the thought that delineates must forever remain limited in time and space and frozen in form and concept into the partial framework of its own conditioning. It may work well in a world that is dualistically conceived, but as for its probing the mysteries of ultimate reality it is by itself an adequate instrument. The powers of the intellect stop short at the point where thought, having reached the limits of its employment, senses that there is still "something other" beyond its reach.

Beyond the illusory nature of the world in which we live and move, mirroring orders of mind and reality that are related to our own neither spatially nor temporally but in another mode of eternal being, there abides the immense, the immeasurable and the formidable subtleties of a universe of pure consciousness. It is the Kingdom as spoken of by Jesus, the Logoidal expression of God's love, the Dharmakaya ("Body of Essence") of Buddhism, the world of real causes from which all visible things are called to form. Within it we are flesh-events, fated to dissolve, losing nothing of our life-essence, only to reemerge like the overnight growth of a whisker with its follicle rooted ever so inseparably with the tissue which supplies it with life. Enfolding and unfolding, dissolving and reappearing, these are the ever-changing seasons of its eternally-unchanging Now. Being eternally Now it contains the whole universe; apart from it nothing has reality or life. In its all-inclusiveness it excludes nothing save the distinctions forged by our insular and arbitrary thoughts. And although vibrating in a wavelength of the mind that for most of us remains a world away, it is the primary postulate of all those disciplines which can rightfully be called esoteric that there is that of ourselves that is identical with its living, numinous presence.

Traditional wisdom holds that from within the sanctuary of that essentially incomprehensible yet all-comprehending universe of consciousness, that aspect of ourselves that *is* Buddha-nature, the *Atman* of the Hindu *Vedas*, the Christ-self of Christian mystics --- in short, that which is the universal Source of mind --- beholds all. It is this that enabled Jesus to see in himself every man, that led Gautama to proclaim in his own words that his consciousness had penetrated countless epochs of the world's past and future, an infinity of time that became to his boundless consciousness the eternal Now. And as part of our given nature, the Solomon Source affirms that there is omnipresent and apperceivable that of the Source within the unmanifest reaches of each individual consciousness: **...there is that in you that can lift the self and the understanding far beyond the manifest, for it has been said again and again that the mind has not the ability to go beyond the manifest to see or experience, to understand or describe the unmanifest. And logic would have it that the unmanifest cannot be understood or described. Yet it is only the manifestation of the mind which cannot understand or describe the unmanifest, and the Source of the mind is unmanifest and can both understand and describe** (Solomon Reading No. 1148. 9/19/83).

Thought, which *is* the manifestation of the mind, is always bounded by a frontier of ineffability, by that "something other" which precedes thought and transcends its grasp. Beyond the reflective, self-conscious activity of the mind lies a vast rolling sea of significance stretching endlessly in all directions. If we are to lift ourselves and our understanding beyond the manifest and into the inexpressible mystery of that something other, then as Paul Solomon himself taught, we must live *in this moment* without binding ourselves in a chain of thoughts, memories and anxieties for the morrow. For as the Source repeatedly insists, the moment of creation is happening *Now*. To swim with the ever-flowing stream of existence, never departing from the unobstructed current of the Now, is to never leave the infinite. For the infinitesimal timeless Now is the eternal abode of the mind's boundless Source.

Hence, "the perfect man," says Chuang-Tzu, "employs his mind as a mirror; it grasps nothing, it refuses nothing, it receives but does not keep." Compared with the mind which "grasps nothing," all forms and categories in which reality appears to our ordinary awareness are illusory because our thoughts, torn out of their organic connections and deprived of their universal relationship, are reactive, attuning us only partially to the world of our senses and contaminating most of it with critical judgement. But the mind that fastens onto no thought and that abandons itself to the creative energy of an ever-present Now no longer sees itself from the vantage point of the ego, but from the universal perspective of its unmanifest Source. He who thus loses his life will have found it. And "that," in the words of Alan Watts, "is the mighty self-abandonment which gives birth to the stars."[54]

While there is no logic or commonly agreed upon method by which we join our energy with the energy of that infinite Presence that surrounds and fills us, nevertheless, as the mystics have told us it is simple: "as simple as flight for the sparrow, as swimming for the trout," writes James Dickey. "You think of God's advice to the millipede, the thousand-legs who asked the Universe that made him how to work all those legs. Does this one go here? If it does, what do I do, then, with *this* one? With all these others? God's advice is... 'Don't think, just walk'."[55] That's us. Like the proverbial fish we are told to just let go and accept. Let go the anxiety, the fear, the endless doubt. Let it all out. Just to breathe is a kind of continuous flow in the unified field of living. Annie Dillard says, you catch grace as a man fills his cup under a waterfall. Let go the questioning, the reasoning, the narrow-gauged logicality that thinking patterns itself on. The Great Flow is just beyond our thoughts. By becoming aware of its fluid and ever-changing movements of energy within ourselves, to that extent we become the aperture through which the whole energy of conscious creation freely and unceasingly flows. "And that," as Paul Solomon puts it, "is the energy which gives birth to the cosmos."

Indeed, we cannot fully understand the cosmos until we have explored all its dimensions --- visible and hidden, unfolded and enfolded, actual and potential --- most significantly within ourselves. For it is here, in the depths of our own being, in the veiled presence of the Source within, that the boundless and implacable force of creation flows. The very same energy that powers the heavens and the infinity of worlds below, the one force in all movement, the one efficient and final cause of all effects, is the nisus embodied by each of us. It is the ultimate Kabbalah, the Logos, the Christos that "was in the beginning, is now and ever shall be;" it is the all-compelling force of the universal consciousness of love.

Were we to lay our minds wide open and peer through the veils receding to infinite depths of being, would we find in the dominion of our own incomprehensible Source the measure of the cosmos, and infinitely more? "Going 'within' is a transcendent journey that can take you beyond heaven and earth," affirms Paul Solomon, "a place greater than the cosmos and can contain it."[56] Standing on a terrace between the earth and the sky, would the scale of the universe remain for us inconceivably vast, or would it come to be seen as proportional to our selves? "Though there may be worlds, many universes, even much as to solar systems greater than our own that we enjoy in the present," declares the Universal Mind of Edgar Cayce, "yet the soul of man, thy soul, encompasses *all* in this solar system or in others. For we are joint heirs with that universal force we call God, if we seek to do His bidding."[57] Confronted with an infinity that lay deeper than our deepest roots and higher than our mind's reach, would we finally come to see the whole of the all-pervading Divine Order as it prevails? The Source tells us that the truth is within ourselves:

> Even in this day you could be one with the universe. At any moment, do understand, at any moment that any human expression of God gives up for a moment any idea or concept, any belief or recognition of the law of separation, gives up the idea that there is something that is opposite of God, something that is opposite Love and Life, when you discard the idea of duality and without resistance in yourself allow yourself to be one with

the universe, then you are now in this moment one with the universe. It simply means being in absolute and total harmony with the Law without insisting that there is something other than that perfect expression of the Law of the Christ within that exists. All that is of darkness, of death, of fear, of hate, all that there is that is not an expression of Love is absolutely and certainly an illusion. It is that which has no power other than that which you give it. And when you empower in your own creativity, from your own belief system, when you empower the absolute truth, the Living Christ, the absolute knowledge of the Law of One, when you experience that without any reservations, you are at one with the universe (Solomon Reading No. 1257, 11/8/90).

In Plato, Timaeus holds that the created world exists because the All-good, which is to say, the original creative force, wants its goodness to flow out upon it. The All-good, which is One in itself without qualification, is, for Plato, the transcendent principle of the whole, the Cause of the being of things, the ultimate Source of all light and life and truth. Likewise, Plotinus writes: "The fullest life is the fullest love, and the love comes from the celestial light which streams forth from the Absolute One" (Enneads, VI.7.23). This ancient and irrepressible truth forms the "genetic code" of all Perennial wisdom which, properly understood, lies at the foundation of the arts, philosophy and of religion. From the "great Tao that flows everywhere" to the Avatamsaka Sutra that transfigures the universe into Buddha's sacred body of light; from the Hermetic Uroborus inscribed "One is All" to Hermes Trismegistus who taught "The One is the father of all...," this primordial knowledge burned bright in human consciousness long before a scientific nihilism in its "quest for truth" degraded the sacramental One of the ancients, prophets, and visionaries into a statistical counterfeit.

Truth is One, states the Source. **And do understand that science...does not in any way mean to be separated from religion and philosophy and understanding. For science is a department of religion, but has in your day been made a separate religion unto itself, rather than serving reunion with the Source. And scientists are priests, priests of a particular order of what should serve the...Law of One** (Solomon Reading No. 1350, 4/20/88). The point is not lost on Sir Arthur Eddington, who writes: "A scientist should recognize in his philosophy --- as he already recognizes in his propaganda --- that for the ultimate justification of his activity, it is necessary to look away from knowledge itself to a striving in man's nature [which is] not to be justified of science or reason, for it is in itself the justification of science, of reason, of art, of conduct."[58] Indeed, if the truth ever is to be known, then science with its hard facts and quantitative abstractions must take its place beside those very traditions that it has worked to exile from cultural respectability. And its treasured idol of objectivity, so ingeniously sequestered from all the traditional gestalts of human understanding, must cease masquerading as the only reliable access to reality. Then, perhaps, "some day," as Teilhard de Chardin writes, "after we have mastered the winds, the waves, the tides and gravity, we shall harness...the energies of love. Then, for the second time in the history of the world, man will have discovered fire." [59]

Part Two
In The Image Of God

Chapter 4

The Fabric Of Creation

"IGNORANCE SURROUNDED BY LAUGHTER"

If the rocks and glaciers, mountains and sands could send us a message, what would it be? That encased within them, in endless strata of time, there lies a human past that denies every conventional thing we know to be true? That remote echoes of mankind's presence resonate through their every geological age and epoch?

The Paluxy River bed near Glen Rose in Texas contains an astonishing mystery. Nearly 100 feet beneath its surface in a limestone ledge dated by geologists and paleontologists alike to the end of the Mesozoic period in the Cretaceous --- some 140 million years ago --- are embedded the clearly preserved tracks of a three-toed dinosaur. Diagonally crossing them in the same stratum are large man-like footprints, the toes and the ball of one foot actually imprinted into the outer edge of a dinosaur track. Stratum after stratum of the dried-out river bed have been carefully excavated revealing hundreds of fossilized tracks of saurians of various species accompanied by the prints of large human-like feet between and next to them in an alignment indicative of a hunter's pursuit.

Standing alone, such evidence might easily be dismissed with the stereotypical objection that it was a hoax or forgery or, perhaps, displaced strata. Many such cases exist, however, adding useful support to the argument that hominids with anatomically modern human feet may have walked the earth for eons. Near Antelope Spring, Utah, William J. Meister reported finding a shoe print in Cambrian shale. The impression, dated to be over 500 million years old, was recovered in 1968 with trilobite fossils clearly indented in the print. In 1922 in Nevada, the fossilized remains of a partial hand-welted shoe sole with a well-defined sewn thread attaching the welt to the sole was recovered from Triassic rock dated at 213-248 million years ago. And in 1931, ten complete fossilized manlike tracks were found in Carboniferous sandstone by Dr. Wilbur G. Burroughs, head of the Geological Division of Berea College in Kentucky. "During the beginning of the Upper Carboniferous (Coal Age) Period, creatures that walked on their two hind legs and had human-like feet, left tracks on a sand beach in Rockcastle County, Kentucky," reported Burroughs in 1938. "This was the period known as the Age of Amphibians when animals moved about on four legs or more rarely hopped, and their feet did not have a human appearance. But in Rockcastle, Jackson and several other counties in Kentucky, as well as in places from Pennsylvania to Missouri inclusive, creatures that had feet strangely human in appearance and that walked on two hind legs did exist. The writer has proved the existence of these creatures in Kentucky. With the cooperation of Dr. C.W. Gilmore, Curator of Vertebrate Paleontology, Smithsonian Institution, it has been shown that similar creatures lived in Pennsylvania and Missouri."[1] All evidence indicates that the prints were formed by compression in the soft weft sand before it consolidated onto rock somewhere around 250 million years ago, a time now gone so utterly that its very light is now traveling on the farther edge of space.

In Greek, "seeing for one's self" is "autopsy." Just how fully prepared are we to autopsy the remains of a past that might conceivably transform our pedagogic knowledge of ourselves in the present? The esteemed American archaeologist George F. Carter discovered that if it is not satisfyingly tidy and complete, if it does not fit current models of prehistory which suggest a simple and scientifically consistent line of descent from ape-like creatures to modern humans, even unambiguous and incontrovertible evidence of remote human antiquity is axiomatically rejected, summarily dismissed, passed over in silence, or publicly ridiculed. At the Texas Street excavation in San Diego in the 1950's, Carter claimed to have found hearths and stone tools at levels corresponding to the last interglacial period, some 100,000 years ago. Given the standard view that humans supposedly first entered North America from Siberia about 12,000 years ago, Carter's claims were heresy to his critics. Although he invited numerous archeologists to study the site firsthand, none showed any interest. His implements and tools were derided as "cartifacts;" he was vilified in a Harvard course on "Fantastic Archeology." Having complied with a request to submit an article about his finds in a professional journal, scholars assigned to review the article rejected it with no credible rationale. Carter's reply to the editor, dated February 2, 1960, bluntly stated: "I must assume now that you had no idea of the intensity of feeling that reigns in the field. It is nearly hopeless to try to convey some idea of the status of the field of Early Man in America at the moment. But just for fun: I have a correspondent whose name I cannot use, for though he thinks that I am right, he could lose his job for saying so. I have another anonymous correspondent who as a graduate student found evidence that would tend to prove me right. He and his fellow students buried the evidence. They were certain that to bring it in would cost them their chance for their PhDs. At a meeting, a young professional approached me to say, 'I hope you really pour it on them. I would say it if I dared, but it would cost me my job.' At another meeting, a young man sidled up to say, 'In dig X they found core tools like yours at the bottom but just didn't publish them.'"[2]

Sadly, Carter's experience is unexceptional. Although convincing, albeit anomalous, evidence exists that anatomically modern humans may have inhabited the earth not merely for hundreds of thousands of years, but for tens of millions of years, any bit of paleoanthropological evidence which calls into question revered theories about human origins is conventionally impugned and subject to disciplinary suppression. As Michael Crèmo writes in *The Hidden History of the Human Race*: "Nineteenth-century scientists found many stone tools and weapons in Early Pleistocene, Miocene, and older strata. They were reported in standard scientific journals, and they were discussed at scientific congresses. But today hardly anyone has heard of them. Whole categories of facts have disappeared from view."[3]

A case in point: in 1866 in Calaveras County, California, a mine owner named Mattison removed a human skull from a layer of gravel overlapped by several distinct layers of volcanic material at a depth of 130 feet beneath the surface. Because regional volcanic eruptions began during the Oligocene, between 25-36 million years ago, and because the gravel bed lay near the bottom of the volcanic sequence, it is reasonable to conclude that the deposits in which the skull was found were somewhere in the range of 55 million years old. Moreover, as Crèmo points out, "the Calaveras skull was not an isolated discovery. Great numbers of stone implements were found in nearby deposits of similar age. And...additional human skeletal remains were also uncovered in the same region." Cremo concludes by saying: "In light of this, the Calaveras skull cannot be dismissed without the most careful consideration. As Sir Arthur Keith put it in 1928: 'The story of the Calaveras skull...cannot be passed over. It is the 'bogey' which haunts the student of early man...taxing the powers of belief of every expert almost to the breaking point.'"[4]

If the earth could speak, what would it tell us? That innumerable races of "mankind" have struggled for love and intelligence under its skies? That perhaps over immense cycles of creation, upheaval, and reformation humankind has been forced, as Plato says, "to begin again like children, in complete ignorance of what happened in early times"?[5] That all things remembered through our myths and legends, through the ancient themes of Genesis, the Popol Vuh of the Quiche Maya, the Hindu Ramayana, through the world's oldest traditions, are but an infinitesimal fraction of all that we have forgotten?

Evidence of technically advanced civilizations of infinitely remote ages has surfaced at excavation sites in every region of North America. In 1829, a quarry 12 miles northwest of Philadelphia yielded from a depth of 60-70 feet a solid block of marble bearing an inscription of letterlike shapes. The consensus is that the formation of the characters was not a product of natural processes, but of intelligent humans from the past.[6] A coin-like object was retrieved from a well-boring depth of 114 feet near Lawn Ridge, Illinois. The deposits containing the coin were dated by the Illinois State Geological Survey at between 200,000 and 400,000 years old.[7] A "small human image, skillfully formed in clay" and "remarkable for the perfection with which it represents human form" was recovered from the 300-foot level of a well boring at Nampa, Idaho. The Plio-Pleistocene deposits in which it was found are dated at 2 million years old.[8] In Hammondsville, Ohio, coal miners working 100 feet below the surface discovered a wall faceted with several lines of plainly carved, though undecipherable, hieroglyphics.[9] And on November 5, 1967, the Dallas Morning News carried a story reporting that ancient fortification-like walls were found buried in Rockwell County, Texas. Four large supporting stones removed from segments of the wall were found to be inscribed by some mysterious and unintelligible form of writing.

Thousands of similar examples of fossilized eoliths, paleoliths, hieroglyphs, and skeletal remains found at sites throughout the world could in fact be cited, leaving no doubt that *some* hominid-like creature(s) inhabited the early predawn epochs of earth's history and that collectively over the course of millions of years we have in all likelihood experienced more than one Apocalypse. More than once has the torchlight of civilization been lit and relit. But all evidence of such is rejected because it upsets preconceived ideas and established scientific theories which tell us in effect what we are; that beginning with Australopithecus afarensis we have steadily evolved over the course of three and a half million years to what we are today; that human civilization is a mere 5,000 years old, having begun around 3,000 B.C. in the Middle East's Fertile Crescent; that we are merely children of Nature, "good enough to survive."

How can Anthropos be understood except in anthropomorphic terms? What is left out is a vast library of rejected facts and realities that have been condemned. What we need is to overcome one of the most powerful prejudices of this century, namely our conviction that we know everything there is to know about mankind's presence on this planet.

"In the topography of intellection," remarked Charles Fort, "I should say that what we call knowledge is ignorance surrounded by laughter." In point of fact, we know more of the beginnings and nature of the universe than we know of the origins and nature of ourselves. It is said that after Plato had defined man to be a two-legged animal without feathers, Diogenes plucked a cock and brought it into the Academy. If man is more than the simplistic measure of Plato's analogical yardstick, then he is something more than a beast. More than simply a concept of fact, human being is being *sui generis*. Are we not equally children of spirit? What of us is nature and what part God? And of that part of us that mirrors the Infinite, how did we come to inhabit *this* human shell? Our genetic link to a three-and-a-half million year old anthropoid named Lucy notwithstanding, what we *need* to know is "something more" than what we've been led to believe, more than what even the most ancient and astonishing artifacts could possibly reveal about our primordial past and our identity in the present.

THE FRUIT OF AN ANCIENT TREE

If the heavens could speak, what would they tell us? That, indeed, while we *are* the fruit of an ancient tree, we are more so the seed of the ancient truth? That all that we are is infinitely more than the sum of all the world has been? That, perhaps, all the greatest mysteries are buried not in the earth, but in ourselves? If an angel reading from the timeless chronicles of an ancient past were to reveal the universal history that lies within each of us, what would he say?

Perhaps this:

> Every living soul has a Recording Angel who was assigned to that soul before time was conceived and who faithfully has followed the experience and the expression of the soul in its unfoldment. Now ... the record looks a great deal like a crystalline fabric, the end of which, or shall we call it the beginning as it issues forth from the emanation of the Divine --- we stretch your imaginations that you may reach back, looking, looking, following, tracing, searching to the Source of the record.... And this great thread of crystals interwoven as a fabric reaches into the morning, the dawn of creation, when the morning stars sang together and the Sons and Daughters of God gathered to witness the issuing forth of the Divine emanations, and the tumbling from the lips of God, the little crystals. We use the word "crystals" as an obviously inadequate term just for the purposes of visualization. Diamonds might serve, again inadequately, to simply give you a picture of that which we speak. Yet diamonds by their very nature are so far less pure and so woefully inadequate as a point of comparison that we use it only that you might stretch beyond words to see the dawning of this glorious morning when Atah Eloheinu spoke and the sound that issued forth with the ema-

nation could be seen; the sound that is the fabric of creation could be seen. And should you see it you would see it as [if] it were a river of diamonds, of crystals, flowing in a great tumbling river.

[I]n your simplicity, you ask, "Lord, let me know the sojourns of my soul from the river of the emanations of light, of crystalline fabric, and of reverberating sound which poured forth from the mouth of Abba Father before time began. What may I know of this record?"

A record of a single soul stretches from sky to sky, from universe to universe, from galaxy to galaxy, from system to system, to worlds that your world has never known and [that] your greatest minds do not yet know exist. [It is impossible] for your mind to even grasp the size of the record without taking from it a single word or concept, just the size, the magnitude of the record of you, [of a] single soul, [an] expression of the Lord in His handiwork. Allow yourself to be amazed....

And then [the] delicate fabric of [this] crystal stretching from sky to sky, planet to planet, of course life to life, woven by the fingers, the hands of Recording Angels as you think your thoughts, myriad thoughts. What have you counted? Twenty thousand concepts your mind is capable of processing in a single minute. See the flying angels' fingers weaving into the tapestry ... of the universe every thought, every feeling, emotion, relationship, discussion, every experience, imagination, flight of fantasy, dream, every experience of weaving such delicate relationships that you call karmic relationships, wrapping and wrapping and touching and bringing together soul after soul after soul in millions, billions --- beyond words! The interaction between the children of God who tumbled from His lips in that day of the morning of the stars, and in your touching one another in what you call karmic relationships through the seasons, the winds and the stretches and reaches of time and space and beyond. You who have tumbled from His lips interact with one another and weave this tapestry which has been called the great Akashic Record. The Recording Angel has set out with a speed far exceeding the speed of light to follow your thread through the tapestry back to its Source as it emanated from the mind and heart of God. How great a love for a single soul had the Source of this universe to weave such a tapestry with your life! (Solomon Reading No. 1261, 9/6/87).

Against this vast enduring background of wisdom, of power, of love, emanations of all the races of mankind begin.

From the almost identical sand grains of a desert, we emerge from the single torrent of our divine creation and, gradually translated to a human center of reference, into the surging flood of the living presence of "mankind." Through all the primordial races of "man," however different from one another and equally remote from ourselves, the Heavens record from the celestial Source of each temporal being the minute distinctive features of each grain. Every least sensation, thought, desire and emotion, every meanness, lamentation, kindness, exaltation, all indelibly written into the great cosmic skein of time and space. From the moment of this bold and deliberate enterprise when we first opened our eyes in amazement upon life, knowing not quite what to do with it, through the suffering of catastrophes and the forging of cultures and civilizations, all the great successive epochal phases of the human spirit have brought us to this most critical moment of our existence as a species. The vision of the Source now rounds back to a close which echoes the opening surge of our creation, but with a difference effected by all that has intervened --- the long sought-after unity with our Source that is of a higher order than the unity we have lost. The great Akashic Record of mankind with all its sustaining visual details is opened as if it were a history book, and from the point of view of eternity we are taken back along the vistas of eons to the living and luminous dawn of creation itself where, seemingly, the whole purpose and extent of existence is unveiled.

Chapter 5

The Day Of Radiance

THE PHRONESIS

From that eternal state of unknowingness ("Prime Central Stillness") before the beginning, before there was matter or any created thing, the Uncreated, Unnamed and immutably Infinite Cause of all causes, or Ein-Sof, contracted into Itself and brought forth the Logos (the eternal creative Word spoken of by John) what is in Itself all light, life, love and truth. From the first light of Logoic consciousness ("primeval inner light", the "infinitely hidden...root of all roots"*) there issued the Sefiroth or ten mystical emanations of light that streamed forth from the original. From these emanations which *are* the Divinity, the interchangeable identity of God with His Names or His Powers, there emerged a kaleidoscopic boundlessness of creation, a vast implicate sea of embryonic spirit from which all orders of spiritual being --- the angelic hierarchy as well as the entire pantheon of god-like beings --- arose.

Among this profusion of non-manifest being, the Logos objectified from Its infinite potentiality the Phronesis, or the Intelligences (Divine-human spirits) which were not as yet *human* beings but rather universal beings, forces of consciousness brought forth in the very image of God in the fullness of that which we call Love. They were beings of pure mind, self-luminous, and by the nature of spirit itself androgynous. Being undivided, they knew not death. Having emanated from the the Sefirotic world of light, they knew no darkness. Conceived in spirit through the infinite power of Love, they knew no evil. Having just emerged from the One, they yet remained immersed in the direct vision of the Source of all light and life and consequently experienced only the mysterious exaltation of life that we call joy. **We will call [this] the Day of Radiance or, as the Hebrews say, the Ain Soph Aur, relates the Source. This is a Day when all the Sons and Daughters of God expressed only as beings of light. And while there was consciousness in this day, it should not be called a self-consciousness for the reason that the radiant light-beings were well aware that they were all radiations of light from a central sun and not separate from one another so that the conscious was not a consciousness of a separate self. No sense of separation** (Solomon Reading No. 1619, 4/2/92).

These, then, were at the beginning with God, before creation. They were given to share in the dynamic unity of God's powers, just as candles being lit from a single flame with no lessening of their cogency or brightness. Here, in that timeless beginning, in the stillness before creation, they anxiously awaited the Divine Fiat that would bring into manifestation their own celestial life-giving powers of Love.

Then as the Word went forth as sound and light, all time, space, matter and energy were sent hurling forth from the fiery breath of creation, the measured

* Kabbalah

increase in complexity providing sequence for the cosmic calendar of events. Souls went out on that day, and in the use of the term 'day' we speak of eons of time. This is the day described by the ancient ones as the Day in which God spoke in creative fiat. And in that Day the radiance from the Creative Source went out and universes were formed, and the ancient writers speak of it as the day when the morning stars sang together. (The Morning Stars, as they watched, burst into a song of praise, and all the sons of God shouted for joy." Job 38:7) There was music in the celestial sphere which was being formed at that time (Solomon Reading No. 1619, 4/2/92).

From the earliest primitive atomic configurations to the formation of stars and galaxies, then at long last to the awakening of a life-bearing earth, the first five eonic days of creation passed into the remoteness of time. And as God smiled upon creation, He called the Sons of God [Phronesis] together. And the Sons of God, all those entities that were part of His Soul, as God moved, these soul entities broke off from His Body and spread about, as you might say, froliking, enjoying the pleasures, the beauty of God's creation. So as the Sons of God, as would be the beginnings of you and me, they moved over the waters and through the light; there was singing and music, the singing, the laughter of the Children of God. And God saw that it was good (Solomon Reading No. 8, 3/21/72).

From the very first moment of creative awareness, the Children of God found in the earth, as elsewhere throughout the starry heavens, a paradigm of the awesome mystery of creation, this planet having been prepared for ... millions of years for the appearance of the incarnation of the Children of God (Solomon Reading No. 1256, 8/22/87). The vast biography of the earth was about to be written, and by bringing their own celestial powers into manifestation, it is they who, as extensions of the Divine, would become its author. Thus, from an eternity which arches over and high above the temporal, as tranquil as the starry sky at night, they descended into the spatial and temporal dimensions of the cosmos and into the yawning abyss of a concrete world of accomplished fact:

So souls entered this earth and began to participate in activities of the earth, even when the most primitive forms of algae had begun to appear on the face of the water in relationship between earth, water and sun. Now, algae and plants would not have appeared on this planet in spite of the combinations of earth, light, and water, if there had not been the projection of consciousness from souls into the earth. This is a secret that soon your scientists may begin to realize, for life comes from the projection of life. Life comes from God. It does not simply spring from the relationship between sunlight, water, and matter. But when the souls began to project consciousness, awareness, life, participation on earth, there began the proliferation of the life of the plant kingdom.

And souls began to inhabit one large island or continent on this planet, the most of which was covered with water.... And as more complex forms of plants began to appear..., there was the group of souls expressing themselves creatively that began this development of unique species, and interactions between species. Even the interaction of soul with soul, resulting in reproduction... (Solomon Reading No. 1296, 3/15/88).

Hence, life is more, far more, than a mere occurrence of spontaneous generation. Using different mixes of what may have existed in the primordial sea and
air, scientists have attempted to replicate the spontaneous generation of life
under laboratory conditions. To date, no experiments have even approached
the compounds that would be required for even the most primitive form of life.
Why? Perhaps it is because, as David Bohm points out, "a deeper generative
order is common to all life and to inanimate matter as well."

> It is not therefore an attempt to explain life in terms of matter, but rather to
> see how both emerge out of a common overall generative order. Within this
> order there is room for new kinds of "pools of information" from which
> life could be generated. The wholeness of the living being, and even more of
> the conscious being, can then be understood in a natural way, rather as the
> wholeness of the molecule and the superconducting system is understood
> (although it must not be forgotten that life is much subtler and more complex
> than molecules and superconducting systems). Life is no longer seen as the
> result of somewhat fortuitous factors which perhaps happened only on an
> isolated planet, such as Earth. Rather it is seen to be enfolded universally
> deep within the generative order.[10]

Thus while nucleic acid in the form of DNA is inherent in the pulsating, vibrating core of matter, the Source declares in affirmation that the illuminative,
life-giving principle is the exclusive function of the deepest, most formative of
all generative orders --- the Logos.

Logoic consciousness is the starting point for all of creation. If, as some
of the world's most eminent physicists believe, the world was created by
thought, the One and Absolute Being's First Thought or Expression was
Agape --- that out-soaring Love that seeks only to give freely of itself. To
this end, Logoidal consciousness sets the Logoidal plasm in motion, thus
producing Logoidal energy, **the raw material from which all else is made.**
The energy of the plasm then takes on form which is the power of spirit to
mold Logoidal force into the shape that it should take to produce a yield
or result which is the physical manifestation of life:

> Now it could well be said that in the production of that First Thought, giv-
> ing manifestation to consciousness, spirit was produced because the spirit
> was the essence of that Thought, giving character and delineation to [Logoi-
> dal] consciousness. And [it] might well be described as [the] first yield. This
> is not totally correct in the sense that it was something of the nature of the
> spirit, as was yield, that prompted the nature of the Thought producing the
> ability to delineate that spirit, you see.

> Then, in this process, there is the point beyond which terminology or de-
> scriptiveness, semantics, cannot take us, for there is, was, the existence of
> both [Divine] consciousness and spirit before the four-fold process [of force,
> form, activity, and yield], and yet there is no process before that process,
> therefore nothing to analyze or discuss. You have gone as near to the begin-
> ning as can be described, for you have gone to First Phenomena, or First Ex-
> pression, First Manifestation, and any attempt to step, then, into the struc-
> ture or analysis of spirit and consciousness beyond that is not something

that either language or thought is equipped to do (Solomon Reading No. 1107, 11/19/82).

Just as nucleic acids and proteins is the basic complementarity of biological life, so the Source reveals this four-fold process of creative manifestation to be the bridge that links life --- all life --- to its Divine origin. It is just this that supplies biological systems with life and binds them to a higher Source.

But the universe is not only unimaginably vast, but unimaginably alive and dynamic, an unbroken wholeness in flowing movement. Between biological life and the Absolute Spirit of creation there is a universe of levels of consciousness and will, entire echelons of supernatural agencies, that far exceed our own capacity of thought. Comprising the role that the Phronesis were meant to occupy in the whole scheme of things was that of evolving consciousness in the spirit of manifestation. Being the Children of God, brought forth as the very image of God Himself, the Phronesis were therefore endowed with that same life-giving potential, the power to manifest life. So as extensions of God and as yet immersed in God they worked through this same four-fold process of force, form, activity, and yield in order to bring what the Source refers to as "secondary consciousness" to matter:

> When in response to the plasm the force produces structure within the plasm, [this] produces activity and there is, as a result, another substance or yield, at this point, perhaps, a structure of matter. Then matter has a spirit. Now this second and third spirit that we speak of are the spirit of the manifestation and are unique to the manifestation. Yet both of these second and third spirits ... partake of the nature of that original spirit, preceding all the tools you have here for defining Divine structure. Consciousness, then, second consciousness, will not again occur in the process at a secondary level until [a] life form begins to express as a result of the interaction of these principles.... As there is the process of form evolving into form, or substance evolving into substance, or yield evolving into sequential yield, the interaction of these yields or products will, at some point, become a conscious process in responding to one another. We then have the manifestation of secondary consciousness (Solomon Reading No. 1107, 11/19/82).

Secondary consciousness makes possible that far-reaching goal of awakening individual self-consciousness to the universal power of Love wherein the Logos Itself could be enthroned. But the long and meandering adventure toward harmonious complexity of form and consciousness had only just begun, and it would be eons before the whole consummate drama of existence would reach that stage.

Thus, in the prodigious tide of this magnificent enterprise, the Children of Light undertook a great campaign of experiment toward which **the evolution of the plant kingdom, and even those processes that you now call hybridization, or the cross-breeding of plant life** [could occur]. Expressing through this same four-fold activity, these first born Children of God were able to effectuate with each fourth step of creative manifestation a yield in the material world of form. And each yield being possessed of secondary spirit, the spirit of each was inclined to interact with the spirit of other yield at its own vibratory level and on those levels of manifestation both above and below, but always within those interfaces of equivalent resonance, thereby ensuring through the unbroken continuity of spirit the integrity of the unfolding manifestation of secondary consciousness at all levels. Hence,

> Your soul was rather an overseeing intelligence surrounding and influencing the plant and its development. The plant, indeed, was your life and your activity.... The activity was co-creation with the Source of all creation on this earth. And as you overshadowed or surrounded plants with which you identified, you were able to shape their form and their destiny as the development of plants on this earth. And this was, in fact, the activity of all entities on earth at that time.... You did not lose in that time your recognition of being one with the One entity alive at that time, the entity being Life itself or what you may call God or Creator. But indeed, the best expression is that which lived in that time and that which you were is Life itself, and life in that day...had the responsibility for proliferating the plant kingdom and the manners in which plants would interact and would propagate.

> Thus ... in that period ... you obeyed the laws of harmony. And because you did not understand light and darkness, you could not imagine darkness, for in your experience it did not exist. Nor did you understand good and evil, for your mind had never expressed, experienced any such concept as there being something relative to good which could be called evil. There was no understanding of duality in your mind, for all was light to you, all was love to you, all was harmony, all was the beauty and the music of the spheres.... And the beauty of that Day in your life and soul growth was the beauty of creation and co-creation, for you worked very much --- not separately at all --- but you worked very much as an extension, if we may call it that, of the Source Itself, an extension of God into the world (Solomon Reading No. 1619, 4/21/92).

No duality, no evil, nothing to misdirect them from the singleness of life's purpose: to manifest the fullness of love! Embodied, therefore, as a great organism "embodies" the cells and tissues within it, the Phronesis or Children of Light were as yet inseparably one in consciousness with one another and with the divine Source of their being. Like the glitter of the sun on the surface of the waters, they were all indivisible reflections of the Universal Mind.

> Using the ancient rabbinical analogy, you might see [each entity] as if it were a desert or a seashore with so many billions of grains of sand. Now we use that analogy, that metaphor, because it was used by the ancients, particularly in speaking to Abraham, that his lineage would be as the number of grains of sand within a desert or seashore. Thus if you consider the desert, one as a multitude of cells or expressions within that one, then there is originally in soul consciousness a relationship only with the desert itself as one whole. And there is no consciousness at all of a grain of sand within that great body being a singular expression. No grain of sand upon this great shore could think of itself as anything but the shore itself. Never self-awareness, until the soul is allowed [this] by the Manu, a word which means literally the elder brothers, but we would point [out] as well that the Manu also are the Lords of Karma (Solomon Reading No. 1629, 4/25/92).

Being selfless, they knew no boundaries, and in the absence of boundaries they knew neither space nor time. This allowed for their expression both as field aspects and as energy aspects of the infinite potential of God for creating the plasmic preforms for various types of structures or species in the physical world. And as emanations of the Logos, they represented God's immanence not only in the world of form but in morphogenetic processes at work in living systems at all levels of complexity. Just as a super quantum potential organizes a quantum field, so from "within" the higher multidimensional field of Logoidal consciousness, these first begotten of God were given charge over the trajectory not only of the biogenetic evolution of plant life but over the dynamic, fluid, and evolving states of higher consciousness as well; first, at the level of physical awareness, and ultimately, at the level of self-awareness where the impenetrable mystery of the human soul could at length be solved. For it was the overmastering "First Thought" which decreed that love, unconscious of itself, should become self-conscious, and with the dawning recognition of love in the life of each and every self-conscious individual that the infinite Love that *is* the Logos should become fully enthroned in the heart of all mankind.

THE GREAT UNFOLDING

As the epochs passed, an evolutionary process synthesized out of the Big Bang and still drawing upon the thrust of that initial burst of raw, unformed energy proceeded to bring forth a remarkable series of increasingly complex, sensitive, and responsive structures of being. But it was through the holistic patterns and formative governing principles of the timeless generative order of the Logos Itself, what David Bohm refers to as the superquantum potential, that these Children of God in their co-creative activities were able to influence and oversee the entire burgeoning manifold of biogenetic life. From the first very simple and fumbling prokaryotes to the emergence of vegetal life in Cambrian times, to simple animal forms (the aquatic, the amphibian, the reptilian), all substages of the Great Chain of Being, the expressions of life, guided and cultivated by these co-creative spirits, underwent a gradual refinement and diversification toward secondary consciousness.

Meanwhile, over the course of unimaginable chunks of time, those spirits which themselves had kindled so many myriad creatures began to enter into imaginative sympathy with them, consciously projecting into them something of their own percipience and will. It was, after all, in the very nature of spiritual being to enter into the experience of the earth in order to become conscious of its own existence. Thus every sensory experience of the creatures of the earth afforded the Children of Light an inebriating although vicarious sense of contact with objective reality otherwise unobtainable. Such fleeting contact with the living heart of matter was but a prefiguration, seemingly, of some more profound and lasting penetration, not yet to be achieved.

It would seem, then, that a nature swayed by providential guidance --- which is to say, a nature made expressly for us --- was indeed expressing itself generation by generation through living creatures that would in some distant age emerge from the purely physical and begin to manifest secondary consciousness and ultimately spiritual lucidity. But that is *not* the way the creative process unfolds. Chaos is as essential to the evolutionary equation as is cosmos. States of nonequilibrium are in fact requisite to the emergence of new structures, new levels of organization, and new kinds of active information. The Source indicates that whenever the potentiality for intrinsic life, be it that of a single specie or an entire ecosystem, is no longer in accord with the canon which the overall generative order has ordained for it, that expression of life must perish from the earth and new emergent formative principles will take its place.

Indeed, more than once has the earth returned to chaos. In Permian time there occurs "the great dying" of almost everything alive. Only five percent of living species escape. Then, at the end of the Cretaceous, 65 million years ago, death struck again in the form of a cometary impact with earth. The cataclysm hurled enough dust and debris into the upper atmosphere to block virtually all sunlight for a time sufficient to kill off the dinosaurs along with three-fourths of the earth's living creatures. Once the earth settled down, life was once more possible for mammals and their descendents, and a new creation began. An earlier reading conveyed through the Universal Mind of Edgar Cayce, states:

> ...you have evolution...you have the mineral kingdom, the plant kingdom, the animal kingdom, each developing towards its own source, yet all belonging and becoming one in that force as [each] develops itself to become one with the Creative Energy, and one with the God. The One then surviving in the earth, through mineral, through plant kingdom, through the vegetable kingdom, through the animal kingdom, each as the geological survey shows, held its sway in the earth, passing from one into the other; yet man was given that to be lord over all, and the *only* survivor of that creation.[11]

From this it must therefore be seen that the world was perfectly formed; and that every misguided creation of these Children of God, however catastrophic it may have been to the suffering of those creatures then living, issued finally, without any miscarriage, in the enhanced lucidity of that eternal and perfect Spirit which comprises all things and all times.

A LONGING FOR CONTACT

A thousand years to the spirit is as an imperceptible instant. Periods referred to by science as geological, containing the drifting and lifting of continents, the rise and fall of species, the Great Uniformity's fathomless rift, the timeless and immortal spirit experiences as we of the flesh experience the hours. Consequently, when the first hominids knuckle-walked their way across the new landscape, in the eyes of the Children of God a mere six days of creation had passed. Organs of perception, of ideation, and of rudimentary language gradually developed and secondary consciousness sprouted and quietly spread in all directions. And of those pre-existing members of the cast --- every beast of the fields and of the sea and of the skies above --- "God saw that it was (all) good."

Continuing all the while to gather to themselves an ever-deepening experience of the earth, these co-creative souls (yet to become human souls) acquired an ever more determinate and vivid insight into the form-giving powers they were endowed with. For all of these entities, as parts of the Creator, of the nature of the Creator, then were in themselves creators through the power of God. We would see, then, that they had those powers of creating forms of their own (Solomon Reading No. 8, 3/21/72). And by virtue of their hard-won harvest of experience, they soon found themselves on a more contiguous co-evolutionary path with the earth sphere itself. Their sense of weddedness to the earth and to its natural forces drew them deeper and yet closer, through a lowered vibratory rate, to the physical life-forms over which they exercised stewardship. Thus, together they descended from the multidimensional heights of spirit for the common purpose of developing their manifold powers and co-creative abilities within the more personal field of self-conscious awareness. Called out of the great mass to experience self-awareness, [each] beheld the earth and influenced activities on the earth, along with the hosts of Elohim, continuing creation on earth:

> Thus, according to the direction of the manu, the Elohim, the expressions within [these Children of God] are allowed to have the experience of moving away from the one great singular body, to project [themselves] into matter, for the purpose of becoming eventually both self-aware and aware of self only as an expression of one singular whole.

> Then as souls are called from this one great body of the Child of God, called by the Manu (literally: "awakeners", or Lords of Karma) into the opportunity for expression, then at that time the soul has its first glimpse of the earth, not only as one portion of the whole, [not] just as another grain of sand in the great body. The soul begins to see the separation between the grains of sand and begins to see the spectacular image of the universe, the glittering and most awe-inspiring experience that one could behold. And the soul even then has quite a strain to gain any sense of the enormity, the complexity, the incredible beauty and wonder of this creation of God. But the soul is called aside from the great body for the purpose of allowing that soul to participate in co-creation with God, because creation is not merely complete, but this is the chosen seventh day in which the One Child (Logos) within whom are the multitude Children of God, it is the decision, the mandate of the Great Creator that each facet of His Being shall work with Him in exploring and discovering all possible concepts, all possible structures, all possible expressions of creation, which might under any circumstances exist. And this one Great Creator of whom all the sands of the seashore, all the stars of the heavens are a part of that Body, this Body, this Creator does not recognize at all the relationships which individuals on this planet have chosen to refer to as good and evil. The Creator, [the] Source, is only interested in the myriad expressions of which His children are capable, including those that from the perspective of an individual on this planet might be seen as lonesome, evil, destructive, and such; they are seen by the Source as [a] growing process of souls exploring all their possibilities, and in their maturity, making decisions as to what is not the best interest of higher creation. And in such a manner the Father, the Source, sees the growth of His children (Solomon Reading No. 1629, 4/25/92).

Thus, creation did not end with God's seventh day of rest. For the Children of God (our own intrinsic selves) were given a mandate as inescapable as the thrust that keeps life begetting more life: the mandate to proselytize the sacred through their every successive re-creational act in the earth. Conceived to be complementary to the creative Source of life, they possessed the ability to mimic the expression and activity of the Maker and thereby contrived to create "another order" in the world of form, an order governed by secondary consciousness through which their own experience of physical manifestation could take place. So through their co-creative urge to express themselves through the activity of the world, the light-beings experienced the second stage of awakening to a form of physical awareness that would involve the risk of alienation from the vast, living Totality of which they were a part.

Filled with a longing for physical contact, for intervention, and sooner or later for bringing something new into being, some of these visionary souls proceeded to propagate by pure thought an increasing host of increasingly individuated and awakened creatures, more patently phantasmal than anything in the zoological panoply of nature. At first, we are told, they simply hovered about, observing from the ambits of their own supernal region the sexual proclivities and endless ritual of procreation --- the spontaneous, tempestuous, all-consuming celebration of the life force --- of the terrestrial creatures of flesh. Seeking to bring forth miracles of their own creation, to create new races and new species, new forms of consciousness, new forms of body, they then proceeded to objectify from their own potentiality thought-forms, each mirroring in itself certain aspects of a variety of creatures all in combination. By identifying with the bird in flight they, in the ecstatic flight of their minds, became in a sense a flying creature. Then again drawn to the wrath and roar of the beast, and yet still identifying with the creature of the air, they consciously projected into being something of the beast, but with wings. Some, moving into the form of the protoanthropoid, subsequently became attracted to the taurian-like strength of the bull with the now fabled result being that of the Minotaur. It was a distorted creativity, at once blind and capricious, caring only to spawn and spawn an infinite variety of composite beings:

> Now that you might understand, these entities were, then, as you might say, thought-forms, but were able to project themselves into material forms. Hence, we would have these beasts, these living creatures that you would consider prehistoric, and many of those creatures that you would consider myths or fables --- the centaur, and satyr, the unicorn, the winged beasts --- these things as have been drawn, things as have [come] from the imagination of man. All these things were beings materialized as thought-forms. And as these Sons of God became caught up in material things about this earth, there were projected through them these grotesque beasts and things lower than Sons of God, as these entities became (Solomon Reading No. 8, 3/21/71).

Of the many monstrosities and prodigies of nature that were brought forth we must perforce say almost nothing, for in most respects they lay beyond our mental reach. What is of significance in mankind's record of sojourn in the flesh is the disappearance of the intrinsic spirit, the splitting off of the soul into an entirely incommensurable mode of eternal being. For as these soul-entities came more and more to identify with the raw nature of the beast, the spirit, residing at the center of psychic totality, became increasingly obscured. Then [each] made a choice to project itself into a physical form, material, matter; the result of creative action, but which in itself is alive and always active. Now when a soul enters into such a body, a vehicle, the sensory faculties of that animal form become [the] primary means of gaining information, whereas before the experience in the body, the information came and appeared as realizations without [the] use of senses.

> Thus, the soul began to explore sensory experience of different types, at least five different experiences of the environment, which were opportunities of the soul to experience other facets of creation. And in the use of those senses, and the experience of the appetites, there is such a deed of the occupying soul to manage such a body and process information coming in through the five senses that in almost every instance the higher senses fade into [the] background only as, appearing as, influences, ideas, not discriminatory, not clear, and not easily accessed, above the [physical] brains [which are] busy processing ... information through the five senses. Now in that manner a soul becomes incaptured or imprisoned within a beast (Solomon Reading No. 1629, 4/25/92).

So as the bridge from spirit to matter was being reinforced by new fibers of consciousness, knowledge, and experience, the sacred light of the soul gradually faded under the mesmerizing glare of the world of physical sense. Overwhelmed by the immense challenges and possibilities of experiences opened to it in the phenomenal world of ceaseless change and finally silenced by the incessant clamor of sensory stimuli, the voice of the Universal Mind was no longer heard. Just as the soul receded into the background of impassive detachment, so the Universal Mind itself seemed to all but disappear into the unconditioned realm of impersonal being. The beast in man had triumphed over the god, and progress in the Great Unfolding had given place to ages-long decay. **This, in fact, is referred to in many forms of scriptures as the Fall of mankind,** observes the Source. Moreover, any prospect of future redemption of these fallen immortals applied not only to the soul of mankind but also to the world of nature which was corrupted at the same time. For these fallen beings had by now interfered with the natural order of life. By commingling and interbreeding with the creatures of the earth, significant hybridization and mutation of species occurred contaminating the bio-evolutionary processes of the planet. All in equal measure now experienced disjunction from the One Reality behind and beyond all phenomenal existence. **The discovery, if it may be called that, or the creation of the idea of separation [from the Source], this was the Fall** (Solomon Reading No. 1619, 4/21/92)

Chapter 6

The Fall

THE SEED OF SELF CONSCIOUSNESS

If, for millions of years, the world had taken the upward road, the summit had been reached and the downward route now commenced. Watching as the veil trembled and gradually became unseen to the mental vision of God's own creation, seeing the earth dissolve into spiritual entropy, other groups of souls began to enter into the dimension of the physical in a manner of providing balance to counteract the declining force of One. So as part of a grand redemptive effort to balance and respiritualize the energies of the earth, a second group of souls now entered from multidimensional realms into the physical in that land referred to by the Source as "Lemuria". Some 800 thousand years ago, midway through the Pleistocene, is the date provided for this entry by the Source. Intent on serving as a corrective for the self-centeredness of those souls which had objectified animal forms to be the medium of their co-creative art thereby willing themselves into impotent drift and spiritual stagnation, this second corpus of souls manifested through the full potentiality of their spirit forms more in keeping with the first purpose of the Creative Forces. Their form, we are told, was not unlike that of the human, but being of a more etheric nature, which is to say, less physically dense and of a higher vibratory rate, it was not perishable in the same sense as ours. They knew neither birth nor death. Still, there was one grave, subtle, and easily overlooked danger that eluded the noblest of their intent. As the Source describes:

> One of the problems in the original manifestation or that which was called the fall of man was that these superhuman bodies as might be called, or these parts of God, these creative forces who looked at these vehicles from these angles (from the multidimensional field of the implicate) were not aware of that which would happen as they manifested through this small copy. Or, that is, they were unaware of the trapped condition within the body, or the inability once they inhabited the body to be aware of that which they were aware of outside the body. Coming into the body placed them under the limitation of the smaller copy of the universe (Solomon Reading No. 2, 10/19/72).

The embodied soul is indeed a microcosm. From an ocean, One, without duality, the soul in its entry into form and flesh becomes as a separate drop subject to the restraints that material nature imposes on it. That it no longer has the illimitable vision to see beyond itself and thus rejects its metaphysical nature and divine ground is possibly its single most debilitating restraint. In itself, the very act of objectifying consciousness tears asunder the unity of paradisiacal innocence. Once formed into matter and shaped, how is it possible to return to the state of the uncarved block?

To their precariously awakened senses, the Lemurian landscape that cradled their race must have greeted them with as much benevolent theophany as that

paradise that embraced Adam on the morning of his creation --- a consummation devoutly to be wished. But that remains in the realm of speculation and
fantasy. For, as the Source points out, their processes of perception, intellection, and even emotion were so altogether different from ours as to constitute
a mentality of an entirely different order. What can be said with assurance is
that in their first act of differentiation, a seed of self-consciousness had been
planted. Gathering purpose and direction over the eons, it might have grown
the way of Jack's beanstalk, reaching deep from within the primordial turf of
their own being into the transcendent atmosphere of the Godhead Itself. After all, it is precisely to achieve this intensifying and universal heightening of
consciousness that the soul sacrifices itself in its initial descent. But in the case
of the Lemurians, although having attained all the heights of philosophy, art,
technology and culture, in the end their world succumbed to desolating self-
indulgence and, through an impenitent separation from the Source, was lost:

[There was a civilization] existing in those times more ancient than you have
record or knowledge [of] in the southern portion of what is now California
and western [parts] of Mexico [and submerged portions to the west]. Now
it [is] here called Lemuria or Mu, [and] this one (individual reading) [was]
in the portion of Mu known as Lemuria, in those times when there came
the height of civilization, the development of science, of technology here.
We find among these peoples a period in which there was the departure,
the rebellion, from both that natural law or that known or understood as
God's Law, and that created by man, or those laws set down as morality or
recognized as such.

Now in the developing of man and in the pride that came from development, or the feeling of accomplishment --- as there was the developing of
such instruments as would ... control the weather, and produce such effects
for weaponry and practices of medicine, control of disease and such --- there
came the pride in the race, or among those peoples a feeling that they had
grown above the necessity of moral law or a moral code. There came a time
when such were given to adultery and this became common. There was not
the respect for the sex of the body and the use thereof and the purposes.
There was open defiance of such given as morals and respect one for another and the worship.

Now these conditions set about conditions of the atmosphere or weather
and that that surrounded the earth. Now in that day --- and it remains true
to this --- that that system by which the universe was set in order and began
to operate was perfect, and it would continue to be so in that day and in
this if conditions were not tampered with by that imperfect or that less than
perfect. That is to say there never would have been the shifting of the poles
upon this planet if there were not the creating of conditions among men that
were defiant to the Laws of God. But when those conditions of law were
subverted among men, and there was the defiance of the Law of God, so
there was set in motion upon this planet an energy that created an imbalance between those forces of good and evil or of positive and negative....
Understand then that the movement, the shifting of the poles was caused
by the activity of men in defiance of their God (Solomon Reading No. 30,
8/11/73).

This disaster was by no means inevitable; but it was brought on by unmitigable spiritual paralysis --- by minds that had become corrupted, hearts that turned hard, a race that had become drunk with absolute sovereignty. Having forgotten their higher origin, they became as contemptuous and profane as those noxious beasts that their entry into flesh was meant to countermine. Only a dying remnant survived, we are told, and migrated to the safety of what is now Peru, Central America, and the American Southwest where the memory of a once mighty past became lost to legend.

With the shifting of the poles there was little left of the old physiographic configuration of the earth's land masses. And along with geological changes came changes in the fauna and flora. Once more there was a great re-making of old types, only less revolutionary than that which occurred during the Cretaceous. Other species, including those of the hominoids, not only survived but actually benefited by the change. The anthropoids had, by the early pre-dawn era of Lemurian civilization, already evolved to the status of Homo erectus, and by the time of the Lemurian downfall their extinction seemed to herald the appearance of Homo sapiens in the form of the sub-specie Neanderthal. Another 250,000 years would pass before the disappearance of the Neanderthals and the sudden appearance of the anatomically modern Homo sapiens sapiens which, by many accounts, evolved partly from the Neanderthal. But recent DNA analysis conducted on a Neanderthal skeleton and published in the journal *Nature* indicates no genetic link whatsoever between Neanderthals and modern humans. The greatest mystery is who or what --- what sense of purpose --- could have transformed Homo sapiens into Homo sapiens sapiens? One moment they did not exist, and the next moment they did! If so, where did we all come from?

THE INCOMPARABLE VISION OF THE ONE

If the Lemurians had struggled slowly from primitive tribalism to civil life only to collapse again over the half-million years of their racial lifespan, the leap into Atlantean civilization was staggering by comparison. The Atlanteans were, as the Source describes, **souls of a higher order,** and because they were by temperament peaceable and of an innately pacific disposition their cultural progress was little delayed. With advance knowledge of Lemuria's rise and ruin, they now had the advantage of sobriety and singleness of purpose. And with the beasts continuing to intermix and proliferate throughout the earth, they entered with the same purpose as their predecessors: to provide a balance to the energies of the earth and through their activities to return the earth to that first purpose of the Creative Forces, that God become conscious and fully manifest through each as an individual.

While there is no fixed point at which we modulated from Homo Lemurius to Homo Atlanticus, roughly 200,000 years ago is the figure given by the Source. The first elements of this new race of "man" began to appear, we are informed, some 100,000 years after the Lemurian disaster. While in semblance the Atlanteans were not wholly unlike their predecessors, they had repeated and far excelled the noble but unfortunate type achieved long before.

Like the Lemurians prior to their fall, the Atlanteans entered into the physical as thought-forms, forms that were by nature etheric. Under this impulse the nonmanifest mind throws off a vibrating portion of itself shaping the plasma through the nature of its vibrations. This sets the elemental essence, or quantum nature, of the surrounding atmosphere into vibration in resonance with the mind's own rate, thereby producing a structure or yield which is an extension of that consciousness that produced it. Being of a finer or less condensed substance than that of the purely physical, the Atlanteans therefore occupied the common frontier of both material form and implicate preform:

> [In] that [early Atlantean] period the incarnation was not such that we would describe it as human incarnation specifically, rather a more highly developed and sophisticated being very much like a human, yet treated not quite as humans by the older influences, or what we may call outside influences. These travelers who settled in Atlantis had bodies made more of light and had little indication of flesh. They were *not* fleshy, physical beings, thus much of the work done in that time was done done by individuals [fully incarnate in flesh] who had much greater influence over physical things, the movement of physical objects and such, while the light-beings had a much greater influence of the mind to cause results (Solomon Reading No. 1677, 5/3/82).

As indicated, it was inwardly rather than in outward physical characteristics that the Atlanteans differed from the earlier race. Possessed with a superb faculty of intuitive insight, they were able to prevail upon their higher Source thereby avoiding most of the carnality and iniquity that had so crippled their predecessors. More extraordinary, however, was that from the immanence of their being their manifested forms were animated by light. **For in the time of Alta, Atlantis, the bodies physical as you would know them were not so solid, material as you know in this time, but were of beings of light; in essence, the light itself forming the configuration of the body...**(Solomon Reading No. 1638, 5/2/92). As expressions of light, the Atlanteans, we are told, were not encumbered by physical limitations as were other beings of the earth. Not only were they able to travel through the air, but interdimensionally as well.

The Malagasy of Madagascar, the aborigines of Oceania, the natives of eastern Indonesia, mythologies of Mesopotamia and Tibet, as well as the Agganna Suttanta ("The Book of Genesis") of the Pali Canon, all speak of the original ancestors as having descended from the heavens, the celestial spheres being nearer to the earth than they are now. Called the "Air-Spirit People" by the Navajo of the American Southwest, these unordinary beings were, it seems, endowed with bodies of light which allowed for the capacity of flight: "They are people unlike the five-fingered earth-surface people who come into the world today, live on the ground for a while, die at a ripe old age, and then leave the world. They are people who travel in the air and fly swiftly like the wind."[12] Indo-Tibetan beliefs likewise refer to Primordial Man as a luminous being clothed in a body called the "rainbow-body," "celestial body," "spirit-body," "Body of Pure Light," or "divine body"[13] with which, according to the Indian epic *Mahabharata*, he "ascended to the sky and returned to earth at will."[14] The Indian text *Dighanikaya* (1,2,2), records that "after the destruction of the World there remained only radiant beings named Abhassara: they had ethereal bodies, they flew in the air, they gave out their own light and lived indefinitely."[15]

Seen by the creatures of the earth, by those thought-formed beasts which over the ages had solidified into forms of flesh, by the more developed species of the hominids, by so many others, the Atlanteans were as gods, their very existence representing untouchable perfection, import, even magnificence. But even more significant, perhaps, significant for the understanding of matters that reached far beyond their own comprehensive and discriminate awareness of themselves and the world they now occupied, is that these beings, much like the earliest manifest appearance of the Lemurians, were androgynous. That is to say, they were, as the Source points out, **all of a common type, or not polarized, but containing both positive and negative polarity; or, though the terms are inadequate, could be described as male and female in the single body. These came not for production, and were not given to reproduction, but had come ... for the experience of creating and recreating** (Solomon Reading No. 196, 7/13/73). Since before the Beginning, *in illo tempore*, androgyny was of the nature of God and of God's ontological expression (the Logos), it should come as no wonder that these Children of God were also united within themselves, both male and female. For just as man is created in the very image of God, so mankind's natural state --- the natural state of each soul being the living pattern of that image --- is androgynous. Thus, in their first appearance in the physical the Atlanteans remained faithful to the divine image of wholeness.

This, then, was the rudimentary beginnings of humankind's sojourn into the flesh. It was seen as a dawning of a new world, a time of re-creation, where the reality of the One was transmuted into the soul's earthly experience. For, partaking of the nature of the divine, these Sons of God beheld God and once more walked with God. Century by century, for thousands of years, souls continued to stream into this seemingly precarious although unshakable equilibrium of physical reality as embodiments of radiant light and wholeness. Countless centuries passed during which the architecture of Atlantean culture and civilization was being fabricated, and because they were fortunate in their almost complete immunity from the lust of power and incurable virulence that cursed the Lemurians, they enjoyed long ages of idyllic peace. This was a time referred to by the Greek poet Hesiod as the Golden Age, "an idealized, remote and unrecapturable dream of man's childhood, when the immortals walked the earth...."[16] This was the original Paradise, the "paradise of the Essence" in Sufic terms, where the all yet remained in the enfolding presence of the One, the ever undivided harmony of nature and cosmos, creature and Creator.

Recorded in the collective memory --- in myths, legends, epics, sacred writings --- of traditional cultures throughout the world is this time of ancient beginnings, when heaven and earth were undivided, when the world and God were one. For the Iranians it was the "Age of Yima"; the Egyptians referred to it as the "Time of Re"; the Hindus remember it as the "Krita Yuga", or Perfect Age. Mythic cultures universally recall it as an age predicated on the incomparable vision of the One, when the unfathomable light of pure spirit illumined the earth.

According to the Hindu epic, the Mahabharata:

The Krita Yuga was so named because there was but one religion, and all men were saintly: therefore they were not required to perform religious ceremonies. Holiness never grew less, and the people did not decrease. There were no gods in the Krita Yuga, and there were no demons.... Men neither bought nor sold, there were no poor and no rich, there was no need to labour, because all that men required was obtained by the power of will; the chief virtue was the abandonment of all worldly desires. The Krita Yuga was without disease; there was no lessening with the years; there was no hatred, or vanity, or evil thought whatsoever; no sorrow, no fear. All mankind could obtain to supreme blessedness.[17]

In the Avesta, the sacred book of Zoroastrianism, it is written: "In the reign of Yima the valiant there was neither heat nor cold, neither old age nor death, nor disease..."[18] Likewise, the Egyptians relate that neither death nor disease was known during the Time of Re. This is quite factually so, explains the Source: **In an expression of wholeness on this planet, there cannot be, in any way, there cannot be any form of disease, there cannot be any form of harm one toward another, of war, or of crime, or of what you think of as life and death. Nor is there a separation in consciousness between one side of the brain and the other, nor is there a separation of the consciousness of mankind with the consciousness of God** (Solomon Reading No. 1643, 5/4/92).

Here apparently were all the requisites of a world rich and unpossessed, and a race of never-aging immortals whose very existence lay wholly beyond our comprehension. Again and again, over a hundred thousand times, the seasons were repeated in the light of a consciousness that apprehends only "Now".

Theirs was not the only theme of this world-biography, however. Succeeding generations of beasts and monstrosities proceeded to intermix and mingle with the creatures of earth, diversifying themselves ever more grotesquely into strange sub-human variants of the natural world. Seen through Atlantean eyes these tranced remnants of an earlier age were not beasts but innocents, lost souls, children of nature who in their lassitude had drifted through spiritual dusk into night, their fate sealed until such time as the gods should intervene. It is impossible to describe the malady of the spirit that undermined these insentient souls. To say that they were suffering a complete severance from their Source would not be wholly false, but it would be a misleading vulgarization of the truth. While the Atlanteans clung desperately to their ancient hope that the light would eventually break in on them, spiritually these genesiological aberrations had so incapacitated themselves that they were calloused against every benevolent attempt to reach them. **This, then, was the reason for the entry into the physical of the first Adam** (Amelius) **explains the Source, for it would be seen that God sent His Son into the world to take charge of the world and subdue the world, for it is spoken in your Book of Genesis that this was God's command to the first Adam** (Amelius), **"Be fruitful and subdue the earth," as it should have been translated** (Solomon Reading No. 8, 3/21/72).

THE DESCENT OF THE GODS

Amelius, who is understood to be the embodiment of the Logos or First Cause, is that same soul who much later would manifest as the Adam of Biblical Genesis and whose series of incarnations would culminate in what the Source refers to as the "Last Adam, or Jesus of Nazareth:

> Then we would see that the one you call Jesus had entered as a thought-form on that land that you would call Atlantis and was known there as Amelius. Other souls, soul entities ... entered the beasts and mutants as they might be referred, that had become grotesque and out of hand. Christ, then, came that these might be released in the earth, and that that higher order of primates, which had been evolved, might be taken as a means of expression for these, that these soul entities might inhabit the flesh forms that were the [humanoids], and in doing so, might walk the earth with an intelligent mind. What we now refer to as the conscious mind was given then.
>
> As the third part, as might be said (sic),... the soul entity ... was thus given this opportunity to live a life on this plane, on the earthly material plane, in such a manner that they (sic) might be purified and gain, regain God consciousness and realize that their soul entity, that which they are, is God; that once again they might identify with God. And in bringing their soul entity back to that level, their thought patterns, their actions, these things might be purified through life on this plane. They would be given that chance to raise themselves back to the level of God and, thus, once again become one with God and know those joys, those pleasures that were theirs before the beginning of the world.
>
> Then ... there were with Christ, through His direction, the other Sons of God that came and materialized in the world at that time in five different places. In five different nations (sic) simultaneously the earth was inhabited. Hence, the five different races on the five different continents, if you would. Now these were Children of God. These had not lowered themselves through the creation and the frolicking in the bodies of the beasts. They came here that those who were so earthbound might be released. Now this you will find in your own Scripture if you read it carefully. All of this, then, might be realized through those words you have recorded in your Bible. There we find that from the beginning that those Sons of God, who still were on the plane with God, were given charge by God of protecting those entities that had fallen. We would find, then, that even in this day there still are those charged on this plane with aiding and seeking to help those of you who would raise yourselves back to this (Source's) plane, and through growth, through spiritual growth, through evolvement, through cleansing the body and the soul, come back to be one with God (Solomon Reading No. 8, 3/21/72).

It was Amelius, then, along with his fellow Eternals, who as emanations of the divine Word took upon themselves that mandate to liberate the imprisoned life force of those of God's children who had become caught in the embrace of Physis --- matter. Charged with the mission of awakening those misbegotten creatures under their gaze, the Sons of God transposed themselves as a great mantle over the ocean of space and time and descended as thought-forms into the plane of earth. Contemplating with deep compassion the host of dissociated spirits over whom they had been given charge, the Immortals then projected radiant light-bodies of their own inhabitation, their perfected forms serving as a reminder to those captive of the flesh, those who had forgotten their Source, of the sacred immanence of their creation. They became the path to regeneration for those souls who had contracted their infinite senses into the bestial world of passions and appetites.

In the presence of these towering messianic figures and under their hegemonic direction there was a widespread feeling among the Atlanteans and those superior races elsewhere that the time had come to gather all their strength in an effort to remake those beasts and "mutants" upon a nobler pattern and to lift them into some new sphere of spiritual mentality:

> And it becomes, then, the work of the elder brethren, those who have been through this experience before and have awakened again to higher consciousness, it becomes their work to take such beasts and expose them to such stimuli as will remind the consciousness within the beast that there is a divine order, that there is an expression of the divine, that there is an indwelling presence that is in fact the true intrinsic soul itself. But this soul within the beast lies completely dormant in terms of activity or influence because it has entered the beast only as an observer, to observe and see and learn of the functions, the activities, the experiences, which are possible upon this plane, this school, this earth.

> This observer self is the one and only true intrinsic self. It is the soul itself, it is the identity. It does not change from one experience to another, one lifetime to another. It is one and the same. It has always existed, and always will; it is incapable of experiencing death. And this observer self, this witness, gathering the experience, exploring the nature of creation, will not assert itself within the beast except in certain important circumstances. Sometimes, though not always, this observer self, intrinsic self, the real and true self, may intervene in survival threatening situations relating to the beast. More often the soul, the intrinsic self, responds to any expression of the divine and expression of the heart of God which manifests within its presence. And such expressions include music as harmony and attunement; such expressions include beauty in the myriad forms in which it occurs. Such expressions are spoken of by the apostle Paul in his writing of the epistle to the Romans in the first chapter, in which he refers to so many expressions of life, so many expressions of God in the environment around every soul that it leaves any particular soul without excuse for failing to recognize and respond to and join with this omnipresent expression of God (Solomon Reading No. 1629, 4/25/92).

In order to lift those souls who had fallen --- the beasts, the hybrids or mixtures, and all others karmically entangled in matter --- beyond their merely visceral and somatic drives and into a new dimension of self-reflective consciousness, the Source tells us that in Atlantis and throughout the ancient world temples of healing were established:

> ...three schools or temples as [they] were called, the Temple of Sacrifice, the Temple Beautiful, and the Temple of Initiation, a purpose of these schools being to awaken a species without self-consciousness and certainly with no

concept of a Source or Creator or God, without an awareness of love and such. You (individual reading) set about in the creation of these temples to expose these creatures, or beasts as you might see them now, you exposed them to beauty in forms of music, of light, of rhythm, dance and such, and when these beings would respond to such an expression of beauty, ...then you, who were of a priest-like status, would explain to that being, although there was not language, the understanding that the beauty that they experienced was a manifestation of God in them and through them; that God had entered into them and was producing beauty, rhythm, emotional response and such through them. They were taken, as well, by others of the priest-like group from Atlantis and were brought into a temple in which their bodies, which would seem so strange and primitive to you in this time, these bodies were manipulated in quite a number of ways. This was the origin, for example, of yoga, of Pranayama, of martial arts, of all forms of exercise and medicine and surgery even (Solomon Reading No. 1643, 5/4/92).

Here in these temples a part of the disorder itself was used to work toward the cure --- a want, a craving, a desire to be made whole like unto that pattern set by the Sons of God. Anatomical and physiological modifications to the physical body were made. Neurological mutations were effected, including changes in the electrical patterns of the brain. And in those cases of the more biologically primitive or rudimentary types, changes in the brain and central nervous system were engineered in order to allow for and awaken the potential for self-consciousness:

[The] minds of these lesser beings were still single but with what you call an instinctual or reptilian brain. And it was in the Temple of Initiation that the Manu, or the priest-like elder brethren from Atlantis and from other spheres, both within and beyond this star system, there worked to create a brain which could acknowledge itself by separating that brain into two halves which would have an ability, then, to communicate with one another, even to argue with one another and have a conversation within the mind and so create quite a new method of thinking which also produced reproduction in combination with the Temple of Sacrifice (Solomon Reading No. 1643, 5/4/92).

Overall, this leap in bio-spiritual evolution achieved through miracles of anatomical and biogenetic engineering opened up unimagined spheres of unconditioned wholeness beneath the chaos of the undeveloped beast. Through the therapeutic disciplines devised by Amelius and the Sons of the Most High and established at these temples of healing, they were given the opportunity to recover their lost unity within the divine hierarchy of creation. Their world became multidimensional, not merely through the acquisition of abstract thought or in the developing stages of self-reflective (secondary) consciousness, but in the very unfolding of their emergent divinity. Among some, flashes and glimmers of godhood began to appear such that, in the words of the Source, "they rose up from that [temple] altar new, in perfected light bodies...."

However, there were many so hopelessly debilitated by their deformities as to be incurable. [These] were bodies which could not be sufficiently molded either by the hands or by color and light and such instruments as they used for surgery, instruments not even known today; not invasive surgery, but instruments which through sound pushed bones into shape and carefully shaped them into new lengths and positions. In that sense, surgery by manipulation we would call it, and by the application of sound and light. However, many, many, many there were who could not, who were not close enough to the human shape to be shaped into this form. They were electively given another option (Solomon Reading No. 1472, 4/91). It was these, the irremediably disfigured, who were to profit from what was perhaps the most important step in the soul's evolutionary return to its Source --- the introduction of death! For, as the Source points out, in that age and time the experience of death among those who were begotten of spirit and who initially had projected themselves into the physical was unknown:

> [These] beings --- unself-conscious and not God conscious --- were incapable of understanding a teaching of God. There was no word in their very simple language ... for God. There was no thought [of] having previous existence or coming from a Source. There was no thought of birth or death. In fact, it may be difficult for you to comprehend that neither birth nor death was known to them. They never died. Neither did the Manu die. Those who came from Atlantis had not experienced physical death, and physical death as such was not known on this earth, this planet (among souls inhabiting flesh) until the establishment of the Temple of Sacrifice. Those souls who entered or left before that time dissolved and replaced their bodies in the earth, even those who were swept away by the earth changes. These electively left the body and ascended not in the form that you now know as death. Now for that reason you will not find their remains. They ascended bodily or they discarded the body, but not as refuse, but rather by disintegrating and replacing it into the earth, quite deliberately. So there was no death as you know it until the time of the Temple of Sacrifice. (Solomon Reading No. 1472, 4/91).

It was here, in the Temple of Sacrifice, that the fortunes of these piteous creatures finally turned to their practical benefit. Ironically, however, the individual's prospect of eternal life now depended on the "sacrifice" of the body. In the Temple of Sacrifice, in order to perfect a body, there was introduced ... a technique of advancement which you now call death, the death of the physical vehicle, the Source informs us. It was *not* an important experience for those in that time, or in the Temple of Sacrifice, and death was quite deliberately induced for the purpose of beginning again with ... a code which was deliberately designed by the priests which you now refer to, roughly, as the DNA chain and the genetic code.... Thus death was introduced for the purpose of rapidly entering again into a new and more perfect life, and the interim period between death and rebirth was only long enough, sufficient time, for the priests [to] use the DNA cluster of protein to punctuate or to redesign instructions in a genetic code for the nature of the next shelter or body, human body (Solomon Reading No. 1619, 4/21/92). The hosts or bodies determined to be most suitable for these now transmigrating souls were none other than the more advanced of the hominids, the most plausible candidate being Homo Sapiens. By employing advanced forms of a technology now referred to as recombinant DNA, designed to modify the information or expression of DNA in plasmid form, these priest-scientists were, according to the Source, able to achieve chromosomal mutation at exponentially faster rates than normal, leading to the sudden and enigmatic appearance of the anatomically modern Homo Sapien Sapiens. **Now at that time in history these things were introduced by the Temple of Sacrifice, not only in Egypt but in Chaldea, in China, in Japan as well, and [in] several places around the earth, even in the Americas. These things were introduced simultaneously throughout the Temples of Sacrifice wherever they occurred** (Solomon Reading No. 1472, 4/91). Hence, the sudden appearance of the five races of humanity, in China, in Chaldea, in the South American Andes, in Atlantis, and in upper west Africa near the Nile. **And so it was that the cycles of life and death on this planet and the graduation, initiation cycles of what you call incarnation, were established by that temple in that time** (Solomon Reading No. 1643, 5/4/92).

BINGING ON THE FRUIT OF THE TREE OF KNOWLEDGE

Well might it seem that the stage was now set for a triumphant progress not only in the re-spiritualization of the earth but in the return of the spirit to its Source, save for one disastrous flaw, an accidental consequence, really, of what was thought to be the all-redeeming virtue of the Temple of Initiation:

> In the Temple of Initiation, in order to establish light --- light as God in the minds of those who were initiates --- in order to establish the concept of light, the concept of darkness was given. In order to establish the concept of plenty and prosperity, limitation and lack were introduced as points of reference. However, there were those who were drawn to fear through the introduction of the idea of limitation. Then there were those who were called the sons and daughters of Bal, or the sons and daughters of darkness. These were those in whose bodies were introduced fear. [This occurred] after the introduction of death as a holy ritual. Having experienced death, those who came through it in new bodies, too often not completing the teaching of the Temple of Initiation, began to find themselves living in fear of death, and fear induced the second death. Fear induced the death of the physical body not as a religious ritual that man might renew himself but as a deterioration of the physical body through thoughts of fear.

> Thus, it might be established and must be established ... that the human body which never, ever, ever experiences a single thought of fear can never die. Only fear can kill the human body. Only fear, and absolutely nothing else! Nothing else is capable of causing death to a physical body. These bodies were made, they were [genetically] designed for eternal renewal. They were designed with systems for resisting any form of invasion, any form of attack, even accident. They were designed to renew and rebuild themselves quite automatically. However, they thrive on a vitality which has become so unknown to man that the closest word for the description of this vitality is perhaps Agape, Love, Unconditional Love. If the body is filled with thoughts of both love, confidence, and absolute lack of fear, the body physical will renew itself through eternity and absolutely will never die (Solomon Reading No. 1472, 4/91).

To embrace such a consciousness of life, to accept unconditionally the Unknowable Source of life, to love life without fear of surrendering it, is to ever be mindful of the enormous sea of energy that exists and moves within and all about us and to draw upon that energy for the continual renewal of life. It is to live in the "Now" without losing the sense of eternity.

On the other hand, a life not measured in love is a life without compensation. By not availing oneself of the energy of life or love, one feels powerless and insignificant, a passive victim of malevolent forces. The fundamental truth about life becomes absorbed and distorted by the fear of death, and fear itself becomes the aggravating factor in death, robbing each cell, stealing life by the minute.

Hence a spirit of competition and of fear deposed the life-affirming force of eternal Love in the minds of many of those who for the first time had experienced death. The contagion of fear spread rapidly, even among those whose bodies had been refashioned and set to rights. It pervaded their habits, their character, their very appearance. In just proportion to their growing discord, their natural radiance grew dim. **They shone, they glowed with the light that all could see until thoughts of fear crept in. Thoughts of fear, you understand, stopped the light process. They stopped the light from shining forth. They make (sic) dense the body, and denser and denser until there are contractions that stop the life process in the physical body** (Solomon Reading No. 1472, 4/91). There now occurs the second death, a perishability induced by fear.

Nor were the Atlanteans themselves, those undivided beings of an altogether higher order, necessarily immune from this growing contagion. They, who were masters of the law, through one single transgression of the Divine Law, would in time become its subjects and subordinates. The Source describes a stage in their cultural development when, seeking like the lower mortals, those now occupying human forms, to beget progeny and companionship of their own, more and more of the androgyny began to objectify something of their own unselfconscious substance in order to produce an opposite. In effect, they dissociated themselves as two independent beings, the one the creative masculine force, the other the receptive force of the feminine. And as related by the Source, the favored sex, the positive force of the masculine, single-mindedly trampled the other into servitude:

> Now we give description in this way only because these were the creative force, and not male or masculine in the sense of the masculine body. Yet these as thought-forms, creators and co-creators with the Father, were able to provide themselves with alternative thought-forms of opposite polarity, or distinguish the polarity within the self by separating the self from an opposite side of self, thus giving an inferior. Now we would see in this manner as it occurred, that the positive or creative force became the greater, and that which he provided as receptacle for himself became the lesser in his thinking, and he dominated the other.

> In such a manner were those first souls or soul mates formed from a single body, ...these [separated] then, being the receptacles --- not necessarily the female in the sense of your time, yet the underlings or the created beings. Now these might have been equipped in the physical sense as the male, yet

that one that was created from the other or became lesser than the master, the creator, became a race unto itself, so that these were considered inferior beings and became beasts of burden or servants to that one the creator.

Now in the giving of selves to reproduction, or in the attempts to reproduce in animal fashion and bring other souls into existence, it became the choice of the creator soul to cause the childbearing to be done by the inferior breed.... In such a manner came those thoughts of the female being considered the lesser within the human race. Now these were not as you would see the female, and had not at that time developed as human or in the perfected vehicle. Yet in those times of Atlantis were these unfortunate creatures used by the creator soul, so beginning those cycles of karma between the male and the female. And we would see that in the adjusting or the righting of that which was created in that time, there must come in these days a ruler of the female; or, that is, that the female will become the superior and will dominate the race, the male, before the ending of this time, for the righting of that which has been created, and we see the beginnings of this in this time (Solomon Reading No. 40, 4/13/73).

Thus, we see that the descent of that soul energy from its First Cause or Principle as a living portion of the whole into its manifested state of two separate polarities resulted in the obliteration of the initial perfection of the divine unity and, consequently, the beginnings of degeneracy among the Sons of God.

To reiterate, separation from the Source, from the eternal I AM, both from within and Beyond --- *this* is the true fall of man. Having appropriated ideas of duality --- good and evil, light and darkness, love and fear --- many of the unfallen Eternals compromised their manifest oneness with God and fell from a state of perfect unity into fragmentation, from eternity into time, over and against which the spiritual cosmos now appeared to them timeless and of another order. As given by the Solomon Source, the path was slippery and dangerous:

[One] was tempted to understand better the relationship between light and darkness, or a relationship that was hardly discernible at that time between one individual and another, and even each individual being androgynous, [for] there was no male or female. And yet the driving force, the highest power of consciousness in each individual soul at that time, the greatest hunger, was for knowledge, consciousness, understanding, wisdom. And this in itself is, of course, good and useful. Each soul was aware of the ability to create and for as long as that awareness was maintained there was never a thought of competition. Because for as long as life-forms on this planet were creative there could not be a thought that, if one should take more, that another would in turn have less.

Thus, there was no thought of competition but there was curiosity, a curiosity of understanding the relationship between light and darkness and what is called love and fear, good and evil. And though those inhabiting this school [earth] were warned against inquiring into such knowledge, the compulsion to know was too great for many to resist, and so there was the reaching into self, what is referred to as eating of the tree of knowledge [of] good and evil.

[It] was actually a partaking of self or selfishness and the separation within [the] self of the two sides, the two hemispheres, the two energies which, as you would see represented in the Tao in this time as yin and yang, are perfectly balanced; there are not two, in actuality, but only one.

Still, the experiment with the curious souls was toward the separation of this yin and yang, which made one, [but] which in turn allowed the separation of the masculine and feminine, the impregnation of the one and the other, but which resulted in the parting of the brain itself, the two hemispheres of the brain, or the cleft brain as we would refer to it. This was the beginning of all thought of competition, of [the] recognition of darkness; it was the birth of fear (Solomon Reading No. 1643, 5/4/92).

"The knowledge of the ancients was perfect," writes Chuang Tzu. "In what way was it perfect? They were not yet aware that there were things. This is the most perfect knowledge, nothing can be added. Then, some were aware that there were things, but not aware that there were distinctions among them. Then, some were aware that there were distinctions, but not yet aware that there was right and wrong among them. When right and wrong became manifest, the Tao thereby declined."[19] Or in the words of Lao Tzu: "When everyone recognizes goodness to be good, there is already evil. Thus to be and not to be arise mutually."[20]

Truth is One, uncompounded, indivisible. This is the Law governing the whole spiritual enterprise. Created in the image and likeness of the One, the soul in itself is complete, being at once solar and tellurgic, logoic and cosmic. But in the moment that the One became two, there commenced *imprimis* the beginnings of all competition, self-gratification, and fear, a beginning that has no ending. The Fall could not be undone.

Beginning with the bifurcation of Self into the opposed yet mutually attractive, quasi-sexual forces of the creative (masculine) and the receptive (feminine), there resulted a differentiated mind which over spans of time precipitated a bicameral brain, its two hemispheres reflecting the duality of consciousness as universally expressed in cultural traditions throughout the world. The left brain, being more concerned with rational, sequential thought, is associated with the masculine, or active, analytical, intellectual modes of operation. The right brain, being more synthetic, is, figuratively speaking, our feminine side, more passive, receptive, intuitive, holistic. When in the beginning the soul began to express the active or creative principle, subjugating the passive or receptive within itself, the active became the dominant force, causing the "masculine", if you will, to become the primary mode of cognitive functioning. Being, therefore, that these two divergent functions are not equally balanced, there has always been a struggle between them as to what is reasonable, "real", ethical, causal, differential, etc., and what is not. All of us suffer in some degree the neurosis of anxiety and fear associated with this incongruent struggle. This, according to the Source, is a consequence of the Fall.

In the case of the Atlanteans, the ensuing disequilibrium between the creative and receptive forces within turned the natural impulse to express without reservation the formative power of Logoic Love into a perverse craving for power, for competition, for selfish pursuit. The cognitive integration characteristic of the androgynous consciousness collapsed into an ever increasing division and multiplicity of psychical functions, of ever increasing remoteness from the One. Like Humpty-Dumpty, who all the king's men could not put back together again, the chrysalis of the cosmic self was irreparably shattered into so many fragments of their own forbidden experience. Self and Source became dialectical images of one reality, a totality divided by the Fall. All that remained was the remnants of a once sacramental vision of the world that up until now had been most faithfully preserved among a unified race of beings of infinite and immortal magnificence. Having lost touch with the living energies of the whole, they now became deaf to the one Law which commanded that they live commensurately with the sacred harmonies of creation.

Perceived as such, the Fall is not so much a single isolated event unique to a specific geographical "ground-zero" as it is the universal conditioning of space-time resulting from the polarization of the One into the succession of twos. For as the principle of opposition became ever more tenaciously rooted in the dualistic consciousness of the bicameral brain, the timelessness of an eternal "Now", once so knowingly manifest to the receptive and intuitive sense of the androgyne, gradually diminished for the rational/deductive mind into a sequential pattern of temporal events. The higher multidimensional vision of the whole hardened into the objective and materialized correlates of self and "other". Hence, [a] race, begun as androgynous or single, one with the Father and worshipping the Law of One, had become a polarized race, or a race worshipping rather duality, a race of extremes (Solomon Reading No. 40, 4/13/73). It was from this uncompromising duality and its continuing division that the Great Reversal of Atlantean culture and society commenced.

The separation of the primal androgyne led inexorably to the division of Atlantean society into opposing castes or groups:

> ...that of the children of the Law of One, or those as you would call the spiritual ones, those attuned to the Father, the Law of the one God and worshipping (sic). And the other, those of the sons of Belial as they have been called, or the humanists in the sense that there was the worshipping of the abilities of the human to the exclusion of a recognition of God or a God force, you see; a worship of power, a worship of control, of selfish control over the lives of others and such (Solomon Reading No. 371, 6/7/74).

The first group were mainly those of the androgyne who had not fallen from the undivided state and who continued to follow the Law of One. The incorruptible standard of these Children of Light was conspicuously reflected in the great priesthoods of the Atlantean world, those whose grand redemptive efforts to raise physical nature to the level of divinity had swayed even the course of human evolution.

From the fragmented and warring inner nature of those "sons of Belial" now in rebellion against the Law, decadence, immorality, corruption, moral dereliction followed. Though still endowed with penetrating telematic power, they ceased to relate their prodigious mental abilities to the whole of a divine order. Although the spirit of the One was still indestructibly woven into the tissue of the cosmos, the providential God of Creation had been replaced by a now fallen race of beings yet in possession of semi-divine characteristics, owing to the extraordinary knowledge they had mastered and the supraphysical power that this knowledge gave to them. But they used their power blindly and haphazardly, to satisfy their own carnal lusts and hedonistic ambitions as evidenced in their brutal exploitation of those as yet unrepatriated beasts.

Having long forgotten that, though simple, these half-human beasts were nevertheless souls conceived of the same Source as themselves, the sons of Belial began to treat them more and more as domestic animals or as beasts of burden, even defiling them as sexual prey. Although the beasts resented the mere presence of these mightier beings, the precarious flicker of their intelligence prevented them from any ill-conceived attempts to resist. Even among the human inhabitants of this world who by now had increased from a handful to a profusion of all five races, the sons of Belial observed no moral or categorical restraint. Admired by these fallen Sons of God for their natural beauty and inward grace, the females of the human species were coveted as wives. "And it came to pass," records Genesis, "when man began to multiply on the face of the earth, and daughters were born unto them, that the Sons of God saw the daughters of men that they were fair, and they took them wives of all which they chose" (Gen. 6:1). It would seem that the priesthood of the Children of Light were no longer the sole trustees of the human spirit.

THE PHYSICS OF THE GODS

Nor were the priesthood any longer the sole guardians of the repository of sacred knowledge, what the Source calls the "Physics of the Gods," which was bequeathed to them by a race immemorially more ancient than themselves:

> We speak now of an age of antiquity lost to your present records, an age beyond the age that you surmise as prehistoric, the times of early Atlantis and Lemuria; we speak of a time yet before these, of an earth before these, before the calamities, the collisions, the malformations caused by life on earth even in that time, the fall before the fall, if you will. All these references we make that you might understand that there were remnants of an earlier race that were seen even by the residents of the great land of Lemuria as the Ancient Ones, the shining beings, the Manu (Solomon Reading No. 571, 4/26/75).

When they were fresher and nearer to their earthly origins, at a time when no separation had yet effaced this past from their memory, the Atlanteans knew that they themselves were descended from gods from infinitely remote ages. Referred to as the Manu, they had vouchsafed with the new Atlantean priesthood a knowledge of cosmic forces that ultimately would transform their world.

> These Manu brought with them, then, the secrets of reflective energy and compressed energy both by the relation of geometric forms and the interplay of reflective surfaces or that [that] you know in this time as pyramid energy and crystal energy. These were not so much developed in Lemuria as in Atlantis in the latter years, [but] first in Lemuria [with] the use of reflective

light in connection with agriculture. At first, then, [there was] beamed...
rather simplified forms of the use of (sic) energy at that time [in Lemuria],
and not so much etheronic energy in that time [of Atlantis] as reflected energy. More sophisticated forms then were developed and given to the people
by the princes of Atlan [in Atlantis]... who were as well priests of Atlantis
who were so named, that is, both as priests and as princes, by virtue of their
heritage as [those spiritually descended] of the shining beings, the Manu,
and were [also] initiates.

[They, then], experimented with, focused, and used both the crystal and
geometric energy for a number of purposes. But central to all use was that of
interplane communication; that is, the originating thought and purpose, intent in the building of the pyramidal temple with its capstone of fire, or firestone, was to provide a chakrum. [It was the] understanding of the Manu
and [so] dictated that there are centers in the physical body of man that are
energy vortices that are the connecting link between the physical and the
spiritual source of consciousness of [any] particular individual. The crystal,
then, [was] an attempt to provide an artificial chakrum of the earth, or a
point of contact, a point of condensation of spiritual energy into physical
form, that [could be] channeled in such ways and purposes (sic). These were
carefully introduced by the Manu in this way: there were built devices of
protection, especially in this sense that there were carefully screened and
selected those who would become aware of the use of such energy. Thus we
have in the beginning of time as you know it the origin of what has become
superstition concerning occult law and [as it] became the practice through
all time that occultists guarded heavily their secrets of communication with
the Divine as a result of these initial attempts to protect such secrets from
the uninitiated. Now the focus in this time seems to be on the firestone itself,
although you should be aware that the earlier devices were of the interplay of
precious metals as geometric forms and particularly of symbols. You regard
yourselves as sophisticated in this time for your opinions that symbols are
only meaningful as mental interpretive objects and have no power in form.
But let the wise one study the Ark of the Covenant and the wings of the seraphim and see what power symbols have, for the focal point of energy on the
Ark of the Covenant was on the mercy seat, not inside the cabinet, and was
a result of the focus of the eyes and the point of the head and the gathering
of the wings concentrating the energy of the ethers upon the placement of
the presence of God in the eyes of men. That is, by the seeing of Him on the
mercy seat, focusing the energy there, if ... seen [through] the power created
by emotion or such, attempt to approach it in the physical and see what will
occur! Now you'll find, then, that there was the use of sources of energy
that you've not begun to consider in this time including the use of symbol,
for you'll find hardly an instrument, whether a flying machine or a source
of treatment for medical purposes or weapons or whatever, from Atlantis
that would not include a carved figure, not simply for aesthetic value nor for
producing a mental reaction but for the knowledge and understanding of
the power of thought-form, of creating physical form, giving command to
[the] etheric counterpart.

[Now], the Temple [of Initiation] lay in concentric circles of protective form,
that is, of walls, a place of mystery to most, though thousands over time

were privy as servants, as workers, all worshippers of the shining ones as representatives of the one God. Most focused on the ideal or thought of the sun as [a] focal point for this temple in this time because of the repute of the crystal as being a focal point for the energies. We find a ... later period in the third dispensation of Atlantis when such instruments were less guarded, yet more sophisticated, and used for a number of other purposes. [We] see these instruments as sitting in a sacred place, a Holy of holies, entered only on particular occasions by the Priest of priests who brought the questions from the people before this [that] is seen as an oracle in this time. And again [in a] somewhat [later period] this crystal [was] far more exposed to public knowledge and used in this time in a medical center both for the purpose of prolonging human life, restructuring physical bodies in ways similar to surgery, though more concerned with burning and reconstructing than with cutting and such as you see it in this time. [It] was used as well for [the] control of weather [and] for [the] propulsion of vehicles, that is, [as] a power center, an energy center, a storehouse for availability of energy in that time. And we find a network of these having been developed in several places about the earth as way stations, though subject to the central energy focus, that is, the largest and strongest of these in Poseidon, in the medical center or temple there; the others dependent on this central focus for their operation (Solomon Reading No. 571, 4/26/75).

From out of an infinite past the Atlantean priesthood had brought forth an infinite power from which, we are told, their technical civilization attained to the highest peak in the history of our world. The Manu had placed energies of cosmic magnitude in the hands of the Atlantean priesthood in the form of the great crystal or "firestone" which **gathered, concentrated, magnified forces of light and universal force [which could] focus in many different ways to provide for travel along the beam of focus, allowing, of course, travel at or beyond the speed of fight. It also allowed to produce (sic) a pathway of focus through matter, through the earth, so that one could travel in such a way through matter, for time and space were not considerations** (Solomon Reading No. 1643, 5/4/92).

Such a predication sounds fanciful it not downright heretical given Einstein's Special Theory of Relativity which holds the speed of light particles in a vacuum (space) to be the only absolute standard of measurement. Nothing could ever travel faster than light, Einstein believed, because at that velocity time barriers simply cease to exist. Unless, of course, there was a deeper "nonlocal" level of reality beyond the quantum. The brilliant mathematical proof now known as Bell's theorem opened the door to the emerging field of quantum mechanics by demonstrating that at "nonlocal" states, faster-than-light communication was possible. It was not until the year 2000 that Bell's 1964 theorem was successfully put to the test. In an experiment conducted at Princeton University and published in the July 20, 2000 issue of the journal *Nature*, researchers sent a pulse of laser light through cesium vapor so quickly that it left the chamber before it had even finished entering, thus achieving superluminal speed. Because the leading edge of the light pulse contained all the information needed to produce the pulse on the other end of the chamber, theoretically the entire pulse did not need to reach the chamber in order to reach the other side.

Far excelling, even by the greatest stretch of our imagination, our own substantial gains in the field of theoretical physics, the highly advanced technology giving rise to the firestone or "great crystal" was based, shall we say, on a similar principle of instantaneous "action-at-a-distance."

> [Thus], the initiates [were] those ordained to the purpose of attuning this crystal for the purpose of providing paths of light without resistance into which a soul might step for the purpose of transportation to a distant, greatly distant, destination, even such as interplanetary travel or interstellar travel which required no time lapse. This was accomplished by the crystal by destroying in its path of focus any forms of energy which would impede the speed of light so that [those] existing as beings of light could step into this pathway or channel which was provided for [them] and [they] could travel instantly, without time loss, to distant locations as the family of the Pleiades or Polaris or other star systems in which they learned more of creation itself (Solomon Reading No. 1619, 4/21/92).

Forming the great capstone of the temple complex at Poseidon, the firestone **did not refract the light into colors**, explains the Source, but by tunable frequency relays of interlocking but reciprocally accommodating patterns --- representing every frequency of cosmic light and radiation --- **it focused the light into a purity of a stream of light most comparable to what you call in this time a laser:**

> Thus, [these] still free, awakened God conscious human or humanoid Sons and Daughters of God learned the properties of the living beings called crystals which had the properties of focusing, magnifying, captivating and holding energy, and concentrating and reflecting the one known energy of that time which was light itself. Thus, the greatest machine, the first machine in all of history was a gathering of crystals which were put together in such a way as to capture the photons or quanta of light and to pass them systematically from one crystal, which had the property of capturing and concentrating the vitality of energy of light, pass[ing] from that crystal to the adjacent crystal which was a magnetic stone. And these crystals obeyed the thoughts and the words of the humans, the co-creators, the Sons and Daughters of God who could then apply even the slightest pressure with mind or physically, applying [this pressure] to the crystal causing a release of piazzo electricity so that photons were given electrical charge which in turn allowed for the creation of atoms which was the property or the purpose of the adjoining crystal of hydrogen and oxygen captured in crystalline form along with other building blocks of creativity and of the planet, the earth as we know it (Solomon Reading No. 1619, 4/21/92).

Being an extremely pure, coherent form of light, the laser can produce wave interference patterns influencing even quantum levels of probability. With a wave buildup, atoms are more likely to be present. Atoms are less likely to be present when the interference of these waves causes a cancellation. And by adjusting the manner in which waves combine, molecular structure itself is altered. Since there is nothing to mitigate against the view that energy, while always conserving itself, can pass from the material to the luminous form and vice versa, theoretically it is possible for an entity to cross one quantized barrier to condensation into the next at a revelatory interval that would essentially be nonexistent. Thus,

> [The Atlanteans] had the ability to fly ... in flying machines or ships which were made primarily of light, light which was made of energies charged in such a way as to produce atoms. These in turn [were] used to form molecular structure, and this, then, was the material of which such ships were made. And these were interdimensional craft, so that in that time [one] would be able to fly through what we consider physical matter, fly through the earth as easily as flying through the air. For in the greatest sense it was not flight at all, but rather the leaving of one dimension and arriving at another without a true passage as is known today as movement through space. Space and time had little meaning in this period. As a result, [one] might leave one location and arrive at another location without the necessity of literal movement through any particular material [or element] in arriving at the destination (Solomon Reading No. 1677, 5/31/92).

It seems, then, that this ancient "Physics of the Gods" was as different from the physics of today as the latter is from the physics of Democritus and the early Greeks. Paradigmatically incommensurable with our own conventional practices, the technology of the ancients, designed **to collect and distribute the greatest power available to earth, the power of light,** represented and in fact utilized the power of life itself:

> [The] instrument of use in Atlantis was a gatherer of [the] positive power of light which in its gathering of power from the universe did not destroy anything for the release of power. Thus it might be said [that] it was operated by positive power rather than by negative power in the sense that [it] is used today. In all forms of science, from the automobile engine to that of nuclear power plants, all of those use the principle of destructive power. The highest of the minds of scientists in this day believe that the only way to make power available for use on this earth is to destroy those concentrations of power which manifest themselves in the natural earth.... All power produced in this manner is dark force power, and so you have an earth today dominated by the powers of the dark or evil forces.

> Now it is a restriction which has been placed upon us since that day [of destruction brought about through the misuse of the firestone] that we are not allowed to unravel for you, to give you the finished work of the formula for this positive release of energy. We can tell you just this much and no more: that the secret of the formula is hidden within the equation six by six by six. We are aware that such an equation or formula is completely occult to your thinking. It gives you not much [with which] to investigate the forces and to teach them, only a piece of observation of the positive expression of energy in the universe, should you look at it. Just keep those numbers in mind and allow your mind to grow until it can comprehend that expression of life not only upon earth, but in the solar system. That is as much as we may say concerning that particular matter (Solomon Reading No. 1235, 2/25/87).

In accord with a technology that was completely assimilated to the grand symbiotic system of the surrounding universe, the highest function of the Temple of

Initiation as a condenser of light, beyond transiting interdimensional barriers, beyond even the regeneration of imperfect bodies, was its use for the further development of the spiritual capacity of an emergent humanity. This means, in the last analysis, the development of a greater capacity for a consciousness of its Logoic Source. For, the sacramental presence of this wondrous instrument provided for these Sons of God the ultimate means of fulfilling their divine mandate: to proselytize the sacred through their co-creative abilities as earthly extensions of the Logos, the very Source of the power of all Light and Love.

> **And we will refer to it in this manner: that in a time when a great culture had been built in a kingdom called Atlantis, there was the rising above Alta of a great mountain, much of it build by man in seven great stages, roughly pyramidal in shape, and with at its peak a great Temple of Initiation. This was a place for the study and commitment of those who had responsibility for the guidance of the nation, the land of that time. And it was a peculiar time, in the sense that this culture consisted of a people advanced considerably beyond the development of other lifeforms on earth to the extent that many of those who have evolved to what you think of as the human state were in that time rather more like beasts of burden to those of the sophisticated culture. But a primary service of that culture was the lifting of the consciousness of mankind. And the primary industry or focus was upon the perfection of character for the purpose that the power of earth might be given into the hands of man (Solomon Reading No. 1319, 3/28/88).**

Because truth itself is a formative power, the energies employed by the ancients naturally entered into such a formulation. But it was power not for its own sake that ordained the work of this temple, rather it was power directed by love into the forms of beauty and truth. **The instrument, however, was finally attuned in such a way as to reveal the separation of light and darkness and the beginning of the understanding of separation came into the consciousness of man.... There was, then, the collapse of that community, that life, that temple that was Atlantis** (Solomon Reading No. 1643, 5/4/92).

Here, once again, we enter upon that time of the Fall.

MEN OF DARKNESS

For over fifty thousand years not merely had these Children of Light been able to perceive the world as One, but they had been able through the audacities of their technological development to act in the same fashion. Ultimately they brought forth the mightiest and most elegant structure of the earth, the Temple of Initiation, capable of ennobling by its awesome power the spirit of every being that availed itself of its sacramental presence. Yet, the cryptic knowledge of those highly calibrated energies concentrated in the firestone was accessible only to the hieratic few lest it fall to the careless and indifferent.

Following the Fall into sexual as well as into material and psychological division, however, their sacred heritage became a repertory of extremes --- light and darkness, good and evil, life and death, love and fear --- forcing choices between absolute incompatibilities and stirring promptings of pride and rebellion. More and more they became desperate assertions of mass egotism, collective power, and aggressive arrogance. And the demon of their discontent in the end focused its rebellion on the great geomantic center of the ancient world, the Temple of Initiation. **Those of the Children of the Law of One [were] alarmed at the loss of the sacred honor and the sacred place of the crystal. We find [many of these] involved in the rhetoric of the times, of attempting to subdue the outrage of the rebels in that time who were preaching to the people that the Manu and those who had gone before had unfairly kept sacred secrets from the people and [that] all should be privy to the knowledge, the understanding, of the Law of One. Many of those even who called themselves Children of the Law of One were preaching in that time that none should guard the secrets, nor should there be secrets, but that all should be brought before the people and such. So then came power struggles** (Solomon Reading No. 504, 4/26/75).

Their antediluvian world was now at a turning point --- a transition from which they could either move forward to a new plateau of technological achievement and social well-being or descend toward disaster of unprecedented magnitude. Given that they were now so totally immersed in a profane consciousness, and given their relative ignorance of the great dangers and great secrets hidden at the heart of matter, they were now treading a path into the midst of an immense darkness. **[Hence], there came a time when the instrument was ineffectively or carelessly used so that those of imperfect character were given [the] reigns of power, and [they] misused much of humanity and [the] earth to the extent that the power turned toward ... these who we will refer to as "men of darkness." Not so much in a sense of evil, but misguided, [and they] attempted to use [this] power for the manipulation of nature and the change of what they considered to be hostile characteristics of the earth. And in so doing [they] released great energies and powers of the earth itself which reacted with the changing of the geological surface of the earth as well as its climatic conditions and such** (Solomon Reading No. 1319, 3/28/88). The result was the first of a chain of major cataclysms to have rocked the ancient continent of Atlantis.

So irreparably fragmented in mind and spirit by ages and ages of fear, lust, hatred, and rebellion, it was now emphatic that this once glorious race would never again embody the light of their lost unity. Nor were the Sons of God any more privileged in their wealth of spiritual preeminence, for they, too, had fallen. **For even the Lord's people [Children of the Law of One] in that time were in those bodies that were susceptible to the drawing of pleasure, the temptation to do this or that, the partaking of self. And there was seen here [the attitude] that 'we can gain for the self by focusing the energy in such a way.' 'I can build for myself those things that will bring pleasure to the self.' Then as there was the partaking of self, there was the taking of the bite from the apple in the garden. Now understand the symbology here. Then there was the separating from the knowledge [that] 'we are of God' and there was the identification of that which was the apple, the physical, that which was taken into the body, into the system. [It was this] that was identified with. Then man, thinking himself man, lost his identity as God** (Solomon Reading No. 176, 6/9/74).

So contagious was the Fall even among those who still considered themselves Children of God, and so widespread had the propagation of the gospel of proletarianism become, that within a few crucial generations (a lifespan extending a thousand years or more) a sweeping revolution of values had, with the bleakest of results, thoroughly secularized society. The sacred rites and holy principles of the old mystery schools, now thrust into the public domain, ceased to inspire by direct insight and instead had hardened into routine gestures and simple mystagoguery. Lacking the vitality of direct experience, the mammonistic priesthood proved less and less capable of yielding the shining human benefits that once fired the mind with transcendent awareness. By this downward spiral, the pedagoguery of religion became the annihilating antithesis of mysteries once acquired on the threshold of ecstasy. It was the tragedy of spiritual blindness elevated to the status of high principle.

Vanity, greed, envy and pride all weighed into the inventory of the iniquitous and now pernicious character of the race, thus producing inequalities among them ultimately fatal to their original innocence and to the freedom of their souls:

> By thus pursuing pleasure they fell into misery. When they sought after wealth, they always considered what they already possessed as mere poverty in comparison with what they lacked, and their acquisitions always fell short of their ambitions. Dreading poverty, they were incapable of being content with sufficiency; fearing death, they took no care of life; seeking to avoid disease, they never abstained from the things that cause it. Full of mutual suspicions, they plotted against most of their fellows.... They hated tyranny and themselves desired to tyrannize; they blamed base actions but did not refrain from them. Good fortune they admired but not virtue, misfortune they pitied but knavery they did not avoid. When luck was with them they were bold, when it turned against them they were in despair. They declared that the dead are happy, yet themselves clung to life, and on the other hand they hated life, yet were afraid to die. They denounced wars and were incapable of living in peace. In slavery they were abject, in freedom insolent. Under democracy they were turbulent, under tyranny, timid. They desired children, but neglected them when they had them. They prayed to the gods, as to beings able to assist them, and they scorned them, as unable to punish, or again, they feared them as avenging powers, and swore falsely, as if the gods had no existence.[21]

With these words the Roman philosopher Maximus Tyrius epitomized the degenerative nature of mankind at the end of the Golden Age.

True, there remained a certain stock of the original race, promiscuously scattered throughout the continent, who proved less susceptible to the vulgarization of truth than the majority. But while still striving to draw back the retreating god, they knew full well that the ethrealization of life was now over. The few remaining roots that tied their visionary energies to the great spiritual tradition of the Manu were by now merely the final glimmers of the failing light. For, without an abiding sense of the Unconditional, the Absolute, the fallen race would inevitably flounder, lurching from crisis to crisis, at the mercy of an uncongenial environment.

Indeed, suffering had become a measure of their remoteness from the Divine Unity, and worsened in proportion as they defied or disregarded the Law. But since they were still in possession of an inexhaustible source of power which could be easily manipulated and easily controlled, the folly and sacrilege of the rashness of their enterprise mattered little to them. Although controllable, once again the power of their technology was used foolishly. The amplification of energies concentrated in the core of the firestone was tuned treacherously high resulting in a global convulsion. Nearly 50,000 years had served to erase from their collective memory the magnitude of the preceding disaster, and this second upheaval was executed with as much reckless ineptitude as was the first. An incandescent hurricane spread over the whole of the earth unleashing in its fury an electromagnetic collapse that only a few remote regions of the earth were privileged to avoid. The immense energy of the central explosions was enough to fracture the continent of Atlantis into three smaller islands. Century by century the pent energy of the massive explosions dispersed itself, but not until many thousands of years had passed did vast tracts of the now reconfigured continent become once more hospitable to life. Thus, a civilization that had taken over a hundred thousand years to spell itself out from its earliest primitive beginnings, and many tens of thousands of years more to reach the crest of its scientific and technological achievement, now faced its impending moral dissolution and physical extinction. Yet another 18,000 years would elapse before that final cataclysmic event that would efface them from the earth.

The history of the Atlanteans, as recorded in the Source readings of Solomon, follows a clearly discernible mythic sequence: the transgression of a certain norm of knowledge and power in combination with egocentric pride and decadence necessarily leads to suffering, chastisement, and finally destruction. This ancient race of god-like beings had penetrated into forbidden territory, overstepped limits considered inviolable, dared to attempt what should not be attempted. Having lost touch with the intrinsic side of their being, they succumbed to the basest part. And as legends of an unfallen world, joyously superior to the enfeebled state to which they had fallen, receded further and further into the realm of myth and imagination, faith in the greatness of God came eventually to be replaced by faith in the greatness of themselves. To paraphrase Abraham Joshua Heschel, "man, who is more subtle than any other creature that God has made, what did he do? He undertook to build a Paradise by his own might, and he [drove] God from his Paradise."[22] Indeed, these images of total catastrophe were the direct result of beings who, through the loss of their sense of reverence for and responsibility to life and to the Source of Life, usurped with defiant temerity the role of the Creator.

This, then, according to the Source, was the reason for the "second" Adam, being the first man of the Biblical Genesis.

Chapter 7

Truth Lay Entombed In
The Grave

THE SECOND ADAM

It is said that God does not will that any soul should perish, but has provided means of deliverance for any who would so choose. Amelius forged the great temples of the ancient world as a means of release for **those who had become captured in bodies and had little or no memory of themselves as an expression of God without boundaries. Thus, it became [His] sacred mission ... to create a series of steps by which these souls captured in matter could again gain self-awareness and the awareness of their Source or God in an attempt to help these entrapped beings return to God consciousness** (Solomon Reading No. 1619, 4/21/92). But as the intrinsic mind became increasingly obscured, the whole venture of the spirit, of exploring the world and its own form-creating potential, eventually brought on evils seemingly beyond remedy. The Logoic Spirit called out for a new man, a new *type* of man, one who, in accord with the Biblical admonition to "keep the race pure," would be incapable of intermingling and crossbreeding as in the past with other life-forms in the physical. More significantly, although it is the soul's birthright, a type of man through which the soul could, in potentia, attain to another and altogether higher spiritual state than that whence it departed, exceeding even, as in the case of the wren out-soaring the eagle, the most highly developed of the Sons of God themselves. Conceived as the meeting point between the heavens and the earth, and the past and future evolvement of mankind, as if in the representational form of a grand cross this new creation would be figured in perfect balance between the forces of the spirit and the flesh. Hence, the new man of Genesis, on the one hand bearing in full the genetic signature of Homo Sapiens Sapiens, and on the other hand one in whom the dawning recognition of love could be exposed to the common light, perfected, and through a series of incarnations in the flesh moved toward its final completion as the Christ. So from that center of psychic totality that is the "I AM", the all-inclusive force of Logoic Consciousness raised from the earth a new expression of Itself through which, through Its grand redemptive journey through the realms of matter, It might ultimately evoke in the world the extraordinary presence of God-in-man.

A Hebrew parable tells that when God was about to create Adam He consulted with the angels, and said unto them: "We will make a man in our image." The angels asked: "What is man that Thou shouldst remember him, and what is his purpose?" "He will do justice," said the Lord. And the ministering angels split into contending groups. Some said, "Let him be created" while others cried, "Let him not be created!". Mercy said, "Let him be created, for he will be merciful and benevolent." Truth said, "Let him not be created, for he will be false." Justice said, "Let him be created, for he will bring justice into the world." Peace said, "Let him not be created, for he will constantly wage war." What did the Holy One do? He hurled Truth from heaven and cast it into the ground. Thus, from the dust of the earth was man created and Truth lay entombed in the grave. Said the ministering angels before the Holy One, blessed be He, "Sovereign of the Universe! Why dost Thou despise Thy seal? Let Truth arise from the earth!" Hence it is written, "Let truth spring up from the earth." (Psalm 85:12)

"I am the way, the truth, and the life," proclaims Jesus (John 14:6). Just as in the first Adam truth was entombed, so in the last Adam, Jesus of Nazareth, the truth is set free. Like the Sons of God before him, the androgynous Adam falls into division: "When Adam looked at his flesh, that was altered, he wept bitterly, he and Eve, over what they had done."[23] It now becomes his task, through a succession of incarnations --- as Enoch, as Melchizedek, later as Zend, Ur, and Asaph, again as Jeshua, Joshua, and Joseph, and finally as Jesus --- to disengage from the physical, to purify the self, to overcome death even, thus circling back to his point of departure in a state of reunified or androgynous consciousness. For, "when you make the two one, and when you make the inner as the outer and the outer as the inner and the above as the below," declares Jesus, "and when you make the male and the female into a single one, so that the male will not be male and the female [not] be female (i.e. androgyne)...then shall you enter [the Kingdom]."[24] Beyond the antithesis of good and evil, beyond the source of all moral values, beyond the world of sexual distinctions, lies the Kingdom --- a realm that is irreconcilable with the world, where opposites cancel out, where conflicting forces are knit into one, where the ineffable absolute being of Truth is actualized in the transcendent experience of Divine Love. **Then that separation of souls into polarity has nothing to do with the sex of the physical body,** explains the Source, **so much as it has to do with the concept that all souls become men, or masculine, in the act of the Fall itself, (or that that is called the "Fall"), in this sense:**

> ...when a soul decided to act upon his own, becoming an active principle, he then began to express the active principle, that which is feminine within himself being set aside. For if one continued as androgynous, active, and yet with the womb of the female, that womb is that which would contain God or the inner Light. It was the loss of this receptiveness of the Will of God that caused man to fall, expressing selfishly; one [single] act without containing the Will of God and [without] expressing it through him. Therefore all souls became masculine in the expression (sic).

> The very act of spiritual growth is the redevelopment of the womb carrying and giving birth to the Christ, so that all souls in the attempt to return to God have felt only half a soul, giving rise to the theory of [the] "soul-mate," or the idea that souls split into a masculine and feminine half, causing all souls to look for their other half, feeling incomplete without it. Then the other half of every soul is his feminine, or mother, or womb-nature, that womb in which he might ponder all things in his heart, giving birth to the Christ within him, causing the soul to be at once complete, and giving birth to that which is androgynous, at once active and yet carrying and acting upon the Will of the Father as that it would give birth to in expression of all things.

There is not, then, the other half of any soul expressed in matter; but the other half of every soul is that [that] can be a part of him that will carry, receive, and give birth to God Himself. Then the soul is married to Christ by becoming His female half, receiving the love flow, or the seed of the Christ, [thereby] giving birth to the Christ, [just] as God the Father, then, went into the Divine Mother impregnating Her with His active principle, and She brought forth that that is the Christ. So that divine drama is reenacted in the new birth in every soul that allows that that which is God re-express in a cycle of return. For that [that] God gave birth to through the Divine Mother was Himself and all that is God. That [that] the soul will give birth to in the new birth is God and all that is God. That which the soul will marry is as well that [that] it would give birth to. That is the expression of the polarity of God and the soul... (Solomon Reading No. 901, 10/21/76).

By thus reconjoining with his true intrinsic self in Christ, the truth entombed within Adam quite literally arose from the earth.

This transformation of the physical into the spiritual and the simultaneous return of complementary opposites into unity must not be dogmatized into an event unique to the physical embodiments of the Christ Spirit in Jesus, for it represents the odyssey of every human soul to the Source of its being. Just as in the beginning God generates Adam in His own likeness, so in eternity does He generate in each of us the living spirit of Truth, the single spirit of the whole. Just as microcosm mirrors macrocosm and earth mirrors heaven, so entombed in our hearts is the Infinite, the indwelling expression of God. Truth, therefore, is incarnate in God's creation of ourselves. Conceived on the analogue of the germination and growth of a living seed which evolves toward its own completed form, Truth, the immanent energy of every human soul, is the Word or Logos, the breath of life itself. "It is the very essence of life," declares the Source.

Now understand that as you would turn back to your source of origin, you would realize that you came from God, that that which gave you life and breath, that which breathes the breath of life into your own body, was God Himself. Therefore, you now breathe the breath of God. If this be so, then does not a part of God, does not the very life of God dwell within you? And realize and be aware that there does not live on your plane any entity who does not have available to him within his own heart all instruction in perfection for living his life on this plane for his development, for his perfection, for his returning to be at one with God.

How, then, comes the new birth? In this manner: when there is realized that the life of God, the very heart of God dwells inside yourself, when He is recognized, when the divinity of God is recognized within yourself, does not it then spring to life? That which was the seed brings forth life. This is birth within, and as you recognize the Christ Force, the Force that made Jesus the Christ, when this is recognized within your own heart and becomes the guiding factor of your life, then this is the new birth (Solomon Reading No. 64, 11/7/72).

The incarnation of the Christ Force, first in Adam and finally in the living embodiment of Jesus, is the prototype for the seed of imperishable life, the manifestation of infinite Truth inherent in each of us. For just as with Adam, within each of us there lies slumbering that divine seed by which the Absolute creates, destroys, maintains, and reabsorbs into Itself the whole of the universal order. "The seed of God is in us," writes Eckhart. "Given an intelligent and hard-working farmer, it will thrive and grow up to God, whose seed it is, and accordingly its fruits will be God-nature. Pear seeds grow into pear trees, nut seeds into nut trees, and God seed into God."[25] This, according to the Source, is the fundamental mystery of our being. Having to do with transformations of being toward and away from Ultimate Being, it involves the entire providential plan of the Logos, beginning with Its physical expression as Adam and Adam's subsequent fall into separation from his Source.

THE NEW MAN OF GENESIS

Now that most sacred one, the first Adam, the Adam which became the Christ, that one had just appeared in these environs (upper Nile region of Egypt), and his son, Cain, was cast out from the Garden of Eden and so as well Adam and Eve. Adam came in his sojourn and so as well did Cain come from the lands of the Tigris and the Euphrates... (Solomon Reading No. 1256, 8/22/87).

Here, roughly 400 miles due east of Canaan, upstream from where the Tigris and Euphrates Rivers adjoin to form the Shatt-al-Arab, we find the Biblical land of Eden. It was this same land which was conquered by the Assyrians in the eighth century B.C. Before that it was a land called "Sumer." In the Sumerian language, the word eden means "plain." Since the Sumerians originally entered this land from the hilly regions to the east, it is likely they thought of themselves as having migrated "to Eden", that is, "to the plain." But the Source places Adam here many thousands of years prior to the rise of the first Sumerian city-state, thousands of years before even the final submergence of Atlantis around 10,700 B.C.

Somewhere in this land called Eden was said to exist a fabled garden, an earthly paradise with its Tree of Life and its forbidden tree of the knowledge of good and evil (Genesis 2:9). **Understand that the Tree of Life is the tree that in terms of the Kabbalistic mystics has [been] referred to as the body of Adam Kadmon, your body,** informs the Source. **Your body a Tree of Life. It is lignum vitae if life lives within you and rules over the kingdom of earth, your body, as it rules over heaven, your crown of light** (Solomon Reading No. 1696, 7/13/92). Symbolizing the absolute life principle established in human consciousness by Divine Mind, the "Tree of Life" represents a kind of axis mundi, the unifying link between earth and heaven, between the physical self and the intrinsic (Christ) self. It sustains the uncompounded and indivisible Oneness of the unfallen world of Eden in which all opposites are contained, but not as yet differentiated. In this sense, Eden, from the Hebrew word "heden", refers loosely to a season, an age, an eternity, with the words beauty, or pleasure, being common semantic variations. The Hebrew word "gan," commonly rendered "garden," means any organized sphere of activity --- a body, a world, a universe. Therefore, "gan-heden," the Garden of Eden, represents the spiritual body of the original prototype of man, Adam Kadmon, or the state of the perfect relation of ideas (thought-forms) to pure Being as it is immersed in divine consciousness.

But another tree stands in Eden, declares the Source, **the tree of the knowledge of good and evil, the fruit of ... which allowed a belief that in addition to good there is something called evil, dualism. [That] moment that man tasted of its fruit he became a cleft-brain species, arguing within one skull --- an army, a battle, a war, a continuous war** (sic) (Solomon Reading No. 1696, 7/13/92). Representing the discerning capacity of mind, the "tree of the knowledge of good and evil" reflects the creative power or energy of the embodied intellect alienated from its supernal origins and held in the grip of Physis. **The fruit of that tree, the bitter, bitter fruit of believing that good has an opposite, equal in strength and power --- no, no, no! It is an illusion.**

> All that exists is God. That which appears to be good and evil is man's observation that some things work in the interest of life and expansion and exploration and some things work against its best expression from the point of view of mankind. In God and His observation or relationship with life, there is no good or evil. There is that which is and that which isn't. Therefore there is only that which is. It expands and contracts. It is binary to that extent; not dualistic, but binary in expression.

> Now if you can absorb this, there is within it all that can be taught and all that can be learned of all religions, whether that taught of the Lord Buddha or the Lord Christ; that which has been discovered and written about by all philosophers, that which has been accomplished by all technocrats and can be observed by the binary or bicameral mind of man. It is that which is and there is no more.

> Now, that which is life, which is the projection of Love into expression, which lives in matter and matter which is alive, may or may not know that its life Source is the expression of love in it. But those who discover that it is, know not only life and love, but truth, and thus become enlightened (Solomon Reading No. 1733, 8/12/93).

The primordial parents were given but one command, one Universal Law to be observed, that they not taste the fruit of the forbidden tree, "for in the day that thou eatest thereof thou shalt surely die." Then came the serpent, offering to Adam and his mate the hitherto unexperienced taste of bittersweet knowledge, a knowledge that divided them from themselves, from each other, and from the primal pre-conscious harmony of Eden. **Now how can it be that the Christ, that one who was perfect, could have sinned in the garden?** asks the Source.

> We would see, then, in this manner: as one who entered on this plane a fleshy body, yet still was God. There was not the possibility for sin, for this was foreign to God. But because it was the purpose of this man Jesus (Adam) entering this plane in order that all others might be given that chance for redemption, Jesus had to lose the God identity which was part

of His nature and become identified with man. Hence, the analogy of the tree of knowledge of good and evil, and the reason for He and His soulmate partaking thereof. We would thus find that the one who tempted Him was another entity like as we are, but one who had fallen. Christ partook of this fruit that He might be complete man. This, then, was the purpose of God, the knowledge of God, that the first Adam might make it possible that in the last Adam (Jesus) all might be redeemed (Solomon Reading No. 8, 3/21/72).

Having thus appropriated ideas of duality --- God and not God, good and evil, love and fear --- the unfallen Adam compromised His oneness with God and, for the sake of those He came to emancipate, fell from a state of perfect unity into fragmentation, from eternity into time.

Hence, divisiveness was not inaugurated by Adam. The cosmic drama of the Sons of God degenerating into the Sons of Belial and the children of men had occurred by stages forgotten ages before. [For] it was from that earliest experience of mankind when there was the taking into [the] self [of] the hemispherical brain, in the moment when there was the seeking among those expressions of God to know what it is like to compare what is with what is not. That experience is described in the Bible as eating of the tree of the knowledge of good and evil (Solomon Reading No. 1457, 11/8/90). Rather, Adam's fall and corresponding return to God as Christ was in calculated response to a fall which had already plunged man into the gross material world of separated and conflicting physical and sexual elements.

Mankind's condition after the Fall is such that he could not prepare himself, by his own natural strength and good works, to re-enter a state of Atonement (at-one-ment) with the Father. Beyond all limitations of dogma and doctrine, precept and conduct, one rises only through the creational force of unconditional love to that state at which God and man exist as one, and where the indwelling Christ is revealed as the intrinsic self within each of us. It was while he was yet in Eden, according to the Source, that Adam learned he was to be the manifestation of the Christ. It was then that he was given the specific purpose of proving to man that he could not earn salvation through the application of law, or living up to a set of standards:

> That is, it was not within the realm of man's nature of possibilities, as lower or fallen man, to follow a set of rules, thereby building or living up to that which would be the expectation to become God; and seeing, then, that proven [through Adam] that it not be so, or would not work.

> Then there was given the new method or the interpretation of that original Divine Plan, or that Master Plan, by which all men entered this plane in the beginning; that is, that as man would discover the true nature, or realize [the true nature], [and] then act accordingly or do those things of the true nature, then the true nature would be activated or revived.

> Then if man were given a series (even as he *was* given a series) of steps that might be climbed, or laws that might be followed, a manner in which true growth might be obtained and one might become one with the Father, or the following of the Mosaic Law as it was given even in this purpose --- even so,

it would *not* work. For there cannot be earned by fallen man that right to act as God; for it is within the nature [of fallen man] that these would fail, then.

But see the teaching of Him who came as the Christ. For it was His teaching that all rules be set aside, all law be set aside, or, that is, brought into one, that "one" being the new birth, or the love of self and others. His saying, then, "unless you be born again, you would not enter the Kingdom of Heaven," would cause man to recognize his deeper nature or true [intrinsic] nature or God nature. And in so doing and [in] so giving birth, then he would feed that life, that nature, upon that which is that nature of God. Then living the nature of God, in such a manner he would develop as God. In such a manner, then, would spiritual growth come. Not that you attain a series of steps or follow a series of instructions, for none can be given, save one: that attunement of self to the truest of self (Solomon Reading No. 198, 7/23/73).

NOTE' not a series of steps —

"This is my commandment," declares Jesus, "That ye love one another, as I have loved you...." This is the Law --- the Law of One, the Law of Love, the one Truth which lay entombed in the Source of the first Adam and which, with the obstinacy of a star, would reemerge and burst forth from the personal core of the last Adam, casting its astounding light onto the world. Through His light, all others could find the light; through His example, the esoteric analogue of the exoteric Decalogue received by Moses, all could achieve redemption. The plan was deceivingly simple. The rays of that evolving vitality would ultimately gather and concentrate themselves in the secret recesses of each peninsular soul such that the energies of Love would cause the birth of love in those invisible depths that really define us.

Following his exile from Eden, Adam's mandate began in earnest. Assuming an even greater significance than that accorded to him by the Torah, it included the transmission of the Mystery teachings through which a spiritual rebirth of "the measure of the stature of the fullness of Christ" (Luke 2:7), the perfected man, might take place throughout the whole of humanity.

[Thus] when Adam appeared on the earth, you (individual reading) had come from Alta in Atlantis. You had come to the area of the Nile with the priests and the prophets who came from Alta for the purpose of establishing those temples of rites of purification that would allow human consciousness to develop an appropriate body for the expression of life on this earth. Now some of the importance of your responsibility in that time was taught [to] you by Adam, for when Adam came into Egypt (what was later Egypt we should say, for the name was not thus in that time) he was by the authority of the priests of Atlantis (now in Egypt) initiated into a new name. He was, for a time, called El Morya, who then became Hermes who established the temples there of Initiation, of Sacrifice, and the Temple Beautiful. You were given responsibility [by Adam] in the Temple of Sacrifice. Your responsibility in that time was ... for refining the physical bodies in what you would seem to think now as strange shapes and appearances, animal bodies which were being refined into more godly form or a human form through the processes of that temple (Solomon Reading No. 1256, 8/22/87).

Seeing after the second destruction of Atlantis that their brethren had almost wholly departed from the Law of One, many of the initiates and priests withdrew from the ill-fated continent and, carrying with them the sacred knowledge of the Mystery Schools, established themselves in Egypt where they became its first "divine" rulers. In point of fact, the ancient Egyptians traced their lineage back to a mythological period when the gods themselves walked the earth and with their own power established the Double Empire of the Nile. Above all, it was in fact Hermes Trismegistus who stood at the very center of an enormous body of Egyptian traditions stretching into an immemorial past. This sublime figure, looming through the mists of time, is exalted according to legend as the bringer to humanity of all the arts and sciences --- of architecture, medicine, surveying, law, astronomy, astrology, music, philosophy, geography, mathematics (especially geometry), anatomy and surgery. Moreover, entire chapters of the celebrated Egyptian *Book of the Dead* were attributed to him. The Source reveals that as the builder of the temples it was Hermes who communicated to the initiates the formulae for spiritual, mental, moral, and physical regeneration. It was this same Adam, according to the Source, who as Hermes restored to mankind the worship of the Law of One, becoming the greatest of all priests and the greatest of the legendary god-kings of predynastic Egypt:

> In those arrivals, then, of the Atlanteans, those from Alta in the great migration following those periods of the breaking up [of Atlantis], [Egypt] then was converted from that of the pagan superstitions, as might be described.... Ara-At, who became Il-Kamin, was [at that time] of the pagan priesthood, you see, a leader of the native people, both politically and in the religion. [Hence] there was trouble here, you see, as those of the Atlanteans came --- [and] Hermes --- bringing the worship of the Law of One. They were resisted then by Ara-At. Ara-At caused quite some consternation for these, you see, in leading the [native] peoples in sabotage of the work of the building of the temples. So it was that Ara-At became an initiate, was trained by Ra and Hermes, that he became a priest of the Law of One, so winning his loyalty and his ability to lead the peoples, the natives, you see.

> So then there became (sic) the change in the religion, the understandings of the people, as they began to understand the worship of the Law of One. So it was in this time, then, that Ara-At, in an attempt to explain or to bring those peoples from the pagan worship to that of the Law of One, instituted that of Sun worship, or that called that one god, the Sun god. So you find that confusion in literature that seemed to be the mixing of the pagan and that of the worship of One as came in this time (Solomon Reading No. 271, 11/8/73).

It is said that if ever God appeared in man, He appeared in Hermes. Now from the Solomon Source we learn that God *in fact* appeared in Hermes --- as the first begotten Son of God in the first man of a re-created race of humanity. It is no accidental consequence of his fall that Adam was exiled from the sphere of Truth. But the ulterior, concealed reality within him of an infinitely more exalted Being fitted him with a new purpose in a world that had become careless of the spirit. It was to become the stuff of prophets. Adam, the builder of temples, would in the fullness of time become the builder of worlds. For it was he in whom the generative force of Life itself would ultimately triumph as the Logos, fulfilling in Him as no one before Him the highest truth: "Before all things were, I AM."

Now there has been questioned whether there was a difference in Him who became the Christ and those others of the masters who seemed equally as great. This, then, would be the answer to that question: that never has there been another who by living his life ended one dispensation and began a new [one]. This has only been done by Jesus, the man of Galilee who became the Christ. There have been other masters who expressed the Christ force and thereby brought salvation to their people and brought example to their people and were great in every sense. And it is being given from these planes that we should not encourage that these be separated or thought of as different or one greater than the other, but that they all are one, they all are the manifestation of the One Force. It is only that this one brought the new dispensation.

This will occur again in that which has been called the return of Christ, the Second Coming of Christ, or the return of the Christ force. This will come not through the manifestation of a single man but from the attuning of the hearts to the Law of One. When the Law of One is expressed, that is, made manifest in the hearts and lives of men; that is, when the will, the soul, the purpose of man is brought to One, the planets will line up one behind the other and express the Christ force in the world. This will be the Second Coming of the Christ, and the man from Galilee will appear and be made manifest throughout the world at all times and all places at one time. This will be the expression of the Law of One. This will be the bringing together, the ceasing of the duality between God and man. This will be the ending of the ages, the ending of the earth as you know it, for this will be a higher manifestation of all that is (Solomon Reading No. 41, 10/19/72).

"IT REPENTETH ME THAT I HAVE MADE THEM..."

Under the leadership of Hermes Trismegistus and those early colonists of the Atlantean priesthood, the indigenous inhabitants of what is now Egypt advanced from an inchoate, unbridled horde and reached at length a certain refinement and equilibrium. Suffice it that the upshot was a very remarkable civilization gifted with long ages of harmony, prosperity, and cultural embellishment. Almost all that could have been achieved by Adam as Hermes in the stage to which humanity had then reached seems to have been achieved.

But if Adam sought to unite the way of the earth with that of heaven in the humanity of his day, we may well see this "first Father" weighing in his soul the foreboding implications of the iniquity and malevolence of his own son, Cain. As the crushing effect of the Fall of that earlier civilization continued to make itself felt even upon this latter-day race, Cain, in his rivalry with Abel to gain the affection of the Creator, brought into a new world the irrational, dark vitality that brought ruin to an earlier world still in its final phase of passing. But the single significance of that first Biblical act of fratricide was to be no more than a dust cloud in the hurricane advance of the barbarism and savagery, the unruly cravings, the fear-inspired aggression and barren lust of power that would come to characterize the generations of mankind.

When at last Adam died after nearly a millennium of service devoted to the intrinsic divinity of man and to the limitless Source of all life, he had fathered a vast tribe of his own, his great-great-great grandchildren themselves grown with children of their own. Very few among them, however, found favor in the eyes of God. And as the generations multiplied themselves and their increasing wickedness starved out their capacity for love, fewer and fewer still were able to enter into that spirit of divine grace wherein God speaks to and acts upon man. Because they had fallen even further into the world of sense and therefore fallen into the same errors as their predecessors, the children of men allowed themselves to become deafened to the Word or expression of the Absolute. Once more, God had become inaccessible to man. This tragic antithesis between man and God and between flesh and spirit, brought on only by the abysmal stubbornness, unyieldingness, and immense indifference in man's heart, had simply surpassed the point of reconciliation: "And God saw that the wickedness of man was great in the earth, and that every imagination of the thoughts of his heart was only evil continually. And it repented the Lord that he had made man on the earth, and it grieved him at his heart. And the Lord said, I will destroy man whom I have created from the face of the earth, both man, and beast, and the creeping thing, and the fowls of the air, for it repenteth me that I have made them" (Genesis 6.5-7). A world full of iniquity, of injustice and idolatry called out for a restoration, a renewal, a purification of the earth such that a new birth, a complete transformation of mind and nature could occur. Not that God's perpetual concern for mankind had ended, for man is a precious factor, an eternal partner in the life of God. Rather that out of the few righteous households that would be spared, future generations might not corrupt their spiritual vision and a divine covenant could be established with them and their descendants. And it was the Atlanteans themselves, according to the Source, a once noble people, who were singled out by God to be the ministers of the unprecedented severity of His divine justice.

For every act of divine justice there is a premonishment which carries with it a measure of hope, an opportunity for change, a chance to prepare. "Have I any pleasure in the death of the wicked, says the Lord God, and not rather that he should turn from his way and live?" (Ezek. 18:23). Hence, there were in this foundering world trumpeters of the shattering cataclysmic experience to come.

Noah, zealously mindful of the great Presence within him, sounded to his people a warning of a coming deluge, and a few sensitive souls took him as their prophet. Most, however, perished in ignorance of the vastness and gravity of the power behind Noah's words. Likewise, among the inhabitants of those remaining islands of Atlantis, **the tendency...was *not* to prepare for what they considered imminent breakup or ending of the land, for as those of the Children of the Law of One were predicting the breaking up, the prophets were saying that the islands are to be destroyed, 'we must prepare communities elsewhere and send out scouts and parties for the establishment of these lands and send teachers and architects that would be for the building of communities in that [that] were considered safe places. So as well, the humanists, those scoffing at [the] predictions [and] prophecies and such, were making arrangements for the protection of self in a physical way. [Others], then, considering only an ending of the world, not believing that there would be opportunity for relocation but only [an] ending of all that was of the earth as known (sic).**

These, then, would be considered in your time [as] dropouts, or those failing to use those of the gifts of the possibilities, failing to see opportunities for the establishment of a new world (Solomon Reading No. 371, 6/7/74).

In the recorded myths, legends, epics, and sacred texts of ancient cultures throughout the world we find that prophecies and warnings had been rendered in anticipation of the Great Flood. In the Americas, the Aztecs, the Mayans, the Apache, Navaho, Hopi, the Huarochiri of Peru, the Papago of Arizona, all speak of a deluge caused by a God whose presence was no longer recognized by the people. Warnings were given and only a modest few, those who were of pure heart, are said to have paid heed. Elsewhere among the native Hawaiians, the Australian Aborigines, the Celtics, the Scandinavians, the Chinese, the Egyptians, myths and legends tell of a fearful catastrophe that finally brought to an all-consuming end the golden days. Although prophets had spoken, in the end all but a scattered few were inspired to turn from their evil ways.

The same ancient traditions that memorialized the Great Flood as a catastrophic consequence of the Fall, all describe with remarkable consistency the same pre-cataclysmic factors that, although recognized in very different settings, would suffice to preserve the seeds of humanity and of all living things. In the Babylonian epic of Gilgamesh, because of the violence of mankind the gods are resolved to cleanse the earth and Utnapishtim is told to build an ark wherein "the seed of all living creatures" could be preserved. Chaldean myths hold that Xisuthrus was warned of the coming inundation by the god Chronos who instructed him to build a vessel for his family, friends, and two of every type of animal. In Hindu traditions it is Manu who, having been warned of the flood, is told to build a ship and to stock it with samples of every species. In the Central American myths of the Michoacan Secs, it is the faithful Tezpi who, with his wife and children, along with a large number of animals and birds and grains and seeds, is spared the flood that destroys a corrupt humanity. In the mythology of Viet Nam, a brother and sister are said to have survived in a great wooden chest which also contained two of every kind of animal. The Chickasaws of the southeastern United States likewise maintain that the world was destroyed by water, "but that one family was saved and two animals of every kind."

Could such chronicles of disaster have appeared spontaneously and arbitrarily in such culturally and geographically diverse parts of the world? It seems too coincidental that inhabitants of lands as extraneous and remote as Greece is from Tibet, or as the ancient Mayans and Aztecs are from the Chinese and primitive cultures of North Borneo, all should have conceived of the same record of the Great Flood at approximately the same period of prehistory. Of the more than 500 deluge legends that are known throughout the world, the vast majority are regarded among scholars as being entirely independent of the Hebrew and Mesopotamian accounts. Attempts to generalize or explain such accounts in terms of superstition, collective archetypal representation, symbols of individual or cultural transformation and the like simply result in conjectural triviality and mentalistic prejudice. All the labored arguments in repudiation of such things and events as the historical authenticity of the Flood or of races and advanced civilizations of our own pre-recorded past, arguments which pretend to be grounded on reason or logic, are merely rationalist devices made use of in the interests of a paradigm or thesis that is to be defended. It is a stupendous hypocrisy, an affective and hollow sophistry bent on sacrificing reality to fact and truth to logic. If we are willing to accept a wider Source of truth, one without prejudice or any preconceived incentive to defend, one that does not degrade the vitalizing force of truth to the function of a method, we need proceed no further than the Source of Solomon in whose Being the memory of the ancient past lives in an eternal "Now." Shifting, then, from myth and recorded memory to the direct vision of the Source, we learn of **those times when there were the attempts...to preserve the lives of the animals in the leaving of Atlantis** (Solomon Reading No. 186, 6/15/73).

It is said that Noah labored for fifty-two years upon the ark, so as to give time to the wicked to repent of their ways. Analogous traditions tell a similar story of the supremacy of forbearance prior to the flood. But when the days drew near and the wicked had not repented, those in whom God had implanted His will were ready to cast themselves upon alien shores, others to take refuge in the still untamed mountainous regions of earth. Then it happened.

AN ENDING OF THE WORLD

Deep in the heart of the Andes Mountains situated more than two miles above sea level on the Peruvian border with Bolivia is found Lake Titicaca. Being 138 miles long and in places 70 miles wide, it is the world's highest navigable lake and the world's largest single body of freshwater. It is also one of the world's greatest mysteries; specifically, how did it get there? The countless myriads of fossilized seashells that litter the lake suggests that at some stage the lake and its surrounding plateau was at sea level, or 12,500 feet lower than it is today. Moreover, despite the antiquity of the event that uplifted Titicaca to an elevation of over two miles, at the present time the lake provides habitation for marine ichthyofauna, including the seahorse and various species of crustacea, leaving no doubt that it was once part of the sea.

Twelve miles south of the lake and more than a hundred feet higher are the ruins of the once great port city of Tiahuanacu, its huge docks, sizable enough to service hundreds of large ships, thrusting indiscriminately over sun-ripened stone and raised beaches, indicating massive and traumatic geophysical changes. Most astounding of all, however, is that Tiahuanaco was not a lakeport but a seaport, meaning that its dramatic change in altitude occurred after the city was built. Judging from the mathematical/astronomical calculations of Professor Arthur Posnansky of the University of La Paz, and of Professor Rolf Muller, the phenomenal upheaval surrounding the mystery of Tiahuanaco and Lake Titicaca occurred relatively recently, around the eleventh millennium B.C.[26]

The standard uniformitarian view among geologists and evolutionists is that mountain building is an exceedingly gradual and continuous process, and that spontaneous upliftings on a large scale simply do not happen, not in geological time and most certainly not within the brief time-frame of the racial memory of our species. The residents of Tiahuanaco must have thought differently. The traditions of the people of Peru hold that the entire surface of the earth was changed in this catastrophe. What violent paroxysm could have suddenly opened great cavities of the sea and ruptured the earth with such incredible force as to raise mountains with a single convulsive thrust?

The Source leaves us no doubt as to the cause. One final bout of insane monkeying with the solar crystal in the great megalithic chamber atop the temple pyramid in Alta sufficed to inadvertently spark a chain of detonations that raged over the entire planet. [Many] familiar with the power of the crystal remained, as others departed, during the [final] periods of the breaking up of the land. [There was] much...destruction then among those in the final days whose physical life was destroyed by the over-focusing, the over-tuning of the instrument producing the final breaking up of the land in that time. [Thus] the loss of life, [the] death and destruction, the burning of people and the city in that time...with the power, the awesome power, of these instruments (Solomon Reading No. 504, 4/26/75).

It is said that the first fury of the vast explosion was unabating, reinforcing itself with fresh atomic eruptions wherever it went. The Atlanteans, now at their final hour, were promptly awakened to the frightful accuracy of their prophets. The atmosphere, a continuous dense cloud of moisture and fumes, churned in ceaseless hurricanes of thunder and lightning, and the earth trembled and was tossed about like a ship in mid-ocean. "The life-giving earth crashed around in burning," wrote the Greek poet Hesiod of this cataclysmic event, "all the land seethed, and the Ocean's streams ... it seemed even as if Earth and wide Heaven above came together, for such a mighty crash would have arisen if Earth were being hurled to ruin, and Heaven from on high were hurling her down."[27] Volcanoes throughout the world became fantastically active. Vast tidal waves engulfed the coasts of every land and floundered up the valleys, as the arteries of the earth broke under the strain of torrential rains and the heaving up of the ocean floor itself. In the six hundredth year of Noah's life, in the second month, the seventeenth day of the month," records Genesis, *the same day were all the fountains of the great deep broken up*, and the windows of heaven were opened" (Genesis 7:11). The Choctaw Indians of Oklahoma, over a thousand miles from the nearest shore, relate: "The earth was plunged in darkness for a long time." Then a bright light appeared in the north, "but it was mountain-high waves, rapidly coming nearer."[28] The world was in flames, record the Chinese annals, and "in their vast extent" the waters "over-topped the great heights, threatening the heavens with their floods." An immense wave "that reached the sky" fell down and inundated the land of China. "The water was well up on the high mountains, and foothills could not be seen at all."[29] Half a world away, Lapland cosmogony relates that a giant sea-wall fell on the continent and the entire world was overwhelmed: "when the wickedness increased among the human beings," the midmost of the earth "trembled with terror so that the upper layers of the earth fell away and many of the people were hurled down into those caved-in places to perish."[30] Last but by no means least, chapter CLXXV of the Egyptian *Book of the Dead* chronicles the destruction of a sinful humanity by a deluge:

They have fought fights, they have upheld strifes, they have done evil, they have created hostilities, they have made slaughter, they have caused trouble and oppression... [Therefore] I am going to blot out everything which I have made. This earth shall enter into the watery abyss by means of a raging flood, and will become even as it was in primeval time.[31]

While the Source does not dispute that it is God who, in His longing for our reunion, is the Supreme Cause, or efficient and final cause, of all such events, the instrument of God's power is most often found in the formal or material cause. Hence, the Source refers us to **that time when the cycles of the rains came, or the time ... of that [final] period of Alta ... when what is called the 'greenhouse effect' first occurred on earth. This again [was caused] from the altering of atmospheric conditions through the overuse of the power of the crystal to concentrate the power of the heavens, when such had been used for the control of the weather. And [man] experienced, then, a period of great destruction and rearrangement of the geology of the planet. [This was] the time referred to as the Great Flood** (Solomon Reading No. 1319, 3/28/88).

The Atlantean death agony was brief. Following Plato's account, the submergence of Atlantis occurred in a single day and night: "...and one grievous day and night befell them, when the whole body of your [Greek] warriors was swallowed up by the earth, and the island of Atlantis in like manner was swallowed up by the sea and vanished."[32] The catastrophe was ubiquitous. Through fantastic storms and oceanic convulsions, through inconceivable inundations and the submersion of entire continents, cultural traditions in all parts of the world tell of the near-total annihilation of mankind.

> **If there might be words that could come from these realms, from these understandings, we would ... show that there *was* an ending of the world, an ending of the earth as those knew it in that time. It was shaken, reformed, their world destroyed** (Solomon Reading No. 371, 6/7/74).

Mountains had collapsed; other mountains were upthrust from the plains, causing faults and rifts, their forms scarred and carved by the Universal Deluge. New alluvial areas were formed. New strata were laid upon one another under new oceans. Massive tidal waves which carried vast quantities of debris and sediment from the ocean floors deposited them thousands of miles away, leaving stranded beaches, some of them hundreds of feet above sea level. Huge beasts were shredded to ribbons by the supersonic winds, piled into mountains of flesh and bone, and buried under avalanches of seawater and mud. Even the atmospheric flow patterns affecting the ancient climates had changed. Indeed, the entire face of the earth had changed. Nearly two hundred thousand years of Atlantean hegemony had come to an abrupt and violent end.

If there is a single and exemplary vision of the Atlantean's mythic quest ending in chaos, darkness and death which characterizes the closing degenerative cycle of this fabled land, their fall away from the Universal Essence is undoubtedly the one. An age of triumphant progress carried out by beings of light whose very nature was godlike had passed into a time of excruciating individualism haunted by increasing pride, arrogance, wickedness, and a common passion for power. Speaking of the Atlanteans, Plato wrote:

> For many generations, while the god's strain in them was still vigorous, they gave obedience to the laws and affection to the divine whereto they were

akin. They were indeed truehearted and greathearted, bearing themselves to one another and to their various fortunes with judgment and humbleness. They thought scorn of all things save virtue and counted their present prosperity a little thing. So they found the weight of their gold and other possessions a light load. Wealth made them not drunken with wantonness, their mastery of themselves was not lost, nor their steps made uncertain.

They perceived with the clear vision of the sober that even these things all receive increase from virtue and mutual love, whereas where the first are sought and held in honor, they decay themselves and the divine strain that persisted in them, their wealth... was still further increased. But when the god's part in them began to wax faint by constant crossing with much mortality, and the human temper to predominate, then they could no longer carry their fortunes, but began to behave themselves unseemly. To the seeing eye they now began to seem foul, for they were losing the fairest bloom from their most precious treasure, but to such as could not see the true happy life, to appear at last fair and blessed indeed, now that they were taking the infection of wicked coveting and pride of power.[33]

Thus alienated from the "divine strain within them" and no longer subject to moral laws, Plato tells us that through the monstrous spirit of that watery apocalypse the gods decreed their extinction.

We have, then, a vision of a final destruction that escapes any individual will, a destruction seemingly present in the very act of creation itself as soon as the paradisiacal vision of the beginning falls apart. It is a vision of a catastrophic end provoked by the transgression of the inviolable norm of the Law of One and the consequential fall into separation:

> [T]his duality, this polarity existed not only in the separation of the sexes, but in the feelings of polarity with the Father [and] between the races [and] between ideas. [Hence]...we would find that the reason for the destruction [of Atlantis] was polarity, or the development of extremes within the people, for these separated themselves into the sons and daughters of the Law of One as opposed to the sons and daughters of Belial. Because of their polarity, because of their separation, because of their insistence on following extremes, so did their times, their lands, become destroyed (Solomon Reading No. 196, 7/13/73).

Perceived in this light, the causes of the end, as given through the Source readings of Solomon, transcend the Atlanteans themselves or even the combined effect of the unlimited force of technology and political power gone mad. Rather, the causality pertains to a fundamental antagonism between the free will of man and the Universal Law governing the cosmos --- an antagonism of which mankind, in the end, can only be the victim.

For many decades the greater part of the planet's landmasses were uninhabitable save for the uplands of regions that an antediluvian humanity might have found too harsh and inhospitable for civilized life. The Chinese annals, for instance, record that for decades following the deluge the land was flooded and water was trapped in the valleys between the mountains. "Destructive in their overflow are the waters of the inundation," declared the Emperor Yahou. "In their vast extent they embrace the hills and overtop the great heights, threatening the heavens with their floods." For many score of years all efforts made by the survivors to release the water by means of digging canals and draining the fields were in vain. It is written that the minister in charge of this immense project, Khwan, was sentenced to death for his failure. His son, Yu, then assumed responsibility for the urgent work and after many more years of painstaking labor he finally succeeded. So honored was he for this inimitable achievement that he was named emperor of China after King Shun, first successor to Yahou.[34]

Conditions throughout the world mirrored those of China. Myths and legends declare that for centuries people of every race and tribe struggled in the flood's aftermath with the formidable task of reclamation, readjustment, and renewal. Although in time the overall level of the seas sank considerably through evaporation, saturation, and the opening of chasms in the ocean floor, for ages the survivors of the human race were subjugated to a very restricted and uncongenial environment. In their isolation tribes lost touch with one another, forgot one another, and because no relics of the ancient order were to be found, they forgot much even of their auspicious origins. Plato writes that "for many generations the survivors died with no power [even] to express themselves in writing." All that could be hoped for on the part of these isleted tribal bands was the persistence of a mere remnant of civilized humanity, one which just might have carried through some tangible shards of mankind's cultural inheritance.

Indeed, in China, in Central and South America, in Egypt, as elsewhere, migrations occurred that preserved not merely the seeds of life, but at least a vagrant few of the ancient seeds of knowledge as well. Many seeking refuge found it in the land of the Maya, according to the Source, **the peaceful kingdom where in that time [they] worked with the wheels of indication of the cycles of earth, the cataloging of the relationship of [the] earth and the stellar system. And [they] worked in ways, not prophetic as you would see them today, but scientific in their own way, for calculating the period[s] of change through which the earth tends to pass.... [These, then], somewhat deteriorated into mystical, magical, and superstitious practices, only because much of the science [was] inherited. [And] though often effective, it was misunderstood and handled as if it were religious ritual and superstition. But still there were the legends that were the teachings of the ancient great ones, legends which gave instruction for the lifting and the development of character and stories which told of the magnificence of the death of the flesh, that the spirit might be born** (Solomon Reading No. 1319, 3/28/88).

Hence, for many long generations thereafter, those factors which earlier had brought about separation between man and his eternal Source were effaced. Not that the Fall was undone, but that unconditioned power had shattered their hearts of stone and fashioned them with hearts of flesh such that a regenerated humanity could once again walk in His path and rediscover His ways.

While God's judgments are not always "wrought in the earth," sacred traditions the world over declare with one voice that in the event of the Great Flood it was God's will that came to expression. The manifestation of God's divine justice enabled the inhabitants of the world to relearn His law, that while choice may determine the shape of events, it is He who shapes man through the illumination of such events. The Hebrew prophet Jeremiah was told to go to a potter's house where he would receive a revelation. "So I went down to the potter's house, and there he was working at his wheel. Whenever the vessel he was making went wrong, as clay is apt to do in a potter's hand, he would re-make it in a different shape, such as he thought suitable. Thereupon the word of the Lord came to me: Am I not able to act toward you, O Israel, like this potter? You are in my hands as clay is in the hands of the potter." (Jer. 18:3-4)

So it was with the flood. Through unimaginable adversity, mankind once again was made fit and pliable, open to truth, sensitive to the divine significance of his soul. **The periods, then, of soul growth**, affirms the Source, **came just following these break-ups, these changes:**

> For it might do well to explain here that there were changes in the nature, the intent, the personality, the concerns, the focus of men's minds following the break-up. For at this time did they seek understanding. The evangelist had gone before in the time of Alta, preaching to the people and saying to those who were callous and hard-of-heart, "It is necessary that we reinvoke our ability to communicate with God." Men were busy about their tasks of daily life, their concerns for the things of the flesh, and while some listened superficially, only the few, so very few, awakened and turned from their self-ish ways toward the establishment of spiritual growth and concern for the true values of life. Not so different from today. After the breaking-up, and during the periods of the trauma and the change, such a release of the energy of earth, such a purity, for that which was separative was destroyed --- the conditions of separation destroyed. And while the sons of Belial still lived, even after the changes, the symbols and the tools of their existence, their cities, and the wickedness of them was destroyed. And at the same time, through fear and through shock of awakening, men began to seek. And during this period, then, the evangelists, the teachers, the prophets were listened to --- for a season. And during this period did many turn, then, toward God, seeking Him actively (Solomon Reading No. 797, 3/26/76).

Once more, God was able to feed His people with the rich and vigorous air of spirit which, above all, reawakened in them the creative principle of love.

But the "season" of mankind's observance of the Law proved to be lamentably short. Inwardly they were a rebellious people, and by the time their great-grand-children had children of their own, the intoxications of the things of the flesh again took hold, and so the prodigal path of wandering and hazards and schismatic dangers opened before them. The great faith of their fathers and forefathers before them became infinitely divided and subdivided into so many superstitious herd-cults. As the venerable cosmogonies of man and of the universal forces gradually sank into crude myth, so too the ancient teachings eventually degenerated into **a time when the misunderstandings of the new birth led to human sacrifice** (Solomon Reading No. 1319, 3/28/88). Their cultures, now split into contending tribes and city-states, became entrenched in bitterly defended anthropogenic creeds and professions of faith to freakish provincial gods.

So as the ancient knowledge of One receded further and further into the realm of myth and unbelief, so too the Shekhinah, the presence and splendor of the Eternal which dwelt with Adam in the earthly paradise of Eden, retired to celestial realms wholly inaccessible to the veiled soul of a divided humanity. And as the degeneration of the already degenerate accelerated, the Shekhinah receded farther and farther from the inhabitants of earth. The Midrash explains that after the fall of Adam, the Shekhinah, or Divine presence, had retired to the first or lowest heavenly sphere. It ascended to the second after the crime of Cain, to the third in the time of Enosh, to the fourth in the time of the deluge, to the fifth when the tower of Babel was being constructed, to the sixth in the age of Sodom, and to the seventh, that is the highest heavenly sphere, when Abraham visited the land of Egypt.[35] So Heschel writes: "The Shekhinah is in exile, the world is corrupt, the universe itself is not at home."[36]

But the Eden of integration is not so distant as we might suppose. For the Midrash also teaches that when just and pious men arise, the Shekhinah once more gradually descends to dwell among men.[37] And it dwelt among them in the embodiment of Buddha, of Jesus, of Mohammed, and those who faithfully followed their teachings --- ordinary men and women who had, as a given fact of direct, unmediated experience, become one with the force of "Love," "Light," or "Truth" on every level of their being.

Truth Shall Rise Up From The Grave

THE LADDER OF LIGHTS

Invited into this infinite epic of creation, farther and deeper still, we find in the intrinsic heart of our being a grand spectrum of illimitable potential whose highest and most subtle regions include the godlike force of "I AM" consciousness. **That which adds to life is by nature the one force,** reveals the Source, **the force of the One known as light, life, love, truth, the I AM, the Logos, the expression of God made flesh and dwelling in you** (Solomon Reading No. 1757, 12/9/93). Just as holographically each of us contains the whole of the Christ force, so too we each are the focus for the absolute energy of the whole that is light, life, and universal love. **Jesus, in becoming the Christ, became the soul of all,** records the Source.

> **Even though the Christ appeared completely in physical form in the body and the life of the man Jesus, it still is also true that the Christ dwells in you. This does not make Jesus any less the Christ, for he was and is absolutely the Christ. And you must understand at the same time that the Christ is one with love, life, light. And if any one man or woman is so given to the expression of that love, life, light as to lose individuality, personality, separation from the One, then that one becomes the embodiment of what the Christ is, and is the one Christ. Yet that might happen in more than one body. That does not make two Christs. It means that those who would determine the succession of the incarnations of the man Jesus as a soul will need to understand that that which was incarnate in Jesus the Christ was the incarnation of the Christ in all of us, in all of you** (Solomon Reading No. 1436, 10/21/90).

Good and evil cease to be when any individual is delivered from Selfhood, when one's solitary and autonomous ego is abolished, and one ceases to be aware of a distance separating the self from the divine Source of one's own being. The smooth waters of inner unity and peace rise up and overwhelm the burdened and unruly beast. The ineffable reality of Nirvana ("Deliverance") ensues. The Christ force manifests as reality itself. Throughout the ages this sense of God's unfailing presence has been the experience of myriads of receptive souls.

What is present in Jesus that is not present in a Siddhartha Gautama, a Krishna, a Lao Tzu, a Gandhi or a Teresa of Calcutta, or even a Cayce or a Solomon? All, according to the Source, were manifestations of the Christ force, by their living example all served as a path by which the "Universal Humanity" could be reached; all symbolized in some fashion the kenotic movement through the totality of fallenness to the final transfiguration of God's only begotten Son within. And their teachings were all of a single voice: that the same endless stream of living energy, the same limitless and liberating life-force that galvanized themselves dwells within our species as a whole. So Eckhart declares: "To deny one's self is to be the only begotten Son of God and one who does so has for himself all the properties of that Son. All God's acts are performed and His teachings conveyed through the Son, to the point that we should be His only begotten Son. And when this is accomplished in God's sight, He is so fond of us and so fervent that He acts as if His divine Being might be shattered and He Himself annihilated if the whole foundation of His Godhead were not revealed to us, together with His nature and Being. God makes haste to do this, so that it may be ours as it is His. It is here that God finds joy and rapture in fulfillment and the person who is thus within God's knowing and love becomes just what God Himself is."[38]

If, as with the Biblical Job, we can with confidence attest, "The spirit of God has made me, and the breath of the Almighty gives me life;" if, as with the mystic George Fox, we can proclaim that "Every Man [is] enlightened by the Divine Light of Christ, and I saw it shine through all;" then why do we not still live in paradise? Why, then, do we regard all existence only through self-as-subject, and not universally, as though through the eyes of the Creator? Why, though gifted with the fullest powers of life and love, are those powers so conspicuously barren?

> Thus says the Lord:
> Why, when I came was there no man?
> When I called, was there no one to answer?
> (Isaiah 50:2a)

Peering out over the terrible ridge of history, the mind can see nothing sure, nothing in all human experience to be grasped as certain, except the cyclical inevitability of suffering and despair. From Cain and Abel to Iraq and Syria, humanity's record, plain for all to see, has been one of ever widening, deepening, and accelerating moral crisis. Ages upon ages of fear, mutual hatred and distrust, and continuous warfare have so crippled us in mind and spirit that we have proved ourselves nearly incapable of sane community, let alone union with the Source of our being.

Simply put, because the mode of our lives is no longer in keeping with the Source of our lives, strife, contradiction, and suffering afflict all of life. The gap between how we live and how *to* live has become an abyss. As children of the Fall, we find ourselves in a state of unmitigable spiritual paralysis, having lost the power to reconcile the duality of living with the reality of the One. For everything that "is" there is an "is not," for every "I" there is an "other," for every fulfillment" there is a "need."

For it was failure to realize the bounty, the unlimited supply, which began the separation of individual to individual in this school, this earth. When there was the perception of limitation which was seen in one person's mind as a competitive spirit, thinking limitation dictates that if I have sufficient

abundance, if I have more, you must have less. Thinking in that manner resulted in what you see now as the cleft brains we see. The mind divided itself against itself. And so the androgynous early manifestations of God in this plane become separated, both in their own minds, and one from the other. This, then, is the very ancient history of what you face today, the separation of the brain-mind from its Source, and [this] requires then the ladder of lights (chakras) which it must ascend from the lowest point in the physical through the highest point you might reach in body, mind, and spirit --- all three. These three [are] related as well to the two outer pillars and that of the [heart] center, the direct path; these [three] again seen in the double helix of the genetic code and its core, or in the serpents, in the rod of Aaron as it was called (Solomon Reading No. 1703, 4/93)

vagus nerve [margin handwriting]

All suffering as described by the Source is seen as a deviation from the primordial state of unity, the Fall being a caesura cutting across everything by which humanity could identify itself with the One --- androgyne and sexuality, love and fear, life and death, joy and sorrow. Ever since the Fall, paradise has been an invisible and embryonic inner state, its gates sealed to all but those who, having harnessed the energies of love, are able to pierce the veils that filter the light of Logoic consciousness. Until those biological filters are surmounted, until such time as the fontanels at the top of the brain, called the Spanda, the primary "frequency realm" that bonds us with the universal Presence, arc the gap to form what the Source calls the "crown of enlightenment," the rest of us must balance between those extremes of being that cruelly divide the integrity of our lives. Until that "crowning of enlightenment" occurs, our interior will be a battleground and the essential tragedy of the human condition will remain unchanged:

For until the mind of man is unified, reunited, until the cleft in the brain, which was separated at that moment of separation of man and his Source, that which is spoken of in the allegory of the Garden of Eden as the Fall, unless that is healed, that separation in the mind and a war within the individual will out-manifest itself into your science, your technology, and all the affairs of men, so that even your judicial system is an adversarial system. You are only beginning to get a glimpse that the healing of misunderstandings and injustice must come through mediation rather than adversarial justice. All these things come from the cleft brain, the separation in the two sides of self, in the separation of man from God and man from himself, for those created and those who first manifest[ed] on this planet were androgynous being[s]. So as the Elohim entered upon this planet to establish it as a place of at-one-ment with [the] Source, those beings were androgynous, whole and complete within themselves. But when the brain-mind became separated and knew itself by points of comparison, by the establishment of light and darkness, good and evil, love and fear, so also the bodies separated into male and female. All of these things have been a process of creating a division between what you have called man and God. Man is a natural expression of God, androgynous in nature and whole within the self.

Then the movement of this species toward the completion of its purpose on this planet will only be accomplished when there is the healing of the separation within the self. The sense of incompleteness because of the separation of the self into male and female, and into right and left hemispheres of the brain, and the separation of the physical from the spiritual, all these things must come together to understand and re-establish upon this planet the Law of One. If one shall understand the Law of One, so shall he be made complete and wear the crown of enlightenment (Solomon Reading No. 1432, 9/22/90).

A QUANTUM LEAP INTO ENLIGHTENMENT

Looking into the abyss of human misery and evil that by and large defines all the days of our recorded past, it is difficult to reconcile over four thousand years of gratuitous violence and unsparing affliction with what the Source perceives as the indefatigable spirit of man striving with a single purpose toward the completion of his final goal: the "Universal Human." Gazing out over the incalculable host of humanity, still only half awake and, though flecked now and then by shreds of higher consciousness, struggling against their impotence and littleness among the stars, we cannot but wonder whether even one human spirit will ever again awaken fully to gather into itself all spirits to become the Soul of All.

And yet, the vast biography of our species is to be judged not solely in respect of its divided past. From the universal perspective of the Source, the purgatorial trials of human history are seen as but a brief episode, no more significant than a violent thundering rain between periods of transforming light. Through Its eyes the contours of the whole are made visible to us all. As though through the eyes of the Creator, we are witness to the entire eschatological drama of our precipitous fall into darkness and our immanent reunion with the One and forthcoming emergence into a wholly new creation capable of manifesting fully and consciously the Logoic power of light and universal love. The Source in fact tells us that we are about to experience an evolutionary leap no less extraordinary or significant than that which in bygone ages brought forth self-reflective consciousness:

> There have been periods in the development of your planet, the development of mankind of the mind and of the spirit, in which humankind have taken quantum steps in the evolution of the mind in its relationship to body and spirit. In these steps individuals have become self-aware. And in becoming self-aware there is an eventual result of [the] breakdown of the tribal instinct, or herding, to individuality, and the swinging back again when this has reached an extreme. You come only now to the point where the swinging back again begins and yet it must be taken to a new and higher level.

> There have been periods then as the mind was opened to art, to medicine, to philosophy, to science and such, that were the development of the powers of the mind, [when] both involution and evolution has occurred. And you come to a time now when the literal

salvation of man and the planet is to take a step in thinking which reaches beyond the brain-mind, the individually contained mind, for the challenges which are before you on the planet are too great for the comprehension of the bicameral brain.

And ... there is that arc or spark of electricity, of energy, of light, which arcs from one hemisphere to the other producing that cap of light or enlightened mind which rests upon the crown, with a knowing that is born of spirit, a "universal consciousness," or the "superconscious," the "spirit of awareness," the "attunement to the Source." All these are the same, that which was described by the ancients as enlightenment or Christ Consciousness. The leaders of your groups, your nation, of the planet itself, must be of enlightened beings to simply comprehend the challenges which are before you (Solomon Reading No. 1378, 7/16/88).

Human reason recoils at the thought that, even under the most favorable conditions, the whole great saga of man as a "crowned" and completed work of art could nigh occur before the great temporal eternities of the evolutionary process have had their chance to redefine us. After all, human anatomy has not altered substantially for the past 100,000 years or so and biophysiological changes, even in small doses, represent enormous "investments" of evolutionary energy over great spans of geological time. In paleontological terms this is referred to as "phyletic gradualism", the idea that evolution generally occurs uniformly and continuously and by the steady and gradual transformation of whole lineages, or anagenesis. In 1972, however, paleontologists Niles Eldredge and Stephen Jay Gould published a landmark paper called *punctuated equilibria*. In it they propose that, based on the geological record, species occasionally experience major changes in very brief periods of time. While they ascribe such dramatic and sudden change to an adaptive process of cladogenesis, the splitting of a daughter species from an ancestral species, they are quick to add that the formative causal principle by and large remains unknown. Indeed, **as science would see evolution of the body, the mind, there comes a belief that such occur only over vast centuries of time,** observes the Source, **and yet there have been periods in Earth's history in which evolution has been assisted, has been speeded, has been used to make a quantum leap. These quantum leaps have been confusing to archeologists, those who study such.** Applied to our own human species, the Source refers to **the leap from a period in which man seemed mostly animal to a time in which there was much accomplishment:**

And the reason for this change was a change in vibration deliberately produced by the Elder Brethren, or the Brotherhood, as you know them, and this change in vibration was brought about on this planet through something akin to music. Now, when we say 'something akin to music', the meaning is this: there is much [that] can be done with sound, with vibration. You do not understand your music. Extremely crude compared to the vibration that can cause stones to float through the air, can cut through marble or steel and such, you see. The production attained can affect all organs, glands, systems of the body, can affect consciousness, can advance thought.

Understand that much of the communication with the Divine in times past occurred through instruments of attunement, some of which are described in your books of ancient history, in your sacred scripture, and such. The Ark of the Covenant's attunement [was] of such a nature, an instrument for communicating with higher force and power, for communicating with the Light that appeared and could be seen between the wings of the seraphim. Now understand, when we say music, we refer here to what might better be called music of the spheres, or a tone quality, a vibration above and beyond that you have at the moment ability to produce (Solomon Reading No. 1000, 12/14/89).

The Source insists that a similar such "quantum leap", this into an enlightened state of reunification with the Higher Self must now occur. Out of necessity, we must raise our minds above partisan politics, beyond all dualistic thinking, drawing from them only what is universal simply in order to overcome the destructive forces of global violence, avarice, and exploitation. We would see that the consciousness of this race must be raised. The purpose of this race in this time is the completion of the mental faculties or, that is, the development of the higher mentality, the realization of [the] Higher Self, the integration of the mental bodies, that is, the ability to turn within and use the creativity of mind. Give all that can be given toward the raising of this consciousness, for the time is at hand. Be aware of the responsibility of the age in which you live; be aware that each is entrusted with his responsibility for completing the Laws of God (Solomon Reading No. 59, 11/2/72).

When stresses impact a system beyond its capacity to absorb without substantial modification, rapid and episodic change occurs, sometimes in sudden leaps. Some present-day species of birds and moths have been observed undergoing major changes in just one generation. Such changes are now incumbent upon us as well:

You stand at the brink of a time when the cleft between the hemispheres of the brain, when the separation, the duality in thinking that keeps man separated from himself and separated from his Source --- you stand at the brink of a time when such duality can be overcome and unity can be found with the self. Within the self, and between self and Source, or the realization of that which has been called the Law of One. Should you reach such a quantum leap in growth, you will enter then in that period that has been called the New Heaven and the New Earth. The ending of the earth as it has been known, and the entering into a new time, a new kingdom, ... an Age of Peace, of prosperity. It literally requires a regeneration of mankind, a quantum leap in evolution.

Yet, this quantum leap could come even in these few short years ... which are the end of this Age. This quantum leap could come were there the understanding of the simple formula of which we have so often spoken --- understanding the Law of Love. If mankind could come to the true understanding, the actual realization that the power of love is, in fact, a stronger force than the power of fear and overcomes it, that the power of life is greater than that of death, love greater than that of fear; and if, then, the consciousness of man becomes confident in the survivability of love as a law of living, of the One Force and harmony, of sufficient protection of mankind to lay down defense and weapon, fear and separation, then there can be the transfiguration of mankind in such an evolutionary step that even literally the physical body of man would be transformed in the movement from Age to Age as you stand on the cusp of this great movement.

It would create literally another lobe, as it were, of the brain, a bridge, a crown that would crown the head and bridge the hemispheres so that it might be seen then as a four-portioned brain, compared to that which is now seen as a three-portion [brain], considering the brainstem and the right and left hemispheres. But that with the crown added, the crown of enlightenment, producing a unified brain, a unified field of thought in contact with its Source. It is this that is meant as an evolutionary step that could come as a result of the initiation of the mysteries, the awakening of the consciousness of a New Age.

Now, this could come in ten years. It can come in a hundred, or a thousand [years]. You must understand that this destiny is not so clearly written as we may say it will happen in ten years. What we can say is that you stand on the brink of it as if you could be tipped into such realization. So close are you to the edge. And so conscious are a few about the earth, here and there, that this glimpse, this glimmer of enlightenment, this glimpse of the possibility is beginning to enter the consciousness. And as it slips into consciousness, as it becomes considered a real possibility, then there is that shift, that movement in consciousness which will happen, as it were, in a flash, in the twinkling of an eye. And those who are so enlightened, then, will be caught up as if they were a luminous cloud in the sky, and others will be left behind in the dark and unknowing. And a new plane of existence, a luminous band about the earth will gather and rule over it in a Kingdom of Peace, and you will have entered a New Age (Solomon Reading No. 1390, 11/7/88).

CHILDREN OF THE GREAT TRANSITION

As the Source sees it, we may be no longer children of the Fall, but children of the Transition, with signs of our transcendent unity having already begun to appear on the horizon. A century ago Richard Burke observed in his celebrated *Cosmic Consciousness* that "there has lived on the earth, appearing at intervals, for thousands of years among ordinary men, the first faint beginnings of another race, walking the earth and breathing the air with us, but at the same time walking another earth and breathing another air of which we know little or nothing, but which is, all the same, our spiritual life, as its absence would be our spiritual death. This new race is in an act of being born from us, and in the near future it will occupy and possess the earth."[39] Teilhard de Chardin, speaking of the impending "great metamorphosis" of humanity, writes: "Everywhere on Earth, at this moment, in the new spiritual atmosphere created by the idea of evolution, there float, in a state of extreme mutual sensitivity, love of God and faith in a new world: the two essential components of the ultra human. These two components are everywhere in the air ... sooner or later there will be a chain reaction."[40] In his last commentary on the Book of Revelation, D.H. Lawrence made reference to the great advent of universal consciousness now underway: "We are witnessing the opening and conquest of the great psychic centers of the human body. The old Adam is going to be conquered, die and be reborn as the new Adam. But in stages. In seven stages, or in six stages and then a climax, seven."[41] The emergence of a new stage of being is similarly foreseen by Henry Miller in *The Wisdom of the Heart*:

> "There exist today all over the world a number of modern spirits who are anything but modern. They are thoroughly out of joint with the times, and yet they reflect the age more truly, more authentically than those who are swimming with the current. In the very heart of the modern spirit there is a schism. The egg is breaking, the chromosomes are splitting to go forward with a new pattern of life. Those of us who seem most alien ... are the ones who are going forward to create the life as yet inchoate.
>
> We who are affected cannot make ourselves clear... This is the era when apocalyptic visions are to be fulfilled. We are on the brink of a new life, entering a new domain. In what language can we describe things for which there are as yet no new names? And how describe relations? We can only divine the nature of those to whom we are attracted, the forces to which we willingly yield obedience..."[42]

This incredible re-birthing of human potential occurs when there is some kind of upsurge of consciousness and exuberance --- what Homer called "menos" --- when some kind of divine influx comes rushing in and sweeps us, so to speak, as inevitably as a ship cutting the sea turns over the waters in its wake. This process of ever-expanding receptivity to a higher essence is sweeping us even now, according to the Source, into planetary consciousness:

> **Dimensions are being added to this plane. They are added first in consciousness... And so it is that a new dimension of consciousness, a new dimension of existence is being drawn closer and closer and becoming a part of the realization of earth. As those who are opening begin to live in the new dimension, so will they bring with them all lesser matter, moving then into a greater or expanded dimension; an expression of a fourth dimension somewhat inadequate. Greater than that shall the change be...** (Solomon Reading No. 604, 5/14/75).

What once was only true for the individual --- for the hermit-saint, the cave-dwelling mystic, the ascetic bodhisattva --- now becomes "writ large" in the greater body of humanity. Just as Jesus or any fully Christed individual transcends the limits of possibility as they appear to our cognitive intellect, so must their epiphany now occur in its universal form as the God who is becoming all in all. **For this race becomes new**, declares the Source, **what the Christ was on the cross, leaving a type behind, a type of race individual. He became the new man of the new race on the other side of the cross. It is at this point that humanity will be lifted through that consciousness to become that new man. Then the new teaching technique of** the young will bring them to that point of evolution that the Master of masters experienced when He died to the flesh and experienced, then, a step through the trauma of crucifixion into the resurrection beyond. If you can then train the children, bring their consciousness to that point, so shall this earth, this planet, step through that hour of sacrifice of self, crucifixion, to the resurrection that brings a new body. For His body was then transfigured --- a new heaven and a new earth. All that will happen to this planet was demonstrated in His glorified body (Solomon Reading No. 953, 6/25/77).

Just as the Christ enfolds the world in a single grasp, so in the end there is one spirit, one universal truth, one Source of life which embraces us all, and all of mankind is needed to liberate it. And the Source proclaims that the hour of mankind's liberation is now at hand. The time of the "second dawning" or birth of a "Universal Humanity" is upon us. Truth must now rise up from the grave:

> Now why is this doctrine coming into the earth at this moment...? In this generation, why has it entered now? It has entered now because the time has come to stop the cycle of birth and death. The time has come to rid the earth of fear because fear has built to such proportions and dimensions, competition has built to such proportions and dimensions, that the very vehicle of earth itself is in danger of dying, of being destroyed by those upon it who have actually learned to believe over time, in spite of the teaching of all the Manu, man has learned to believe that fear, resistance, power, authority are more effective than love.

> Your ... purpose is to teach with utter certainty that the power of love is more powerful than fear and can overcome it if mankind would understand the power of love as a science, ...not as an emotion, not as a gushy affection, not as a feeling, not as lust, not as something that is simply pleasant, but rather as the power of life itself, that which generates life, that which generates light.

> Without love the sun would not exist. The gases that you think feed the sun are the expansion of love itself pouring out of the heart of God. It is for that reason that the ancient teachers pointed to the sun and said, "There is Light. That is God." And from that came a corrupted teaching of Ra the sun god as being something to be worshipped until Akhenaten came ... and attempted to understand it as Aton, more than the sun itself, but light itself, the One, the One and Only.

> There have been attempts to renew love. There have been attempts to describe it through music and through the arts, for music and arts enliven the soul when they are properly applied, you see. And touching and loving between one another lift the spirits. Compliments lift the spirits. Laughter lifts the spirits. All of these are techniques of the science of love. When the science of love is understood, there will be an energy source so powerful that the forces of destruction which are now used for the production of energy... ---this is a ridiculous concept in itself! Please hear it and please preach it and teach it. Destroying and burning things on this earth, killing them to release their life that it might be used to power machinery --- this

is utter degradation of the earth. This is the opposite of its purpose. This is [the] creation of hell on earth.

Man must come to know the loving God who did, in fact, give His Son to die for all of us. But we are not teaching here Christianity. We are teaching that ... His only begotten Son was love itself, you see? Love, the Living One, was sent and made flesh and dwelt among us. But we killed Him inside ourselves by giving power to fear instead of love. And when fear is alive and runs the body, the Son of God inside is dead, and the body itself must die. The temple of the Living One cannot live when it is abiding fear.

Now ... this is the time to extend the sight, not for the purpose of making the physical bodies more important than they are. That is not it. But rather understanding that we no longer have to go through the cycles of birth and death, and birth again, and repeating the same mistakes over and over and over in our journey to know God.

Now make your life purpose not so much the teaching of physical immortality, but rather the teaching that nothing other than fear can destroy life. Physical immortality --- to try to achieve that for its own sake, as if retaining the same physical body throughout eternity is so vitally important --- this is not the point. That one can maintain the same physical body throughout eternity, that is well enough to teach, but that is not the point. The point rather is to overcome the fascination and drawing to the things that cause death.

Then [the] teaching [must] be the teaching of love, life, light, enlightenment. These all are the same things, and these are the unutterable name of God. God is life, but to utter His name you must live. You see, life itself utters His name. Words cannot shape it in the throat. The name of God cannot be produced by vocal cords and the movement of the mouth and the lips. The name of God is called by the projection of love from the instrument that is the temple of God. This is the unutterable name of God.

Teach love, life, light, joy, happiness, support for one another, abundance on the earth. Teach ... that laughter and song, that touch and joyous living without fear, without lack and limitation, without withholding the forces of life, that this is that which make men and women utterly alive in the highest and truest sense. And where there is a body built of pure love, it is also a body of light. And there will come a time when you will know one who has achieved physical immortality because their body will glow like a light. You will see a light body, unmistakably, for all to see.

Now that time is coming, and that is the Second Coming of the Christ, that is the Second Coming of life without death. Life without death is the Second Coming of Christ. It is the end of time because time in a world of physical immortality is insignificant and does not exist. Concepts of time will be wiped out and all [will] know themselves to be both immortal and light bodies which can pass through darkness. Which is to say, bodies when perfected in the light will be able to pass through the earth itself, will be able to travel interdimensionally. These things (Solomon Reading No. 1472, 4/91).

"For the end is always like the beginning," observes Origen, and in the New Earth "that dispersion and separation from the one beginning" will undergo "a process of restoration to one and the same end and likeness." [43] That likeness being God's first expression as light: ...for never have there been men so blessed as you who come in these last days to learn these last few lessons that would transmute those physical vehicles that you inhabit into vessels fit for children of the King. For in so changing these vessels ... by blessing them with so much love, even the vibrations of thine body will be changed to so much finer, higher rates of vibration that these physical bodies will become light bodies, and they will become not akin to that which is the physical earth, that which is material. And as the heaven and earth shall pass away, and all shall be made new, so shall you be in that body that would be a part of the new and carrying His likeness into the higher manifestation of all that is (Solomon Reading No. 148, 3/28/73).

While the highest reaches of Solomon's vision transcend all that we can know or experience insofar as we remain limited by a mind manifest in duality, they nevertheless give promise of an ultimate liberation, one that will not simply recast but will wholly transform all that we immediately and naturally are. Just as the individual will be brought nearer to his Source, so, we are told, Truth must be linked once more back to the Eternal.

Mankind's eschatological end comes to be seen, therefore, as inseparable from the great outpouring tide of its creation, for the beginning and ending are the one truth to which all existence aspires. The overall course of our descending trajectory into materiality and flesh and the impending reintegration of spirit and substance can be figured, therefore, as a circuitous journey --- out of (away from) God and back again, to the prepotent but hidden order of our unbounded Source. The one spirit is all there is in the story:

The history of the planet, from your perspective looking into millions of years, is virtually incomprehensible. And yet you [now] come to a point in time in which time itself has so accelerated in the furious activity of man attempting to reach his final initiation on this planet to make the planet as it exists ... now obsolete, you see. For you will have gone the step beyond the movement of matter with matter. That was an initiatory phase in the entering of man onto this material planet, and exiting from it will require the relearning of the movement of matter with that which is not matter, [which is] the formless.

Then your study is the impression of the form from the formless, from the formless into form and from form into the formless, returning again to the form. That is the triangle, the apex that is the purpose to lift mankind and the planet through its initiation, the thirteenth path into a new state, a new expression, a new dimension, a new heaven and earth in a very literal sense. For the character and nature of the earth itself will change in its healing and in the final step of initiation of mankind as humankind now exists. That is the summons to the high crusade that is before you (Solomon Reading No. 1416 7/2/90).

Part Three

Suspended Between Two Worlds

Chapter 9

The Age Of Darkness

PROGRESS AND PERIL

Mystics of all ages and, now in our own time theoretical physicists, tell us that the world is one. One life, one mind, permeates the entire universe. At our core there is no difference between I and not-I, between you and me. Duality, the sense of separate existence, is simply due to name and form --- different waves in one and the same ocean. It is, as Einstein stated, all an "optical delusion of consciousness."

A delusion to the deluded nonetheless appears real, however, and it is central to the question of how we treat the world and one another. While instinctively we may know of the emotional bonds between ourselves and life as a whole, a secular humanist establishment devoted to the skeptical, the empirical, the scientifically demonstrable, tells us that the universe is merely a random assemblage of dead matter and empty space. It is a view that has dominated our thinking for the past 400 years and has rationally convinced us that, as islands unto ourselves, alienated from the world beyond our skins, we are entitled to withhold all moral sanction from the transcendent needs of ourselves, our fellow creatures, the Earth upon which we live. By virtue of a superior intellect, we are little gods locked within the gated communities of our own skulls, free to exploit whatever our ingenuity can bring under control all in the name of "progress".

Conventional wisdom states firmly and confidently that, owing to the immense benefits of the technological virtuosity of our age, we in our time are riding atop the crest of the historical wave of human development. Our triumphant "march of progress", from fist-hatchets to computers, from our anthropomorphic and Neolithic beginnings to the Industrial Revolution, from the Wright Brothers' first flight to a moon landing less than 70 years later with yet ever-widening cosmic aspirations before us, has been unremittingly obstinate, exponential, and nothing short of astonishing. "Bigger and better." The "law of accelerating returns" and the record of improvement in the conditions of human life bear justifiable witness to this self-evident conviction. After all, who among us romanticizes the short, brutish, disease-filled life of the Late Middle Ages as anything to be longed for? We have surpassed that, and so much more.

We've developed and direct tremendous power, produce consumer goods on a mass scale, exercise an unsurpassed degree of control over disease and physical pain, and have created the conditions for comfort, abundance and continuous advancement in every area of life. Science has given us supremacy over nature, and with its objectively demonstrable knowledge has liberated us from the esoteric and imaginative superstitions of our earliest ancestors and the gods of our failed past, de-mythologizing virtually every aspect of our lives. Proven ignorance and error lay everywhere in ruins leaving us in the undiminished and dispassionate light of pure scientific truth.

It's not that there aren't any risks and dangers that ensue from our progress. But if perils are intertwined with the benefits that our world-engineering technologies afford us, where else are we to turn for the guidance we need to navigate past them then to the wisdom and prowess of that very authority that ultimately provides all sense of meaningfulness and value in our lives. Given enough time, money and research, eventually science will provide us with all the answers. Moreover, we've already crossed the Rubicon of technological development and there simply can be no turning back without imperiling ourselves even further. So it is that through the post industrial blessings of security and all social good that it promises, science has become the god of our salvation. We, the beneficiaries, are living in the age of enlightenment.

Ancient traditions from cultures and regions of the globe as hetero genetically diverse and geographically distinct as Greece is from China or as India is from the Americas or the Aboriginal Australians tell a quite different story. With astonishing continuity, they all speak of our age as one of ignorance and darkness, an age when human consciousness will have declined far from the sacramental vision of the One to a state wherein humans would through their greed exercise their capacities to violate and disrupt all that was perfect and beautiful thereby throwing off the balance of Creation.

According to Greek poet Hesiod in his moralizing epic, *Works and Days,* the Golden Age of the Gods, an age of perfect virtue and simplicity in which humans lived in the company of the gods, was followed by the Silver Age, an age characterized by a deepening awareness of opposites and by increasing imperfection owing to its purchase of progress at the price of moral decline. With its disappearance came next the Bronze Age, a period drudged even further into degeneracy by the mindless, violent conflicts that ensued from their growing technology in the fabrication of metals. In the end, they annihilated each other. The inexorable decline would proceed to our present Age of Iron, the darkest and most wretched of all ages given the convergence of a highly sophisticated technology with a viciousness, a merciless cruelty and barbarity unknown in all ages of mankind.[1]

Close parallels abound among other cultures. In the Americas, for example, the Hopi refer to four successive worlds (ages) which, as in the Greek and Vedic records, are identified with gold, silver, copper, and a mineral mixed with clay, the latter being our own world. Each was "purified" or destroyed, they say, as will be our own prospectively, because people had disregarded and separated themselves from the order and harmony ordained by the Creator. The Iranians, likewise, knew four cosmic ages that, in a lost Mazdaean book, the *Sudkar-nask,* are referred to as the ages of gold, silver, steel, and "mixed with iron." As with other accounts, each successive age represents a step further in the world's deterioration into ignorance and savagery, with the last and furthest from our enlightened origins being our own.

In virtually all accounts --- Chinese, Siberian, Scandinavian, the Chins and the Twyan of Indonesia, the Aborigine of Australia, the Mayan, Toltec, Aztec, and Lakota (Sioux) in the Americas --- the Heart-intellect or pure consciousness that so typifies the perfection of our earliest beginnings, that which sees directly the undivided Essence of Truth, becomes increasingly earth-bound and materialized until finally that which once connected us with the subtlety and intimacy of the web of all creation and with the inexpressible Singularity from which all things are generated is inaccessibly absent. Invariably, it is our own age, the "Age of Iron", that the time-honored myths and sacred scripts of antiquity refer to as the Age of Darkness. It is we, the modern savage, who bear witness to a divided and discordant world.

UNDER A STORMY SKY

One need only look to the daily news, growing stale with reiteration, for the ominous signs that our days of undiminished progress are nearly over. Under the veneer of orthodox optimism and the ad-mass images of new cars, computer games, and pharmaceutical wonder drugs, all intended to tranquilize our anxieties, lies the precarious and pathological state of the world we have forged. The disequilibrium of environmental systems, threatening the natural foundations on which we and all species depend for survival; terrorism along with the ever-present threat of "leaked" nuclear weapons falling into the hands of terrorists; the runaway growth of mass consumption and rapid depletion of natural resources; the exacerbation of racial, cultural and national tensions; global poverty and international inequality, to name but a few, are crises so catastrophic as to threaten our existence. Moreover, in the pursuit of or in subservience to wealth and power, they are all self-created and inextricably linked. We who bear witness must also bear the responsibility and blame. For modern technology itself is the result, not simply of the impersonal law of supply and demand or of triumphs and changes in modern science, but ultimately of the collaboration of all of us in our myopic pursuit of plenty.

If ever there was doubt that ancient prophetic traditions carried with them a relevance unique to our own time, the brutal results of our headlong descent into barbarism, compulsive irrationality and collective spiritual decay over the course of the past 100 years should serve well enough to erase them. Like no century before it, the Twentieth Century has proved to be a testament to the savagery of our age.

What began as an era baptized in the name of peace, the inevitability of mechanical progress, and the perfectibility of man began almost immediately with the First World "War to end all wars" in which over 20 million people lost their lives. By the end of the Second World War the number of deaths had climbed another 55 million --- 6 million exterminated in Nazi death camps, 10 million imprisoned, many to die, in Stalin's gulags, 4 million dead in the famine that British rule brought to Bengal in the early '40s; hundreds of thousands incinerated in the bombings of Dresden and Hamburg, and in the atomic holocaust of Hiroshima and Nagasaki. Torture, murder and genocide had been officially condoned and in fact sanctioned. In the unspeakable savagery of the Second World War, bottom had been reached, and reversal had to be at hand, or so it was thought, if only because mankind could sink no lower. But this, the most murderous period of time in all recorded human history, did not end here.

Since the end of the Second World War more than 250 major wars have been waged, in which 23 million people have been killed, tens of millions made homeless, and countless millions injured and bereaved. Apart from war, genocide and other mass murders have killed more people, an estimated 80 million, than all wars in the history of our race. Nor has the crossing of the cusp into the peaceful Age of Aquarius spared us any mercy. Following 9/11, along with wars in Iraq and Afghanistan, Sudan, Syria and the rise of Isis, there are over 35 major armed conflicts ongoing in the world today with 90% of the casualties being civilians and 3 out of 4 fatalities being women and children. So writes Juarès: "Exposed on the one side to hunger and on the other to hate, how can humanity be thinking of the infinite? Humanity is like a great tree, a-buzz with angry flies under a stormy sky; and under this clamor of hate the deep and divine voice of the universe is no longer heard."[2]

If for all our power and cunning that great and ancient voice eludes us, it is not simply because of hatreds and rivalries among nations or the destructive powers at their disposal. Rather our deafness is more directly a consequence of the final indignity to the human spirit: the callousness, the insensitiveness, the blindness, the lack of empathy and concern toward the needs of the most vulnerable and least fortunate among us. In the same world where 99% of the world's wealth is owned by 1% of the world's population, where global military spending has now topped $1.8 trillion per year, half of the world's population, over three billion of us, continue to live in conditions of poverty so extreme that they can barely survive. Half that number, mostly children, face daily starvation.

It is now known, as a matter of fact, that we can abolish poverty and hunger worldwide. We have it within our means. There no longer exist any insurmountable technical, resource, or logistical obstacles to achieving it. All that would be required is an additional $265 billion per year on average. Of this, $89-$147 billion would need to come from public funding, putting the total annual public funding requirements at $156-$214 billion.[3] This amounts to approximately 10% of global military spending. Imagine reducing our hatred and fear by a tenth (a mere tithe from global military budgets or from the coffers of even the three wealthiest individuals in the world who control more wealth than all 600 million people living in the world's poorest countries) and increasing our capacity for empathy and humaneness toward all of our human family by an equal degree. The result would be a life more peaceful, more abundant and more fulfilled for everyone on the planet. And if our fears are so deeply rooted that we fear fearing that much less, consider this: one-seventh of our global population cannot read or write and 72 million children don't even have a school, let alone a school lunch. Every child on earth could be educated for scarcely $12 billion, which is only 1.7% of the annual U.S. military budget by itself.

Laying all sophistry and conscience aside, we simply must not fail to realize that what we do to nature or to members even of our own human community we do simultaneously to ourselves. We reap what we sow. We are now irreversibly depleting the earth's resources at an unsustainable pace, nearly 40 times faster than in 1970, with the world's richest countries consuming an average 10 times as many materials as the poorest countries. Competition among human societies and nations, the haves and the have-nots, for a meager slice of the world's increasing wealth and rapidly depleting resources (Middle East oil, for example) has already and will continue to exacerbate social tensions and disintegration that could very well trigger conflict on a scale threatening the very existence of human civilization altogether. We would only too late come to recognize that all the military forces so designed and arrayed for self-protection of our society and way of life would have proved incompatible with a preventative and more equitable distribution of resources and with the very functioning of the economic system itself. Falling short of such a recognition, the Solomon Source forewarns: **You will see turmoil and difficulties, a continuing build-up, agitation, involvement of other nations in a holy war in the Middle East involving the Eastern and Western blocs of nations...** (Solomon Reading No. 1147, 9/3/83). **And you will see bloodshed as has never occured on this planet...** (Solomon Reading No. 219, 8/21/73).

Prophetic warnings such as this have been sounded again and again for more than a century: that lacking insight and the will to respond, our frail loyalty to love and reason will once again surrender itself, as it has so often over the past one hundred years of unspeakable cruelty and systematic atrocity, to those demented gods that rise up from our baser nature whenever we sever ourselves from the common Source of all life. Perhaps we have simply failed to remember the lessons of our ancestral past. Possibly it's because we've become so paralyzed by moral numbness, inertia, and suicidal isolationism that we find ourselves helpless to avert the catastrophes that our irrational pursuit of power and wealth have prepared for us. Whichever is the case, it has become manifestly clear that the unpredictability of events is precipitating greater hostility and fear among not only individuals but religions, ethnicities, and nations. The result is all too obvious:

> **There is coming and all too soon upon you a world wide war. As it begins as skirmishes between borders and such of small countries, it begins to pull into the battle activity, the war activity, the allies of those countries, and more and more the dividing line between the two warring forces will be primarily based on ethnic and religious factors. Meaning, that those of the nation of Islam about the world wherever they exist will become one faction, and the other side the Christians, Jews, and many other faiths ... including those without religion, no particular religious interest. But as this shall be considered a holy war, particularly by the Islamic World, it will take on overtones of [an] ethnic and religious battle** (Solomon Reading No. 1653, 5/30/92).

To be sure, given the seemingly endless and rapidly intensifying state of conflict and chaos now raging in the Middle East, the outcome of this prophesied development is already clearly visible. But if we mistakenly equate the "coming" of this war with its inevitability than we will most certainly have done not only the Solomon Source but ourselves a great injustice. Prophecy is given as a warning of the conditions that confront us and the almost certain fate that awaits us if we fail to alter our course in the light of its message. But if the unraveling of Middle Eastern events is of concern to us, then as the Source points out how much greater of a concern should we have for the fate of the entire planet?

Chapter 10

The Inextricable Complexity

A FATAL LEGACY

Unlimited and undirected power has in fact brought us to the very edge of an abyss. For the first time in human civilization the power over life and death, that of our own and of the basic life systems of the planet, rests firmly in our hands. Those delicate skeins which inextricably unite cultures, link species with species, and bind humankind with the living earth in an intricate web of interdependence have begun to unravel. The Source tells us that through our irresponsible and catastrophic interference we have brought virtually all the life-support systems on which humanity depends to a state of near collapse:

> [You stand] on the brink of destroying the balance of the natural energies in and about this planet. And, indeed, affecting the balance of the entire system --- the solar system, the universe itself. For you cannot destroy one of the bodies in such a balanced system without destroying the balance of the [entire] system. Then the destruction of weather patterns, the imbalance of nature, the use, the burning of [fossil] fuels has produced a difference in your atmosphere, both in temperature and the filtering of the rays of energy to your planet --- all of these become threats to the existence of your race as it now manifests (Solomon Reading No. 1068, 1/23/81).

In our dysfunctional and ultimately destructive relationship with our natural environment and with the living body of the Earth, the Source tells us that **the stability of the environment is already lost…, that much of the effect upon the environment, the damage to the systems on which you depend in this time, much of this already has been damaged irreversibly** (Solomon Reading No. 1282, 3/5/88). If we do not soon rediscover our role in the larger evolutionary process, if we fail to regain our intimacy with the Earth, the Source tells us that this planet will be incapable of sustaining life in the century now before us:

> There will come a time when the Earth has darkened, and the energy and the climate of the Earth have changed. The rain has become acid and is destroying crops. You will find that it is already being said about the Earth in those days that it is too late to save the atmosphere, that already the food and the plants about the Earth are dying. The predictions and assessment of conditions will be heavily pessimistic, and the assessment of nations and governments will be that it is too late to reverse the damage (Solomon Reading No. 1069, 1/24/81)

Moreover, warns the Source **you will see those times that even [the] Earth underneath your feet would seem unstable, and you will see the Earth breaking open as its crust would shift and move, and there will be the noxious gases coming to the surface, the entire atmosphere will smell of the sulfur fumes and there would be taken much of the plant life from your plane and the ma-**

jority of life as you know it will be taken, will be destroyed, will be changed into other forms (Solomon Reading No. 90, 12/4/74).

"Science," we have heard it said often, "will solve all our problems." But the powers of darkness and destruction have been multiplied by the very scientific advances that most modern thinkers once believed would ensure the coming of an age of universal peace and felicity. **Your ability to release power is so far beyond your ability to understand the nature of power at the moment,** declares the Source, **that there is a terrible imbalance in your science.** (Solomon Reading No. 1390, 11/7/88). Like the Sorcerer's Apprentice, we no longer know how to control the power we have fatally invoked and which now threatens our existence and the existence of the world we live in. The French poet, Paul Valery, put the situation very clearly some years ago: "...we are blind and impotent, yet armed with knowledge and power, in a world we have organized and equipped, and whose inextricable complexity we now dread."[4] The Source suggests as much when It warns: **A scientist who knows not God is a danger to mankind** (Solomon Reading No. 1318, 3/27/88).

Moreover, forces driven by power and greed that bait us with the promise of the Fat Life, a life mesmerized by images of opulence, luxury, sexual fulfillment, ease, and entertainment, continue to feed our infantile fantasies and appetites while unchecked industrial exploitation frays the natural basis of life and drains the ecological systems which sustain it. Fully co-opted, tranquilized, and integrated into the all-inclusive apparatus of the consumer economy, we stand full square upon that very scaffolding that underlies the despair, the anomie, the apathy, the irresponsible drift, the resignation to fate, which make significant and critically necessary change all but impossible. The fallout is all around us: a quarter of the world's mammals are threatened with extinction; more than a quarter of the world's known 10,000 freshwater fish species have already become extinct while 75% of the world's fish stocks are on the verge of collapse; 50% of the world's plant species are at risk of extinction while aridity and land degradation threaten nearly one-quarter of the land surface of the planet, putting more than one billion of the Earth's population at risk; over half of the forests that originally covered 46% of the Earth's land surface are now gone, and as the Source warns: **They [the forests] are being lost so fast [that it] endangers the lives of your children, and threatens that your grandchildren's children will not see the light of day.** (Solomon Reading No. 1332, 4/3/88)

In a mere 25 years humanity will consume 80% more of the world's natural resources than the Earth can replace. But we don't have that long to respond. The earth and climate has already changed; the damage we all spoke of only a few years ago as being in the future is here, now. As the Source points out:

> **You have prophets who have spoken of the changing of the natural balances of the rain, which has throughout history always been alkaline for the renewal of the earth, and is now changed in ph balance to become acid, and increasingly acid with each day that you live, in the manner in which you live, with the burning of fossil fuels [and] with the uses of unnatural substances changing the nature of the environment about you. Even the production of oxygen which to every school child is obviously necessary**

for breathing upon your planet; there is already a measurable change in the oxygen/carbon dioxide ratio about the earth in your day.

We do not speak of the future when we speak of these things. We speak of what has occurred and is upon you already. These things already have changed and continue to change at an alarming rate. The very spin of the earth upon its axis becomes slower with each passing decade, and this too is measurable. These things are upon you, these imbalances.

We mention this [time] as a critical point for this reason: your climate has changed the earth, the climatic conditions, the zones of weather, of rain, of dry, of desert, these things have been altered dramatically --- the relationship of carbon dioxide to oxygen has been altered dramatically. Both of these, the effect of the destruction of your forests, of the alteration of your rivers and your streams, [and] of the balance of nature. The oxygen on which you depend for your very breath is provided by your forests, your trees. Your ability to breathe is being lost, taken away, robbed with every tree that is cut.

It is suicide to maintain the rate of destruction of the natural surface of the earth, that which holds together the skin of this holy planet upon which you live. This living, breathing being on whose surface you live, is being destroyed, being made sick systematically by your relationship with your Earth. You must walk upon her as if she were a holy altar, and as alive as you are, and knowing that her surface is a skin as alive, and breathing, and vital, as the skin of your body (Solomon Reading No. 1282, 10/28/89).

Our global industrial culture, as the Source so urgently warned over twenty-eight years ago, has now surpassed the climatic danger zone, and ironically, the potentially fatal legacy we now leave to our children is destined to be the most thoroughly documented disaster in human history. Despite this, many of the wealthiest industrialists in the world have weighed the fate of the Earth and every living thing on it for untold generations to come, and they have come down on the side of more profits for themselves.

If we do not immediately challenge the ideologies that dominate the world industrial economy as a whole as it races toward global integration and mount a massive salvage operation for the reclamation and renewal of the life-supporting systems of the planet, this physical body of Earth, like a human body subjected to similar torture and abuse, will die. If in the next few years we fail to confront the facts now before us, if in our soporific refusal to sacrifice our privileges and luxuries we turn our backs and ignore the consequences altogether, the end result will be apocalyptic: pestilence, war, disease, famine, and extremes of global desertification and massive flooding will have dealt with the majority of humans. If for some this sounds like hyperbole, the Source tells us we need only look for the signs: **You will see [first] a recurrence of 'dust-bowl' conditions in the [American] Midwest and periods of unusual drought in areas known for rainfall, and rainfall in areas normally arid and dry. Cold in areas that were warm, and unusual warmth for periods in areas that have been cold. Do not look for such total changes as alternating polarity during your time, or the literal disappearance of a nation, or the freezing of the** whole of Europe, though those things come, sometime after the turn of the [20th] Century. (Solomon Reading No. 1147, 9/3/83).

It now seems that the great task of our day and age is to prevent the human race from committing suicide and from seeing the world around us dying. Very shortly, declares the Source, we will have reached **the zenith, the pinnacle of destruction in this generation...** We will have **gone as far as the creative energy of man can lend its power to the power of darkness, to create forces of economy, energy and such which, even this day, threaten the survival of this globe of earth and mankind upon it** (Solomon Reading No. 1642, 5/4/92). The consequences, we are warned, may be catastrophic: **I declare unto you, you've entered the times when the changes come. You'll begin to see features on the face of the earth that will startle men and begin speculation that the end of days are at hand. You'll see it in your newspapers. You'll hear it talked [about] in places you had never suspected that men would speculate on such things, but it comes.** (Solomon Reading No. 662, 1975)

Divorced from all spiritual sensibility and set against the cumulation of scientific advancement and human error, the world, we are told, is saturated with darkness. The Source does not sentimentalize our plight. Unless we abandon the pathological habits of the old consciousness that divide us from all the unitive dimensions of our existence, unless we act immediately and with a clear will to free ourselves of all signs, memories and expressions of human separateness by which we deny our interrelatedness with the sacred whole and our natural connection with the Divine, an apocalyptic destruction must and will occur:

> Now, we do not exaggerate the seriousness of the situation, though we know that prophet after prophet in every generation of recorded history has suggested that the world would end with his generation, or the next. Still, yet, knowing that we say that you've come to a time now when you need not listen to the prophets to see the handwriting on the wall, as it were.

> Your scientists are your priests of today. And those who do research and who see these results are warning you in as loud a voice as they can --- that destructive elements currently in motion must not only be stopped, but must literally be reversed lest we lose this living being that is our mother.

> There are those who have spoken of the crucifixion of the Son of our Father on this earth, but there is at your hands in this day the crucifixion of your mother. Better know that she is a living being who tolerates your presence, and which should be a symbiotic relationship. But when there is the devastation of her skin, her circulatory system, her respiratory system, all of the systems that keep the earth alive, then you will find that you have crucified the mother as well, and her children will die. <u>Do not let that come upon you</u> (Solomon Reading No. 1332, 4/3/88).

We who now have the power to prevent the impending disasters that lie plainly and seismically before us will very shortly be called to account by our own grandchildren with the damning truth: How could we have demonstrated such disregard and contempt for their future?

FIRE AND FLOOD

According to the Source it has happened before: **[Mankind] has destroyed the earth as we know it already once in just beyond your written history. The evidence [for this destruction] is about you in the crust of the earth. See that you have destroyed the mantle of it once, and can again** (Solomon Reading No. 1390, 11/7/88). Responding to the objection implied by the theory of continental drift that, as one questioner put it, "the coastlines of North and South America fit neatly together" with their counterparts in Europe and Africa, and therefore "there is no room for a continent of Atlantis in between," the Source replied: **The [continental drift] theory is not so far off as that expected. Nothing particularly wrong with the understanding that these have been a portion of the same [continental] mass. [This] does not make it at all inconsistent that there is below this plate or below these plates that have fit together another, [and] that as these drift apart, rises between them occur even at this time... Both, then, are quite true without any inconsistency** (Solomon Reading No. 741, 1/22/76). Having violated the sacred principles of his stewardship of this earth, mankind perished. **There was an ending of the world, an ending of the earth as those knew it in that time. It was shaken, reformed, their world destroyed** (Solomon Reading No. 1068, 1/23/81). In fact, the Solomon Readings portray a long succession of previous worlds, each having succumbed to a cataclysmic fate when its inhabitants, having exempted themselves from universal law, become incorrigibly deaf to the emanative Word, the Logos, of their creative Beginning.

The Source recapitulates an ancient theme. Extant traditions from all parts of the globe refer to a plurality of worlds and recreations that would succeed one another in the course of cosmic revolutions. The cultural memory of successive creations and worldwide catastrophes is found preserved among tribal islanders of the Pacific --- in Indonesia, Polynesia, and Hawaii; in the Americas among the Incas, the Aztecs, the Mayans and the Hopi; in Asia among the Chinese, the Hindus, the Tibetans, the Lao-Hmong. Nearly all testify to the destruction of previous world ages or "Kalpas" either by fire or by flood. "He made several worlds before ours, but he destroyed them all," writes the Jewish philosopher Philo. "Some perished by deluge, others were consumed by conflagration."[5] Similarly, in the tradition of the Greeks, "there is a period called 'the supreme year,'" writes Censorinus, "at the end of which the sun, moon, and all the planets return to their original position. This 'supreme year' has a great winter, called by the Greeks *kataklysmos,* which means deluge, and a great summer, called *ekpyrosis,* or combustion of the world. The world, actually, seems to be inundated and burned alternately, in each of these epochs."[6] Hence, Plato recounts in the Timaeus: "There have been, and will be again, many destructions of mankind arising out of many causes; the greatest have been brought about by the agencies of fire and water...[J]ust when...nations are beginning to be provided with letters and the other requisites of civilized life, after the usual interval, the stream from heaven, like the pestilence, comes pouring down and leaves only those... who are destitute of letters and education..."⁷ Likewise, the Codices of Mexico record: "The ancients knew that before the present sky and earth were formed, man was already created and life had manifested itself four times."⁸

In hymns, prayers, and psalms, in legends and myths, in historical texts, philosophical discourses, and by oral transmission the ancients insistently conveyed to succeeding generations the teaching that whenever mankind cuts itself off from its timeless spiritual Source, invariably there opens before it an abyss into which all the storied experience of mankind's historical achievements, the sum of human knowledge and wisdom vanishes. The ancient Greeks identified four previous ages or worlds, the violent destruction of each having been brought about by the widespread deterioration of human conduct and character and mankind's flagrant disregard of the universal laws of order. The Persians, the Babylonians, the Chaldeans each had preserved the memory of four successive world cataclysms, all said to be for the purpose of the purification of the human race. By the time of Noah, the malice of man was so incorrigible and the degeneracy of all living races so complete that once again a rending and purification of the earth was necessary: "In the eyes of God the earth was corrupt and full of lawlessness. When God saw how corrupt the earth had become, since all mortals led depraved lives on earth, he said to Noah: 'I have decided to put an end to all mortals on earth; the earth is full of lawlessness because of them. So I will destroy them and all life on earth" (Gen. 6:11-13).

Now again, warns the Source, we are at the brink of one of the great fracture point of human history:

> You stand at this moment in time at a precipice. You stand at a moment in history when this planet, this mother upon which you live, has been so scarred, so abused, that it is as if the soul of this great mother has been made sick and must erupt to shake off the abuse so that it may be made new.

> Now this precipice, this critical moment in time, may be experienced as a great cataclysm, for it has happened, you see, before in history, or prehistory. This earth was, and then was in essence destroyed. There was an age in which man as you know mankind did not live on this planet, and so she renewed and a garden grew in Eden. And that was the dawn of this age (Solomon Reading No. 1280, 3/5/88).

Thus, the concluding stage of the last great epoch has rounded back. We now face a time of unparalleled chaos, of tremendous discontinuity with all that has been:

> [T]he time is finished when there will be the progress in scientific and automated methods on your plane. There must be the turning to the natural methods. This race must prepare itself for living without those artificial disciplines that have been developed. Hence we find those ... with the natural desire, the memory, the innate desire to prepare self for those days when that which comes, as so many artificial methods, the machinery, the technology of your day will be destroyed. The earth will be devoid of that which you depend on in this day for sustenance... (Solomon Reading No. 98, 12/15/72).

Indeed, prophetic references common to cultures throughout antiquity point to a time at the end of the cycle of cosmic ages when mankind, in possession of forces beyond his moral comprehension or rational control, would be poised at the juncture of self-transcendence or self-obliteration.

The sacred calendar of the Maya calculates a "Great Cycle" of 5,125.40 years, the most recent beginning in 3113 B.C. and ending in A.D. 2012, closing out not only the "Long Count" of this age but the entire evolutionary span called Homo Sapiens. Here the Mayan calendar ends, sealing the destiny of a nearly infinite expanse of cosmic history. The final period ending in the year 2012 prophesied not the ending of the earth on that date as moronically inferred, but rather the beginnings of the time of "Great Chaos" marked by catastrophic earthquakes and geophysical upheavals unparalleled in the ages of the earth. Quetzalcoatl, the divine hero figure of Mayan tradition, is said to have prophesied of this final period of darkness that "the equipoise of nature will be lost, ...the ocean tides shall obey no more." Mountains would collapse, cities would lay in ruins, leveled by great earthquakes. Vast explosions would decimate the earth, and fires would "leap forth on the forests and grassy meadows, wrapping all things there in a winding sheet of flame, and melting the very elements with fervent heat."[9] Following this cataclysmic interval, humanity will either ascend to a heightened level of attunement with universal forces ("The Coming Sixth Age of Consciousness") or, through its rejection of the sacramental unity of all life, the dissolution of civilization promises a new age of mindless savagery and annihilating despair.

Likewise, the ancient Indian Vedic system of cosmology teaches that an entire Age of ages, the "Great Cycle" of mahayana, is now at an end. If humanity would but turn within to the spirit of integration, to that seed (Atman) of inner truth, then as the present dark age of the Kali Yuga ("Age of Iron" or "Chaos") draws to its tumultuous close, a regeneration of the Age of Gods will dawn. For just as chaos is prelude to cosmos, so it is from the twisted ruins of the Age of Iron that the new Golden Age of the Gods will rise.

You are at the cusp, declares the Source, **the place of ascendance, to begin a new world, that referred to by the Hopi prophecies as the result of the four worlds and the entering into a fifth** [world] (Solomon Reading No. 1609, 3/31/92). The third world, that prior to our own, relate Hopi myths, was destroyed by flood. Now as the fourth world ends it is joined to the future fifth world by a final interval of cleansing, what the Hopi refer to as the "Day of the Great Purification." The fourth world, they say, will end in fire. Near Oraibi village in the American southwest is a pre-Columbian Hopi petroglyph depicting the prophetic life-plan of the Creator. Two horizontal lines of the petroglyph represent the two divergent paths which it was foreseen mankind would embark upon and which would foreshadow his ultimate destiny: the sacred path of harmony and reverence for life, and the path of materialism and invention leading to what the Hopi call "Koyaanisqatsi" --- "world out of balance". Two circles on the lower path represent the first two "world purifications" --- World War I and World War II. A vertical line intersecting both paths signifies one last fork of the road, one final opportunity to reestablish the natural balance of the earth through a spirit of loving stewardship before the third Great Purification, brought on by the moral neutralism of science and the entire technological enterprise of modern culture, consumes us all in a sacrificial holocaust. In his article "The Essence of Hopi Prophecy," Tom Tarbet writes:

> The final stage, called the "great day of purification", has also been described as a "mystery egg" in which the forces of the swastika (Nazi Germany) and the sun (Imperial Japan), plus a third force (yet to come), symbolized by the color red (Communist China? --- 'The red hat and cloak people will have a huge population" relates Hopi prophecy) culminate in either total rebirth or total annihilation --- we don't yet know which, but the choice is ours. War and natural catastrophe may be involved. The degree of violence will be determined by the degree of inequity caused among the peoples of the world and in the balance of nature. In this crisis, rich and poor will be forced to struggle as equals to survive.

> That it will be very violent is now almost taken for granted among traditional Hopi, but humans may still lessen the violence by correcting their treatment of nature and fellow humans.[10]

The same ancient cosmological traditions which tell us that the ages of the world unfold under the aegis of a divine plan, concurrently declare the coming New World to be a provisional result of the collective will and consciousness of mankind. Because we, in our divinity, imitate the creation of the world by our active aesthetic response to nature, we become the essential factor of Creation. Thus, human deeds and thoughts have a compelling influence on a world that is tentative, open-ended, unfinished.

Acting hedonistically (without regard for the basic conditions of interrelatedness that are indigenous to life itself), mankind has flagrantly interfered with the spontaneous arrangements and symbiotic associations of a living planet which now hangs in the balance. As we confront a biospheric emergency unknown in all the life-sustaining ages of the Earth, our anticipated new age of spiritual regeneration may yet become a paradise lost, a fallen creation founded in human desolation.

Acting "cosmically" (from a mindfulness of the internal logic of a sacred whole) and in harmony with the balanced forces of a divinely ordered universe, mankind becomes a responsible agent for peaceful change to a new age of enlightenment. **"[Y]ou will find that [if] there has been a change in the consciousness of man, a change in science and technology, that you [will] have been able through the re-establishment of plant life, the trees, to reestablish your oxygen and ...[to] make of the deserts a place that blooms, and of your earth a planet of wholeness again. It will be a day when there will be dismantling of unnatural structures about the earth, and a time of man entering a period of time of living, as it were in Eden again"** (Solomon Reading No. 1282, 3/5/88). As indicated, our responsibilities to the Earth and to the creative dynamics and multivalent meanings inherent in our relationship with the Earth call for something more than simply an eco-spiritual awakening on our part. At the very heart of our responsiveness to and interactive participation with Gaian ways of being lies the epiphenomenal Law of One and our stewardship of the limitless power that it implies.

ONE ENERGY, ONE LIFE, ONE LAW

"Surely this law which I enjoin upon you this day is not too baffling for you, nor is it beyond reach," says the Lord. 'It is not in the heavens, that you should say, 'Who among us can go up to the heavens and get it for us and impart it to us, that we may observe it?' Neither is it beyond the sea that you should say, 'Who among us can cross to the other side of the sea and get it for us and impart it to us, that we may observe it.' No, the thing is very close to, in your mouth and in your heart, to observe it." (Deuteronomy 30:11-14). "Closer than your jugular vein", states the Koran. **There has never been a set of rules or principles laid down by Him who is God that we must follow for God consciousness,** observes the Source. **All that was laid down [is] the Law of One, the Law of the universe, the spiritual law that [deals] in concrete reality** (Solomon Reading No. 45, 10/23/72).

There is but one Law, therefore, and just as with the unfathomable unity of God, so it is written that the Law is one, undivided, beyond both faith and reason, good and evil. It is the Way of Tao, the path of Dharma, the Word, or Logos, which leads us to the Kingdom spoken of by Jesus. It is that Law by which the world is restored to its primordial unity and by which the generative powers of universal life are returned to mankind. As all-pervading and immediate as the air we breathe yet do not see, the Law is the very *life* of our life which at the same moment illuminates the mystery of being which we share with all things. This single universal imperative, called the Law of Love or the Law of One, **is the recognition that there is one power only, only one power, one force, one energy -- only one!** declares the Source. **And that one which is called by some the Absolute, that absolute singular energy or force is given into the hands, the minds, the lives of humans, those who live on this particular planetary mystery school. The power of the one energy which may be called love or life, is called the light or the truth, all of these words used only to express the nature of the one and only singular force that is available in this life, this universe, and this experience** (Solomon Reading No. 1709, 5/5/93).

We mistakenly conceive of good and evil, love and fear, as polar opposites, contending forces so intimately related that one cannot exist without the other. Confronted as we are by all in life that is hateful to us, it is hard to think otherwise. But as the Source tells us, we can no more equate the force of fear to the power of love than we can liken the force of the Devil to the Power of God. It is an absurdity, an ideological thought-crime against the energy of life itself. They are rather, as the Source points out, substance and shadow, fear being only the absence and dearth of love. With this comes an understanding of the Law of One:

> **It is critical that you understand the principle described as the Law of One. The Law of One states that there is only one primal energy, only one, not two. The appearance of two energies is a result of the functioning of the bi-**

cameral mind of the species. Thus there is a great difficulty, an overwhelm-ing difficulty in the minds of most, to understand that there are not two equal and opposite energies in the earth, in the solar system, or in the uni-verse. What appears to be positive and negative, light and dark, good and evil, love and fear, life and death, all these things are one energy relating only to absence of it. That is to say, light exists, darkness does not. And so it is with all opposite forms or opposite appearances of form of the one energy.

What needs to be understood beyond this then is, there being only one en-ergy or force, how is it that some are capable of applying energy in a destruc-tive manner? The answer to this is that the one energy which is variously described as life, light, love, consciousness, sometimes described as good, life force, dynamic force, primal force, and such, this one living force can be applied through the creative mind to any purpose including destructive purposes. This is the creativity of the mind applied to the one force, which in and of itself is neither good nor evil. It is beyond such comparison or judge-ment as good and evil. It is what it is. It is life force. It is primal energy. It is light. It can be misapplied and in misapplication it appears to be a destruc-tive force. It is destructive only to the extent of the limit of man's imagina-tion. The limit of man's imagination or creativity extends to just less than equal and opposite force.

Let us state that in this different manner: the one force cannot extinguish itself. Thus the principle is that man can misapply the one force, the vital force, the one life energy to the extent of coming what might be described as one step away from extinguishing that force. Yet the one energy cannot overcome itself. This then deduces that what appears to be an equal and opposite force is a misapplication of the one force. It can be applied to the extent of coming near to extinguishing the force itself, but the ability or the power to misapply the force can never be stronger than the force itself, you see. Thus the appearance of equal and opposite force is a false appearance. There remains then one energy. It is life and inherently moves to greater ex-pression. It can be misapplied, but not to the extent of extinguishing or even matching the power of the one force.

Now this is a simplified statement of the Law of One.... All energy is moved by the creative mind of man which is, in man, the expression of God, and [which] has the freedom of will to apply and/or misapply the one force in a creative manner reaching to the limit of extinguishing itself, but falling just short of that limitation. That is to say, the creativity of man extends to a point just short of matching the creative energy or vitality of God, the expression of the one force. These things, then, should be known and under-stood as a basis for understanding for the teaching of the laws of application of energy (Solomon Reading No. 1407, 4/1/90).

A CHRONICLE OF HUMAN MADNESS

Once upon a time a king received a shocking report about the new harvest: Whoever eats of the crop becomes mad. So he called together his counselors. Since no other food was available, the alternative was clear. Not to eat the new harvest would be to die of starvation, to eat would be to become mad. The decision reached by the king was: "We will all have to eat, but let at least a few of us continue to keep in mind that we are mad."[11]

This parable, as told by Rabbi Nahman, holds a certain poignancy for the times in which we live. It reminds us of what we as a race have become. From the moment when in defiance of God's will Adam ate of the forbidden fruit, the characteristic lure of self-consciousness, of a knowledge that separates the knower from the known, the above (shekhinah or divine presence) from the below (ego-personality), and good from evil, set in motion a psychological chain of causation which has plunged us deeper and deeper into a forgetfulness of our undivided origin. The Biblical prophet Isaiah therefore teaches that the world is not one and so is not to be trusted. The psalmist tells us not to rely on man, for he is divided within himself. Then, from Cain's fratricide began the history of the human race as a history of evil works. When after many generations the prophets of Israel opened their eyes to the world, they beheld "distress and darkness, the gloom of anguish" (Isaiah 8:22). Ages upon ages of fear, mutual hatred and distrust, and continuous warfare have now so crippled us in mind and spirit that we have proved ourselves nearly incapable of sane community.

Brought forth as an irradiation of divine light, we have descended into darkness. Nourished by the inexhaustible sustenance of love, we have drugged ourselves with customs, ideologies, and principles so alien to the essential Source of life that by our ruthless aggression toward each other and the Earth we now threaten the survival of our world. Fashioned by the Source of all cosmical being with the fully awakened powers of co-creative love, we have sunk slowly and tragically from a heightened sensitivity to the whole into the single dark cell of our separate 'self'. Having lost touch with our Source, we no longer recognize that in our tribalism and religious fanaticism we have surpassed the bounds of sanity.

Six thousand years of bitterness, bloodshed and brutality plainly reveal the extent to which sacred truths, universal principles, and rigorous codes of morality have served to enhance our wisdom, secure a measure of collective justice, or even mitigate human suffering. Civilization has not made us more humane. In fact, the presence and devastating consequences of evil have never been so evident as in our own time, **worse than in the times of Noah,** declares the Source. While in our conspicuous advances in science and technology we seem about to be tipped into a new age, morally and spiritually we are no further from Cain and Abel than an apple is from the tree from which it was dropped. That is why to some the history of our race has from the very beginning seemed no more than a chronicle of crimes and human madness.

Commensurate with our capacities for unifying and uplifting ourselves, one another, and the world around us is our potential for creating ever-increasing possibilities of chaos, mutual destruction, and indeed for bringing about the final collapse of the Earth itself. As in ages past, so it is true for us today: our exercise and deployment of this single inexhaustible force of life --- for good or ill, for the self-fulfillment of a New Eden or for perpetuating the lethal conditions of the current state of our existence --- determines the level and extent of our apostasy from the One. And if our collective fear, magnified by the cold-blooded weapons of mass extermination we ourselves have voluminously been producing, is any indication, in our consciousness we are as far from the outpouring spirit of our Source as is ice from fire. All the collective evils --- war, genocide, lawless dictatorship --- that went into mass production beginning in 1914, all the steadily augmenting horrors of our age, from Auschwitz to Vietnam, from Kosovo to Aleppo, leave no doubt. "Is it not evident," writes the artist Eugene Delacroix over a century ago, "that progress, toward good or toward evil, has brought society to the edge of an abyss into which it may very well fall, to make way for a state of complete barbarism?" On countless occasions the twentieth century's "March to Progress" has in fact plunged us into the abyss. Life so misdirected and so misconceived, so immersed in Satanic realities on so colossal a scale has only served to undermine our resistance to forces of disintegration manifest in our brave new world's erosion of values, dissipation of humane purposes, and denial of any distinction between good and evil, right or wrong. While the edifice of our social and governmental institutions may appear sound, the foundations of meaning and value are all but eroded. We are, as the Source would see it, teetering on the brink of total madness.

Policies and decisions which are today made ostensibly only in the "national interest", which are cogently and manipulatively expressed in the language of cosmopolitan idealism or religious faith, are in fact inspired by nothing more than national aggressiveness or fear, or by some even more disreputable private motive. The religious creeds and beliefs that establish barriers between people, that seal them in isolation from each other and bind them to a hatred generated by fear, continue to produce the conditions for the dominance of war and chaos which, as the Source sees it, serves merely to perpetuate and reenact our Fall.

Nowhere is this more bitterly objectified than in the Middle East which has spiraled into the bloody mire of sectarian disorder. More than nationalist sentiment, it is religious extremism that is tearing apart the multi-ethnic countries of the region with tribal and sectarian identities becoming ever more firmly shaped in relation to the current enemy du jour. While the U.S. continues to loom over the rest of the planet as the "sole superpower" with its military on constant interventionist mode, rising nation-states such as Russia, China, and Iran closely monitor Middle Eastern developments to determine whether the political disequilibrium in the West give them opportunities to advance their own interests. More broadly, while for more than a quarter of a century the nations of the world appeared to be on a trajectory toward ever greater diversity, multiculturalism, liberty, solidarity, and equality, the dream of integration, transnational cooperation, and "globalization" has now given way to increasingly populist movements championing the erection of walls, the enforcement of homogeneity, and an implacable sense of national, ethnic, and sectarian preeminence. The result, as foreseen by the Source, **will be turmoil and difficulties, a continuing build-up, agitation, involvement of other nations in a holy war in the Middle East, involving Israel and her neighbors and as well involving the Eastern and Western blocs of nations with increasing concern, particularly because of ... a growing hostility** toward America... (Solomon Reading No. 1147, 9/3/83).

Until our own time, wars have always been waged in the shadows of recon-
struction. They've carried with them the implications of recovery. Ours is the
first civilization in human history that can literally end in wholesale human
slaughter. What we now see before us are merely the beginnings of what the
Source refers to as the "Great Tribulation":

> You live in the last day. Look for changes, for war as it comes, and par-
> ticularly know that the time is near when those acts of terrorism that have
> seemed to occur in other countries become rather commonplace in your
> own [U.S.]. Know that if you do not have the power, the love of God, to
> survive, you will be in sore straits in these times and question yourself now if
> during these times of plenty, if during this moment when so much is bloom-
> ing, so much is yielding harvest.... If you yet have difficulty in this time
> maintaining a spirit of joy, of happiness, of radiance, how difficult will it be
> when you are confined by your government to the limits of your property
> lest you encounter guards and soldiers who will search you for weapons and
> bombs. Know, *know* that it is tomorrow that these things occur. You have
> a message, you have a message that the world has not. See ye to it that you
> apply it in your own life. Find the joy that is spoken of, then share it. The
> time is now upon you (Solomon Reading No. 1187, 1985).

THE LAST DAYS

In the broader sense, what we have now entered has been referred to as the
"end times." In his letter to Timothy, St. Paul declares "that in the last days
dangerous times will come." Christ said also that in the "last times of the
world" there "shall be great tribulation, such as was not since the beginning
of the world to this time, no, nor ever shall be. And except those days should
be shortened, there should no flesh be saved: but for the elect's sake those days
shall be shortened" (Matthew 24:21-22) The "last times," thereby, would be
witness to a specter of destruction unknown to our collective cultural experience:

> Has it not (already) begun? asks the Source.

> Do you not see in this moment the fulfillment of prophecy that brother shall
> take up arms against brother? Does it not happen in this day with those ac-
> tivities in the Middle East even to where you go now to worship in this time
> of gathering? Are there not cousins, brothers, here in your country (United
> States) --- brothers to those slaying those of your own brothers, sisters, cous-
> ins, families --- does it not occur to you that it has been spoken that brother
> will take up sword against brother in this last day, and is it not true as well
> that your young men begin to dream dreams and your old men to see vi-
> sions? Is there not a reawakening of the interest and the understanding of
> magic of occultism, of the hidden things of this world? Is there not a great
> curiosity not only to know God but also to be able to communicate and to
> do His work? And where are the prophets, where are the teachers? (Solomon
> Reading No. 1187, 1985).

Specifically based on that enigmatic period of "tribulation" spoken of in Matthew and in the Book of Revelation, the Source tells us that the force released from that equation that identified mass and energy definitively heralded the times of Great Tribulation: **Called a time of tribulation by John ..., the period of trial for mankind began with that descent of fire (atomic blast) upon these people (of Japan in 1945)** (Solomon Reading No. 1304, 3/27/88). From that time to this, we have been forced to regard the world in apocalyptic terms. And the heir to that vision has become "Armageddon."

Indeed, the great war of Armageddon, its seeds planted long ago in the lethal divisions of a biblical past, may already be upon us, warns the Source, its shoots having burst forth as recently as the Persian Gulf War. In a reading delivered January 21, 1991 at the very onset of the Gulf War against Iraq, the Source responded to the question, "Is the Gulf War Armageddon?" with **a very certain YES, that this is an initial phase of the war of Armageddon. ...And while it is in fact the sounding of the trumpet for the beginning of the orchestrated action of Armageddon as it would appear in the physical, still,** the Source qualified its answer by stating that **this war fought with missiles and guns is [but] a small portion, and [only] one battle of the greater conflict to come. Then expand your consciousness beyond your concern for this current battle, for it is only an initial battle of the way.... [Armageddon] will be a different battle, for then the players will not be the nation of Iraq against a coalition of others, but rather it will begin to involve all nations of that region and beyond to virtually every nation in the world. As to this beginning, the beginning of hostilities in the Middle East, you will find that the war has begun that will involve nations in what might be called World War III, or the Great War of Armageddon, and so shall it be a war to end all wars** (Solomon Reading No. 1466, 1/21/91).

> **We have given emphasis in this time to overcoming differences attributed to religion, and attempts to avert what you refer to as a Third World War, but it is virtually inevitable that these forces aligning in such a manner will create what appears to be a Holy War. The opportunity to avert such a holocaust comes in more appropriate alliances with those countries, the overcoming of fear and misunderstanding in the western world toward Islam...**
>
> **During this period of realignment of nations, it is important that you reach out not only to Western nations, but [you] will find a need for a balance, an awkward balance, perhaps, with the Islamic world as well.**
>
> **. . . then . . . play a meaningful role in assisting the development of those countries, to reduce the anger of isolation and prejudice. For you will find an Islamic leader emerging, and this will lead to that we have spoken of before, an attack on Israel, which will be a major threat of the use of nuclear arms. The recent [Gulf] war is a portion of the balance of which we speak, and will be re-encountered** (Solomon Reading No. 1518, 9/1/91).

And so it has. Islamic extremists are now confident that their time is near. Arab governments throughout the Middle East and regimes as far away as Afghanistan, Pakistan, Libya, Somalia, and Yemen are under siege by militants who condemn their Western influences and who conceive an idealized version of an Islamic superpower rivaling, in its might and sweeping political influence, the United States. "The worst-case scenario," writes Tom Hundley of the *Chicago Tribune*, "is that Algeria, Egypt, and Jordan will fall into the hands of Islamic radicals, joining militant regimes in Iran and Sudan to form the core of a geopolitical movement that sees the West as the embodiment of all evil."[10] Saudi Arabia likely would be the next to fall, followed immediately by Kuwait, then other Arab oil-producing states. Given the West's vital dependence on Middle Eastern petroleum, such a prospect is an almost certain prescription for war between the East and the West.

THE TEMPLE OF SOLOMON

To date, there exists no one central organized body or hierarchy that can claim to represent, let alone to mobilize and regulate, a pan-Islamic movement. But as warned of by the Source, the West should not be lulled into believing that in the complex and quickly changing world of Middle Eastern politics a tidal wave of Islamic fundamentalist fervor could not suddenly and powerfully erupt to produce the kind of military-ideological dictatorships that would turn a jihad or "holy war" into World War III. All that would be called for to ignite such a catastrophe would be the introduction of nuclear arms into the hands of fanatical fundamentalist regimes. And **unfortunately**, the Source adds, **the introduction of nuclear devices into Arab hands comes very soon and is upon you:**

> **Now, it is this that the prophets have referred to as an earthquake on the Holy Mount. We would see it as a nuclear detonation affecting the Holy Mount which will cause Israel to seem justified in reclaiming . . . the rebuilding of the Temple of [Jerusalem].**
>
> **... look for the time when world speculation turns to the possibility that a nuclear device has come into the hands of the nation of Syria. And when there is discussion of that possibility and the denial of it, and the tension mounts, know that here is upon you that devastation that begins a major war among nations** (Solomon Reading No. 1332, 4/3/88).

The exalted status placed on the Temple of Jerusalem by the Jewish people cannot be overestimated. It represents the holy place of God's "indwelling" from which He would appear, counsel, and command His people: "There I will appear to thee, and I will commune with thee from above the mercy seat, from between the two cherubims which are upon the Ark of the Covenant, of all things which I will give thee in commandment unto the children of Israel" (Exodus 25:22). This holy Temple, which united God with man, spirit with matter, heaven with earth, what is above with what is below, was to serve as the fixed "center of the world" --- Jerusalem. "Since the day that I brought forth My people out of the land of Egypt, I chose no city among all the tribes of Israel to build an house in, that My name might be there; neither chose I any man to be ruler over My people Israel. But I have chosen Jerusalem, that My Name might be there." (II Chronicles 6:5-6) The Temple of Jerusalem, then, became the outward and visible expression of God from which the spirit of Israel and all humanity might be raised once more to its original state of purity before Him.

By the hand of man, by the Will of God, two Temples were constructed, the first by King Solomon, the second following the Jewish captivity in Babylon. By the hand of man, by the Will of God, both were destroyed because of Israel's sins. The third and last Temple, as foretold by the prophets, will be completed in the day of the Jewish Messiah. For nearly two thousand years the Jews have awaited that day, and according to the Source, that day is now upon us.

Thus, in the wake of a nuclear detonation "affecting" the Holy Mount, look to the rebuilding of the ancient Temple of Solomon. This indignity to the faith and pride of the nations of Islam, the Source tells us, will be the final prophetic event signifying that the great struggle of Armageddon is at hand:

> Now as there is the taking of that Mount and the destruction of that Temple now placed, then look for the beginning of that war of wars. For as there is the destruction of that Holy Place, now set on the Mount, and the attempts to rebuild the Temple of Solomon, so in that time will there be set in conflict man against man, for religious purpose, religious causes. And will you learn from history?

> Then see that that occurred in Atlantis. And has it not often been described . . . that that law, that war that came and was the destruction of that time, was concerning the beliefs within the self? Or the sons of the Law of One and the sons of the Law of Belial, pulling, then, apart within the self? And there will then be that war for no other cause, but rather for the belief, for the religion, for the attempts of these to convince the others and pull this way and that.

> So that in the destroying here and the rebuilding of the Temple, will be the fighting with passion, and will be the resentment of the many nations, saying that this one has usurped that that was holy to another. And there will be joining in of the many nations, the many powers here, [and they] will be centered in their concentration on this point in the East (Solomon Reading No. 241, 9/20/73).

THE PLAINS OF MEGIDDO

As with a pebble starting a landslide, the restoration of Solomon's Temple will bring about a war of unbelievable magnitude. And as foretold by prophets of a more venerable time, it is on the strategic plain and over the skies of Har-Megiddo that the armies of the world will clash. In the words of Paul Solomon, "In the Book of Daniel and in the Book of The Revelation, in both of these books, we have references to a great war that will be fought on the plains of Megiddo or Armageddon, as it is called in the New Testament, referring still to the same place. And there are some interesting things about this battle that is to be fought there. Perhaps the most significant words recorded say that the battle will be fought in the air.

"Now, can you imagine that being written 2,500 years ago? There was no way to fight a battle in the air at that time, and yet the prophets that wrote about this great last battle to end all battles said that it would be fought in the air. And it will be fought by some kind of thing they described as being rather like a giant locust with a chest of metal and with metal armor that would fly through the air and encounter the armored locusts sent to meet it. Now the interesting thing is that if you aim a scud missile from Baghdad to Haifa, and if you intercept it with a Patriot missile, the interception will happen over the plains of Megiddo."

No battleground has ever received the same strategic attention as that which lies at the foot of Mount Har-Megiddo. And if what Solomon implies is correct, following the Great Battle to come none will ever compare in its infamy. For as the Source affirms, **nuclear arms will be used against her [Israel]. And she will return in kind. You will see the plumes of fire and smoke that are spoken of in the Revelation. You will see this coming out of this war. . . . So in all of these battles which are a part of the Great War, you will see all of these things used (biological, chemical, nuclear weapons), and not the least of them biological** (Solomon Reading No. 1466, 1/21/91) Thus, the plains of Megiddo will be strewn with more bloody corpses than in any battle in mankind's violent history.

THE RENDING OF THE VEIL

In a reading that adds an entirely new dimension of meaning and immensity to this impending world conflict, the Source tells us that **you will see bloodshed as has never occurred on this planet. . . .**

> **For this war will surround the earth and there will be found now ... that as such eruptions take place on this planet, then there is the removal or the rending of that veil ... between the physical and the spiritual.**
>
> **So then will the Hosts of the spiritual be entering into that of the battle that will not only be between those in the physical body; but there will not be seen the difference between the physical and the spiritual. So has been described that Battle of Armageddon: as these entering from the air or from the spiritual, will be taking place in a battle upon this physical earth. So will there be the rending of the veil, or no longer the separation between the physical and the spiritual, but all will take new dimension in such revelation.**
>
> **These come then, and are developing quickly. Observe the speed with which such come. And as there come the times, as statements are issued forth from those leaders of the nation, saying, "We will build the temple in this spot," look then for the end and watch for His glory, for His light in the clouds. For it exists even now** (Solomon Reading No. 219, 8/21/73).

So profound will be the release of energy throughout the Earth, the Source maintains, so great a rupture will occur, that those inaccessible realms of the spirit, remote from all human experience, will be opened wide, giving rise to an entirely new cosmic dimension of conflict.

As impossible as it might seem, the Source assures us that it is actually quite reasonable. A whole world --- a subtler realm of spiritual reality --- remains hidden from our ordinary physical senses by relatively stable patterns of electromagnetic force active throughout the physical universe. When a sufficiently massive discharge of energy occurs through seismic or volcanic activity, nuclear explosion, etc., these stable patterns of force can be disrupted, causing the distinctions between matter and energy, space and time, electric charge and field, to resolve into configurations of an underlying implicate order. The resulting breach or tear in the fabric of physical reality allows for an interactive convergence between two separate worlds and realities --- the enfolded and unfolded worlds of spirit and matter. According to the Source, it has happened many times before:

> Now understand that which occurs in the period of an earthquake. For [it] has occurred each time [that] as the earth would break open on this plane, you would see [it] as if this were a chakra of the body of the earth, or [as if] this were an energy center. And in the breaking open of the earth, as it happened in the time of Christ, at the time of the crucifixion of the Master, so did the earth open. And in that time of the opening, so was there the rending of the veil between the physical and the spiritual, and so will it occur in this time, in the beginning of that war of wars, so will there be that rending of the veil. And you will see no difference between those walking alive in the physical body and those of the dead that would rise up or would walk from the graves, and those places where they are found and would walk among you.

> Now understand [that] this has occurred even in this time, in this day, in that portion of South America... you have so seen it happen, that in the rending of the veil the third eye is opened, and these [whose sight is opened] are unable to deal with reality and are unable to deal with that which they see. For there is not separation between the reality and the unreality. Then these who have seen the spirits of the dead during the earthquakes begin to take their lives. If you would understand the truth, then study that rate of suicide that came following those quakes in Managua, Nicaragua, or in Greece, or in those recent times when there have been the quakes on your plane (Solomon Reading No. 241, 9/20/73).

Given the immense destructive capability currently at our disposal, therefore, the merely human margin of this struggle will thus be joined in battle by forces from a world beyond, by strange and unseizable potencies that quite literally will shake the world to its primordial core.

> Now understand that we give these things for this reason; that in the rending of the veil in the time of the beginning of the building of the Temple in Jerusalem, so will you see among you those that appear as spirits, or have been

dead, and these take a part, then, a portion of the fighting that will come. And this has been described by those writers of the Scriptures as that time of Armageddon, and it is that time of the ending here, or the transformation of all that is (Solomon Reading No. 241, 9/20/73).

Look toward the building of the Temple as your most important sign of these coming events (Solomon Reading No. 1560, 9/16/91).

THE HARDNESS OF OUR HEARTS

If the prospects for a peaceful world prove to be as dim as the desert prophets of Israel or the prophets of an even earlier world have foretold, the cause will lie not within the labyrinth of the world's competing national interests or sectarian creeds, nor with the ever escalating destructive capacity that nation-states continue to amass. It will lie ultimately within ourselves, in the transcendence that has faded from our awareness. It is the bestial component of ourselves that continues to wage its wars --- with itself, with others, and with the planet. While there are many who may exempt themselves from the faults that they see in others, yet they cannot see that it is beings in no way different from themselves who are doing what they despise and who themselves despise it even while they do it. Clearly there are some who are possessed of greater intelligence and far more integrity of will than others, but we are all men and women with the same power to create and destroy, with the same gratuitous grace of understanding mocked by the same bestial blindness. We are one and all condemned to a desperate struggle against the same impulses which we are accustomed to regard in others as self-serving, hate-filled or contemptible. It is with these impulses stirring in regions deeper than consciousness that we as a species face perpetual war and the devastation of our terrestrial home. Only the awakening of the mass of men and women into a new and greater Intrinsic awareness can avert the huge disaster toward which our world is heading.

The greatest measure of our Fall, therefore, is the sheer hardness of so many hearts. While the numbers of truly awakened personalities have begun to multiply, still, for the vast majority our incapacity to act or even to feel, our morbid tendency to avoid or to transfer blame or responsibility in the face of the world's pain and suffering and privation betrays our detachment from even the most minimal sense of a consciousness of love. Surrounded by materialism, moral relativism, and consumer-egoism, by the breakdown of absolutism, a profound crisis of authority and the resulting general decay, by all-powerful media and a decline of the power of the state, by the rise of a technical civilization and now its own beginning disintegration, by the rise in ethnic hatred and the eclipse of religious tolerance, by the snapping of the links between generations and the severing and dissolution of families, mankind's moral and spiritual self-affirmation is deeply threatened; relatively in terms of emptiness, absolutely in terms of meaninglessness. Hundreds of millions have turned to violence (at least vicariously), drugs and pornography in a neurotic attempt to find refuge from the increasing impoverishment of their own lives in a world seemingly gone mad. Societies saturated with violence and drugs, societies that venerate homicidal imagery and prurient sexual voyeurism, are societies in crisis.

As violence and injustice continue to pervade our irreparably fallen world, the inexorable questions of human purpose and responsibility seem to be leading in circles, again and again to the intersection of nihilism and dogmatism, to emptiness and to vulgar caricatures of a divided truth. Both paths leads us further and further into the desolate wastelands of a truly moral life, the essential life of the spirit and of the spirit's will, until once more we find ourselves at a crossroads, helpless either because we can grasp nothing or because in our prejudicial beliefs we cannot let go of anything. Either leads to a lack of human-heartedness. The reason for this should be plain: no longer feeling any sense of control --- over our own personal lives or the margins of our freedom --- we're simply worn down to lassitude.

What we in fact see in this Brave New World's present state of technological consumerism and corporate wealth, however, attests undeniably to who in fact *is* in control: it is those whose religion is greed and whose only god is money, power, and self. There is scarcely anyone alive who has not experienced the consequences of their dark diplomacy: the programs of fear, the lust for the natural resources of the planet, the unimaginable wealth of the elite few, the rivalries and conflicts and wars and bloodshed and deaths of hundreds of millions for the benefit of the industrial affluence that feeds on war. They are as insatiable as they are ruthless. Even though a few may actually imagine themselves as servants of the light, yet in their blinkered self-deception they merely deny in themselves the subtly disguised temptations of the lure for personal aggrandizement and dominance. In their narcissism and deceit, they have utterly corrupted the Divine Laws upon which their wealth is predicated thereby predisposing us all to the undeviating fate toward which we in our disingenuity and ignorance are heedlessly advancing. **We will describe that danger in this manner,** explains the Source:

> The Laws of Prosperity are laws governing the movement of energy, a very real energy which does in fact move with ebb and flow and with purpose. These laws work with mathematical precision. If applied totally, thoroughly, completely and without any distortion, without failure in the application of these laws... you will have, certainly, sufficient result to establish opportunity that you may even take the understanding of these laws to others and assist in their experience of trying and proving such laws. [But] because the law is a law applied to the movement of energy with purpose, there is a violation of the law when one would seek to accumulate an energy which, being kinetic in nature [and] purposeful [instead becomes] related directly to the accumulation of money and material values in particular.

> Now, while we do not criticize the desire or the application of the law for the drawing of money to self (the application of money producing results), we do warn against an attempt simply to accumulate money without a purposeful flow [or] movement. We speak of energy which is alive and which is teleological in nature. Money is but a symbol --- instruments, papers, coins, and other forms of money as such. Money itself has no inherent value. The values are determined and attached to these symbols all too often in violation of the Laws of Economics. These factors must be considered particularly at this time in history. [You] are at a moment in which the Laws of Economy and Prosperity are being falsely manipulated by political contriv-

ance rather than the pure application of the Laws of Economy.

We cannot fail to warn you in this time that these laws as were stated in the ancient Greek teachings as "Ecos Nomia" and which are Universal Laws, which were universal laws before those early observations, these laws which are designed to work with mathematical precision are currently being violated, are being manipulated politically. The laws of politics conflict considerably with the laws of economics, particularly as politics are currently expressed.

Now, it is essential to recognize that in your operation of these laws, however perfectly you operate them, you operate them in a hostile environment which threatens the precision of the Laws of Money, of value for value exchange; that is to say, an exchange of equal values. And furthermore, we find in approaching this record that a part of the purpose involves the present practice of gambling in high stakes which are in turn politically altered in the result of your approach to such government supported and politically manipulated gambling. Now, by gambling we do not refer to what are commonly called gambling dens or to participation in games of chance. It is rather to that respectable form of gambling which is now referred to as a market of stocks and bonds. We find this practice, as it has been developed and as it is practiced at this time, is not only a practice of gambling by its very nature but it is also subject to manipulation in terms of applications of energy which violate the Laws of Economy... (Solomon Reading No. 1693, 6/6/92).

Today's global economy can hardly be described as anything even resembling the kind of value for value exchange spoken of by the Source. With over $30 trillion invested in equities and other assets, financial institutions and governments around the world are now the dominant players in the stock market, thereby literally controlling the "free" markets.

Following the Great Recession of 2007-09, central banks with their monopoly over currency and credit set record-low interest rates supposedly in order to help stimulate a "recovery" from the very financial crisis they and others through their own greed and irresponsibility caused. Then, in order to compensate themselves for their loss of income in the bond markets, rather than invest in failing infrastructure these same privately owned financial institutions along with governments bet on the stock market, OTC (over-the-counter) derivatives and credit swap derivatives, using fiat credits (promises to pay) that are either borrowed or printed. (While it's estimated that the total exposure that global banks now have to derivatives contracts exceeds 710 trillion dollars, the fact is that there is not nearly that much actual "money" in circulation today.) Fiat currency is now being printed on an unprecedented scale, much of it being used to artificially boost stock prices while eroding the value of real assets through inflation of the currency supply. This is euphemistically referred to as "quantitative easing" or monetizing debt. (Wall Street, meanwhile, depicting itself as that part of the economy that's helping the body commonwealth to grow, is in fact the parasite that is taking over the growth)".

The reality is that global bankers, operating in a feudalist fashion secretly and in concert through central banks of the world, are using taxpayer money --- and the money of many future generations --- in a global casino royale that enriches the investor class at the expense of the middle class. In layman terms, our whole monetary system is nothing more than a house of cards. The entire global equity market is now one massive Ponzi scheme based on debt and paper promises in which almost all the economic growth in the last decade has gone to the 'One Percent.'

While credit continues to flow freely and everything today seems fine, when its earnings are far less than its payments how much debt can the global financial system take before it utterly collapses? The Source tells us the day of reckoning is at hand:

> We have spoken often of a time when a piece of bread would buy a bag of gold. You are upon those times now. This means for so many that the understanding of success must be changed, must be changed from the concept of money which no longer has real value. It always has, of course, been only symbolic of value, but there was a time when that symbol was a symbol of real value held. [But now] the currency has been disconnected from real value and does not symbolize a true portion of wealth. That is to say, in your economies ... the governments are bankrupt, the economies are a shambles. And the result of that, the fallout from that, in markets such as real estate, will clearly come upon you.

> Then the time comes when a piece of land that will produce a bit of bread will be worth far more than gold, for gold cannot be eaten, cannot feed the world, and is no longer the standard for the economies of the world. Economies are now politically manipulated rather than being representative of a value held. Those who have so heavily invested in buildings and investments and have left themselves no room to move this way or that, these [will] become caught in the collapse of the economy. And only through barter will those of you who are wise enough to understand that real economy consists of value for value exchange. Through that knowledge you may win, in the sense of being able to divest yourselves of such things as become, as they were, stones, millstones about the neck that weigh you down, that keep you from being able to move. And do prepare to divest yourself as much as possible or to become liquid, in the jargon of those who deal with finance, except to hold that land which will replace money as value. Particularly food-producing land will be essential to stability.

> You are on the brink of a collapse in so many ways, but those of you who understand the laws governing success will realize that the laws continue to be the same, for the laws of success are Universal Laws. They are not tied to the economies. They are not tied to the symbols of wealth (Solomon Reading No. 1332, 9/22/90).

Given their complaisant faith in the smooth curve of progress and the triumphant gains it has afforded them, the apostles of convention blindly close their eyes to such warnings. They see no need to risk their social status or accumulated wealth in behalf of human ideals simply on the presumption of more apocalyptic futurism. But if the Source's diagnosis is correct, they will become the suffering heirs to their own deeds. The calamities which they've brought to us all and to the world and which through their brigandage they continue to bring forth for all our posterity contains within itself the germ of its own retributive reaction. It carries within it the curse which will fall upon their own heads:

> I declare unto you, you've entered the time when the changes come. You'll begin to see features on the face of the earth that will startle men and begin speculation that the end days are at hand. You'll see it in your newspapers. You'll hear it talked about in places you have never suspected that men would speculate on such things, but it comes. And the beginning of a famine of seven years, a time when men will begin to fight in the streets over scraps of bread. You will see men lining before the doors of institutions finding their currency has no value. You'll see a time when the judgement of God will say, "I have indeed heaped upon you blessings that you were not able to receive. And in mockery you have despised them. And if it must be that in order to hear the sweet prayers of My children, then I must take away all things, and leave them bare and wanting until they cry out unto Me, so be it." And so it has begun (Solomon Reading No. 662, 1975).

In the meantime, each year the economic wealth of the world becomes more narrowly concentrated in the hands of the few while billions of people worldwide live in unalleviated poverty and tens of millions more, mostly children, die of starvation. As the homeless, the hungry, the poor struggle against the irresistible current of obsessive greed and the ideological assumptions upon which it is justified and propagated, so through our complacency and indifference we have assaulted life and the one Law which gives meaning to life --- love of the Infinite and impelling Good, of neighbor, of nature, of enemy, of self. Our cities are eroding with crime, drugs, mental imbalance and physical rot while the walls of our rooms and the screens of our smart phones, iPads and video games define for us the limits of our moral vision. Far easier to cast blame on inevitable Fate than to accept responsibility or guilt for our indifference.

Thus, if in our apathy and resignation we are loathe to look to our destiny straight in the eye, it is perhaps because of our unwillingness to assume responsibility for the transgression of our own passivity. We have made covenants with death, the Source declares, and through our lack of compassion and concern, with hell we have made our peace. **Now there have been the warnings given,** admonishes the Source. **There have been the many who have been lifted to this plane and have seen the awesome sights and have reported those things that were to come.... And it has been given: unless you place your value on those things of value, those things even of value shall be taken away. And that you might know and recognize value, we give these indications even at this time that you might be aware of that path for which you are given responsibility and the narrowness thereof:**

> Now you have made the Word of God a weak instrument. You have made it impotent by declaring there is no hell. You have denied the wrath of God or the possibility of punishment, but we would have you open your eyes in this moment. We would see the black river Styx. We would see its murky depths flowing through the crags and the rocks, and we would see perched at in-

tervals in this black and filthy mess those urchins, those angles of hell, those imps that would laugh and delight at the suffering of those of your race and on your plane. And yet we would see those even in your day clambering with delight and throwing themselves into its murky waters, and carrying even their children into its black and disgusting depths. And we would see only one fence that need be crossed from the birth on your plane to the river. We would have you realize that no one could reach this black and murky river that you might see as hell, as everlasting punishment, we would have you realize that it cannot be reached without trampling upon that which God put in the way. That which you must trample upon to reach eternal punishment would be a bleeding body on a cross.

Then would you declare that a just God would not create a hell if He would put such an awesome figure in the way to protect you from the depths thereof? Would you then deny its existence? But know that there are even now in this moment below your plane those souls bound in chains that clammer even in this second for an opportunity to take up that body in which you now reside, feeling of a certainty that they could please their Creator and raise themselves a little higher, a little closer to the Godhead if given another opportunity. And yet you take this incarnation so lightly.

Now search your hearts and see your concerns, for your concerns are for material things. They are for income, for personal satisfactions, and lusts and pleasures. Now we have you realize in this moment that thou art weighed in the balance and found wanting. You speak of balance; you speak of service; you speak of love; how oft would you step from the way and look for [an] opportunity to help a brother? How oft do you trample over the body or go around when you see one dying? [Is] there not more time spent in condemning another than in searching the depths of your own heart?

Now when you speak of love, know what love is. And when there is an opportunity to lift the spirits of another, turn not thy back, for his blood will be required at thy hands. There has been given sufficient warning; there has been given sufficient instruction.

We would see those who understand the messages of the stars, even in this day, being able to see that which comes upon you. And we will find that, and it has been predicted that, even your largest cities in this time will fall away into the sea. And you have not begun to understand the implications of those times... you have not prepared yourself for their occurrence. Now study the life and realize that you may look forward to the time that even a scrap of bread would bring a bag of gold. You will see children dying in your streets. You will see your moon turn to dripping blood. You will see the atmospheres of the planets collide one against the other. You will realize that that which is the mass of earth in this day will take new form and new shape and will be unrecognizable to those who inhabit the earth planet in this day.

...To whom do you owe your allegiance? I say to you, if you speak not the words of God, that you are of your father the devil. He who is not for Me is against Me. There is no middle road. You have a charge to keep. This is a sacred trust, and woe be to him from whom it is taken away. It is written in your Scripture: "My Spirit will not always strive with men." (Solomon Reading No. 88, 12/3/72).

If complacency and indifference to the increasing misery, suffering and hope-lessness of others is poison to the life of the spirit, then surely by now we have assimilated enough of its toxin that already we are spiritually half dead. And in that death is encompassed our own doom. "The great mass of mankind," writes the novelist Henry Miller, "destined in our time to suffer more cruelly than ever before, ends by being paralyzed with fear, becoming introspective, shaken to the very core, and does not hear, see or feel anything more than everyday physical needs. It is thus that worlds die. First and foremost, the flesh dies. But although few clearly recognize it, the flesh would not have died if the spirit had not been killed already."[13] So far have we regressed in our heartless-ness and passivity into the spiritual equivalent of decomposition that we are scarcely conscious of the depth of our present degradation or nearness of our own final undoing. **As has already come to your attention, you are living in the last age, the last day, and very near the dawning of the day of our Lord,** observes the Source. Viewed from a vantage point of an eternity above and beyond history, the Source affirms that the "last days" are now upon us; the fulfillment of God's Law is immanent. Very shortly, we are told, the wicked-ness and corruption of the world will be called into account. Evil will be con-sumed in "agony, death and desolation."

Even now God's judgment is being enacted; in these prophesied "last days" His presence is coming to expression in the pulsations of accelerating change in the unfolding events of our time:

> So that all that you see in the latter time will be accelerated; experiences and changes will occur more quickly. Evolution, as you know it, will be speeded beyond that you have ever recognized in this life wave, in this root race. A period of counting down, as it were; a period of acceleration of the changes until they reach that dramatic point when there will be no more earth as you know it (Solomon Reading No. 645, 7/4/75).

Thus, by all signs, visions and prophetic indications, the final hour of our choosing has arrived. According to the Source, **"the ending of the times and the times" as given in Scripture has now passed. [These] are the years, a change and a great tribulation, then a change, and the dawning of the New Age. These are the times you have entered the half-times.** (Solomon Reading No. 645, 7/4/75). We have now reached the edge of that mythic landscape set forth in the writings of Daniel, in the Revelation of John the Divine, and in the apocalyptic visions of prophets from around the world and from every previ-ous age. **Now if you would listen, listen not to one prophet, not to what one man would say,** urges the Source, **but read in your Scriptures and see those words of old and the many who have appeared and warned here, the many of the different faiths, in those ways that have been described....** In particular, directs the Source **...be encouraged by that you have called the Holy Mother from earliest times, ...that expression that is the Mother of all and more than Mary** (Solomon Reading No. 364, 5/24/74).

Chapter 11

A Woman Crowned By
The Stars

SPIRIT BREAKING ON THE COASTS OF MATTER

Given that our age has mystically assigned to blind chance the role of Divine Providence, perhaps it is not so much the number of warnings we have been given as it is that through our fanaticism of scientific rationalism we have unconditionally rejected or arbitrarily ignored them all. Any epiphany of the transcendent that seeks to interpret God's intentions to us and to make our values and behavior fit into a larger scheme of probation and salvation simply represents a betrayal of realism and sound logic. The irony is devastating. By denying the inner dimensions of ourselves, we thereby deny the source of the warnings, either because it is too fantastic to believe or because we have simply disciplined ourselves to a view of the world in which miracles, prophecies, and divine apparitions play no part in coloring the results. To all but the most incorrigibly skeptical, however, something strange indeed is happening across the entire face of the globe, and we must wonder what it means not only for ourselves but for the larger destiny of the earth. For those who can even partly grasp something of the harmonious, inter-dimensional, many layered complexities of the world as a reflection of the Divine Source of all Being, these astonishing events may hold the secret of our fate and may now be a necessity of our survival.

What began on the night of April 2, 1968 as an attempt by two mechanics, on duty at a city garage across from the Coptic Church of Saint Mary in Zeitoun Egypt, to stop a white-robed nun from committing suicide from atop the church's large central dome soon led to the witnessing by up to two hundred thousand visitors per night, an estimated 15 million in all, of what was described as the "magnificent, wondrous, glorious form of Our Lady from Heaven," along with apparitions of Joseph and Jesus in blessing the huge crowds. The appearances usually were heralded by mysterious lights, glowing clouds and, more frequently, by large luminous birds which were seen to fly swiftly in the formation of a cross or triangle, only to disappear abruptly, then reappear in yet another formation. The Lady herself seemed to be composed entirely of light and was seen to move serenely from atop one side of the great dome to another, as if responding to those who called to her to "come their way." To those who chanted or sang she would bow in acknowledgement, greeting, or blessing, or make gestures of prayer, or at times wave what appeared to be an olive branch. At other times she would appear bearing the Christ Child in her left arm.

There were yet other effects, seen and as a matter of record photographed, which seemed to occur in accordance with their own supernatural laws and for which there were no physical explanations. Anba Samuel, Coptic Bishop for Theological and Educational Institutions, recounted that on a certain night, for instance, light was seen to pour from beneath one of the small domes of the church and gradually creep over the entire church roof. The light, possibly a form of intense ionization, was evidently not reflected, but emitted from the very air surrounding the roof and domes. On yet another night, great luminous clouds of red incense billowed up from the area of the central dome of the church. Given that the glass windows of the church were as always sealed, and that in the words of Bishop Anba Gregorios it would have required "millions of sensors to produce that amount of incense," any possible source of the phenomenon from within the church itself was thoroughly discounted. Furthermore, on still nights the glowing vaporous incense would drift down from the Lady's mantle onto the crowds gathered in the streets below.

While the apparitional events varied in length from night to night, from April 27 to May 15, 1968 the appearances were reported to be even more spectacular in their intensity and longer in duration. On the night of June 8, 1968 the apparition could be seen continuously for seven and a half hours --- from 9:00 p.m. until 4:30 a.m. -- allowing some members of the crowd to go home to rest and to return later to the ongoing spectacle.

Official investigations by the Coptic Church, the Evangelical Church, and the Egyptian Government each separately and unequivocally affirmed and documented the happenings as authentic apparitional occurrences. Photographs taken by Mr. Ali Ibrahim of the Egyptian Museum, and by thousands of others, all appear to substantiate the written accounts of these events. More recently, apparitional events similarly visible to all have occurred at the Serbian Orthodox Church of Saint Peter and Saint Paul in Beirut, Lebanon.

In trying to imagine the overwhelming effect of such visions on those who actually witnessed them, we are simply out of our depth. The sudden detachment from one's consensual reality, from one's entire universe of conditioned belief, would be as disorienting as vision flooding the system of the congenitally blind. On the other hand, the notion that one's senses may be engaged in any sort of treason against the actual facts would surely be eclipsed by the corroborating testimony of so many millions of fellow witnesses from every continent and religious background --- Muslims, Copts, Hebrews, Catholics, Protestants, and many others. While there are those who would dismiss such phenomena as the aberrant effect of "swamp gas" or relegate them to the metaphysic of the mind's ability to hallucinate en masse, such paralogical and utterly desperate explanations are all too often conceived of a specious need to defend and secure the borders of one's own preconceived view of reality. What we give in such cases to the process of inquiry is precisely and to the same extent what we receive from it by way of accommodating solutions. The only sensible alternative is simply to accept that the multitude of witnesses knew clearly and reported accurately what they saw, and that every feeble attempt to explain otherwise could in no way improve upon either the quality of their vision, their collectively shared experience, or, indeed, the actual photographic evidence. If we can accept these events for what they are, as "spirit breaking on the coasts of matter," then the question becomes: What is their purpose? What in human affairs is of such far-reaching significance as to compel a manifestation of such magnitude to transport itself upon the shores of our physical world? What manner of mystery could fill the margins of such a prodigious miracle? It may be more than we ever care to face.

THE HEART OF A MOTHER'S LOVE

Seen from the perspective of the Source, the figure of the mother of Jesus, having appeared first in the expression of Eve, stands at the very center of a vast mythico-historical universe that stretches in time from creation to apocalypse and in metaphysical space from supreme abode of the heavens to earth. In this universe which spans all the dimensions and levels of our own being is enclosed all our concerns, hopes, anxieties and potential as well as the vision of all that was and is and is yet to come. As the "second Eve", Mary's enduring connection with and abiding concern for "her children" should come as no wonder. She is, after all, quite literally the mother of all humanity. **Hold fast to such images as would come,** advises the Source, **and know that ... presence of the Holy Mother as she expressed, ...and be encouraged that she be about for she would love and care for you even as the Christ** (Solomon Reading No. 364, 5/24/74). It is thus that she has appeared time and again throughout this age bearing a message not of fear, or of war, but of a mother's love and a warning to us all of the need for greater love and peace among the whole of her human family. For love, she continually submits, is the one power through which all things are made possible. "Wars can be stopped and even weather controlled by these means (fasting and prayer through the power of love),"[12] declares Mary to a visionary in 1992. But of course as with all teachings and traditions both ancient and modern, the choice is ours. "What happens to the world depends upon those who live in it," says Mary offering herself as Our Lady of America. "There must be much more good than evil in order to prevent the holocaust that is so near approaching."[13]

The same theme accompanies every visitation, dominates every vision, even when it is communicated symbolically through signs and gestures as with the more recent apparitions at Zeitoun, Beirut, Bethlehem, Tel Aviv and elsewhere. Where there are no words, but only the silence that marks the possession of words, the relation of symbolic gestures to the human spirit becomes an infinite relation. Words prove insuperably inadequate. A condition of pure reciprocity is established between the symbolically sovereign center of the apparitional event and every eye to which it is offered, so that as with the sign of the olive branch, an obvious warning of a need for peace, its meaning spins out from the very midst of the heavens into the depths of human consciousness at every level of being. It was through the medium of this universal language that the apparitions at Zeitoun allegedly forestalled a planned mass persecution by Muslim extremists of Christians whose homes had already been marked by blood and that was on the verge of a murderous outbreak.

But for every Zeitoun-like Marian event that occurs there is a parallel series of apparitions that speak plainly enough in words that even a child can understand, as they have, effectively and uninterruptedly, for over a century. In fact, among the increasing proliferation of Marian apparitions in our own time, the most remarkable and auspicious have appeared to simple peasant children. Indeed, if the Son of Man sought to apprise the Sons of Men that they must become as children to enter the Kingdom, then it was his Mother who brought the principle to life. Over 300 cases of individual apparitions to children have occurred in the twentieth century alone, each bearing with it a warning for what Mary refers to as the "last days of the world." "I am warning you that difficult times of trial are coming on this godless world," she declares. "[P]eople are not aware that the prophesied times are upon them... I tell you the final times are near."[14] The signs written of in the Gospels and in the Book of Revelation are now before us, she tells the young Korean visionary Julia Kim in 1994. "...As I told you before, the natural order is now being disturbed and abnormalities are occurring frequently: floods, fires, famines, earthquakes, droughts, tidal waves... large-scale destructions, many kinds of environmental disasters, and unusual weather. Also, many people are dying because of wars, incurable illnesses and contagious diseases. When snow falls and cold wind blows, you know winter is beginning. When new buds sprout, you know it is becoming spring. Then, why do you not understand that these disasters are SIGNS?"[15]

SIGNS OF THE TIMES

Beginning with the events at Fatima, Portugal where in 1917 over 70,000 people --- atheists, "freethinkers," skeptics, clerics, pilgrims from every land --- are reported to have witnessed the "great miracle of the sun," the mother of Jesus has chosen the meek, the innocent, the unworldly to deliver to the world the message that the last days are at hand. It was to the children of Fatima that she appeared "more brilliant than the sun" wearing a crown of twelve golden stars and with the moon under her feet. More than serving merely as a messenger of these "final times," Mary proclaims herself to be the very fulfillment of prophetic "end-time" scriptures. "A great sign appeared in the sky," declares the Book of Revelation, "a woman clothed with the sun with the moon under her feet, and on her head, a crown of twelve stars." (Rev. 12:1). "I am the Mother of everything created by God," Mary declared to the visionary and stigmatist Gladys Quiroga de Motta in 1988. "I am the 'Woman Clothed with the Sun,' the 'New Eve', who will lead mankind to Light...."[16] "I am the Virgin of Revelation,"[17] she tells Father Gobbi in 1980. Through her role as the Great Sign to humanity of the times in which we now live, Mary is consecrated to, in her words, "bring you to the full understanding of Sacred Scripture. Above all, I will read to you the pages of its last book, which you are living. In it, everything is already predicted, even that which must still come to pass."[18] And the fateful character of that which "must still come to pass" has no equivalent, so we are told, to anything that has ever come before. "So, be ready," another young visionary is told, "because Great Tribulation is near, such as has never been since the beginning of the world until today, and which will never be again...."[19] As Mary repeatedly insists, "My times have come."

THE NIGHT OF THE SCREAMS

From Beauraing, Belgium in the 1930's to San Sebastian de Garabandal, Spain in the 1960's, and from the 1980's to the present in Kibeho in Rwanda, Medjugorje in Croatia, Oliveto Citra, Italy, Cameroon in Africa and elsewhere in the world, children have been the recipients of visions and increasingly urgent messages that warn us, as Mary put it to the children of Kibeho, that we are on "the edge of catastrophe." "Great times of tribulation are coming," Mary reportedly told one young visionary in 1988. "Natural catastrophes and those created by man, and the third world war are near."[20] The apparitions warn that the survivors of this coming apocalypse, far outnumbered by its victims, "will find themselves so desolate that they will envy the dead."[21] But from the time of the miraculous events at Fatima in 1917, the precise nature of this coming apocalypse has remained a mystery.

During one of the apparitions at Fatima, Lucia, the eldest of the three young visionaries, took a deep breath, went pale as death and, along with the other children was heard to cry out in terror. The children later explained that they were given a terrible vision, and that its message was to be kept secret until its release in 1960. Millions of people the world over from many different faiths anxiously awaited the Vatican's release of the secret, but when 1960 came and went with no disclosure and with no explanation as to why a message given in the name of God should remain sealed, speculation as to the contents of that letter written by Lucia bearing the secret message began to mount. As if in response, only a few months later, on June 18,1961, another series of apparitions of Mary "dressed in a white robe with a blue mantle and a crown of golden stars" began a short distance from the village of Garabandal in Spain. The Garabandal apparitions, more than two thousand separate events over the course of four years, seemed to echo with an even greater urgency the warning given at Fatima: "Before, the chalice [of Divine wrath] was filling," Mary told the four young visionaries, "now it is overflowing."[22] And as at Fatima, the children of Garabandal were likewise "called" to receive an awesome vision of the coming chastisement. The vast crowd which normally followed was told to wait while the four girls proceeded alone to the small grove of pines outside the village. Their voices, customarily ecstatic, turned suddenly on that night to a series of terrifying shrieks. "Let the little children die first!" one of the girls was heard to plead. "Please, please, give the people time to repent!" Their sobs and screams continued unabated for a period of hours while the crowd sank to its knees and fervently prayed in fear and bewilderment. Finally, their eyes swollen from tears, the children returned to the village. They had been given, they said, a vision of the chastisement that would come to the world unless humanity turns from materialism, greed and selfishness. Then on the following night, the feast of Corpus Christi, the terrible vision was repeated in what has come to be called "the nights of the screams." Speaking of the vision of the chastisement she witnessed, one of the young visionaries reportedly confided: "It would be worse than having fire on top of us --- fire underneath us and fire all around us. [I] saw people throwing themselves into the sea, but instead of putting the fire out it seemed to make them burn more."[23]

But of course this served only to fuel the already excessive apocalyptic flames of anxiety and anticipation that had been ignited by the still undisclosed portion of the secret of Fatima. What was it that evoked such terror in the children of Fatima, that was recapitulated in the visions at Garabandal and elsewhere, that now looms with ominous foreboding on our horizon? By what manner of scourge, by what unearthly efficacy of dispensation would the rod of divine justice be drawn down in Mary's words, "For [our] total purification through darkness, through fire and through blood"[24]? The answer seemed as imponderable as the source through which the warnings were given. But an answer would surely come.

While millions could only guess at the unbeknownst fate that threatened to lay their world to ruin, the warnings grew more and more insistent that "the time that you have left is short." Ever increasing references to a "great tempest" or "storm" which "will break with unprecedented fury" --- "As in the days of Noah...", did little to ease the confusion, particularly since they seemed defiantly in contrast to God's unyielding promise that "never again shall all flesh be cut off by the waters of the flood; never again shall there be a flood to destroy the earth" (Gen. 9:11). Then finally, in 1973, on the fifty-sixth anniversary of the miracle of Fatima, Mary specified for us in prophetic terms the wages of our sin. Speaking to the visionary and stigmatist Sister Agnes Sasagawa of Akita, Japan, Mary disclosed: "As I told you, if men do not repent and better themselves, the Father will inflict a terrible punishment on all of humanity. It will be punishment greater that the Deluge, such as one will never have seen before. Fire will fall from the sky and will wipe out a great part of humanity, the good as well as the bad... The survivors will find themselves so desolate that they will envy the dead."[25] It seems that in the old Negro spiritual there was truth after all: "God gave Noah the rainbow sign. No more water, the fire next time!"

MERCY OR JUSTICE

In retrospect, it is evident that this vision of chastisement was not born in Mary's heart. Surprisingly it has been warned of by prophets and visionaries throughout the ages. The renowned visionary Marie Julie Jahenny of La Fraudais, France, the "Stigmatist of Blain," foresaw in 1891: "There will come three days of continual darkness... During those three days demons will appear in abominable and horrible forms; they will make the air resound with shocking blasphemies. The lightning will penetrate the homes... Red clouds like blood will pass in the sky, the crash of thunder will make the earth tremble; lightning will flash through the streets at an unusual time of the year; the earth will tremble to its foundations; the ocean will cast its foaming waves over the land; the earth will be changed into an immense cemetery; the corpses of the wicked and the just will cover the face of the earth. The famine that will follow will be great. All vegetation will be destroyed as well as three fourths of the human race. The crisis will come all of a sudden and the chastisement will be world-wide."[26] The same message of warning has for the last twenty years been reported through Mother Elena Leonardi of Rome, Italy, through Father Gobbi, through Maria Esperanza, through the visionary experiences of the children of Medjugorje, only now with a supreme urgency: "The great trial has arrived for all humanity. The chastisement, predicted by me at Fatima and contained in that part of the secret which has not yet been revealed, is about to take place. The great moment of divine justice and of mercy has come upon the world."[27] If there were any remaining doubts as to the contents of the unpublished portion of the third secret of Fatima, Mary recently laid them to rest on the Feast of Our Lady of Sorrows when, in a locution to the Marian Movement of Priests, she stated: "A chastisement worse than the flood is about to come upon this poor and perverted humanity. Fire will descend from Heaven and this will be the sign that the justice of God has as of now fixed the hour of His great manifestation... Even now, that which I predicted at Fatima and that which I have revealed here in the third message confided to a little daughter of mine is in the process of being accomplished."[28]

Indeed this is at the very root of Mary's anguish. Again and again for generations she has delivered her watchword, hoping against hope to see a righteous world forming: "You live unconscious of the fate which is awaiting you. You are spending your days in a state of unawareness, of indifference and of complete incredulity. How is this possible when I, in so many ways and with extraordinary signs, have warned you of the danger into which you are running and have foretold you of the bloody ordeal which is just about to take place?"[29] Mankind's suffering is Mary's grief. God is about to bear His might before the eyes of all nations, and her grief is more that her soul can weep for. "[A]t least try to understand the reason for my concern," she implores. "It is dictated by love for man, for all that is human and which ... is threatened by an immense danger."[30]

Like a mother, I am telling you the dangers through which you are going, the immanent threats, the extent of the evils that could happen to you, only because these evils can yet be avoided by you, the dangers can be evaded. The plan of God's justice always can be changed by the force of His merciful love. Also, when I predict chastisements to you, remember that everything, at any moment, may be changed by the force of your prayer and your reparative penance.[31]

Herein lies Mary's role as the Mediatrix of divine graces and Advocate for humanity. Appearing before her children she pleads for God. For as awful a chastisement as this would be, for Mary our apostasy from the One is incomparably worse. Standing before God she pleads for her children, even though she knows that the pattern of our unrepentance is set and that it is unlikely that mankind will turn from divisiveness and self-will to love and grace. While there yet lies within her the ultimate hope that the whole world will be transformed, she leaves with us the promise that at least a remnant will remain: "In all the land, two-thirds of them will be cut off and perish," she tells Father Gobbi in 1992, "and one-third shall be left. I will pass this third through fire; I will refine it as silver is refined, test it as gold is tested."[32] She knows the divine justice to be an instrument necessary for redemption and sees these few, having been tried by fire, as but a foretaste of an abundant harvest of blessing. While the preeminent meaning of this great chastisement cannot be fully disclosed until the hour of our redemption, Mary assures us the great theophany is sure to follow: "From the perfect fulfillment of the Divine Will, the whole world is becoming renewed, because God finds there, as it were, His new Garden of Eden, where He can dwell in loving companionship with His creatures."[33]

> These are the times of the great return. Yes, after the time of the great suffering, there will be the time of the great rebirth, and all will blossom again. Humanity will again be a new garden of life and of beauty... You will at last see a new earth and new heavens.

> These are the times of great mercy. The Father thrills with ardor and wills to pour out upon this poor humanity the torrents of His infinite love. The Father wants to mold with his hands a new creation where His divine imprint will be more visible, welcomed and received, and His fatherhood exalted and glorified by all. The breath of this new creation will be the breathing of the love of the Father who will be glorified by all, while there will spread everywhere in an increasingly fuller way, like water which springs from a living and inexhaustible fount, the fullness of His divine love.

> ... And creation will again be a new garden where Christ will be glorified by all... It will be a universal reign of grace, of beauty, of harmony, of communion, of holiness, of justice and of peace. [34]

To Mary our time is an emergency, one fragile instant away from a cataclysmic event. Even more ominous, perhaps, than her warnings for these "final times" is her declaration that she would cease to manifest herself to the world when the ordeals of divine justice would begin to unfold and the calamities of tribulation were about to descend. Her voice is now all but silent. The hour of darkness has arrived. Throughout the world the apparitions as foretold are now withdrawing. The significance cannot be overstated. As the Source emphatically advises, **A time of redemption, or of destruction is at hand. Hear these words... those who have ears to hear** (Solomon Reading No. 1300, 3/17/88).

Chapter 12

Only Two Paths

Seeing that the courses of action are many and that our days for acting are numbered, the tragedy or triumph of our world lies in the power we possess to interact with the prophetic warnings that have been given, and in the extent to which we are able to embody rather than merely ritualistically mimic through the false piety of doctrines and dogmas the true faith that teaches mercy, kindness and love. It is the choice of each individual and of mankind as a whole:

> **The step of mankind into the Age of Enlightenment or destruction ... both of these paths lie before you. The step into the Age of Enlightenment, the step into the destruction of the planet, either could occur in this critical time, and in fact both can occur in the sense that many may be caught up, and the others left. And yet, out of it all will be produced a new Eden, a new blooming of a new planet after the time of transition** (Solomon Reading No. 1390, 11/7/88).

If the Great Awakening is not too late to somehow still regard these apocalyptic messengers, as Jonah was to Nineveh, as accessories before the fact, then perhaps they may yet succeed in arousing us in sufficient number to examine and weigh the probable ill-fated course that we are piloting. But let the truth be told: if in bringing our ship to port we cast aside sextant, compass and chart --- if we turn a deaf ear to the call of love --- then we are surely approaching the last leg of a fatal voyage. Echoing the assessment for human survival expressed by prophets throughout the ages, the Source emphatically warns that only two paths now lie before us: transcendence born of a creative love and utter destruction as a result of hatred and fear.

Fear is the source of all disorder and disintegration we are told. It is that which brings about the malignant aggression of crime and war, that which gives rise to all forms of exploitive control from domestic violence to despotic rule. It frustrates growth, dissipates energy, creates permanent unbalance, and denies all that is intensely good in itself. In the words of the Solomon Source, **fear and destruction are one and the same. That which destroys is fear. Thoughts of fear will destroy the mind and body. Thoughts of fear, thoughts of worry and disharmony will destroy mind, body, spirit, science, technology, environment, the planet itself** (Solomon Reading No. 1559, 9/15/91).

The Source in fact tells us: **This world has been a world ruled by fear. Fear is the destructive energy. A divided or bicameral mind can only create destruction** (Solomon Reading No. 1518, 9/1/91). Plainly, the corrosive effects of fear and spirit of destruction are evident in the continual rise and fall of civilizations, the pathological turpitude of kings and tyrants, the chronic unhappiness and degradation of the masses, and the barbarism of over 15,000 wars from the beginning of recorded history.

The greater sum of individuals, in every age and historic civilization, have lived only partial, fragmentary lives, beset by anxiety and fear. Whereas in times past, however, humanity could suffer the ill effects of fear --- of war, crime, famine, economic impoverishment --- survival and recovery never seemed to be an issue. There was always the assurance of some continuity to life, the assurance that the present would not cease to bear in its womb the seed of tomorrow. Such an assurance can no longer be confidently espoused. For at no previous time in human history have we been endangered by a crisis which threatens altogether the very conditions of life on the planet. Writing at the onset of the final fifty years of this past millennium, social critic Lewis Mumford observed: "If we continue on our present downward course, at the accelerated rate that marks the last half-century, the end of Western Civilization is in sight: very probably the end of all civilization for another millennium: possibly even the extinction of life in any form on this planet. For the first time in history, man has the means in his possession to commit collective genocide or suicide, on a scale sufficient to envelop the whole race. 'The end of the world' is no longer an apocalyptic hyperbole...."[35] Nearly fifty years following Mumford's ominous warning, the Source grimly advised: **If this earth is not healed within twenty years, you will not have a habitable planet for 2,000 years. After 2,000 years life would appear then once again, pristine, beginning to grow as Eden again.** (Solomon Reading No. 1248, 10/31/90). The conditions aggravating our potential for extinction evidently have worsened. Never before, in fact, have so many potential paths toward points of irreversible decline or wholesale destruction been opened before us.

By contrast, the equilibrium of the entire world, not merely peace, but collective justice, not only religions that are capable of filling the human heart with the spirit of universal fellowship, but a science and technology that are life-enhancing, rests on our capacity to achieve wholeness. And wholeness is impossible to achieve without giving primacy to the integrative elements within the individual: love, increasing self-awareness, the impulse to perfection and transcendence. Therefore, all that exists within us as diffused and contradictory first must become crystallized, purified, hard as a diamond, made brilliant through the power of unconditional love which *is* the power of One.

Then, affirms the Source:

> ... **if there can be a lifting of the level of consciousness, if there would not be the accepting of fate as it comes in this ending of time, but rather the belief that we can prepare, ... then we can relate to those who have given up hope for the salvation of this civilization.... Man, then, lifting himself nearer to the Godhead, will evolve. This planet, this universe, even the stars in their paths will be changed to that higher level of manifestation that will be a new formation, a new expression of God, of all that is** (Solomon Reading No. 1066, 1980).

The Source tells us that this power, the power of agape love, is at once the ground and the issue of the infinitely diverse host of all life. It is that which enhances growth, integration, transcendence, and renewal. It is the energy which powers the cosmos. It was Teilhard de Chardin who defined it as "the fundamental impulse of life...the one natural medium in which the rising course of evolution can proceed." Were we to grasp the depth, the perfect harmony, the profound significance of this one Law which embraces within its own comprehensiveness the essence and complexity of all universal law as it pertains both to the flesh and the spirit, through us would flow all power, a power that is at once energy, beauty, and force, a power that is alive and is life itself. **The power over life and death, over disease and destruction, over war and peace, that power is given to those who know love as the power of life and who do not entertain thoughts of fear,** declares the Source. **If you can give up your belief in fear and believe instead in the Law of Love, you can become enlightened beings** (Solomon Reading No. 1282, 3/5/88).

> If you may live as one whose heart, mind and life are so filled with the power of love, then you may also claim the promise of the Master [Christ] who promises only to the wisest of the wise. He has made the promise that, should you claim it through His nature, you may so, and so it will be true: "All power is given unto Me both in heaven and in earth." And this is not for the reason that you become a powerful force in world affairs or such particularly, but only that in your creativity, in your loving communication with the Source of life, you might always make petition for all beings on this entire planet and for this living earth herself; that you might claim all power in heaven and in earth to empower the healing of both the planet and her people; that the people of the earth gain knowledge and experience and the wisdom of knowing, finally, that the power, the force of love as an energy, a vitality, is far greater than that force related to fear, power, destruction, death, darkness (Solomon Reading No. 1642, 5/4/92).

Fear brings about separateness, teaches the Source, and with it violence which depletes our moral energy and power to change. By sheer force of habit if nothing more, radical transformation, so deeply alien to a culture of fear and violence, becomes impossible. The impetus of the force of life itself, in most of us, is limited by inertia, and the accepted pattern of fear and response, far from allowing for dynamic unity and synthesis, creates a static monolithic body of dogma marked chiefly by a paranoid isolationism that divides us --- sect by sect, religion by religion, nation by nation. Thus we condemn ourselves by our denial of a truth that is single, and by our implacable unwillingness to fill the space of the eternal by plunging into the world's fate. Instead, we invest our hope for salvation in science, in political leadership or ideology, in the return of a Messiah, to relieve us of the responsibilities which are ours alone to bear, of the choices which we alone must make. "The task of the individual Messiah of the past now devolves equally on all men," writes Lewis Mumford, "likewise the burden of sacrifice. No Diogenes need run through the streets with his lantern looking for an honest man: no John the Baptist need perform a preliminary cleansing and absolution upon others, while waiting for the true prophet to come. Those are the images and expectations of another era. Today each one of us must turn the light of the lantern inward upon himself; and while he stays at his post, performing the necessary work of the day, he must direct every habit and act and duty into a new channel: that which will bring about unity and love. Unless each one of us makes this obligation a personal one, the change that must swiftly be brought about cannot be effected." Echoing the Source, Mumford concludes: "The new age will begin when a sufficient number of men and women in every land and culture take upon themselves the burden men once sought to transfer to an Emperor, a Messiah, a dictator, a single God-like man. That is the ultimate lesson..., the burden cannot be shifted. But if each one of us, in his own full degree, accepts this desperate condition for survival, that which seemed a threat to man's further development will be transformed into a dynamic opportunity."[36]

The Source maintains, therefore, that for each of us, for all of us alike, the moment of reconciliation and renewal has come. The day and the hour are at hand when we must choose between the forces of darkness and fear and the power of unconditional love. Both paths lie before us; one leads to death, the other to life. "If", in the words of Jonathan Schell, "we choose the first path --"

> if we numbly refuse to acknowledge the nearness of extinction, all the while increasing our preparations to bring it about --- then we in effect become the allies of death, and in everything we do our attachment to life will weaken: our vision, blinded to the abyss that has opened at our feet, will dim and grow confused; our will, discouraged by the thought of trying to build on such a precarious foundation anything that is meant to last, will slacken; and we will sink into stupefaction, as though we were gradually weaning ourselves from life in preparation for the end. On the other hand, if we reject our doom, and bend our efforts toward survival --- if we arouse ourselves to the peril and act to forestall it, making ourselves the allies of life --- then the anesthetic fog will lift: our vision, no longer straining not to see the obvious, will sharpen; our will, finding secure ground to build on, will be restored; and we will take full and clear possession of life again.[37]

We now find ourselves, as Matthew Arnold would say, suspended between two worlds: one dead, the other powerless to be born. The old world with its accumulation of knowledge and mastery over nature, in which the pathologies of power and fear have shaped the destinies of individuals and nations and the fate of a living Earth, is coming to an end. But if we do not seek immediately to renew our human participation in the grand liturgy of the universe, the new world may be powerless to be born. **For you live in a time, a day when the people of earth are destroying earth and self through the manner of relationship with the planet, the care, the responsibility for this earth, this temple,** declares the Source. **You live in a time when changes will frighten many. You live in the time of Armageddon. You live in a time of increased activity of volcanoes, of earthquakes, of disease, of the realization that man in his responsibility for the planet has lost control; that the relationship has been a destructive one because of fear, because actions and thoughts and relationships are molded by,**

motivated by, built of fear, and there is a better way (Solomon Reading No. 1173, 8/84).

Therefore we must overcome all fear. We must "find a way beyond the continuous chain reaction of craving, jealousy, ill will, indifference, fear, and anxiety that fills the mind." writes Charlene Spretnak. "Find a way that dissolves the deeply ingrained patterns of negative, distrustful behavior caused by past cruelty and disappointment. Find a way that demonstrates to you that ill will and greed are damaging to your psyche. Find a way that grounds your deeds in wisdom, equanimity, compassion, and loving kindness. Find a way that reveals to you the joy of our profound unity, the subtle interrelatedness of you and every being, every manifestation of the unfolding universe. Find a way that will continually deepen your understanding of that knowledge. Then we could build a community without hypocrisy. Then we would have a chance."[38] If we are to find the way, we must **first understand and reestablish upon this planet the Law of One,** declares the Source. **For the Law of One is the ruling law of the universe to which you must come in harmony** (Solomon Reading No. 1069, 1/14/81).

Part Four

Awakening:
From The Beast To The Gods

Chapter 13

Mark Of The Beast

A BIRD IN THE HAND

The New York Zoo had some years ago installed in its Great Ape House an exhibit entitled "The Most Dangerous Animal in the World." Situated squarely between the gorilla and the orangutan compartments, the exhibit consisted of a full-length mirror with the text:

> YOU ARE LOOKING AT THE MOST DANGEROUS ANIMAL IN THE WORLD. IT ALONE, OF ALL THE ANIMALS THAT EVER LIVED, CAN EXTERMINATE (AND HAS) ENTIRE SPECIES OF ANIMALS. NOW IT HAS ACHIEVED THE POWER TO WIPE OUT ALL LIFE ON EARTH.

Looking into this mirror we are confronted with a contradiction. Concealed beneath a thoroughly civilized veneer lies an estranged and murky assortment of mad passions. What essentially is this elusive, paradoxical and often malevolent human something that peers back? Who are we really? Which is the substance and which the shadow?

We are pursuantly led to ask: with the means it has already devised for our ultimate extinction, is this beast fated to return the earth to a primeval incandescent mass? Or does it have within itself the ability and will to choose conscience over cunning? And if darkness, war and self-destruction are inherently locked up within its nature, then how much time have we left before it employs those means for our ultimate extinction?

For several centuries we have operated under the assumption that we can understand the universe without understanding ourselves, and have in fact exalted change in everything but ourselves. What a fantastic irony that we have leaped centuries ahead in inventing a new technological world to satisfy our material wants, but know little if anything about our part in that world. Figuring into all the other equations that portend our return to a new stone-age future --- politics, religion, corporate imperialism, militarism, nationalism --- the one great unknown remains the very nature of ourselves. This, despite the fact that all of human history has been nothing more than an exteriorization of ourselves, of human thought and intent. What perpetually goes on in the human brain manifests itself in the patterning of human events. It is therefore here, within our nature as the human animal, that the whole drama of our existence as a species and our world will play itself out. No amount of tinkering with our institutions will be sufficient to ensure our survival unless we can make the necessary changes within ourselves, among ourselves, and in our own relationship with the earth.

Beginning with mankind's initial "Fall" from a conscious union with his source and into a subsequent blindness and insensitivity to his own divine nature, we have become creatures wholly wedded to the flesh, subject to the limitations of corroding fear, ignorance and narcissistic deceit. That is what makes us so dangerous, and why the angels, the forces of truth and justice, were opposed to the creation of man. It was foreseen that mankind's divided and polarized self would create nothing but evil and destruction. And it is why the history of mankind has been a history of God's disappointment.

> **Then, has it not inspired the wrath of God even as in that time of Noah, that He would repent to the opportunities given to men for their despising of what is set before them so clearly? Has not even the Apostle written that the very wonders that stand before you are witness against you for your refusal to recognize their message of truth and that that they teach?** (Solomon Reading No. 895, 10/21/76).

Once already the world was destroyed --- by flood. But through Noah a second opportunity was afforded. Noah and his descendants, however, offered in their thoughts and actions little in the way of assurance that God's covenant would be honored. So again He revealed His will to this people at Sinai, transforming them into a holy nation, that through them the world might come to know the Lord and follow His ways. If His covenant with its Royal Law, "Thou shalt love thy neighbor as thyself", were to be followed, the world would survive; but if it is not, if mankind continues to be ruled by hatred and passion, it will be turned back into chaos.

Judging from the less than favorable directions to which a seemingly incorrigible humanity is currently headed, it is self-evident to most of us that, collectively, its virtues have lost out to brutishness, ignorance and, perhaps, annihilation. "An important question to consider today," reflects Solomon, "is how nearly that describes where each of us is in this moment. If we are indeed God, children of God, why do we not think with the mind of God and express all the attributes of God? Why are we not creative in the greatest sense of being God? Why are we not aware of being one with the body and mind of God? Why are we limited to the five senses of the flesh? The Master of masters who was the greatest initiate of this world, said, 'That which is born of the flesh is flesh; and that which is born of the Spirit is Spirit. Ye must be born again.' (John 3:6) You must be reborn into who you were in the beginning. Essentially, those creatures of the Fall who originally were imprisoned in the flesh were creatures that were being held under the mark of the beast, as mentioned in scripture. (Revelation 20:4) They were trapped within the body of the beast, slaves to the five senses of the flesh. And we might ask ourselves where we are in relation to that? To what degree are we slaves of the senses, the appetites and the flesh in this day?"[1]

The answer, as implied by the question, not only speaks to the prophetic times in which we live but may hold the key to our fate. The prophet Isaiah foretells of the "last days" that "the Lord shall lay waste the earth, and shall strip it, and shall afflict the face thereof, and scatter abroad the inhabitants thereof.... With desolation shall the earth be laid waste, and it shall be utterly spoiled: for the Lord hath spoken this word. The earth mourned, and faded away, and is weakened: the world faded away, the height of the people of the earth is weakened. And the earth is infected by the inhabitants thereof: because they have transgressed the laws, they have changed the ordinance, they have broken the everlasting covenant. Therefore shall a curse devour the earth, ... and therefore they that dwell therein shall be mad, and few men shall be left." (Is. 24:1 ff). Is the living Earth not already in mourning? Infected like a malignancy of cells by its own inhabitants, is the earth not already being poisoned, stripped and made desolate? Having transgressed the Law of Life, have we not broken the covenant with He who is the Giver of life itself? And if the ever darkening shadows of hatred and fear continue to thicken into the fatal storm of what the Source has foreseen as a globally apocalyptic war to dwarf all others, insanity will have indeed seized the minds of those few remaining. As Albert Einstein once warned: "The unleashed power of the atom has changed everything save our modes of thinking, and thus we drift to unparalleled catastrophe."

Yet it need not come to this, for as the Source reminds us, **"where there be prophecies, they shall fail."** Put in another way, *any* prophecy that has come to pass is a prophecy that has failed to bring people to a needed awareness of change --- in themselves, their character, their behavior, their spiritual attitudes --- without which the inexorable momentum of future events will continue to form and unfold into tragic consequences:

> This is meant to say to you, you are given a measure of free will. It is the purpose of this channel and these Readings to look at the moment now, the moment at which the Reading itself is given, to look at the direction being taken, the decision being made by the consciousness or consciousnesses of the individuals in the moment. Now, as a result of the Reading giving warning in prophecy saying, "Your actions and thoughts up to this moment have decreed that there may be in this incident or that which will occur within a year, two years, or five years." The information given is accurate, completely, at the moment given. Do understand that after five minutes it may no longer be accurate, for it is the nature of your minds to sometimes heed warnings, to change the mind, to make plans, to move in different directions. Then, that record, written on the skein of time and space, must be consulted again to see if such result of actions and thoughts have been altered by different directions taken, by decisions of mankind or a single individual. So it has been that the prophecies given through these Readings, these Records, have been accurate for the moment in which they were given and never intended to be accurate any longer than that, for they were given for the purpose of influencing the consciousness and the direction, the intent, the action of the individual. They are not given for the purpose of being accurate.

> It has been said before through these Readings, "A prophecy of discomfort, a prophecy of dire circumstances, of hunger, of starvation, of tragedy, such a prophecy, should it come true as prophesized, is a prophecy that has failed." It failed to cause individuals to change thoughts and action, thus tragedy was not averted even though the prophecy was given.

> Then do understand that it may appear from time to time that these Readings are inaccurate. They are not. Assure yourself of that for we come to you as a result of the prayers of your attunement; we come to you strictly regulated by the wishes and the Will of the Christ. This is a barrier beyond which we cannot cross (Solomon Reading No. 1167, 12/04/84).

Hence, the visions, as given by the Source, of impending cataclysmic change
--- geophysical, geopolitical, or otherwise --- *will* come to pass "as prophesied." The pattern of such events is already established. The actual timing
of their occurrence and manner of their fulfillment, however, is never firmly
fixed. Rather, it is dependent on the free will and determination, on **the actions, the reactions, the thoughts, the purposes of man.**"

The Solomon Source has stressed repeatedly that we are living in the "last
days", and that God has provided prophets in these final days that we may
have the opportunity to know, to prepare, to change our thoughts and attitudes to a greater awareness of the universal order. This is exactly why the
Source has manifested its presence among us --- to influence our minds in
their effect on the unfolding course of future events. And just as Nineveh was
spared its destructive fate by heeding God's warning as delivered through His
prophet Jonah, so too we are given the same warnings and opportunity for
change as delivered through no less a prophet than Solomon. This time, however, it is not the fate of a single city that hangs in the balance, but that of an
entire world:

> The step of mankind into the Age of Enlightenment or destruction ... both
> of these paths lie before you. The step into the Age of Enlightenment, the
> step into the destruction of the planet, either could occur in this critical
> time, and in fact both can occur in the sense that many may be caught up,
> and the others left. And yet, out of it all will be produced a new Eden, a new
> blooming of a new planet after the time of transition (Solomon Reading No.
> 1390, 11/7/88).

Gerry Spence, a self-described "old country lawyer" from Wyoming, tells the
story of a wise old man and a smart-aleck boy who wanted to show up the
wise old man as a fool. One day this boy caught a small bird in the forest. The
boy had a plan. He brought the bird, cupped between his hands, to the old
man. His plan was to say, "Old man, what do I have in my hands?" to which
the old man would answer, "You have a bird, my son." Then the boy would
say, "Old man, is the bird alive or dead?" If the old man said the bird was
dead, the boy would open his hands and the bird would fly freely back to the
forest. But if the old man said the bird was alive, then the boy would crush
the little bird, and crush it, and crush it until it was dead. So the smart-aleck
boy sauntered up to the old man and said, "Old man, what do I have in my
hands?" And the old man said, "You have a bird, my son." Then the boy said
with a malevolent grin, "Old man, is the bird alive or is it dead?" And the old
man, with sad eyes, said, "The bird is in your hands, my son."

So it is with us. As the old song goes, "we've got the whole world in our
hands." For Spence, the story is an effective tool for transforming a purely
rational closing argument into a persuasive emotional plea. With a defend-
ant's fate now in their hands, a jury is more inclined to mercy, to "set the bird
free." But what about the fate of the world? The choice is ours: malevolence or
mercy. It is we who future generations will put on trial, not so much because of
the enlightened choices we failed to make as what the reflections of the mirror
have revealed to us about the battlefield of contending forces within our nature. Having closed the true "doors of perception," we are no longer open to a

higher undivided truth. And so, even though the destiny of the world remains in our hands, history will record that we've shown it little in the way of mercy. How much should we expect in return?

If the fate of the Earth looks grim, it is therefore not that in our mercy and concern we would choose for things to be the way they are; rather, we've failed to confront and transform what *we* are into beings that are even *capable* of single-minded choice. For in our divided nature it is the predatory part of ourselves, the dark part that we simply ignore or deny, that rules the vast range of our incapacity. Its appetites are healthily and daringly omnivorous, and to the extent that it requires persistent feeding, it will, if compelled, ravish and devour even our sense of humanity as it has indiscriminately over the course of the past century. A story, believed to be of Cherokee origin, tells of a young girl troubled by a recurring dream in which two wolves fight viciously. Seeking an explanation, she goes to her grandfather, highly respected for his wisdom, who explains that there are two forces within each of us struggling for supremacy; one embodying peace and the other, war. At this, the girl is even more distressed, and asks her grandfather who wins. His answer: "The one you feed." It is this that determines whether our hopes and dreams and aspirations for an awakening of the flesh to the collective life-affirming genesis of a new spiritual Eden ends in fulfillment or in the doomed failure that is our final tragedy.

YAHOOS WILL BE YAHOOS

What we call the future is in a sense always an illusion, it having no being whatever until the present has already ceased to exist. And the greatest disillusion that we suffer from, more so today than perhaps at any time since the days of Noah, is the assumption of the continuity of our civilization and, beneath our saber-rattling superficies, mankind's continuing development toward a relatively sane and survivable planetary culture.

On the surface, the assumption appears worthy of credence. By means of the internet and all of the informational and digital communication devices by which we are globally interconnected, the human world is becoming one system. Its regions have become interdependent economically and, to a certain extent, culturally. An article posted by an online blogger in one part of the world immediately becomes part of a system accessible to anyone with a PC and an internet connection anywhere, rapidly becoming part of the common conversation for millions. Even China with its strict censorship will sooner or later democratize, not because its Communist leadership are looking to extend the cause of human liberty, but because its young, entrepreneurial, net-savvy population will demand it. The World Wide Web with its fiber-optics, ethernet cables and satellite links has been likened to cells firing across synapses in the human brain, a globally ubiquitous nervous system connecting all of humanity into a unified organism. A wishful thought.

Yet beneath it all, the world continues teetering fitfully, lurching from crisis to crisis. The redivisioning of the world into rich and poor states; the appearance of radical fundamentalist movements; the rise of ethnic hatred and xenophobic nationalism; terrorist movements in the ascendancy and the collapse into chaos of nearly the whole of the Middle East; the degeneration of politics into the art of evasion, with politicians as assuagers rather than leaders and power-brokers rather than healers; the rule of international banks and transnational corporations --- all raise fundamental questions about the future of the human race, now clearly experiencing a renaissance of ignorance, barbarism and deceit.

And of the great transparency that optimists envisioned the internet would bring to the world? Most users log onto sites and read only that material that supports their preconceived prejudices, opinions and beliefs, linking them with others in a continually reinforcing feedback loop that tends to harden ever more into a cyber-conceptualized world of polarized extremes. Rather than uniting us, the internet has played a key role in further dividing us. We may sincerely yearn toward a vision of universal peace and understanding, but distorted by preconceptions and predilections forced upon us by our own flawed and fragmented nature, we yearn in vain. Neither within ourselves nor within the race of humanity as a whole can we attain it.

Our nature, it seems, is made up of antipathies. We are taught to think, and are willing to believe, that our rational intellect subdues the beast within us and that love, above all, has its seat in the human heart. Time and again, however, our frail loyalty to love and reason has surrendered itself to our basest nature. With the least indulgence love turns to indifference or hate while the trammels of civilization along with all its intellectual refinements --- the flimsy veil of humanity --- yield themselves to the rooted prejudices and deadly animosities of sects and parties in politics and religion and in the brute force of contending nations at war. As much as we'd like to place our trust in the innocence and inherent goodness of others, still, we teach our children to "Beware". We know all too well the truth, that the world suffers from evil people ruthless in their pursuit and exercise of power. Vigilance is born experience. "Be ye therefore wise as serpents, and harmless as doves," (Matthew 10:16) instructs Jesus.

In the acclaimed thirteen-part BBC television series *The Ascent of Man*, the mathematician, poet and historian Jacob Bronowski is filmed scooping a handful of muck from a dead and dismal swamp. Slowly looking up into the camera, he speaks to the audience: "This is the concentration camp and crematorium at Auschwitz. This is where people were turned into numbers. Into this pond were flushed the ashes of some four million people. And that was not done by gas. It was done by arrogance. It was done by dogma. It was done by ignorance. When people believe that they have absolute knowledge, with no test in reality, this is how they behave. This is what men do when they aspire to the knowledge of gods." [2]

Unravelling the web of human nature into its various threads, we find woven among the higher virtues those of arrogance, vindictiveness, shallowness, untruthfulness and unforgivingness, false pride, want of feeling, and indifference towards others, and ignorance of ourselves, revealing nothing more than that we are creatures who lie to ourselves about who we really are. We suffer from a crisis of identity, no less than Gulliver in Swift's allegorical masterpiece, when he travels to the land of the Yahoos and the Houyhnhnms. Here Gulliver finds the mirror depictions of humanity, reason and passion, precisely separated and embodied respectively in these two creatures. Whereas the savage Yahoos are beastly, detestable and un-civilized, a wholly degenerate species of man, the Houyhnhnms, though led by a life of reason, are simultaneously exempt from all love, friendship, fear, sorrow, anger and hatred, save for their anger and hatred toward the loathsome Yahoos. Following his sojourn, Gulliver resigns himself to the idea that we are all just a bunch of Yahoos, the personification of the beastial in human nature. Whereas reason may mask our natural deprav-ity, nevertheless it only enables humans "to aggravate their natural cor-ruptions and to acquire new ones which Nature had not intended." The beast that is the lower self continues to run the show. What's more, in be-ing too arrogant and proud to accept the rational absurdity and animality of our nature, as a race we are, it seems, cursed for all time to be our own worst and perhaps mortal enemy.

Paul Solomon looks at it this way:

> Humans are naturally capable of more thoughts, moods, emotions, feelings and appetites for good and bad than any other living being on this planet. Included in who you are is the ability to express a range of so-called negative emotions including anxiety, resentment, anger, jealousy, hurt and hate. All these expressions are perfectly natural.

> It is natural for you to feel, think and do all the things that you feel, think and do. It is natural for you to feel angry and vengeful, even to fantasize about killing someone. It is even natural for you to kill, given certain circumstances. It is natural for you to have sexual urges and fantasies because all these expressions are natural and are all right to experience. You cannot express incorrectly. You can only express what is in your nature.

> However, it is important to know that you did not make that nature. That nature is an aspect of this planet earth. It is an aspect of a liv-ing beast that occupies this planet and lives within its inhabitants. It is natural for you to express that beast within you, which includes the complete range of emotions and feelings that God ever created and put on this planet.

> Here is an important key for understanding this point. Outside this planet, you would not experience the nature of this earthly beast. It is a consequence of living on this planet.

> As a result of living on earth, you express the beast nature that rules this planet. The king or ruler of the beast nature of this planet is called by many names, including Satan. Satan's kingdom is the king-dom of Earth. And all of that is all right. It is natural for the beast

to act like a beast, which means to participate in the life and death cycle of this planet.

Consider the lesson of the frog and the scorpion. The scorpion wanted to get to the other side of the river, so he asked the frog to carry him across. The frog answered, "You'll sting me if I let you ride on my back." The scorpion responded, "Surely I wouldn't sting you because then we would both drown." The frog, trusting in this logic, allowed the scorpion onto his back and began the journey across the river. Halfway across, the scorpion stung the frog. As both began to sink below the surface, the frog cried out, "Why did you sting me? Now we will both die." The scorpion stated matter-of-factly, "I couldn't help myself. It's my nature."

It is important, even crucial, to understand that your personal beastly expressions are natural and that they are all right. A scorpion can be nothing but a scorpion. Individuals who resist that part of self will wrestle needlessly and unsuccessfully, so it is important to accept all aspects of the beast nature within you.

Confusion arises when you try to put all of this into a religious context, believing that you are supposed to behave in a "morally good" way. It is impossible to force the beast to act in a way that is not like a beast.[3]

In short, Yahoos will be Yahoos, and there's not a damned thing any of us can do to change it. It is an undeniable part of our terrestrial nature. It doesn't really matter who we are --- academicians, aristocrats, ecclesiastics, salt-of-the-earth types, or those of us who may think we may have a smidgen or more of polish --- we know in our genes and in the dirty back roads of our minds that we are all a bunch of Yahoos. And the mess that we've made of our disordered world stands as grim, irrefutable evidence. So rooted are we in the nature of the beast that we fail to even realize that it is nothing less than the beast of Revelation that lives within us. Like an active volcano that smolders even when not actually erupting, Paul Solomon tells us that the smoldering fires of Armageddon are already upon us:

The Great Creator of this planet Earth gave us the responsibility for her care. She is a living, breathing, conscious being, at the mercy of our actions.

Interestingly, in this [past] century we have manipulated the environment so that the climate and the temperature of the planet have been altered. We fill the atmosphere with pollutants, putting filters between the earth and the sun --- our planet and her Father, so to speak. We have altered delicate balances between carbon dioxide and oxygen, acid and alkaline. We are the dubious inventors of acid rain. As we destroy trees without replacing them, we alter the delicate balance that sustains this planet, and we leave her surface, which is her skin, to become hard, brittle and cracked.

The order of this Eden was so specifically designed and set in motion that, left alone, a perfect balance would be maintained to produce and sustain life. But humankind continually attempts to improve what is perfect by manipulating it. We create acres and acres of one kind of plant, providing a banquet for certain insects and inviting imbalance in the delicate symbiosis between plants that naturally grow side-by-side to nourish and protect each other. Then we use chemicals to destroy those insects, and we poison our children and ourselves simultaneously. The patterns of destruction go on and on. We are destroying our own life support system --- the planet for which we were given responsibility --- and ourselves along with it....

More relevant to each of us personally, even more relevant that the ecological issues, is another factor: anything that destroys the life of our planet is the expression of the beast. Anything that we use as an opportunity to escape responsibility for the maintenance of this planet, its health and its joy, is the very nature of the beast, the enemy in the battle of Armageddon.[4]

TAMING THE ENDOGENOUS BEAST

As we sink further and further into our obsessive need to conquer, subjugate and master the physical world all for our own use, the earth continues its inexorable slide into environmental collapse --- a consequence of the insatiability of an omnivorous beast. The crowning vulgarity, however, is a cynical justification of our militant and apocalyptic inveteracies premised on our own superiority, that we are uniquely conscious beings, a creation precious in the eyes of a god conceived in our own image. Through the eyes of the ego, we find nothing companionable in all the vast spacial world outside our senses. Though we may gaze with wonder into a night sky rippled with stars, still, our fascination is rendered upon nothing more than an appreciation of the vastness of the great mechanism of natural forces. The earth, stars, galaxies --- all but lifeless clumps of inert matter and gas, each traversing its seasons, each blindly conveyed by electromagnetic waves in its purely mechanical and gravitational path through the heavens. We've cleverly convinced ourselves that we alone are sentient beings trapped (perhaps with others amongst the stars equally so advanced) in the desolation of an infinity that offers no warmth, no consolation, no love.

"The modern industrial societies have been reared on a vision of nature that teaches people they are a mere accident in a galactic wilderness," observes Theodore Roszak: "'strangers and afraid' in a world they never made. What stance in life can they then take but one of fear, anxiety, even hostility toward the natural world? Like children who see their parents as remote, powerful, and punishing authorities, they will feel they have no choice but to stand defensively on guard, looking for every opportunity to strike out. Their encounter with nature will not be grounded in trust and security, let alone love. This is the point where epistemology, cosmology, and psychology intersect. The picture of the cosmos we carry in our minds can dictate a range of existential conditions. We may live sunk in bleak, defensive despair or we may find ourselves gracefully at home in the world. In addition to *what* we know, there is *how* we know, the spirit in which we address the world."[5]

What we are in need of most is a sense of connection with the ineffable source of ourselves which is harmoniously synchronized with the source of all being. Without that we cannot in the deepest sense be said to be truly 'aware'. In fact, were we for one brief instant to awaken from the almost miraculous stupor of our vanity and ignorance which are but the veiled culmination of our fears, perhaps we would see what Plato saw more than 2,000 years ago when he described the entire universe as "one Whole of wholes... a single Living Creature that encompasses all of the living creatures that are within it." Perhaps we would come to know what mystics have known for millennia and what biologists such as James Lovelock and others have been telling us for decades, that our Earth is a living conscious being that needs to be recognized and trusted as such. Maybe we would experience what Apollo 14 astronaut Edgar Mitchell experienced in 1971 on his return trip from the moon, "an overwhelming sense of universal connectedness" with "an intelligent and entirely conscious universe." Or maybe, just maybe, if we were not so ignorant of our own essential inner being we would not be so ignorant of the inner sentient being of the Earth.

So long as we accept that "reality" is ultimately determined by nothing but a strict and precise description of the world as perceived through our senses, we will axiomatically reject as irrational and unreal anything that defies our measurement and control. We will remain as prisoners of our own bestial delusions. What looks unreal within the limits of the senses, however, may be luminous within the scope of an eternal Self. Though we continue to live through the impoverished state of our senses, we but live as beasts, surrounded by a wilderness of our own superficial lies. It is this that has twisted and distorted the very basis of our lives, deceiving us into believing we live in a reality that does not exist. This, according to Solomon, is the natural consequence of our 'Fall'. It is the mark under which we all now live:

> It is observable that almost everyone on this planet is already living under the mark of the beast. People are living in such a way that the beast, which is also named fear, is dictating to them whether they are happy, whether they are contented with life, whether they are afraid of life. People are living in fear, as victims. And that is the mark of the beast....

> We are children of fear, living in darkness. It is a serious matter. Billions of people on earth, 99.9% of us, are living under the mark of the beast. Armageddon is already here. Do not give into the conspiracy that warns against some future event, a rising dictator, a world economic system that employs tattooed numbers. That would be too obvious. Satan is clever and deceitful, and knows how to appear as the prince of light. The personification of evil, darkness and fear can disguise itself to look like anything other than what it is.

> We are destroying our planet by the methods we use to manipulate her ability to grow and provide for us. We assume that ecological matters are for someone else to solve and that it has nothing to do with Armageddon. Better rethink that one!

It is time to realize that whatever gives you a reason to express anything other than total love to yourself, to other living beings, to Mother Earth and to your source of life is a part of the great conspiracy that creates hell on earth. If we are supporting the enemy in our relationships with each other, we are engaged in the battle. And we are on the wrong side.[6]

This is in no sense an exaggeration. Humanity from the beginning has been plagued with darkness and fear. This is the one coherent pattern that stands out in all of human history, no more so than in our own time.

From the rise of our self-consciousness, the result of our Fall into separateness, and the ensuing terror at finding ourselves alone and cut off from our fellow beings and from our inextricable unity with the world, the beast in us took hold. From that time to this, as our self-conscious pride has grown, so too our alienation has grown ever more harsh and discordant.

Satan has had plenty of time to perfect his techniques. He rules us with ever greater ease because we no longer know or believe or even care if he is there. Nor is the underlying principle of our spiritual unity with life any longer believed in, nor the fellowship of our humanity. The myth of Satan has been laid to rest alongside all the sacred myths and ancient teachings of our "primitive" ancestors. But this has not freed us, rather Satan. He rules us through our pride, the deadliest of deadly sins, the sin by which Satan had himself fallen. And he rules through the beast, the beast that lies within us. Hence, the battle of Armageddon is upon us now, for as St. Paul tells us, "we wrestle not against flesh and blood, but against principalities, against powers, against the rulers of the darkness of this world, against spiritual wickedness in high places." [7]

For those hopelessly old-fashioned believers who look forward to the day when the final establishment of a Messianic kingdom will put an end to all sin and suffering, they too must know that by meritoriously numbering themselves among the "chosen few" and cynically abandoning responsibility toward the things they inwardly loathe, they are merely subsidizing the whims that arise within a community of certified beasts. We are simply on the wrong side if we support fear; the wrong side if we give energy to pride; the wrong side if we passively abdicate to the powers of evil the fate of our world. Solomon places the responsibility squarely on our own shoulders:

> Many of today's prophets predict that a world dictator will take power soon and that the inhabitants of earth will be forced to wear tattooed numbers, necessary for buying and selling goods. By interpreting the message of John's Revelation of Christ to mean that there is a ruler who is going to threaten the whole world, we can effectively externalize the message and make someone else responsible for it. We can look at nations with suspicion and fear, and justifiably add millions to our military defense funds. We can watch dictators and rulers who rise to power around the world, wondering if he or she is the one. We can watch for the number 666, believing that its appearance will confirm our identification of the beast. Yes, then we will know who the beast is.

Searching the horizon for the beastly dictator is part of the great conspiracy, because it keeps our attention turned outward, and it sustains the battle between love and fear that rages within us. Two mistakes are commonly made in interpreting the warning of John's Revelation. One is to externalize responsibility. The other is to cast it into the future.

The beast is here now! His power is already revealing itself. He is already dictating to people whether they may live or die, whether they may feel good or bad, whether they may feel loved or rejected, whether they may feel alright or not. The beast is the animal nature within you, and it uses the senses and the appetites of that nature to rule over you.

When the appetites of the beast dictate whether you can feel good or whether you can feel happy, joyous and alive, or whether you can express your true self, you are already tattooed with the mark of the beast. The beast is alive, ruling your thoughts and your actions. The vile dictator has claimed power over the world --- your world.[8]

The beast is dauntingly clever, using any ruse of self-deception or camouflage in order to survive. While outwardly and collectively its footprints are well-defined in the toxic soils of the battlefields of the earth, in cults, religions, and nations and in the cold-blooded rape of our planet, it is completely obscured from our own consciousness. It is ironic indeed that, outwardly so clearly visible in the character and conduct of others, it is rarely seen for what it is within ourselves. Nevertheless, it is a force of our raw nature. We, too, are stumbling in the shackles of our beastial quiddity, staggering through a world where heavenly virtues are few and where our inherited fallen nature, even though unrecognized, has so often brought us nothing but misery in our personal lives. The lineaments of whose countenance we see in others may be prefigured in our own --- appetites and addictions, lust for power, possessiveness, manipulative agendas, deceit, chaotic emotions, and so forth. The more we deny them, the more they weigh us down. The abject negativity and destructiveness of the beast is a function of the degree to which we neglect and/or refuse to take responsibility for it, only inflaming its ferocity and pernicious power.

As Paul Solomon explains:

When we enter this material universe, we must use a body to experience the laws of this planet and to learn the lessons that this planet presents. Our spirits are housed in these bodies for a time, yet these bodies have a nature of their own that is not the nature of God. It is a beast nature. It is an aspect of the living beast that occupies earth and lives within its inhabitants. As long as you inhabit the body, that beast nature will be a factor in your experience.

Rejection of any kind of animal causes problems. Without understanding and acceptance of its ordered nature, the animal will rebel. In gaining control over a wild animal, there are a couple of options. The spirit of the animal can be broken, pitting will against will. Or the animal can be tamed through a gentle, tolerant process of winning trust and cooperation.

Most often, when a horse is broken, control is gained through brute strength and illusion. Horses are physically stronger than humans, but they are made to believe the opposite through methods that can be cruel. Similarly, the beast in you is naturally stronger than any fabricated or forced desire within you to change your nature to something you consider to be good. Trying to break the will of your beast will not work.

The goal is not to change wild tigers into docile pussycats. It would be an insult to the creator of those beings if we did. When we try to discipline our minds and our bodies into a forced obedience of rules and codes of behavior that are contrary to our natural desires, yearnings and appetites, we get restrained, inhibited, explosive, unnatural human beings. Religions produce them. Society produces them. Families produce them.

When we try to control our natural yearnings and instincts by force of will --- by saying, "I will make myself behave so that I can fit into society and meet the criteria of religions and laws," --- we fight against our natural will. And when we fight against something, it perceives that it is unacceptable, condemned, feared and hated. Any animal sensing those feelings in an owner will become stubborn, or will do the same thing. It is the nature of the beast to do so.

As you exist in this physical body, it is not wrong for you to experience your nature in all its aspects, including your emotions, your feelings, your instincts and your expressions. However, it is inappropriate for you to believe that the nature of your body, your animal, your beast, is your only or true nature.[9]

THE INTRINSIC SELF

If all that we know is not all that we are, what, then, of the veiled presence of our true Self? If it is indeed a being other than our conscious self, imperceptible to our senses, yet dwelling in the depth of our own nature, is it somehow ourselves though infinitely more? If we could reach back through time to the moment of creation, Solomon tells us, we would see it as the very child of the Source of all light and life and love. If not narrowed and corrupted by fear, we would be raised instantly from our obsessive individualism into its universal radiance. "The other nature is not a participant in the life and death cycle of this planet," Solomon informs us. "The other nature is a continuous, sustaining, creative consciousness. It does not grow through the death of other things. It has no natural instinct to kill and eat, to cause death and recycle life. It has no appetite for reproduction. That which does not die does not need to reproduce. The other nature can only create.... It is an archetypical, everlasting nature --- and it is yours. It is your intrinsic divine nature."[1]

It is the ultimate Principle, the Atman of Hindu teachings, the Solomon "Source", the Intrinsic Self that is the essence of all human existence. Untouched by age or death or sorrow, it is our macrocosmic being suffused with eternal life, the still, silent, unchanging ground that is wholly present in every living and conscious being which is itself subject to perpetual change. As Solomon describes it:

The divine nature that lives within you wants it to matter that you were alive. There is something in you that wants to make a difference that you were here on earth, beyond the fact that you attended to the creature comforts of your body. There is something in you that wants to make a magnificent contribution to the world.

That divine part of you cannot be killed, but it can be overruled. You can overrule your real self so that it stays entombed. You can lock your divine nature away in a tomb, and the stone rolled in front of the door is called "behaving according to expectation." The stone that hides the magnificence that you are is your conformity, your submission, your refusal to do anything that is outside the bounds of acceptable behavior. You cannot let the divine spirit in you rule without being extraordinary, because the divine nature in you is not an animal nature. It is not even a nature of this planet. It is the nature of the Creator of this planet.[11]

Both the Intrinsic Self and the earthly material self have their foundation in our nature, and both exist and exert their influence. But is our human existence to be eternally torn by these two contending forces? "There is a continuous battle raging within you between these two natures," states Solomon. "That is where the real battles of life are being fought. The bumps and nicks and scars occurring on the surface are outward manifestations that reflect your struggle to regain control of a beast that has grown seemingly insurmountable, lifetime over lifetime. That is where madness is. That is where heaven and hell lie. That is where God and the devil meet. You can continue to believe that they [both] exist out there, outside yourself. Maybe they do. But those externals are not the ones influencing every thought, feeling, mood, interaction and circumstance of your practical daily life. The God that lives within you causes you to feel uplifted as you respond to a divine presence. That God is alive, and there is no need to question it."[12]

As Solomon makes clear, we are in no sense exempt from the vicissitudes of biological existence common to all forms of animal life. So long as the True Self, the Self that imprimis chose to enter the beast, continues to occupy the body of the beast, the influence of the beast will continue to exert its restrictive power. If we do not "have dominion" over the beast, everything that lends stability, harmony, continuity and integrity to ourselves and that of the world we live in will be decisively threatened. The beast will continue to shape-shift into ever more horrifying forms and proportions as the drama of our species continues to race against the looming threat of a global Apocalypse.

The alternative, states Solomon, is to confront the radical absurdity or "madness" of the world's spiraling descent by pacifying within ourselves the very force that brought us to this crucial threshold to begin with. "Let the beast be loved and accepted by the God in you," Solomon tells us, "by the highest part of yourself, by that in you that loves naturally. Let the beast in you be accepted, loved, appreciated and approached gently with confidence and reassurance. At the same time, let the warm, beautiful, loving parts of your nature that you want to encourage be nourished, robustly and regularly. Christ taught, 'Resist not evil' (Matthew 5:39). Do not give the beast nature in you more power by trying to force it to behave differently than it does. Your nature, in all its oddities, is acceptable to its Maker. The beasts and the animal natures exist as part of a beautiful and harmonious plan, a divine plan. While that is the nature of the animal, the body, the planet and the universe we live in, know that it is not inherently your highest aspect. There is within you a creative being. It is the part of you that wants to love. It is the part that wants to participate in creation. If you will allow that part to come forward, as you love and accept all the various parts of yourself, you will know who is in charge. The spirit of love, which is the source of life, will hold dominion over all the beasts.... In the presence of living-love, without fear, even the lion will lie down with the lamb."[13]

Fear is a conditioned impulse in the heart of the beast, an actionable part of our everyday lives. As a contagion it resonates collectively resulting in racial prejudice and war. Particularly susceptible to the contagion are religious groups that tend to judge and condemn other religions that differ from their own in core matters of belief. Christians have carried out pogroms against Jews, Roman Catholics have had their Inquisitions, Protestants have beheaded Catholics, all in the name of the love of Christ. Now, in the most benevolent name of Allah, dogmatic and radicalized sects of Sunnis and Shias are committing similar atrocities, not only against each other but against all others whose beliefs fail to agree with their own.

But if fear is a motivating factor in the state of our lives, then so is the perfect eternal presence of the Good which is an expression of living love. Both are sown separately into the whole of who and what we are. As Solomon explains:

> Only two powers exist on earth. And everything derives from those two powers. We can call them the expansive force and the contracting force, or life and death. Life includes anything that grows, supports growth, expands, increases and builds. The energy of life includes joy, healing and health, happiness, effectiveness, expansion, abundance, prosperity, productivity, growth, encouragement, support and power. Death is an energy that contracts, decreases, hinders or destroys growth. It includes hurt, pain, limitation, competition, dis-ease, illness, worry, negative emotions and negative perspectives.

> Those two powers that enliven the universe are in constant war, battling against one another. Each attempts to recruit you to its camp, meaning your vitality is invested on one side or the other of these two expressions of power. You believe in one or the other. You accept and depend on one or the other as your source of security, vitality and life. You have confidence that it will support and sustain you. Whichever of the two powers you have confidence in will motivate you and empower your life.

> These two forces can also be called love and fear. The term love means everything within you that is expansive, everything that makes you feel better, more alive. Love nurtures and sustains.[14]

Hence, anything within that makes us feel good about ourselves and about life, that makes us respond with hope and healing when we see particular images, when we hear particular music, when we encounter particular people, when we experience particular events, or when we just pay attention and appreciate life as it is --- that, says Solomon, is the force of life. It is that force that awakens us and makes us alive to the present, without regret for the past and without fear of the future. "That creative, life-giving force," Solomon tells us, "is God within us." Standing in opposition to the force of light, life or love, is that within us that evokes dreads, fears, and worries, that judges, condemns, hates and becomes melancholy and depressed. "You can call that force Satan, the devil, the lower self, the beast nature, or any other name you prefer," states Solomon. "The truth is that it exists. When you talk with that force, you feel worse. And that is the definition of evil. All the studied categorizations of morality and sin provided by traditional religion --- this is good but that is bad, this is acceptable but that is not --- are unnecessary. The definition of evil is very simple. Anything that makes you feel worse is evil because it is the opposite of life. It does not enliven you. It un-livens you. Whatever takes your life away makes you more dead, and that is the nature of evil. Anything that gives you liveliness, that makes you more alive, more life-filled, is Life and God. Scripture tells us that when asked to identify Himself to Moses, God said to him, 'I am that I am' (Exodus 3:14). 'I am that which lives. I am life. I am the living one. I am what makes life live.' Let that be your definition of God."[15]

The war --- against our own holy planet, against our fellow humans, the war that rages within ourselves --- all these must end if the river of human history is not to plunge finally over the precipice of our apocalyptic fears. In our hearts the spirit must claim us from the forces of darkness and death. To do so, we must first awaken the phoenix of our inner life from where it has long been lying as if dead. This, according to the Source, discloses our mission. We must reconcile spirit and matter, essence with ego, the godlike with the beast; that is, we must realize atonement (at-one-ment) through the force of life --- the force that has given us life itself --- if we are to survive the sophisticated barbarism of our age.

SEARCHING FOR THE LIGHT

To begin, it may need be that we disinter our ancient wisdoms and raise them to a new level of respectability that allows us to expand, first ourselves. "To put the world in order," teaches Confucius, "we must first put the nation in order; to put the nation in order, we must put the family in order; to put the family in order, we must cultivate our personal life; and to cultivate our personal life, we must first set our hearts right." "Setting our hearts right" means, as with Plato, that we must unchain ourselves from our own subjectivity if are to reach finally the depths and heights of a human potential which neither psychology nor Western religion seem able to reach. It's no wonder that so many have become disillusioned with more conventional forms of religion which exhort and command us but provide no instrumental means of actually transforming us through the life-energy that lies at our very core. Their concern with starving and merely stifling the beast as some sort of atavistic defilement simply makes the animal within us go hungry and crazy. To direct that energy toward integration and awareness requires a practical method and discipline, not simply a system of moral behavior which few can or will follow.

Precisely how to invest ourselves with the ability to master the conflicting forces of our nature has been the supreme challenge of the great spiritual teachings and disciplines of all ages. Lying hidden in these ancient vaults of visionary knowledge are the secrets of human nature and the methods of reclaiming the sacramental truth of our divine potentiality. But navigating through these perennial waters is tricky business. Inscribed thousands of years prior to our own time, many are so weighted down by veiled anthropomorphic imagery that we find them inscrutably alien to our own cultural transparencies. Others, perforated through and through with misinterpretations, mistranslations and misrepresentations, leave us with nothing more than their garbled and ossified remains. While an occasional sliver of truth may reach us, still, deformed to the point of caricature it's hardly enough to satisfy the hunger which our Intrinsic Self stirs in us. Many of us, searching for a technique or resource we can actually work with, are drawn into a maze of curious off-beaten paths and blind alleys only to have found everywhere among them apotheotic swamps, unprolific mystagogic disciplines, both traditional and experimental, secular counterfeits, and betrayals of our faith. We are like the blind searching for the light.

The Source tells us, however, that it is only our own fears and beliefs that blind us to the light. We do not need new religions or ancient messiahs more glorified and godlike than ourselves to reveal to us the light. **The experience of God is not dependent on simple belief or blind faith, but is rather an experiential reality. Believing without experience builds fantasy.** The Source enjoins us, therefore, **to free the life from tyranny of belief, from tyranny of religion, into the direct experience of life, the direct experience of reality, the direct experience of God, so that one no longer needs to believe in this or that set of beliefs, ideas, faith and such... but knowing through direct experience.** (Solomon Reading No. 1154, 10/83).

It all sounds right, we tell ourselves. Far easier, however, to acknowledge a truth than to find a way of fulfilling it. Inevitably, the question we ask is, is it even possible? How can we transform a life that is tangled, fierce, and capricious into one that is intricate, wise, and benevolent? How can we rid ourselves entirely of fear in order to bring about in ourselves the changes that will finally make possible a new world unfettered from the anxieties and hostilities that now so cripple us? Is this not simply manna before our eyes?

Solomon's reply is that our lack of trust in our own powers is at its heart a lack of experience, either in defect or in accomplishment. In short, having never made a serious effort, we simply do not know whether we have the power or not. It's not so difficult as one might imagine. "All enlightenment means is to wake up out of fantasy into reality," Solomon tells us. "That is all you have to do. You already are --- always have been and will be --- God-conscious. You do not have to work at enlightenment. All you have to do is stop the fantasy of something else and experience reality. Metamorphosis occurs when fantasy and fear die, and love lives. If you are not introducing limitation, limitation will not exist. If you are not introducing fear, fear will not exist. That is what life is about --- being as alive as we can possibly be in every moment and supporting life in everyone and everything around us. That is what it is to be God."[16]

Chapter 14

Anamnesis

THE OCEAN OF ETERNITY

From our original stewardship over the total genesis of creation, the Source explains that we fell into a trance-like attachment with the manifest forms we were given to minister. Whereas we were intended to remain hegemonically discrete, merely guiding and overseeing the unfolding process of an ordered complexity, we bungled it. We separated ourselves from our own co-creative Source. From that day to this, we have been children of the Fall. Interfused and identified with the beastial bodies we inhabit, we are merely alienated fragments, hidebound and entombed by the sleep of forgetfulness of our eternal origin and consequently by the mortal fear and horror of the final severance we call "death". So as earthly creatures we struggle against death in the name of life.

Wherever there is separation there is fear, but as the Source points out, there need not be. For in reality, death is nothing to be feared. **We would have you see it in this manner,** describes the Source:

> If we could just create here an extended metaphor, perhaps in this manner. If you would visualize a group of a few individuals in a pleasant tropical setting on a boat with a view of the beauty of the palms on the beach, of the waves on the water, perhaps the beauty of the sky, the clouds, a small island, and those on the boat have made a decision concerning some excitement and experience, a joyous experience. To have the experience, they must strap onto their backs some rather heavy weights, tanks of air, and on their feet instruments which would make walking very difficult on the shore. And before their eyes, tight fitting goggles which do not allow for water to penetrate, and placing in their mouths an instrument to allow them to breathe from the tank, they will then fall over backward, over the edge of the boat and into the water. And having descended below the surface, they will encounter quite a different world, different in every way, different in appearance, in the rate of motion they can experience --- the challenge of maintaining sufficient buoyancy to lift from the bottom, and opportunities to explore the world around them for a limited period of time, knowing that in perhaps an hour and a half, they must return to the world they had left behind.

> For the time that they are exploring the depths of the coral reefs and the beauty and the dangers, including those of sharks, of moray eels, of other such things of which they must be aware ... they explore for a time, and when the air in the tank has run a bit low, they return quite willingly to the surface. And as each boards the boat and removes the heavy and awkward weights which would make it considerably difficult to walk in the world above the water, they shed the heavy instruments, the blinders of goggles, and the flippers on their feet and they talk excitedly about the foregoing

experience.

And if you can imagine their conversation, they will speak most of the dangers they faced, for these are interesting and have some excitement.

So it is, so very similar, that you and others have left a world where breathing and movement, should it be necessary, are so easy and simple that it requires only a thought to take you to a distant place, without travel, [for] travel is not involved, but instantly at one place, having thought of it and then at another place in space or time, for you are backward in time with complete freedom. But if one desires the adventure of this world with its atmosphere, one must then put on the equipment which is heavy, cumbersome, awkward, but allows for experience within this atmosphere.

The equipment is alien to the individual, and at the beginning of the experience, it is thought of as such. "I will put on an alien piece of equipment to allow me to function in this environment for a time." And then with no real sadness on the part of a soul who remembers taking the plunge, as it were, [one] will return to the surface as the time is completed, and excitedly share the experience of descending into that world with its atmosphere, its environment and its experiences.

And then, the soul will be off to other experiences in other places. Even within your own solar system, there are various schools, this particular school being one of cause/effect relationships and it is the purpose of putting on the equipment and descending into this world to learn to move physically with force material things with the material body and [with] senses which communicate of matter and material things. One does not, in putting on this equipment with five senses designed for experiencing a physical world, one does not give up the five subtler senses which already existed for experiencing and exploring a world not of matter, but of images, ideas, and experiences of various kinds.

One might visit another of the schools and learn there assertiveness and some sense of boldness and adventure, and in another school, one might review the karma of the soul's experience for a time. And eventually, a soul, having experienced these schools sufficiently of this system will exit directly through the sun itself and on to other systems somewhat similar.

So we have gone to some length here to say to you that the experience of death will be a great deal similar to removing last year's overcoat which has become quite heavy and a bit tight, too snug to be comfortable. And shedding the garment, you would feel light and free and breathe more easily. And as your physical body should tumble perhaps to the floor or if you leave it in a hospital bed, then others would gather with some concern and grieve. And you would attempt to reassure them and find to no avail, for they think that you are the body which has stopped breathing and they will forget that they can communicate with you and have through subtler senses in many occasions.

And having seen what you have left behind, usually with no particular regret, you will see before you a bright and shining pathway and a bright and shining city, and there you will meet the Lords of Karma and make some decisions of your own. And understand that the decisions will not be imposed. You will be given opportunities to re-experience lessons which you feel incomplete with. And so you, yourself, will design the nature of the karma of the particular lifetime you are about to experience should you return to this particular school of cause/effect. Or you might make a decision to go to one of the other schools to gather a greater understanding, to complete, to flesh out your character and your understanding of yourself and nature.

But in all of this experience for the one experiencing what you call death, this transition would hardly ever seem a tragedy at all, but rather an experience of lightness, freedom and leaving behind something which had become cumbersome, tiring, a bit old and finished with its ability to serve you.

It is quite simple (Solomon Reading No. 1588, 11/5/91).

While for some it may be difficult to accept, it is not death itself, but the death *of* self, of the trivial familiar separate identity of body and of experience that we call "self", that we most fear. Though we may perceive ourselves to be its rightful sovereign, the Source tells us that the *real* drama is behind the curtain of the ego's struggle to maintain itself in a dreamlike world of abstractions made concrete. The eternal world is *the* reality. All else passes and becomes as though it had never been once our minimal consciousness becomes enfolded into the vast dimensions of the greater self from which cycles of life and death and of successive personalities have unfolded. It is, as reflected in the Sufi allegory "The Tale of the Sands", a simple existential truth:

A stream, from its source in far-off mountains, passing through every kind and description of countryside, at last reached the sands of the desert. Just as it had crossed every other barrier, the stream tried to cross this one, but it found that as fast as it ran into the sand, its waters disappeared.

It was convinced, however, that its destiny was to cross this desert, and yet there was no way. Now a hidden voice, coming from the desert itself, whispered: 'The Wind crosses the desert, and so can the stream.'

The stream objected that it was dashing itself against the sand, and only getting absorbed: that the wind could fly, and this was why it could cross a desert.

'By hurtling in your own accustomed way you cannot get across. You will either disappear or become a marsh. You must allow the wind to carry you over, to your destination.'

But how could this happen? 'By allowing yourself to be absorbed in the wind.'

This idea was not acceptable to the stream. After all, it had never been absorbed before. It did not want to lose its individuality. And, once having lost it, how was one to know that it could ever be regained?

'The wind,' said the sand, 'performs this function. It takes up water, carries it over the desert, and then lets it fall again. Falling as rain, the water again becomes a river.'

'How can I know that this is true?'

'It is so, and if you do not believe it, you cannot become more than a quagmire, and even that could take many, many years; and it certainly is not the same as a stream.'

'But can I not remain the same stream that I am today?'

'You cannot in either case remain so', the whisper said, 'Your essential part is carried away and forms a stream again. You are called what you are even today because you do not know which part of you is the essential one.'

When he heard this, certain echoes began to arise in the thoughts of the stream. Dimly, he remembered a state in which he --- or some part of him, was it? --- had been held in the arms of a wind. He also remembered --- or did he? --- that this was the real thing, not necessarily the obvious thing, to do.

And the stream raised his vapour into the welcoming arms of the wind, which gently and easily bore it upwards and along, letting it fall softly as soon as they reached the roof of a mountain, many, many miles away. And because he had had his doubts, the stream was able to remember and record more strongly in his mind the details of the experience. He reflected, 'Yes, now I have learned my true identity.'

The stream was learning. But the sands whispered: 'We know, because we see it happen day after day: and because we, the sands, extend from the riverside all the way to the mountain.'

And that is why it is said that the way in which the Stream of Life is to continue on its journey is written in the Sands.[17]

Intrinsically, therefore, we are immortal and eternal, belonging to an imperishable world. Death is simply the great awakening. Once the physical form has been discarded, we are pervasively aware of what we are in reality. In the world of the spirit, unlike that of the flesh, it is not possible to pretend to be one thing and actually be another. As we are opened to our true nature, we drift toward what we really are, over and above the minor obstacles and accidents of social and cultural conditioning and personal life circumstances. At death we are ushered into the unimaginable expanse of a spaceless and timeless reality no longer fragmenting but total. It's all-revealing light illuminates to our consciousness the universal indivisibility of eternal existence:

> Because time and space appear as illusions here [the state of pure spirit] it follows then that all lifetimes lived are lived rather at once. However, in relationship to moving bodies through time and space they are seen as a succession. Then from your point of view it is not a fragmentation of self

but a succession of lifetimes. From our point of view all these lifetimes appear simultaneously, thus appear to be a fragmentation of souls. However, understand that this is an illusion. There is one soul, one lifetime, then, that you think of as a soul rather than a fragment of one. Only in this manner does fragmentation go beyond illusion and even this illusion [as well] when you see that we really have not even left the Heart of God but are still experiencing as expressions of Him. Then all of time and all of space and all of fragmentation and all of separation and all of polarity are but illusions, [merely] a means of learning that which we are and have always been. And when we learn no longer to accept the illusion of separation from God we'll find that we are and always were one and at one with Him (Solomon Reading No. 522, 3/4/75).

Now looking back, our physically restricted lives seem as but an instant. There can no longer be any romanticizing of the faults and failings that separated us from our true selves. As beasts of flesh, our spirituality is not a given fact; we are spiritual beings only insofar as we manifest ourselves as such, insofar as the spirit within us gains possession of the natural elements. Ignorant of our own nature, ever racked by inner conflicts which eluded our apprehension while on earth, our physical lives end not as revelation but as self-judgement.

TRY NOT TO FORGET

While it is the birthright of any child eternally begotten of spirit to remain open to the universal context of his or her existence and to "remember", we now see that we were thwarted into a forgetfulness of ourselves, again and again and again. Through a network of multitudinous relations beginning with our birth into flesh, we can now see that we not only took on the roles and attitudes of others, but at the same time we took on their limitations, indeed, their world. We allowed them to define for us our "rightness". Out of a fear of disapproval, abandonment, or the judgement of others, we abdicated to *them* the possibilities and choices of our life. From them we learned not only what, but how to see; not merely what, but how to think and believe. The entire socialization process that structured and warped our days now becomes glaringly plain and simple.

So from the pre-incarnated existence of our source we decide once again to immerse ourselves into this denser world, but this time to remain "awake". The awakening of spirit in matter, however, is a risky venture, for with each stride forward into awareness we are thrust back yet again by the pressures to conform and by the limitations of our own fears. Hence, with the mandate: "Do not forget your true nature and purpose," we again exchange the elysium of that higher world for a new body on earth.

"So you got back in the body," relates Paul Solomon, "and you tried to stay there as much as possible. You practiced operating it for longer and longer periods each day, leaving it less and less as time went by. You got better and better at making the parts do what you wanted them to do, when you wanted them to do it. The body required a lot of your concentration to make it work. Over time, you began to lose consciousness of anything else. You even began to forget where you had come from, who you had been, and who you really are. And you definitely forgot the Lords of Karma and the all important list [of lessons to be applied]. The instrument required so much investment that you began to identify with it. 'This instrument is who I am. I *am* this body.' You began to accept, as everyone around you did, that 'If I want attention, I have to use this instrument to get it. If I want to communicate, I have to do it through this body. Because of their limitations, these people believe it is the only way. So to exist here, I'll have to adopt the same limitations.'"[16]

When a soul first enters this world from higher realms, the newly acquired brain-mind begins immediately the process of structuring and synthesizing its experience from all available sensory feedback of its physical environment. And yet, as the Source explains, **the seals of the body by which the soul is connected, being like tunnels to other realms of space, are yet in contact with other planes and that activity on other planes.** Until approximately age 7, when a concern for social consensus leads selectively to the screening out of certain kinds of experience, the child, through the free and as yet unconditioned play of its consciousness, is still in rapport with the marvelous heritage it has left behind.

With what he refers to as "primary perceptions," the perceptual abilities that arise from and affirm our biological bonds with the implicate state of nature, Joseph Chilton Pearce cites several studies that clearly indicate a prevailing patterning of telepathic ability in young children. "'I see white light coming out of your head and fingers', reports little Jessie. 'There are bright colors around your face and body.' Larry, aged seven, sees white light around trees and orange light around dogs. Brynn, seven, sometimes sees specks of color float around her bedside."[19] Reports culled from the studies of James Peterson, Eloise Shields, Van de Castle, Gerald Jamplosky, and others, indicate that telepathic/clairvoyant ability tends to peak at age 4 and generally fades by age 7 or 8.

But why should our ability to "see" in certain ways, and to experience heightened forms of awareness, simply disappear as we emerge from our early years of childhood? Why, indeed, if as Pearce contends, "Primary perceptions are as biological as any other form of perception; are almost surely genetic to our species (as well as many other species), rather than space-age esoterica, spiritual gifts, or psychological aberrations; and are (or should be) clearly developmental, as all intelligence is."[20] Part of the answer seems to be simply that our experience, however personal, occurs in a social field of reciprocal influence and feedback. In his *Analysis of Perception,* J. R. Smythies holds that while hallucinatory experience is a normal part of a child's world, to the extent that social agreement dictates what is real through "positive reward," the child selectively represses or learns to ignore aspects of his reality that are regarded as illusory or "fictitious" by the prevailing standards of "negative social value."[21] While shared experiences reinforce a child's consensual reality and his need for parental bonding, selective inattention results from the failure to gain sanction for experiences that cannot be defined or affirmed by others. The child learns simply to screen out that for which there is no common ground of acceptance or approval. Consequently:

Peterson showed some older students pictures drawn by his seven-year-olds showing various odd colors around things and asked them if they had ever seen such things. "Yes," they replied, "but not anymore. Caused too much trouble." And it had taken Peterson some time to win the confidence of the seven-year-olds so that they would confide in him all about the colors and things. They all had said that when they told their parents about it, their parents' colors changed --- to red.[22]

Not until the seventh year or so does the dramatic shift of a child's neurological functioning occur that enables him to relate to and "re-present" his environment logically and analytically, something Jean Piaget calls "concrete operational thinking." Here the child enters into the discursive and analogical universe of rudimentary adult thinking. Before age 7, concepts are formed directly from the child's sensory interaction with his environment; at 7 years, the brain-mind forms concepts based on its ideas of the world. The concrete perceptual receptivity of the child gradually comes to be functionally dominated by the creative capacity of the adult mind to synthesize its contents and furnish abstract perceptual experience entirely from within itself. The brain-mind's capacity for abstraction now allows for an endless series of operational changes to occur in the structuring of information itself.

But the patterns for synthesizing information and mediating the operational flow of concepts are neither genetically determined nor do they simply arise in a vacuum. Rather, they are conditionally determined, as Benjamin Lee Whorf points out, by the obligatory and pre-established forms of cultural agreement. While such patterns give structural integrity to the conditions of experience and provide for the transmission and legitimation of social and cultural demands, nevertheless they constitute reality not as it is, but as a construction. The "world" becomes an invention, a conceptual fabrication.[23]

The child's primary bonds with the implicate order have now been broken. Culture becomes the surrogate matrix. No longer does the child have any ground for spontaneous outbursts of intuitive expression or gratuitous explosions of vision. The child's sensitivity and responsiveness to the world "as it is" comes to be continually altered by the internal dynamic and contour of the mind's own network of causality and belief. The pure data of experience become subject to the relative attributes of culturally orthodox patterns of expression and traditional normative standards of belief that are completely at odds with our natural interconnectedness in the holographic order. As David Bohm puts it, "... conditioning blocks us (from that deeper order), because it creates a pressure to maintain what is familiar and old, and makes people frightened to consider anything new. So, reality is limited by the message which has already been deeply impressed on the brain cells from early childhood."[24]

So as Paul Solomon observes, to exist here in this physical realm of experience, we feel the need to adopt the same limitations that confine and restrict everyone else: "By adopting the same limitations, you yielded to the false beliefs of the people around you and manifested again what is called the 'fall of man'. The fall occurs every time man affirms himself as matter, denying his true identity as a wondrous divine creator --- *in* this world, but not *of* it. Unless the parents involved are highly aware and able to help the soul maintain an awareness of its true self, the physical, mental and emotional bodies will mature while the unconscious, spiritual aspect spends the rest of the lifetime attempting to spark a memory. For most of us, this is the pattern that our lives take. The conscious self skips along through life with comfort and happiness as its primary goal, while the unconscious spends every moment of the day and night, year after year, decade after decade, trying to get our attention, to wake us up and remind us of the truth."[25]

THE GREAT CONSPIRACY

To the extent that we accept limitations imposed by others or by the norms predicated by society in general, our consciousness becomes saturated by worry and fear: fear of losing love and approval, fear of nonconformity, fear of the loss of self-esteem. Externally and internally we are surrounded by the supreme fiction --- fear. No matter how confident a person may seem, everyone experiences fear. The vulnerabilities and limitations that feed our fears are now seen as the natural state for most people, as something which is intrinsic to our identities and personhoods and which are recognizable through our beliefs and actions. Fear, the great emancipator for the influence of all evil, has become a means through which we respond to and make sense of the world.

Hence, fear is not something natural or purely psychological. It does not just happen. It is shaped and determined by and through our interactions with others and by a cultural script that defines for us the boundaries of "normal" behavior. Outside of these boundaries we crouch before the serpents of condemnation and abandonment. So we yield to fear, and in so doing, accommodation becomes the norm. In other words, fear is socially constructed and then manipulated to the reciprocal advantage of each of us in ways that sustain and reaffirm our limited self-concept. It is what Paul Solomon refers to as "The Great Conspiracy":

> You have the right to be totally alive on all the levels of your being, physically, emotionally, mentally and spiritually alive. This right to be alive on all levels can be called your 'alrightness'. The very fact that you are not dead should confirm to you that you are all right, perfect as you are. Being alive means being all right.

> On the other hand, you can also choose to experience life according to the dictates of others, letting others determine how you should feel, think and act. If you do, you also give them the right to hurt you, the right to make you angry or sad, even the right to make you happy.

> If you choose to surround yourself with people who decide whether you are all right, it means those people are important to you. It is a system that serves all of you because those people want to be important to you, particularly because they have probably given you the responsibility for their alrightness as well.

> If those people are important to you, they can assume that you will give them what they want and need, which is your assurance that they are all right. As long as you remain important to them, you can expect them to give

you what you want as well. An unspoken agreement is formed. You all agree to pretend responsibility for each other's alrightness.

The conspiracy consists of an agreement to pretend that you determine my alrightness and that I determine yours. It is not a conspiracy to believe that this is so. It is a conspiracy to pretend that this is so. No one really believes that their alrightness is dependent on what other people think of them, but almost everyone pretends that it is so.

The truth is that your alrightness depends on absolutely nothing but your decision to know that you are all right. You are inherently all right and cannot be otherwise. It is your choice to recognize it. You can choose to know that you are all right, or you can leave the decision to someone else and join the conspiracy.

We teach children to sell out to the conspiracy through our examples, through the values we set, through the messages of our media, through the means to our goals. We teach children far more by who we are and what we do than by what we say. We teach them to conspire for alrightness. We teach each other in the same way we teach children. Sometimes, we try to convince others that "I'm not important, but you are." Other times, we try the opposite: "You're not important. I am. And what I say goes."

The biggest contribution we make to the conspiracy is that we remain victims ourselves. Each time we allow ourselves to be hurt by someone, we buy into the conspiracy and we model the conspiracy for our families and our friends....

The amount of power that I agree to give you is the amount of importance that I give you in my life. Then we call that loving each other. What it means is that I will give you the power to control my life and I will make you prove your love for me by testing how far I can push you. I may need to prove my importance to you by saying, "How important am I to you? Am I important enough for you to put up with this?" Zap! Lovers do it regularly.

If the beast in me is fearful, and I make you responsible for the way I feel without taking care of my own love needs, because I am too busy participating in the conspiracy with you, then I can call you wrong, bad and evil. I can blame you for the quality of my life. And then we can have a family feud.

I can even call you an agent of Satan, and we can have a "holy war." Have you ever wondered how two such contradictory words can stand side-by-side in a rational sentence, in a rational world? I can go to war with you. Satan does not care on what scale the wars are managed. Small, seemingly insignificant family feuds feed on fear and hurt, on suppressed, unconscious resentments. And they keep the planet in a state of disharmony. Strife is expected and reasonable. Hate and conflict are so seemingly innocuous that they continue without resistance and become habitual and commonplace, a way of life. In other words, the beast reigns in his kingdom.[26]

In short, fear is something which makes and shapes our identities as much as it does the state of our world. And whenever consciousness is pulled by the strings of fear, fear becomes our master. It controls us through the self-monologue that rings incessantly in our brain, perpetuating and strengthening the same kind of self-defeating limitations that occasioned our loss of self-confidence to begin with. As Paul Solomon points out, fear-based self-talk, conditioned by our earliest childhood experiences, has become so ingrained and habituated that we're often no longer even aware that it's happening:

For most infants, the first encounters with the world bring love, nourishment, attention, warmth, security, admiration, praise, even worship. Further on, that experience changes --- even though the needs of the individual do not. People continue to need love, attention, admiration, even worship, throughout life. The biggest challenge comes as those who are providing love and praise to the infant begin to express disapproval. To regain their approval, children must begin to act differently. Children must begin to act according to the expectations of those who are disapproving.

For the first time, an artificial element is introduced into the child's life, something unnatural. As love and approval are withheld, a fantasy called fear is introduced, a fear that something needed will be withheld. If children decide to supplant their own desires, aspirations, even intuitions, with the desires of others in order to get the love and approval they need, they join the conspiracy to act as if others determine their alrightness.

The fantasy of losing what is needed for survival can develop into an energy of fear that becomes a focus of life. The constant conversation occurring in the minds of all individuals known as self-talk can become dominated by this fantasy. As children grow into adulthood, their self-talk will express as fear thoughts. "I'm afraid of being rejected. I'm afraid they won't like me. I'm not worthy. I feel so guilty. I don't deserve to have a good life."

Thoughts born out of fear of lack or limitation have two things in common. First, they are lies. They do not tell the truth about you or about others. Second, they either devalue something that has value or they limit something that is limitless. Negative self-talk will devalue you by depreciating your inborn value as a human being. It will also devalue the possibilities of your future. Negative self-talk is false, yet it has the power to impose effect on reality because you accept the false limitations as real. The result is decrease and death. If the source of your self-talk is fear and its content is limiting or critical, it will make you feel lessened. All thoughts coming from limitation produce death.[27]

Thoughts of worry, guilt, self-doubt and fear produce the negative feelings, moods, attitudes and emotions through which we objectify our
world. The thoughts come first, the feelings of lack --- of self-worth and
of self-confidence --- follow. Were we to look beyond ourselves, we would
see as the Source sees that **this is the pandemic of this age, that those of
the family of this planet in this time suffer more than any other ill the lack
of understanding of self-worth, self-esteem, self-love, and confidence, and
particularly personal responsibility for all that comes into life.** (Solomon
Reading No. 1593, 11/28/91).

Etched into our brain patterns and hammered incessantly through sustained and unremitting inner self-talk, our negative thinking becomes for
us a mantra, a form of negative meditation. As Paul Solomon himself
tells us, "worry is the most practiced form of meditation in the world. It
is carried out more regularly than positive meditation where the mind is
focused on good, body systems are strengthened, and stress is reduced.
Worry is a universal religion, subscribed to by millions of people, mainly
out of a feeling of obligation. 'If I don't worry, it means I don't care. If
I don't worry, I won't be ready when it happens. If I don't worry, who
will?' Worry is faith in evil, believing in darkness, expecting the worst. It
is the one god that almost everyone on the planet worships, regularly, at
least once a day. The effect is predictable. The rewards reaped are tensed,
stressed bodies and contracted, diminished lives."[28]

Moreover, as given by the Source, we are told that the voice of fear is quite
literally the voice of death. With the inevitable stress that its reverberative
dissonance produces, it is threatening to the very life of our bodies:

> Every thought, literally, every thought is accompanied by a mus-
> cular movement. You cannot think without moving muscles. The
> related muscles are within and throughout the body. It is such that
> every thought which involves stress or worry results in a muscular
> contraction only, never expansion. Thoughts of joy and laughter
> and the resolution of conflict, these result in muscular expansion.

> See then the implications of this direct relationship between mind
> and body, and the fact that a worrying mind will create muscle
> spasms, often tiny, almost microscopic muscle spasms throughout
> the body, but particularly following the spinous process where they
> may easily be observed and have been in post mortem examinations.
> Such encrustations around muscle spasms have closed off the life
> lines, blood, lymph, nerve supply to organs, thus becoming the cause
> of the death [of the body]. Meaning that this is literally embodied
> thought expressed through musculature in contraction which does
> not release again until there is a corresponding thought of resolu-
> tion or joy related to the same concern.

> Thus there are muscle spasms which may be as old as thirty years
> or more within the body. Now in the truest sense this is the cause
> of death in virtually all internal illness, the breakdown of internal
> organs. It is not yet described that way in the current medical para-

digm. We are simply proposing a new medical paradigm which will recognize that stress is by far the greatest factor in disease and healing. (Solomon Reading No. 1678, 5/31/92).

Like everything else in the universe, our thoughts and feelings possess energy and vibrational frequency. Negative thinking and feeling affects the vibration of our whole being predisposing us on every plane of our existence to weakness and ill-health. On the opposite end of the spectrum of frequencies is a life motivated by the expression of love, a life undiminished in which the narrow boundaries of the ego are absorbed into the unlimited expression of joy and freedom. This is the inherent natural state of our Intrinsic being, the suchness that we "forgot" in our return to the flesh.

NOTE Joy

The full realization of our betrayal of our true nature becomes evident, then, on every level of our being --- physically, emotionally, psychologically, spiritually. When the ego and its sense of personal worth becomes threatened, we barricade ourselves behind a network of false and spurious value attachments that form the basis of our compliance with the "great conspiracy" and that therefore blind us to the truth of our own essence. Honesty, responsibility, and integrity become expendable under the emotional pressure and stress. Reality becomes the enemy and truth becomes conditional to the counterfeit reality of a separate self with its face-saving pretense of artificially concocted self-esteem. In this complex process of self-deception we capitulate to values and standards that we ourselves do not honestly respect, thereby compounding the torture of our distress making us ever more vulnerable to illness and disease.

LOVE AND FEAR

While the limitations precipitated by our fears merely perpetuate the self-destructive spiral of our personal descent into fragmentation and blindness of our true nature, the Source tells us that we have within us the power to reverse the spiral and to open ourselves to an unlimited dimension of conscious freedom. To awaken to the autonomy of a self born of the inimitable power of love, we must begin first by recognizing and acknowledging that we, each of us, live our lives by default; that we live not authentically but parasitically off the thinking, values, needs and expectations of others. We are sacrificial animals, sacrificing our own worth and relevance to that of others, to the extent that we often blatantly imitate the manners of those we admire, coming close to losing the value of our own original nature and way of life. This is perhaps the greatest curse to living autonomously and without limitation. Furthermore, the Source tells us that a life so dependent on the choices, decisions, and examples set and determined by others is a life incapable of love. It negates the very possibility of love.

> If there would be the love for God, the love for the Father, there cannot be the lack of love for the self or the expression of self. Then see in others that "I AM" and know these to be a portion of that same body. How can the hand despise the foot of the same body that I am and know that until

another is well I am ill or I would share his illness? As there is the entering
into realization of being cells, or units, or parts of a single body, then love
will begin again to increase one for the other. Then if there would be the
increase for self or of respect for the self, begin to bring comfort or happiness or the smiles to another and see that that I have caused. I will begin to
respect the self when I know that self has caused happiness in another. I will
begin to love that instrument that produced happiness and love in others. If
you would love the self, then cause others to love the self, and as they love
you so then would you respond in kind and begin to love thyself as thou
art loved by others. Again these are the laws of tenfold return: that which
you produce in others will return to the self tenfold. Then make ten others
happy and see if you could stand that love that would return to self from
such an act (Solomon Reading #258, 10/15/73).

We must first love and respect ourselves before we can love and value others.

We all suffer from a thirst for approbation, from an eagerness to please and
to receive the approval of others, in order to reaffirm our own sense of "rightness". But as Paul Solomon points out, we simply cannot afford to dispense
with the spontaneous freedom that rises from within us, simply for the sake
of acquiring approval in an artificially contrived relationship, qualities that
hardly express the essential nature of our true selves. Doing so makes us psychologically invisible to ourselves. Through an intense sincerity of commitment to living consciously and to achieving our highest potential, however, we
can reclaim our right to exist as free, independent beings, thereby bringing a
deeper existential unity to our lives.

As a basic requirement of our survival as autonomous beings, therefore, Paul
Solomon tells us that we can and must end the conspiracy:

> All you have to do to step out of the conspiracy is to become conscious. Be-
> ing conscious of what you are doing is called enlightenment. Just admit what
> you are doing and name your action. Call it what it is.

> Here is the good news. Admitting what you are doing will cause what you
> are doing to change.

> You cannot change your actions through trying. If you try to stop an action,
> you will make it more important, and it will grow larger and more dominant
> through your attention. You will become more entrenched, and it will hurt
> you more.

> Recognizing that it is a game that you and your cohorts have been playing
> will steal its power. Like a deflating balloon, it will look silly. The action will
> become futile and foolish as you acknowledge that it does not serve you any-
> more. And you will no longer give it energy and importance. The very act of
> performing the action will remind you of its senselessness.

> Buying out of the conspiracy means being conscious. Enlightenment does
> not require learning great truths. It only requires that you turn on the lights,
> become conscious, acknowledge what you are doing, and be honest with

yourself. Enlightenment is simply shining a spotlight on the truth of your actions.

By acknowledging the conspiracy, you will begin to notice what others are doing as well --- not the feigned interpretations that the conspirators have agreed to, but how things truly exist.

When you observe the conspiracy that others are playing, resist the temptation to suddenly blow the whistle on everyone's game. Just see it for what it is, make note of it, even laugh at it. It, not them. Remember, you were just there.

Individuals may say to you, "That means you don't love me anymore." That is not true. It means, "I don't need for you to tell me that I am all right anymore. I don't need to give you the power to hurt me in order to feel important and loved anymore."

Stepping out of the conspiracy may seem lonely because there are so few doing it and because you no longer get to depend on others for your alrightness. Beware. The feeling of loneliness is part of the conspiracy, because loneliness is a feeling-reaction based on the belief that others are responsible for your alrightness.

Removing yourself from the conspiracy results in independence, which does not equate with loneliness. Not having needs that others must fill is not a problem. It is an advantage. Only then can you love because you want to and because you choose to, not because you must in order to get your needs filled. That is real freedom.

There are only two choices, love or fear. If you serve love, you serve life. If you serve fear, you serve death. By serving fear and death, you remain a slave no matter how free you think you are.

You do not become free by breaking the rules. You become free by choosing to respect the rules, the universal principles on which life on this planet is based. You do this because you want to, because you recognize that they are authentic and work effectively for everyone simultaneously. No one is free to live in abeyance of these principles, except to the extent that we choose our master.

Who is the master of your life: Love or fear? Life or death? [29]

Caught in a web of psychological entanglements, torn by conflicts of desire and ambient loyalties, we are for the most part oblivious to who and what we are as independent beings. We have allowed ourselves to be marginalized, manipulated and shaped by relationships we ourselves have formed and consented to. In failing to know ourselves independently, we further alienate our intrinsic nature and impoverish our capacity for unconditional love. Hence, we find ourselves on the knife-edge of choice: self-surrender or self-determination; death or life.

Solomon tells us that by letting go of our attachment to fear, we can emancipate ourselves from the overly restrictive beliefs of who and what we are based upon how we believe others perceive us. Only then will we be able to awaken ourselves to the previously hidden powers of an unlimited self. It is from this threshold that a truly conscious life becomes possible.

BECOMING CONSCIOUS

Mind is the builder, the Source continually reminds us. The importance cannot be overstated. Nothing whatsoever happens to us outside of our own consciousness. Since nothing hurts us or saddens us or gives us pleasure or joy except within our own minds, the supreme importance of being in control of the mind is obvious. The idea is as old as the Upanishads, but it is an idea whose profound truth and urgency most people live and die without ever realizing. If, therefore, we are to awaken to a more integral and universal consciousness of our being, then the pattern of uncontrolled fear-based thinking, the cycle of thought that has us trapped in an endless loop of 'should-haves' and 'what-ifs', must be broken.

To those who doubt the possibility of controlling one's thoughts, the Source tells us that it is simply a matter of effort and choice. By abdicating ourselves to a belief in insufficiency and to our own limitations, we predispose ourselves to the power of fear. To lift ourselves from the ordinary into a marvelous new state of change and awareness requires only the willingness and commitment to change the conversation within our own minds. As Paul Solomon so insistently emphasizes, "there are only two powers. There is love, and there is fear. If the conversation in your mind is coming from heaven or love, then you are supported. You are supporting yourself and your whole life, including your health, your prosperity, your feeling of security and confidence. You feel supported, and you can handle life no matter what comes along. If the conversation in your mind is coming from fear, you will fear life. You will feel inadequate because that is what fear does. It tells you that your future is limited, that you will never accomplish your goals, that you will always be poor, that life is not yours for enjoying. Talking with fear is talking to hell. It means living in hell while on earth. Talking to love makes you feel better, simply because you talked to it. It makes you feel good about yourself and life. Love never limits you. That is how simple it is. There is no mysterious technique. If the conversation in your mind makes you feel better, it is coming from love, and it is supporting you. If it makes you feel worse or makes you feel afraid, it is coming from hell, and you need to get hell out of your head. Let it exist as a fiery pit down below for others if they want, but eliminate it from your life."[30]

Enslaved by the inner voice of the ego's tyranny, most of us would acknowledge that we're living in hell. We are confined to the limitations of worry and fear and to our agonizing subjection to its constant assault of our self-confidence and self-worth. We are all to some extent bound by these same limitations. Imperceptibly, and for the most part unwillingly through its subliminal influence, we become guilty of deceiving others to the same degree as ourselves. How easily we consent to the mendacity of our thoughts as an indispensable fact of life.

But the very fact that we, as an ego, would even attempt to free ourselves from the prison of our own fears and cravings is a certain sign that we are more than our limited selves and that there is that in us that is beginning to awaken to our intrinsic nature. Such an awakening to the unlimited power within us is, according to Solomon, the most exalted art and craft of living:

It's called becoming conscious and that's all it really amounts to. When we become conscious we become something that has been glamorized as "enlightenment", God consciousness, cosmic consciousness. There are all sorts of other words for it but what all of those words are really talking about is nothing more than waking up out of fantasy into reality. That's all we have to do. As far as being God consciousness, cosmic consciousness, enlightened, all of those things, who you are is all of those things. So you don't have to do a lot of working for it. You've already got it. All you have to do is stop the fantasy and experience reality.

Emotionally, spiritually, on every other level, you will experience a recharge like recharging a battery. That's what love is. *Not* the emotion, but the energy. The energy is the energy of life. It will heal you, it will enlighten you, it will give you life, it can perform miracles, all sorts of miracles. It's the source of the metahuman, it's the source of transformation. It can allow you to experience a metamorphosis. In fact, the metamorphosis occurs at the moment that fantasy dies, fear dies, and love lives.

When that happens what happens in you is a metamorphosis, meaning that you become alive in a new way. And that you had identified as you is now dead. Metamorphosis is a combination of words, one meaning life the other meaning death. Through death I become alive. That is what metamorphosis means. It produces a transformation. The transformation is that I become the cause of my body and what it experiences instead of being the result of the functions of my body and its brain-mind and emotions. I go through the created to experience being creator of it. That's metamorphosis.

In a very practical way how can I do it? There are some keys that are very simple. It's a matter of giving love to all that you have created. That means, your body, your mind, your personality, your habits, abilities --- everything that you have identified as you needs to be given love. That sounds like it will keep it alive. If I want that to experience metamorphosis, how's that going to help?

Love is the source of life, will in fact keep it alive, but the death/birth experience will not mean that the body crumbles and dies, and it won't mean that the mind dies in the sense of annihilation, in the sense of not existing anymore. What it really means is that it dies in the sense of being my identity. I die to it and I become born to a new relationship with it. So I'm giving it life, love, in a new way. To say that another way, there are six things that you have in order to survive: air, sunlight, shelter, water, food. Those five you've been aware of for a long time. There's a sixth one and that one is love.

We have before us in this moment the opportunity, the challenge, the responsibility to create a new Heaven and a new Earth. That's what this is all about.

The power of this impersonal love resonates to the greater beauty and harmony of a higher world wherein a truly conscious life becomes possible. Without it, we are doomed to a woefully constricted and self-destructive state of perpetual misery. It may take perseverance, but the Source assures us that we do have the ability; and the rewards, of unqualified joy and freedom, are simply beyond the mind's grasp.

While at first we may not have gone ten paces before the mind's untrained conditioning drifts back to the thinking of a beast, the Source tells us that through constant discipline of shaping the coordinated powers of the brain the mind will at length reconstitute itself and yield to the command of its own higher source of consciousness:

> Then decide anew, for the mind must be trained, you see. You have allowed yourself to be the product of uncontrolled thinking that was allowed to go here and there according to its own will, not bent to the will of the Father or anything created within the [Intrinsic] Self, so that beliefs, reactions, responses are built into the very cells of your body and consciousness or brain-mind, and there is the learning of this submissive self through repetition. For many times you have given the message to that that you call the lower self or the submissive self, to that portion of self, saying, "I wish to change," but then have demonstrated through action that that wish was not correct. Then decisions made lightly or with words, with idle thoughts, make little impression on the submissive self. Then training comes by destroying one idea or manner of response and reaction again and again until that submissive self begins to understand, to comprehend, to form a new pattern, becoming automatic until you become new --- a new self.

> The decision, then, begins with setting a new ideal and insisting each time that that ideal is met by focusing again on that ideal. Become new again and again and again in consciousness, in ideal, until you become new in fact and reflect His glory (Solomon Reading No. 954, 6/25/77).

The key to achieving this, therefore, lies not only in the relinquishing of all fear-based motivation with its narrow emphasis on the avoidance of pain, but in our unqualified faith in ourselves as divine elements called to a creativeness that first and foremost implies the transfiguration and illumination of our own created nature.

Thought, be it voluntary or involuntary, is absorbed by the brain and remains there. Because the brain cannot disentangle itself from the confusion of thoughts by which it is conditioned, it causes no transformation of the person. The ego stays the same. If we are to overcome the anonymity of our thoughts, we must keep our heads clear of all digressions that prevent the mind from becoming aware of itself. Only then will we begin to transform ourselves from the dismal and diminished human image we inherited from our fall and achieve what even death cannot undo.

All our efforts, then, must be inspired by the will to subdue the self-assertion of our wild, uncontrolled thinking. All our focus must be that of freeing the mind of the dark chaos of its conditioned fears and of consciously awakening ourselves to the experience of unconditional love. Should our vigilance weaken and occasionally be overtaken by fear, failure, and self-doubt, the Source tells us to notice in those moments there is fear, Satan, death, destruction, limitation that is speaking to me, attempting to channel its power, its energy through me. You see, you are all channels and when you are not channeling the Christ, you are channeling that opposite energy, the anti-Christ or Satan. When you are motivated, controlled by fear, you become a channel of fear or destruction or death. When you are motivated, controlled by love, then you become a channel of love and love is Christ, Christ is living love through you. In all those moments in which you become a channel through which love flows, you invite the Christ to manifest His Second Coming into the earth. Then look carefully with each moment of life as you live it. What is motivating me in this moment to cause what I feel emotionally, what I think mentally, what I feel and express spiritually. Become conscious (Solomon Reading No. 1173, 8/84).

Become conscious, that is to say, of the unlimited freedom that we from our own divine heritage are endowed with. Love, Light, Life Itself --- that is the infinite river of the Logos, the expression of the I AM that is our source. We are of Its own essence. Like a stream separated from its source, our spiritual being wanes and withers when severed from what is greater than itself. Trapped in fear, we are cut off and confined to an ego that by its limited nature betrays its own unlimited source of freedom.

THE LIMITLESS FREEDOM OF BEING

In truth, our egoic consciousness, which is the ground of our earthly experience, is a mere trickle of the Reality which underlies our human awareness. Innumerable worlds, an infinity of infinities, according to the Source, coexist with and interpenetrate the levels of our own consciousness. When we think and believe the narrow range of stimuli reflected in our senses from the external world is the sum of our consciousness, we limit ourselves by default to a faith in a world shaped by fear. What we perceive of the world, then, becomes merely an abstraction, processed moment by moment through what the Source calls the "reducing-valve" of the brain and nervous system:

> The brain is not an instrument to extend man's consciousness into the sensory world around him. It is instead a filter, if you will, a condenser for the purpose of taking the magnitude of what is happening around you and reducing it to a level of tolerance which the physical body can manage.

> Thus the brain of man is a reducer, not an expander of consciousness. And it has become separated upon itself as man confused his rational logic with his intuitive mind and began to argue within himself, stepping from the androgynous being, single-minded with single purpose, an extension of the Christ, to the time of the fall when man sought to see himself as separate, individualistic, and become a champion of free will and separation from God.

So [then] did his brain separate one part from the other (Solomon Reading No. 1466, 1/21/91).

With separation, then, there arose fear. And as long as we channel fear, we become blinded to anything beyond the matrix of the sensory world that we inhabit. A stream channels what it is fed from its source.

A universal consciousness of Logoic love, on the other hand, cannot be truly manifested without relinquishing all fear. This presupposes an unconditional faith in and loyalty to the power of unconditional love and to its divine Source within each of us. This is a love that surpasses human comprehension. It is, in the words of Paul Solomon, "the vital energy out of which the world was made. It is the living-love that dwells in a sacred place within you."[31]

As finite selves, we are merely isolated analogues of a transient love conditioned in some sense by the love of a self mired in egotism and pride. In extremis, it is its own enemy. But as mirrors turned to the sun reflect its light, so does the impersonal love that faith empowers us with become a reflection of the unlimited Christ-Source of our own creation. Within ourselves, declares the Source, lies the boundless possibilities of this power of love. We need only summon the faith to reveal once again the Word become flesh. But as the Source emphasizes, such a faith can only be awakened by a leap, by a springing clear of the fear-based motives and lack of belief that feed the self:

> These, then, who are created by the Master's hand, these expressions of God in earth now that are a part of this race in this time have often found the self limited and use those limitations as an excuse not to be perfect. There is no excuse for a lack of absolute perfection in that which God has created. Then it is not sufficient for anyone of you to say as an excuse or as a reason: "My thoughts failed me. I fell into confusion, not thinking deep enough." If you fell into confusion, then it was laziness and habit. There is not an excuse for it. Simply, then, use the tools at hand and do not accept that. Require the more of the self, for your ability is to receive and understand all things.

> Then begin to think in a new manner, thusly: that the confusion I now experience and perceive is not an adequate response and does not serve me well. I will, therefore, not accept this state of affairs as being normal or natural to me, but I will clarify this thought. I will see sharply with the eyes even of a master and begin to perceive through pure intent and by decision, thereby overcoming those things I had settled for simply because the world accepts them as excuses. The culture, the race, has taught you to accept limitations and you find them perfectly natural.

> Your natural state is the state of the Father, the state that Jesus Christ experienced on this earth. The natural state of man is that which He demonstrated for you and to settle for less is a lack of belief. Again and again the scriptures speak: "Believe in this name, this experience of the Christ." Then what is belief? Believe that He told you that you have these capabilities even as I have these capabilities, and to experience less is to experience a lack of belief.

Begin to believe differently, for you do not believe that your thinking can be more adequate. You have the ability to believe that another's [thinking] can and that Christ's could. 'Except ye believe, you shall not in no wise enter the Kingdom." That is spoken. Begin to apply belief in that manner and be lifted to a new expression of that that you are and can be (Solomon Reading No. 954, 6/25/77).

Armed with nothing more than a mustard seed of faith, Jesus assures us that absolutely nothing is impossible. Though we may hear the words, yet within the limits of everyday life they become lost amongst the perplexities that surround us. A mind habitually reinforcing the inadequacy, guilt, and self-doubt that efficates its sense of limitation is a mind groping in vain. If we cannot even trust ourselves, how much can we entrust ourselves to embody a faith as unwavering and infallible as that lived and spoken of by Jesus?

In an 1982 interview, however, Paul Solomon stated his firm conviction that all human limitations are merely self-perceived and self-imposed. Human nature can indeed be raised to the level of greatness, but only when through an act of faith we join in intimate relationship with our source to make it possible:

We have had some irrational beliefs that do not work drilled into us while we were growing up. In fact, they work against us. We are taught, for example, that Einstein was a genius, and in giving him that label it separates what he was from what we are, as if it were a different species. If, instead, we realize Einstein was a man who used more of what we also have to use, then he isn't qualitatively a different kind of being. He is what I am.

That same thing is true about Jesus Christ. Throughout the world, especially with religious people, one of the most heretical statements that you could possibly make is that the average human being could do everything that Jesus Christ could do. The interesting thing is either that's true or Jesus Christ lied. If Jesus Christ lied, we have a problem, especially Christians. Yet in order to be a good church-going Christian you have to believe that Jesus lied when he said, "All the things I can do you can do and greater things than these." You're not really supposed to believe that. In fact, you could probably get thrown out of church for believing that.

So we have these beliefs that are tailor-made to give us an excuse for not accomplishing what we came here to accomplish. I think we each came here to be a master. There have only been a few masters in history --- though many people would argue that there's only one, Jesus Christ --- but in any case we can count the number of real masters on our fingers. About four and one-half billion people are alive today and nearly that number have been alive in history. If we look at these nine billion people and we can count the people who actually accomplished what they came here for on our fingers, it's staggering. It makes history look tragic.

If we came here, intentionally and purposefully, to a planet run by the laws of cause and effect, we must have come here expecting to learn the right causes and produce the right results. Otherwise we would be very foolish to come to a planet that is run by those laws and not expect to be able to learn and apply them.

That suggests that our specific purpose for incarnating on this planet is to become a master, and yet even religious leaders will tell you that there is nothing more presumptuous and that there have only been a few masters and will only be a few. But if we change that belief system, if we change the old-fashioned concept of humility to a new kind of humility that works for us, we can recognize the very basic truth --- that a human being is a delicate, complex, fascinating absolutely wonderful creation. And if I admit the truth of that, I become responsible for doing wonderful things. Real humility is recognizing truth, taking responsibility for it, and saying thanks to the Source.[32]

From the standpoint of our own pre-incarnated existence the concept of non-limitation is no paradox but simplicity itself, and the mystery of our origin and identity with the Christ spirit is no fanciful speculation but clear certainty. Even while confined to a physical body we are under no necessity to abandon ourselves to the finite order, for as the Source points out:

All things the Christ may do, you can do, and you must do even, not for your own aggrandizement, but for obedience to the Source of all, God, His expression the Christ. The Christ will not be enthroned until one understands and completes precisely what He taught. This, the body you live in, is the body of the Christ. The blood coursing through your veins is the blood of the Christ. Thus, you can and you must do all things He did and more. And in so doing, you vindicate His life, complete His teaching and usher in the Second Coming, the higher initiation of this entire planet, this world of people. Take that as literally as you can understand it and apply it, and in doing so, cease from criticism of self or the humility that causes you to make less of self. Making less of self can only prevent you from being all that you are and can be. It is a false humility that must be left behind. True humility is understanding that you are no less than the Christ of God and with it, a humble appreciation for the gift of God to know your body to be that of the Christ and your blood to be His coursing through your veins.

Digest that. Understand it, and you step into the ranks of the enlightened (Solomon Reading No. 1717, 7/10/93).

Chapter 15

The Pearl Of Great Price

"BEHOLD BUT ONE"

As Christians, we are taught to believe in the historicity of Jesus as the God-man, the *only* Incarnation of God. It is blasphemy to think otherwise. As the Word made flesh, Christ is to be enshrined and adored and in that adoration we express our humility. To draw any equivalency is nothing short of heresy. Although the Scriptures tell us that we are made in the image of God, yet as fallible and fallen creatures drawn from the dust of the earth, we could make no such claim without laying perjury upon our souls.

Jesus is regarded as divine insofar as He became the complete human receptor of God's love, the one who, more than any other, was so totally open to God's love that He became its bearer and its vehicle. As God is the Source of all love, light, life, truth, so Jesus became the very child of that Source. But just as we praise and deify Him as our Savior, so we squander something essential within ourselves: that is, the same power of that life-impulse by which we may become as Jesus Himself was --- the perfect expression of the Logoic energy of love. **So many among you would set the Christ incarnate apart, believing that it only has happened as a phenomena once in history and never would happen again,** declares the Source:

> So that my elevation of Jesus who expressed the Christ causes me by necessity to bring to lower estate those who would attempt to teach and express His presence in this day. Now it is hardly possible that such ideas can be productive for they are contradictory in fact. For the Master of masters, the Christ, first said that the Son of God is that only Son become flesh and dwelling among you even now. If the belief, then, is that I will recognize an historical figure but refuse to recognize Him in anyone who expresses Him in this day, then I have relegated the Christ to being a has-been. Once was, is not now. If you would elevate and recognize the Christ, recognize Him when He speaks through a being to you. And at the same time if you would believe that you can recognize and honor that spirit without honoring it within this channel (Paul Solomon), then recognize that you are creating the fall, the separation from God anew and afresh, and perpetuating that that you seek to end. Look for at-one-ment in that which is before you and whenever it is expressed notice it and be inspired by it. So shall your joy be increased by the experience of seeing the face of the Christ often. So as well will your belief, your faith, your ability to express the Christ be increased by the knowledge that it does occur often. And when you see less than the Christ in these, set that aside as being misperception, whether in yourself or in them, but look for that that is the Christ, not discounting the form in which he presents Himself to you. For these are mirrors, points of recognition, and know the parable of the Christ Himself who said, "The owner of a land sent his servant into that land to collect the first fruits, that owed by the tenants on that land. The servant then was destroyed, not honored among

the people but killed. And he sent another and another and even his son."
And so the parable expressed that those who have no respect for the servant
neither has respect for the son, nor respect for the Father. Do not fool yourselves by saying I respect God, I respect the Christ, but I see the imperfection
of this servant sent to teach me. Your honor and respect of God is reflected
in that that you direct toward His expression in this time, in this plane. This
is not to suggest a worship of any human form at any time, whether this or
that teacher or another, but that you begin to love and respect one another
as He has loved you and as He commanded that you love Him (Solomon
Reading No. 964. 7/77).

It is only by virtue of our misguided and mistaken understanding of the nature
of the Christ Itself that we separate ourselves from Its truth in both ourselves
and in others. The essential truth of Christ is the living energy of Divine Love
without which Creation itself could never have occurred. It is the very Source
of our source, the Logos of our timeless origin and the ever flowing spirit of
Divine Love for life. Martin Buber relates to us the teaching of Rabbi Bunam:

> This is how we must interpret the first words in the Scriptures: "In the be-
> ginning of God's creation of the heaven and the earth." For even now, the
> world is still in a state of creation. When a craftsman makes a tool and it
> is finished, it does not require him any longer. Not so with the world! Day
> after day, instant after instant, the world requires the renewal of the powers
> of the primordial Word through which it was created, and if the power of
> these powers were withdrawn from it for a single moment, it would lapse
> into tohu bohu (chaos).[33]

The primordial Word, which is the expression of God's power and energy
manifest in and through Christ, constantly sustains every atom of His creation. It resonates at the very heart of any religion that proclaims God as One.
As the Source points out, **one who knows the Christ as He is will know that
He is not labelled by a Greek name, or even a Hebrew name, nor is He of
the Jew, or the Greek, or the Christian, but in all men everywhere who have
learned the nature of love, of light, of the Source of life, and have worshipped
that and have sought to introduce it to the world wherever man has sought to
understand God as God. God has revealed Himself and so the child of God,
the child that is born of God, has expressed Himself in many lands, in many
religions** (Solomon Reading No. 1368, 5/15/88).

> Now those followers of those Masters of the ancients, whether of the Christ
> as expressed in Christ or as expressed as another ... understand that these
> are words, attempts to express a concept. That which made Jesus the Christ
> was that same force that made Mohammed able to bring the light to those
> of his people. And these followers, whether of the Mohammed, the follow-
> ers of the Christ or the followers of Moses, if these then worshipped the
> man and those legends concerning the man, then it is of little good unless it
> awakened within the self that that made the man. It was the force that these
> were able to see, to direct, or that they became that should be worshipped,
> that life force that made these the Christ.

> And believe not that Jesus only was the Christ, for it was the force of the

Christ that struck water from the rock as Moses held the rod, was it not? And it was that Christ that Moses believed in and worshipped that you would worship in this time. And that same Christ was that force worshipped by Jesus. Jesus then became one with the force, manifesting it. This is not a different force or a different Christ than those followers of Mohammed would find or those followers of the Buddha.

Then that force, that life force, that that is the Son of God, is that universal One that made available that light that these used and would point you to. Then if Mohammed points you no further than Mohammed the man, then he has failed. But if he would point to that that made possible his salvation, then he would point to the Christ. And whether you would know this as Jesus the Christ or only as that God force that existed in Mohammed, you are worshipping that same force as you understand that light as the Son of God (Solomon Reading No. 240, 9/13/73).

That force that is the very expression of God cannot be divided --- it is singularly One. But what have we done? We've externalized It in the embodiment of a single man and dogmatized It into a sectarian figure, arrogating onto ourselves an exclusive entitlement to the redemptive fruits It offers to those of a single faith. Much the same holds for every great religion. While for most Muslims the whole idea of divine incarnation is anathema, as early as the third century of the Mohammedan era the Prophet Mohammed, or rather the 'truth' or 'light' of Mohammed, became endowed with all the attributes of the Christian Logos. He had become the pre-existent "center and animating principle of the whole created universe, the spirit of life of all things, and secondly... the Mediator of Divine grace, the channel through which God imparts knowledge of Himself to his worshippers and endows them with every spiritual gift." The same is true of Hinduism with its allegiance to Vishnu and Siva, as well as Buddhism wherein the Buddha, meaning simply 'an enlightened one,' becomes in the later Mahayana schools the Supreme Deity in trinity, manifested in the Body of the Law, the Body of Bliss, and the Magic or Transformation Body, the last of which enabled the triune God to adopt the human form of Sakyamuni.

Any religion, be it Hinduism, Christianity, Islam, Judaism, or any other springs from a faith. Beneath each faith are the non-rational dogmas or first assumptions on which all else depends. But the faith that each so cherishes is based on nothing more than hearsay and rumors: it is a faith in a belief in the unique divinity of its founder and an attachment to the symbols, rites and ceremonies surrounding that belief. In the words of the Source: **Each discipline that has appeared on the face of the planet from its inception as it now appears, each discipline that taught a single God, the One, has begun with a great pearl, a pearl of great price. Then in the course of attempts to explain and apply, has gathered about itself the dust of the thoughts of man, buried as it were in the dirt, in the earth** (Solomon Reading No. 583, 4/30/75). The 'pearl' of truth that lies at the core of each has been skillfully trapped and imprisoned in synagogues, temples, mosques, and churches the world over. We would rather believe in dogmas than in God, serving them not for the sake of awakening ourselves to truth but for the sake of a creed. The husk of religion remains, but unless the precious life in its germ is given a soil in which to grow, it will forever remain dormant. The point is contained in a parable given by Paul Solomon:

A wise man once walked among God's people. The people wanted to know God and to grow spiritually, so they said to the man, "Master, give us rules by which we can live." He consented and began to list some rules that, if followed diligently, might lift the people's consciousness to the level of God-realization.

He said, "One day a week should be kept holy. Let it be a time when you set yourself apart and forget everything else. You should spend a seventh of your time doing absolutely nothing except sitting still, listening and worshiping, thus making your creator and source most important in your consciousness."

"Yes, we will do that. Now, tell us more," said the people. They wanted to know exactly how they should worship. How should they prove that their creator was most important?

So the wise man said, "On the seventh day, you may go only a few yards from home. That is how precious this holy day is. You cannot travel, and you cannot buy or sell on that day."

"Yes, we will do that. Tell us more."

One rule led to another, and the list grew and grew. Soon the rules extended into the personal and private lives of the people. The wise man said, "Your body is precious because it is the temple of God that lives within you. Thus you should have rules about diet and rules about exercise." He set up a program of nutrition for the health of the body, and the people believed that they must eat according to these rules to grow toward God.

On and on grew the list. There were rules regarding cleanliness, and rules regarding fair exchange, and rules regarding marriage. There needed to be an official name, so the rules were called "laws and commandments." For every rule, there were a dozen guidelines for their application. The rules extended into every area of life as they became more complex.

By now, the wise man was gone and could no longer interpret the rules for the people or help them in the application. So the elders of the community pondered the importance of the rules. A university was established where the rules could be studied and wise interpretations of the meanings behind the meanings could be determined. Churches evolved around the rules, and some leaders of the churches said, "The rules mean this," while others said, "The rules mean that." The rules became points of contention. The differences in thought engendered hate, and wars broke out.

God was no longer most important in the people's consciousness. The rules had become most important.

Eventually, another wise man came and walked among God's people. This new wise man saw that the rules had become the people's god. He said, "Understand this. It is not through following rules that you will come to know God. You may believe that you seek him through your rules, but you will not find him there. It is only through a transformation, which occurs within you, that you will come to know God."

So the second wise man instituted a new form. He said, "Come with me to the river, and there I will put you under the water and bring you up again. It will be as if the old you who is fascinated with rules, the old self, will be dead. A new self will come up out of the water. Think of it as a burial and resurrection. The new self will live life in a new way because a transformation has occurred within you."

He led the people to the river and taught them about the futility of their rules. Many were baptized and experienced burial and resurrection. But soon, the people turned baptism into the new rule. Everyone had to be baptized to be saved, to become new, to know God. The people had discovered another rule to worship.

Over time, another wise man came and walked among God's people. This new wise man saw that the people had complicated God with rules. Worship was no longer joyous because it was burdened with restrictions. He said to the people, "All these rules and laws and commandments can be summed up in one simple statement. It is not a new commandment, but a fulfillment of the old. *Love one another.* Love your neighbor as you love yourself, and love God most of all. That is my only teaching. Having mastered this one thing, you can then do all other things. With love, you can accomplish anything."

The wise man taught the people on the hillsides and in the town squares. The people listened, and they were astounded by his simple words The wise man taught that if the people would simply love one another without condition or restraint, all the rules would prove unnecessary. There would be no need for the old laws in an environment of love.

The wise man used his experience of life to demonstrate this truth. He was love personified. At times, he deliberately broke the old laws to reveal their impotence. The people saw that he was a holy man, yet the old laws had no bearing on his holiness. He was God-like, not because of the rules, but because of what lay beyond the rules. Because he lived the purpose of the laws, the laws had no power over him.

Then he was gone. So his followers taught the people and said, "You only need to experience within yourself a living presence. There is no need for laws of worship. The only sin is selfishness. If you insist on your selfish ways to the exclusion of others, and their way, and their happiness, it is wrong. There is nothing else that is wrong, so you do not need rules."

But the people said, "We understand about love, and we will be loving. We understand about listening within, and we will do that also. But give us some rules. Life is simpler when we have rules to tell us what to do. Should we be vegetarian?"

The wise followers said, "It is not what goes in your mouth that defiles you, but what comes out."

"Well then, should we keep the Sabbath?" the people asked.

"Make every day holy," replied the wise followers.

"Should we wear certain clothes?" they asked. "How often should we pray? Must we have steeples on our churches? Is it better to laugh or be somber? Give us some rules. We must have rules!"

"You must find the soul behind the laws, beyond the customary dos and don'ts and shoulds and shouldn'ts. You must look past the practice to the essence of the law, beyond the regulation to the spirit of the law. When you know the spirit of the law, you will know the creator of the law, the Initiator. You will be one with the law, and it will be for you a way of life, not a dictate. Then you will know that there are no rules."

But the people dismissed their words and made rules anyway. They divided into groups and built structures and jurisdictions around their rules. They established hierarchies and granted the leaders of their churches piety and the right to know God, while they deemed themselves unworthy and unable. They formed judgments of others who practiced a different set of rules. Judgment often turned to persecution, and persecution sometimes turned to war. But they were only following the rules, so they were justified. They did it all for the glory of God, and they called their handiwork "religion."[34]

How often do we barter the inalienable truth of our own hearts for the spurious idolatry of a creed?

Religions are dead and separate the truth, declares the Source, **thus bringing confusion. Yet they are born of ones who knew** (Solomon Reading No. 1352, 12/12/89). If a spiritual teacher from some distant time --- Jesus, Buddha, Krishna, Mohammed --- were to step forward into our century and behold the proliferation of conflicting doctrines and separatist creeds that have coalesced around the seed of truth originally sown by him, he would have good cause to doubt either his sanity or that of our own. Each in his turn lived through the One, declares the universal Source of Solomon, **and know that if you walked with Moses, and if you walked with Elijah, and if you stood with Samson and you stood with Daniel, or if you walked with Zoroaster, or studied with the Buddha, if you were the student of Confucius, or the pupil of Ra, know that ... you walked with one of those who became one with Him, and there is none other.... That is to say, all lies in the understanding of One** (Solomon Reading No. 75, 11/19/72).

Each of these prophets and teachers, having bequeathed to humanity the spiritual blueprints for personal transformation, individual immortality, and universal brotherhood, would now find those same teachings so ineptly altered and narrowly misconstrued as to defy the very principles upon which they were originally set forth. Each would behold followers of every sect and creed summarily occupied by the vain and tedious complexities of religious ritual against which the founder himself had gone out of his way to warn them. Each would witness over the span of centuries mankind alternately building and destroying, killing and being killed, all in the name of the universal truths originally posited by the founder. Looking back, each of them, from our time to their own, they would no doubt sadly nod in agreement with Aldous Huxley:

> The atrocities of organized religion (and organized religion, let us never forget, has done about as much harm as it has done good) are all due, in the last analysis, to "mistaking the pointing finger for the moon" --- in other words to mistaking the verbalized notion for the given mystery to which it refers or, more often, only seems to refer. This is one of the original sins of the intellect, and it is a sin in which, with a rationalistic bumptiousness as grotesque as it is distasteful, theologies have systematically wallowed. From indulgence in this kind of delinquency there has arisen, in most of the great religious traditions of the world, a fantastic overvaluation of words. Overvaluation of words leads all too frequently to the fabrication and idolatrous worship of dogmas, to the insistence on uniformity of belief, the demand for assent by all and sundry to a set of propositions which, though meaningless, are to be regarded as sacred. Those who do not consent to this idolatrous worship of words are to be "converted" and, if that should prove impossible, either persecuted or, if the dogmatizers lack political power, ostracized and denounced. Immediate experiences of reality unites men. Conceptualized beliefs, including even the belief in a God of love and righteousness, divide them and, as the dismal record of religious history bears witness, set them for centuries on end at each other's throats.[35]

Beginning with the idea of the unity of mankind and of a unifying spiritual principle underlying all reality, the world has degenerated into a welter of confusing and uncompromising claims to truth. "Generally, above and below, thou shalt find but the same things," wrote Marcus Aurelius. "For all things throughout, there is but one and the same order; one and the same God, the same substance and the same law."[36] But the all-embracing unity of the One has been inexorably eroded by a multitude of discrepant and incommensurable absolutes, each with its own territorial prerogatives, each arrogating divinity exclusively to itself. "Behold but One in all things," taught Kabir; "it is the second that leads you astray."[37] But religions have divided the One, and from it they have created a world of an irreconcilable duality to which we have not only committed our faith, but to which we have surrendered, even within ourselves.

The true mystery of ourselves begins where the limitation of all doctrines, dogmas and beliefs end. Beyond limitation lies, in the words of the Source, **the understanding of that which is self, that which is real, that which should be cultivated; that one who could learn the importance of individuality or the casting away, the rejection of the necessity to manifest individually. The importance of this has separated man from God. The greatest lesson of all life would be to learn that lesson, 'I am God'** (Solomon Reading No. 186, 6/15/73).

THE SEED OF GOD

Just as Truth is the Word, or Logos, from which all creation came forth from Eternal Being, so is mankind the language of God. When one individual, then, perceives the power we call Christ as separate from his or her self, or when one religion places the human Logos of another religion in hell, we close ourselves to the limitless dimension of our source, or to the pearl of Truth upon which any religion stakes its claim to legitimacy, thereby recreating the fall. The dogmas, creeds, and beliefs that teach us to be less than what we are need to be abandoned and, as the Source affirms, the pearls need to be extracted and brought [to light]. For if among you one man will point to the one way and say this discipline in its manner of presentation is exclusive, then much understanding will be missed and men will be narrow of thought and will never discover the union, the at-one-ment of all things. But if there be only one door and one way, and there is of course, then that one door, that one way will be reflected in all these pearls. How much greater, then, the opportunity that all men might find that single way (Solomon Reading No. 583, 4/30/75).

> That truth as spoken is that one central truth. There is no other Name given among men whereby we might be saved. This, then, would be individual with every man. If you would understand the many different religions, or ways, or means of working out the salvation, then count the stars, count the sands on the beach, count the number of human souls that have and will come to work on this plane, for God has chosen that system and set it in motion, that there are as many systems for working out that return to Godhead as have been sparks of life come into creation. One for every one, yet still all come back to one. There is only one realization, that I am God, and that all other is excess coldness around me. All else is separation from God, and if there be awakening of that spark, that realization, then all else is only a means for attracting, for awakening. These rituals, these concepts, these teachings as have been given can be nothing more than tools. It is not the acceptance of the tool, it is not acceptance of a religion, a theory, a law, a concept, but the manner in which it works, that which the teaching leads to.

> Then see religion only as a concept, a means of interpretation. It would not be the interpretation of the thought, but the thought itself that would attract the mind. It would not be the interpretation of God, but God Himself that would be that belief, and that which causes Him to be awakened in thine own heart. This would be truth. This would be the Church of God. And in establishing His Church on this plane, He established not a religion, not a system of teaching, not a system for understanding truth. That Church was established in each heart, in every heart and only in the heart. Then in the establishing of that within the heart, or the awakening of this spark, so did that Church grow to become a multiple thing or a body of believers in the manner that the awakened spark in the life of each one might attract that similar spark to himself. So then might these aid and assist one another, being of common faith or common understanding, so that each may grow in fellowship. So then the bringing together of the sparks broke down that separation between these and all realized, "As I am God, so thou art."

> That separation between souls, then, breaking down, so does God and the body of God become more complete. In this manner understand that the Church is the body of God, not a body on this earth, not an organization, not a system of belief or teaching. Ever is the individual responsible for working out, that bringing out, of the nature of God within himself.

There is, then, one system, one way, yet at the same time, as many ways as there are sparks of God in manifestation (Solomon Reading No. 186, 6/15/73).

If, then, we can liberate ourselves from all limitations --- of fear, of self-doubt, and of those restrictive beliefs imposed by religious doctrines and creeds --- we will already have achieved some degree of enlightenment. For the degree of one's awareness of such freedom is a clear measure of the degree of that person's power of enlightenment --- that is, of one's openness to the unmediated love and inspiration that radiates directly from the higher world of the source or Intrinsic Self.

But the power itself is wholly impartial. We must still deal with the ego and its self-will. As the Zenist would say, "after enlightenment... more dirty laundry." What we _do_ with that power still lies entirely with ourselves. We can aggrandize ourselves or we can become a more perfect expression of love for the sake of Love Itself. We can channel the Devil or the power of a Christ. Hence we must through the conscious control of our thoughts, feelings, and activity continually commit and recommit ourselves to the living Being of Love, the Supreme Source of our source. Once the seed of love has become firmly implanted in our consciousness, only then can it find within our own responsiveness the fertility to take root and produce what the Source calls a "metamorphosis of the human spirit":

It is possible for any one of you to become consciously aware that there is always a divine desire inherent within you that impels you toward good, toward God. There is a spirit, or a presence, or a consciousness within each one of you. It causes within every man, woman and child an inherent seed of desire to be what you might call an expression of good, or of God.

There is inherent within you a portion of yourself which desires to be the best that you can be in all aspects of endeavor. It is a seed of your Source that desires to germinate and to bear roots, and boughs, and fruit --- to grow and to mature into that possible being, that one you could be, who through complete harmony would be an expression of the highest and the best that you might have potential to express in the earth.

In moments of quiet and peace, there is often a consciousness in your heart of the existence of such a seed. And you desire to feed, to water, to nourish that seed so that it might express. In other times, desperation within you drives you to awaken that seed of consciousness in order to establish a communication between that seed and its source.

It is the nourishment and the awakening of this seed of source which allows and causes the experience known as "regeneration," "metamorphosis", "transformation," and "the new birth."

The first step in this experience of transformation is a moment of evocation. There are times when you desire to express totally that which is good, that which is unselfishly of God within you. There arises a need in you to express perfect love, harmony and peace. The dreamer in you dreams of being all that you can potentially be, as an expression on Earth of the Divine Creative Principle, the Creative Fiat.

In those times when you experience that desire or quest, those moments are called the evocation of the highest or the divine to be in you and speak through you (sic). You seek the highest that is within you --- the creative nature, living love made manifest. You hunger for the true nature of your heart of hearts, where the only desire is to express on Earth as a presence that will contribute to life on Earth --- a light extending from yourself to burn as a candle in the darkness.

There manifests within each of you a presence which is the seed of your source. When watered by your expression of desire and prayer, there is awakened a need to express your holiness. This is the transforming experience. The seed that is planted in you is fed and watered by the transformation of all else that has been self. As self falls away into insignificance, it becomes like compost to this seed of the divine. The seed, sprouting as it were, reaches for its source, for it is a seed of a tree that is planted in heaven whose boughs, leaves and fruit extend into the earth.

The seed of God in you cries out to its source for the creative awakening spirit, the Divine Fiat. It is the extension of God that allows the spirit of creation itself to germinate that seed in you. And in that moment in which the best and the highest in you, that which is good and of God in you, that kernel or seed of God himself that he has planted in you, begins to awaken, there is the calling toward you of all the beings of the universe.

There exists a Great Cloud of Witnesses, which has been spoken of by the Apostle Paul as those who have gone before you from Earth's experience to become the heavenly witnesses of the times when the Source of Creation reaches its points of love into the hearts and activities of men, to empower life in a man or men, in a woman or women, and even in children, to express themselves in such a way as to lift the entire race a little closer to the perfection of the expression of God on Earth.

This Great Cloud of Witnesses surrounds the earth with its presence. These witnesses to the power of God are responsive when any one of you cries out to know the spirit, the presence, the power of God. These witnesses are drawn to the light which occurs in the moment of evocation of holiness, when self seeks its source so that it may germinate and express its potential of allowing God to live in and through the body. In that moment, the seed becomes active through the intentional evocation of that which is of God, of creativity, of good and growth.

A light is created in dimensions hardly known to you, but which are occupied by this Great Cloud of Witnesses. This light, or spark of light, comes from the intent of one individual to know his source, to discover his creator, to discover the source of love in himself, the source of motivation to turn away from alternate lovers, distractions of the earth that keep the mind bound to things, that allow the mind to be so occupied with things not of God that there is left little room in consciousness for this seed to have that bit of attention that it must have to become activated.

This tiny seed, which is of God, is surrounded by a boundary, born of the insistence of God himself. Your source, your creator, has insisted that this seed be surrounded by a barrier that consists of your own freedom of will, so that you might live your life according to a will that is separated from the natural fruit of this seed of God within you.

In those moments when any man gives up his separate identity, when any woman gives up her will that is separate from the will of the source contained in the seed of God within, when the barrier of self-centeredness and self-interest is pierced to explore the presence of light, of love, of goodness in self, when the consciousness is turned in full desire without reservation, when all other things become insignificant in comparison to the discovery of the potential of this seed of God in self, when evocation has occurred, invocation takes place.

The seed of God draws to itself its source of divine nourishment. There is created between the individual being, the human, a living link between the seed and its source. This, in turn, creates a light in dimensions hardly known to you --- a light which draws to itself that great host of the angelic kingdom, the Great Cloud of Witnesses. There is drawn that presence that has been described as the spirit of holiness and that presence that has been called the expression of God. There is called ultimately to this flowering of God in a man, the presence, the wisdom and the nature of the divine Source itself.

So as we speak, we attempt to explain who we are. We are that in the unseen that are attracted to a prayer, a request, a commitment, a dedication --- an emptying of all that is human self, presenting for a moment only that seed of God, with all else of the self lying dormant, unconscious, having given up its own thoughts which remain contrary to one another because of the nature of the cleft brain of man. And going beyond that mind, the seed of the source opens communication with those gathered here who are all presences, dedicated and committed to that one who has before him the records, the book and the books, as called in The Revelation. These are opened before him --- the books giving the thoughts of the source of creation itself in the Creative Fiat when the worlds were spoken into being.

His purpose in so doing is recorded here, and the history of the development of his creation is laid before him here. We, the witnesses, are gathered to be a part of this divine experience, to contribute to it and to bring our strength as witnesses to affirm and confirm to you that it is possible for the mind of man to be influenced and directed by the spirit and presence of God.

We would draw your attention to the prophet Daniel and the manner in which, by entering a sacred sleep, he allowed the communication of divine source to fill him with inspiration of the instruction of that source that he might then be a channel of the guidance of the divine.

This process has ever been available to mankind, and is. We seek not in this moment to describe for you some special gift, something that you would think of as supernatural or psychic in nature. But rather we present before you that which can happen and does happen when any one among you enters a moment in time when your very heart seeks to know experientially and personally the presence of good and God --- the manifest presence of holiness of the universe, available to you, that you might attune to His presence.

The seed in you is awakened through experiences such as this, in moments when you set aside all thoughts and opinions, all appetites and expressions of the body and the mind separated from its source. It is awakened as you enter into a time of utter stillness, listening with every part of the self to the expression of the source, listening with a request from the heart, not the mind, but from the very depth of self, the soul, the heart of self crying out to know its source and to be an expression in perfection of that source so that it may reach itself into Earth through you.

That experience of awakening is called by some, "transformation." By others, it is called "metamorphosis of the human spirit." By others, it is called the "experience of the new birth." All of these link the consciousness of man with its source and produce potentially what has been spoken of through this source and this channel as the Meta-Human. It is the birthright of all mankind to know, to be in tune with, to be an expression of and filled with the presence of, the divine to the extent that the limitation of what you can experience and express through human life is not the limitation of human possibility or capacity.

We have attempted to explain that what is occurring in this moment, the words that come and that you record, is not a phenomena for entertaining the fancy, for channeling the words of consciousness of an ancient being who will give his opinions of that which occurs on Earth today. We do not purport to be a psychic source speaking through this channel or individual through whom we speak. We express ourselves only as a response to proper prayer --- proper prayer being the setting aside of the self that is a distraction from the perfect inner desire to know God and the crying out sincerely from that heart of self that seeks to know God and asks, "Will you respond through me?"

Our words are a response to that prayer made possible by the setting aside of the limited consciousness of the brain's activity, ideas, prejudices, opinions and beliefs, that there might be produced a clear channel for all that is of God, all that there is of good and living love, to operate the consciousness and speaking mechanism to speak words of divine guidance. This should not be any more uncommon among you than the practice of the ministers, the preachers and priests who claim to speak the words of God before congregations of virtually every religion and creed about your planet (Solomon Reading No. 1413, 5/29/90).

Chapter 16

Fire In The Mind

THE CROWN OF ENLIGHTENMENT

Conceived through the limitations imposed by its own conditioning, the ego is formed out of separation. It is really nothing more than a facade of accumulated fears, a shield or defensive barrier contrived as a safeguard against the perceived threats of a hostile environment. The tension, anxiety and stress by which it maintains its separate identity is like a clenched fist. Relax the fist --- the mind and heart --- and there is nothing and no one inside. **For all that stands between your realization of who He was and is is that which you know as ego, or personality, or self,** states the Source. **For as long as you value identity, personality, or self, you find that barrier between one's self and the expression of the Divine. And [in] that moment that [that] identity is lost and thou shalt become Him, in that moment shalt thou express Cosmic Consciousness and His presence on this earth plane. And in that moment shall the scales be lifted from your eyes and you shall observe the Second Coming of the Christ** (Solomon Reading No. 385, 7/2/74). The more we become free of fear and of the other limitations of self, therefore, the more we become expanded vessels for the expression of the unlimited power that we call the Logos or Christ. And the more that the energy of love comes to permeate all levels of our consciousness, the more of all that is past will dissolve into the immediacy of the timeless present. As the whole substance of mind is of the past, so it dissolves, and with it the self, disclosing the presence of the greater Self. It is this the Source refers to as the "new birth". Or in the words of the Maitrayana Upanishad: "Having realized his own self as Self, a person becomes selfless.... This is the highest mystery."

There are so few capable of understanding that mastery can be achieved, and so few willing, then, to accept that challenge and create that expectation (Solomon Reading No. 9367, 3/12/91). If we are among those many who see it as so mysterious or esoteric or otherworldly as to be utterly unattainable, then by the limitations of our own lack of faith in ourselves we merely render ourselves impotent and incapable. As the Source points out:

It is not uncommon for men to cut themselves off from their source of communication, from hearing the presence of God, as is the natural condition of man. Do understand that it is the natural condition of man to live in the presence of God and to have a connection with Him for communication. But we are taught so, in our society, to cut ourselves off from the Source of inner creative being by the superstition that those guidances as come from within are mere imaginings, and have little to do with truth. Understand here that it is not difficult for a man to reconstruct in his life what he has lost through practice, through belief. That is to say that there is actively in your being, even in this moment, a communication going on between the parts of self, as it might be called. This in fact, communicates throughout the night, yet at night it might be heard better than during the day, the part of that communication that is at peace with God with little resistance.

Now this means if you can withhold the constant chatter of the mind, and rest it in moments of meditation then you can clearly hear the voice that comes from the Source of man, the creative Source, the Presence of God. There are several reasons why most men do not recognize this ability and think it unusual. It has been thought that no one particular man could actually hear the presence of God. The thought is based on the idea that man is insignificant, particularly in such numbers as are on the earth to have a direct link with the consciousness of God. It is often thought egotistical and selfish. Do understand that it is not because of the importance of one individual, yourself or another, that you have the opportunity to speak with God. It is not man's greatness; it is God's greatness that He can speak with so many as will listen at one time.

And when those do, from time to time, stop to listen, they are considered, then, channels. And too often people listen to them rather than to Who they are listening to. This is to suggest, then, that [although] you have available to yourself those abilities that you need to hear the presence of God in your coming to meditation, you will have a bit more of a challenge toward listening. And this is a bit of a self protective mechanism that you've had to separate yourself from an inner voice at times when it seemed to produce feelings of guilt, or lack, or unworthiness (Solomon Reading No. 1203, 6/25/90).

As we believe, so we become. And if we are not masters of ourselves, then, as the Source points out, we must ask ourselves, who controls us? Love or fear? Life or limitation?

But the mind of each of us is not only capable of this prodigious leap from the human to what the Source calls the "meta-human", it is literally hard-wired into our DNA. It is our birthright and the very reason for our physical being on this earth --- to know ourselves. Moreover, it is our responsibility, both to ourselves and to the world we live in, to live consciously and in clear realization of our divine nature. It is simply a matter of having faith in our unlimited potential and in the willingness and commitment to control the irresponsible nature of our own thinking. By so doing, the Source tells us that the integration of the brain-mind with the higher mind of the Intrinsic Self becomes possible:

Now, we would attempt to describe the necessary process of mastery in this way: inner peace and serenity are results; cause is integration. That which is referred to as the Intrinsic Self is certainly the God within, the Higher Self, the inner Christ. Understand its nature in this manner: it is intrinsically you; it is by nature non-assertive. That is key to understanding the means for invoking and integrating with this Christ-self, this God-self in you. We give emphasis to this for this reason: the non-assertive nature of God, of Christ in you, of the highest in you is so because God in you seeks that you might have limitless expression of your own will --- not your will as opposed to Divine Will, but in the opportunity to integrate all portions of yourself with that nature. Thus it requires this: being non-assertive except in survival situations means that the Christ in you will not control you except as you seek that It do so.

And you might find steps to enlightenment in this manner: understand that this Intrinsic Self will not impose itself upon your feelings, emotions, inclinations, beliefs or your thought. Thus the integration with it occurs when you seek that integration above all things. It must be the highest desire of the heart, and all factions of self must be in harmony in seeking it. All incarnate individuals have factions or incomplete personalities within the self which must be integrated, and in the integration, must dissolve into the Intrinsic Self incarnate. That is the state of mastery --- when there is no portion of self separate from the expression of the Intrinsic Self.

Thus, it is the requirement in your prayer, in your seeking, in your communication with the highest within you, that prayer must be that every portion of yourself, needs and desires not excepted, seek to integrate with God in you. The result of this, then, is inner peace and serenity. Integration with the inner Intrinsic Self is the path of mastery. It may be stated in many ways including the description of the Crown of Enlightenment. The Crown of Enlightenment is, as well, a result of integration with the inner Intrinsic Self.

Steps to that include asking first. Might be stated in this manner: you begin by talking to and with the Inner Self or the Intrinsic Self. Then, asking that the Intrinsic Self do more of the thinking for you which integrates the hemispheres of the brain and thus creates an integrated mind. As you continue in the path to mastery, the Intrinsic Self replaces the hemispheric or cleft-brain thinking that is typical of the species. The resulting integration is the Crown of Enlightenment.

When the separated self --- the self separated from the Source --- disappears, you are then, to use an ancient term, a Christed being. You are the Christ. When there is no separation between that which is incarnate and expressing in the created from the Creator Self, when this is integrated, there is then the Crown of Enlightenment, inner serenity and peace, at-one-ment with source, and there is no identity separate from source within you. This, then, is mastery, and is the accomplishment of that that your soul entered to express.

Let us, however, take a step further in saying, it is essential that you become totally aware of your inner conversation, for the inner conversation is a dialogue. The dialogue will result in a unilog when the brain is integrated and the Christed Self is the thinker. In the path to enlightenment, one must first begin with the dialogue, but causing both sides of the dialogue to seek the same result. That is integration, transformation, metamorphosis as the dialogue disappears into the expression of the Higher Mind, for it is only the brain that is separate. The mind is not separated from itself. The brain-mind is a result. The Cause Mind is the creator of the brain and transcends it.

Then as to creating clear, conscious thinking --- as we would refer to it as full-time thinking, without lapses in responsibility for thought --- begin carefully, addressing the Source of your mind, asking that Source to ever more each day take over the thinking process. Not that you would give up self to something outside of the self to control you, but rather that you would end the separated nature of thinking by dialogue merging into integration with the Higher Self, the Intrinsic Self, the God within, the Crown of Enlightenment.

Seek clarity by knowing your thoughts. Knowing the thoughts, then, take control of the thoughts. Think what you wish to think rather than thinking what comes to mind as is the nature of irresponsible thinking. For most who are incarnate, thinking is not intentional, meaning that most are carried by their thoughts not knowing that they can master thought.

Think on purpose. Fill your mind with what you choose to fill it with rather than allowing thoughts to come randomly and without control. Know your inner dialogue. Recreate that dialogue so that you harmonize the argumentative nature of the dialogue. Seek that the cleft brain create neurotransmitters from one side to the other to integrate the brain. Then transcend the brain-mind by allowing that the Cause Mind, the creator of the brain, becomes the thinker within you. This is the Crown of Enlightenment (Solomon Reading No. 9367, 3/12/91).

If what is contained in this reading seems baffling or perhaps even incredulous, consider that modern neurological research tells us very much the same thing: that not only can we create new neural networks within the brain, but through a conscious focusing of our attention and mindfulness of our thoughts we can create them to be so powerful as to overcome even our most basic instinctive emotional reactions. Contrary to earlier held beliefs, modern research indicates that even in old age the neural cells of the cerebral cortex (the 'intellectual' part of the brain) respond to our thinking patterns by forging new connections to other cells.

In brief, this is how it works: in the brain-mind, consciousness is mediated by the interaction of electrical impulses and neurotransmitter activated buffers and filters. It is a self-generating, self-regulating electromagnetic field potential modulated by the action of conductivity sensitive chemicals in the spark gap of the synapses. Synapses are the infinitely small gaps separating neurons across which information travels by way of chemical changes. When a thought is generated, a sufficient buildup of electrical intensity triggers a cross-synaptic firing forming a pattern in the brain that is imprinted, either temporarily or more permanently, in protein and other macromolecules, at and around the synaptic junctures. Studies indicate that when a thought is repeated, neurons increase in dimension and activity, glial cells (which support neurons) multiply, and the dendrites of neurons (branches of neurons which receive messages from other cells) lengthen. The dendritic increase makes for a more entrenched and more conditioned pattern of communication with other cells. Memories become 'fixed' such that any form of learned behavior (i.e., riding a bike, playing a piano, etc.) need not be relearned over and over. Hence, not only does the brain shape thought, but thoughts quite literally shape the brain.

Bearing all in mind, the Source tells us that thought manifests both physically and psychically: the brain which processes thought being the physical-cerebral organ and the mind as the conductor of thought being that of the psychic.

When the mind allows thoughts to randomly and uncontrollably roam free, the brain's nervous system patterns itself accordingly, resulting in a semi-conscious and involuntary state of mind, the neuropsychological analog of an unconnected or 'fragmented' sense of self. Uncontrolled thoughts based commonly on fear, anger, sadness, or any form of negativity then repeat themselves over and over in a constant and perpetual stream of inner dialogue, reinforcing and deepening the same neural pathways of the brain. If, for instance, we hear someone say something offensive, we have an emotional reaction. Our bodies tense up and our inner thoughts play out in dialogue, looking for a response. The longer the troubling thought persists, the deeper the associated stress embeds itself in our cells and in the brain's neural networks in a self-perpetuating cycle of reiterative memory and emotional response.

Neurological research demonstrates that stress response patterns cause a dominance of high frequency beta waves in the brain. While in the beta state, the brain is capable of nothing more that primitive stimulus-response patterns adopted largely from our environmental conditioning, making any significant change or transformation impossible. The transcendental realities of the undifferentiated Cause Mind of the Intrinsic Self are simply obscured by our own subjective thought patterns and remain wholly inaccessible to awareness. Our day-to-day behavior has, for the most part, become reflexive and fear-motivated starting as far back as our earliest childhood memories and experiences. As a race it extends back through to the mists of our collective childhood, to the time of our fall when all contact with the Causal Mind or Infinite Source was lost. Not a tithe of the experiences of our own Transcendental Self are any longer communicated to our limited and sleep-induced consciousness.

Mankind's fall broke up a seamless cosmology into a universe of fragmented pieces. Had we not experienced such a fall, we would be able to see with our god's-eye vision "what Adam had seen on the morning of his creation," as Huxley puts it, "the miracle, moment by moment, of naked existence."[38] No words, no human expression, could contain the immensity and power of such a mind and heart perfectly integrated with the entire stream of life. No divided mind could possibly fathom the vast, incomprehensible, power of a Christ.

... in a being without the separated cleft brain, but with the wisdom of an androgynous being, energies and powers beyond any that you know now could be called upon with something similar to what you now call thought.

Now we resist using the word "thought" because thought is accomplished by interaction between two hemispheres through conversation in a brain. But before that separation, before the cleft brain occurred in the human species, before that moment of selfishness which resulted in this separation, there was an expression of ... single minded creation with no resistance, no force working against other forces. You could call upon the power to travel, to fly, either about the Earth or even through the Earth itself. But when there developed a kind of competition between individuals, the organ known as the brain in all mankind was severed at that moment. Cleft right through the center and from that moment were known male and female which had not before existed. And also was known selfishness, competition, expressions of power and such. And what this seer has told you of the past is an attempt to explain to you that, as you recognized this so-called fall of mankind, you immediately set about attempting to heal this cleft in the brain, that it might once more act as one single unit which was not even created for thinking in reality. The original use, purpose of the brain, and the reason that so little of the power of the brain is used, is because the brain was originally something of a transformer of such enormous power of the universe that it was necessary to be reduced to levels manageable by physical bodies upon this planet. And only then when the selfishness, the cleft occurred, only then, was the thought of religion a necessity, a practice, as you would say. Although even before that there was a worship, [a] singular worship of the One --- it was an adoration. It did not have a point of comparison between light and darkness which is that knowledge of good and evil. Without the partaking of that fruit there was no ability to discern darkness or evil. Darkness and evil do not, in fact, exist, but having eaten of that fruit they appear to exist and have even caused many to learn fear and danger and such to a much greater degree and extent than they learn love and beauty... (Solomon Reading No. 1642, 5/4/92).

Like the starry sky on a clear night, the unconditioned unity of Paradise may indeed surround us, but we simply cannot see it through the neon glare of our own projections of language, thought and discrimination, modalities of perception and awareness which we take to be the whole of reality. Beyond the manifold of our thought and conditioning, however, there lies the unconditioned matrix of the world's reality, the "unfallen" world beyond time, space, and polarity. And there it remains, as a background to the broken world of egotistical rebellion and despair.

The flesh-and-blood body of the human beast has not changed in the last several thousand years, nor has its mind changed. The beast of a hundred thousand yesterdays is essentially the same as today --- a tangled mass of contradictions filled with the same limited attributes, motivated by the same impulses, and chained in the circle of its own habitual feelings and thoughts. Its sense of self is produced in these thoughts which come into it by association it knows not how or from where, and which over the course of its life play themselves out entirely disconnected from the intrinsic Source of its own creation. By virtue of its somnolence and insensibility, it has become alienated from the surrounding universe and from its own true nature.

Few men and women who have ever lived have known that they were living their lives as in a dream. The visions of their humanity, the apparitions of their imaginations flooded with the fears and passions of obscure impulses inscribed indelibly on their faces, all speak clearly enough to the inner demiurges that control their lives. Faces twisted by depression and pain, faces of terror, hate, meanness, faces impassive and expressionless, faces wrinkled, sagging and sealed against experience, all appear as those of sleep-walkers constantly influenced by the trance-reactions of emotion and thought. Even the most advanced among us inhabit worlds of thought entirely primitive to the illuminations of the spirit.

One can only imagine that like the blind man who knows the night to have no end, we are all, save for a very few, bound by our fears of the darkness, possessed only by the fantasies of our egocentric dreams. Blinded by a cloud of unknowing, the mind projects onto the world its own reflected images. Through the temptation to create a world in thought, it tyrannizes by bringing the world's creative flux to an end. In short, it has ceased to lay claim to its original spiritual freedom and has instead asserted a new and dreadful liberty --- the liberty of privilege, of distinction, of egotistical ambition, of the deification of self. The mind's strength is at the same time it's ailment. It gains its knowledge and its power of becoming at the expense of, and in exact proportion to the intoxication of self and its irredeemable blindness.

In the words of D.H. Lawrence, "Knowing and being are opposite, antagonistic states. The more you know, exactly the less you are. The more you are, in being, the less you know." In other words, the self's inseparable attachment to its conceptual creations --- to its thoughts, beliefs, dreams, fantasies and fears --- only thickens the veil of separation between our divided selves and our source. We can no longer recall ever having known good without evil or perfect love without fear.

"Sleeper awake!" In the Gospels as in fairy-tales and in the world's most ancient religious texts, it is always the same admonition. Imprisoned in the mind of a beast, we are wholly unaware that the earthly aspect of our nature is but a vast slumber of the spirit. And until that ineffable moment when the spirit within us awakens, we will continue to be carried away by momentary cravings and long-festering fears and animosities, by simple acts of heartbreaking ignorance and by secular allegiances and tribal hostilities that threaten our world, all of which are ludicrous even by our own estimation.

In a passage from the film They Might Be Giants, George C. Scott, fancying himself as the legendary Sherlock Holmes, turns to Dr. Watson, the female psychiatrist assigned to relieve him of his delusions, and declares, "If God is dead, then He laughed Himself to death." A cryptic glance from the provisional Holmes at lengths piques the inquiring mind of Watson. "We've never left paradise," he informs her. "It's all around us! Moriarty has made fools of us all! But tonight, my dear Watson, we'll bring him down."

Like Maya, the goddess of illusion in Hindu mythology, the shadowy Moriarty has blinded us to a paradise, masked only by the illusion of separateness, that has surrounded us all along. So it is that Holmes, fulfilling his tragic destiny, goes forth to battle the villainous Moriarty. Only in conflict with as worthy an opponent as the infamous Moriarty, in the conflict with his opposite, can Holmes truly complete himself.

Moriarty's shield is darkness, his weapon is illusion, which leads us ultimately to a delirium induced by spiritual density and self-ignorance. Herein lies Moriarty's greatest strength, that there is that of us which craves the shadows of self-ignorance and the great majority of us who, though regarded as quite sane by conventional standards, have neither the courage nor the will to battle our own fears. Consequently, the paradise that everywhere surrounds us has been turned into hell by the enemy within us.

It is tempting to suppose that Holmes' deduction is correct: that we are all merely blind, or perhaps asleep --- a sleep of forgetfulness of our true center, our eternal being --- to the paradise that exists "just beyond the thin veil" of our insentience. Our "Fall" consists of nothing more than our falling asleep. All fear and suffering comes from this. Having lost contact with the sacred light of the Source, we wander through life in darkness. Estranged both from God and nature, we are now caught in an addictive cycle of fear and desire that shrivels our sensibilities and narrows to a thin wisp any least glimmer of the failing light. Unless and until we can arm ourselves with a love so fearless that it casts its searing and irresistible light into the very source of the mind's dark filters, the shadow will continue to master its substance, the beast will rule the god, and paradise will forever remain an "open secret."

But as the Source makes clear, the higher Causal Mind is not so far removed as we might imagine, nor is it all that difficult to reach. Paradise lies just beyond the threshold of our preconditioned thoughts and fears. Heaven, in fact, is *not* a place where one "goes", but a consciousness of One with no separation. That is why Jesus said, "Heaven is within you." Through a conscious and committed effort not merely to control our thoughts but to transform them from fear to the higher frequencies of love, new feedback loops of positive transition enhancing neuro-chemicals will form that will literally repattern the brain's neural networks. Fear and anger shut down communication to the prefrontal cortex and anterior cingulate, the areas of the brain responsible for mediating empathy, love, intuition, compassion, and the ability to regulate emotion. But when through the mind's conscious intent thought is transformed to a higher frequency, the activity in the amygdala, the primary fear center of the brain, subsides, and new channels of communication are opened to the prefrontal cortex, eventually becoming permanently etched. As emotion and fear cease to dominate thinking and behavior, deeper brainwave states result increasingly in the mind's awareness of itself and of its experience in real time, the ever present and eternal "Now" of a Heaven within where Love is the natural condition and climate. Love in such a state is not a verb or an activity, but a state of being. In the absence of fear (anger, sadness, etc.) there is only peace. **Then the single most important key, emphasizes the Source, is the profound release of all the bonds, the ties to the physical body, particularly expressed in embodied thought. This occurs at the threshold of the alpha and theta levels of consciousness with relation to biofeedback. Remember that relaxation is of the mind first, the body second; the mind at total peace which requires profound release. This is release from guilt, release from any regret, release from anxieties, all release, all those thoughts and concerns related to success or life in the physical --- all this must be released. Total release of concern will bring the mind to peace. When the mind is profoundly at peace, the body will respond to the peace of mind.** (Solomon Reading No. 1717, 7/10/93). It is precisely this that makes for the integration necessary to achieve an attunement with the Causal Mind.

FORTY DAYS AND FORTY NIGHTS

The Causal/Intrinsic Mind or Self is uniquely each of us. It is the essence of oneself as a newborn, before the consensus trance of social and cultural conditioning --- before fear --- has begun to re-form and redefine us in its image.

It is only when we have awakened ourselves from all "entranced" behavior, habits, thoughts, and learned feelings --- when we have become conscious --- that the Causal Mind is most accessibly within reach. It is at this point, from the deeper brainwave states of love and awareness that, as the Solomon Source puts it, a distinct, personal, experiential relationship with the Source of life can be acquired:

> Now we begin with describing a manner of exhorting this presence to assert. The non-assertive Presence feels no need to control. It has given, has granted opportunity to the embodied personality and character to experience the world through the senses, to follow the teacher known by and through the sensory awareness. For as long as you so desire, the sensory teacher, the witness of the actions, activities of God in creation about you, this teacher has been and is to the untrained or to the once born the most obvious and most available teacher. We refer now to the sensory mind, not preferring one hemisphere of the brain over the other, for it is not the brain precisely of which we speak, but rather the mind as it discovers and teaches through the use of the senses. This teacher, called "the witness", can describe only to you, can teach you only of those things which can be seen, heard, experienced through the senses. This mind, the sensory mind, will not fail in any life, in any human, to from time to time assert.

> Within the self, within the mind, there is a greater teacher than the mind. Some choose to believe that this inner prompting comes naturally through the mind of the senses, and those who do so believe are sometimes prompted, enticed, sufficiently intrigued, sufficiently inspired and moved to seek out the non-assertive higher teacher. It is the one of which the [sensory teacher] has spoken, "There is a teacher greater than I, one who can teach you things not of this world, but who can teach you the presence of the Source of all life, for He is, at all times, with that Presence, the Source of all life." Then the sensory mind will not fail to produce such prompting, an urging, that one seek such a higher teacher, and those sufficiently inspired, determined, committed and desiring to know the higher teacher above all things [will begin] "the search" as it has been called, the search for the Holy Grail, the search for the pearl of great price.

> Then [you are brought] to ask: "How can I know, experientially, directly, personally, how can I know you, my source? How can I become familiar, conversant, committed to following and to discovering the purpose and the highest path to the Kingdom, to the Crown?" We respond by saying: "Set your priorities straight." This is an absolute. Never bother to set priorities as you feel they should be. It either is your priority or it is not in your life to know the non-assertive, creative source of yourself and Christ's teaching, direction, and guidance and purpose for your life. Make straight the path. So it is written as the Apostle John has said, "And in so doing, in so setting aside all other desires, all other wishes, all other purposes, all the alternate lovers, should you understand their nature through the Song of Songs attributed to Solomon, setting aside all other priorities."

> Then, simply address the non-assertive, intrinsic expression of the Christ who is the You of you, who is the Intrinsic, the manifest. The Intrinsic is

called the Christ or the child of God, for so it is. This child of God might better be expressed as the expression of God in you, lest you think of this non-assertive self, the Intrinsic you, as being another or someone else, for it is not. It is rather the You of you, the impersonal life.

Address, then, that non-assertive factor in you which has caused in you from your earliest awakening the possibility that your life could in fact make a difference; that your being manifest in a physical body on this earth with your ability to speak and to act through that body could matter; that it could make a difference, could accomplish even something which would raise the consciousness of the race of mankind closer to the expression of the Source of creation.

We declare then, that your first and immediate step is commitment, a commitment which is made by considering all things important to you and eliminating all which may by any means appear more attractive than knowing your Source. This step of commitment is referred to appropriately as the Abrahamic Sacrifice. It requires that if you wish to both know and to manifest God in you, your own Intrinsic Self, if you are to manifest even who you are, you must eliminate all attractions which compete with that determination to know. This commitment then, this sacrifice, is the first step of the knave to the beknighted who seeks without distraction the Holy Grail.

Having made such commitment, you need only then as a next step to speak. It is written, "You have not because you ask not." Then ask. Ask that the non-assertive Intrinsic Self, the Self of self, the Intrinsic Creator of all that is you, ask. Ask, saying in your own words, "I seek to know You," even saying strongly enough to express: "I demand my birthright to know my Intrinsic Self, the expression of God manifest through me, the return of the Christ in the flesh. I seek to know You, my Source, my Guide, my highest and closest connection with the Source of my soul." This was the instruction given in response to the question of the Apostles of the Christ in their asking Him, "Teach us to pray." Jesus responded in this manner, giving to them the Lord's Prayer. Not at all the Lord's Prayer, but rather His teaching, His teaching of a formula of prayer saying simply, "Begin your request by addressing to whom you speak."

Say that. Write it, for the writing of the prayer will bring it from the formless into form; from vision into manifestation grounded into the world of formation, creation. Write it. Speak to the Source of sources, the Source of Self, and say as simply as this: "I ask to know You, to know You better. I am sufficiently committed in my seeking that I will begin my experience of consciousness upon awakening in each day to repeat my request, asking, "Are You there Source of myself, Creator, Guide, Highest Teacher, Master of Masters? Are you there? I would speak with You. I wish to know You, to know You even better." Be sufficiently committed to begin each day with such a request, setting aside all other questions for the moment, for a time of at least forty days, and ask no further question than, "I seek to know You. I request that You manifest, that You assert that You are there."

The non-assertive self is non-assertive only because all kingdoms, the supernal, the higher kingdoms, those of whom you refer as angels, angelic beings, the spirits of nature, of creation, the multitude of life and kingdoms of life which reach to the Sources of the universe and beyond, all of these, including the non-assertive within you, have a commitment which is in fact in obedience of Universal Law, the Law of the Source of all that is, that Law being that God has placed upon Himself a restriction, a limitation, a chosen limitation, a Universal Law which says: "I will not force any of these creatures which I have fashioned in my own image and expression, I will not force any one of them to acknowledge My Presence, to be controlled except that they seek to be and that their seeking be the highest motivation of life."

This, then, is that which is both simple and complex. That which is at once easy, the yoke is easy and the burden is light; and yet at the same time, to one who does not yet know, it would seem that setting aside all other values in life for this one pearl of great price is a very demanding request. Then it is simple or complex, it is easy or difficult, but it is, in the end, your choosing; it is your will. If, then, that will is at the level of the heart, if that will, not contrived but of essence is to know, to be, to do, what you are, who you are, why you are, then simply ask. Ask as your soul is returned to you from the School of the Divines at the dawning of each day that you refer to as awakening, that We refer to as resurrection. Upon the changing of your consciousness from the state of sleep to awakening, at that moment, make known your request immediately. "I seek You. I seek to know You. I ask You from my will. I yield to Your Will in this moment. I seek that You assert." For He will only assert by request, unconditionally.

Thus, if your question, if your asking be from the heart, then you have your instruction. "Ask, and you will know. Knock. The door shall be open. Seek. You will find." Recognize that these are three statements of promise. Absolute. There is not a maybe; there is not a caveat. There is a direct promise. If you seek, you shall find. Then it is yours to seek. It is that simple.

Now let us build upon that by saying that if you so seek at the beginning of each day and maintain your seeking as an underlying drive of the heart and the soul to know, which does not interfere with all other activity but which does co-exist as a foundation beneath all other activity, you will find, perhaps to some amazement, that the activities of your day will be accomplished more effectively --- immediately. The quality of your work, your life, your expression will increase in effectiveness, in efficiency, in order. It will become a quest for excellence in all that you do.

Now this is only the slightest evidence of the manifest from the non-assertive Intrinsic Self. If that underlying request, desire, holy quest, is maintained throughout the day and spoken even in consciousness as often as it comes to mind, then when you lay yourself down to return your soul to His hands in the altering of your consciousness from what you call awake to sleep, then in the time of your sleep, your training, your schooling, it will be, and through the night you will be taught. Your knowing will grow. And after a time of forty days and forty nights of having walked and talked with the Master of Masters, you will know Him, you will know Him as certainly as you have ever known a friend, and you will know this being whose name is

Truth, whose name is Love, whose name is Life. You will know this friend. For within this time, the non-assertive will begin to assert at your request, and only at your request, and the only exceptions are moments of survival emergency.

Then shall you develop the mystic experience, that is to say, an experience of knowing directly, experientially, personally knowing, not believing, but experientially knowing this Source who will walk and talk with you. The conversation which comprises your thinking will be altered dramatically, for you will cease to send thoughts from one hemisphere [of the brain] to the lowest point of connection between the hemispheres to reach the other and to answer back again. The conversation between the inherent child and the imposed parent, this conversation will alter dramatically until it become a bridge, a bridge above the activity of the brain-mind, a bridge which is a bridge of light, similar in analogy to an electrical spark or current which produces a glow, a light, a Light of lights, a light which is as a crown, a yarmulke of light resting upon your crown, the Crown of Enlightenment.

Now this is an ultimate knowing. We do not suggest that such a permanent bridge of light which will unify the cleft brain to become single-minded will be permanently built in forty days, and yet, it is possible. As the Christ said, "This temple you have been forty years in the building, I will resurrect in three days." Such was the initiation of the Master of Masters. What will yours be? Forty days is essential to establish such a bridge of light. Maintaining it, then, will be a result of commitment and direction.

We will move if we may to that which you would ask, "How may I escape this prison which I experience as laziness, hedonistic, meaningless activity, the result of a bored mind? How may I escape into the freedom to express who I am?" And the answer is this: When your communication becomes vertical as we have described, invoking the non-assertive Intrinsic Self, evoking from within you a desire to be one with that Intrinsic Self, your circle of friends will change. Of those who have been an influence, some will be lifted to another level because of you. Others will drift away. It will be rather an unconscious experience. It will have been done likely before you notice. In such a manner will virtually all activities and relationships in your life be altered, your system of values overturned and replaced and ordered in a thoroughly new manner as a result of this commitment.

We challenge you, charge you with responsibility for being that you came to be (Solomon Reading No. 1694, 8/11/92)

HE WHO SEEKS WILL FIND

The neuro-physiological changes associated with the transcendence of the brain-mind into a fully integrated state of enlightened awareness have been known among various spiritual traditions throughout the ages. Each in their own way found inspiration from the example and teachings set forth by those supremely awakened minds whose legacy provided them with the blueprints for spiritual freedom. Gautama said: By self-denial, seek that annihilation of self which is the way to universal being. Socrates said: Let us fulfill ourselves by embodying in ourselves, and in the world that is our city, the true and the Good. Jesus said: Love one another; love God above all; for God is love. From each there developed methods and disciplines for awakening the mind and for escaping the limitations of the flesh and individual consciousness in order to be gathered once more into the Absolute Being. No doubt the followers and practitioners of each separate discipline were entirely unaware of the physiological changes that would accrue from their efforts. But enlightenment is enlightenment, by whatever path it is achieved. And in every case, if approached single-mindedly and with the yearning of an open heart, their efforts led to the same result: a subtle alteration in the electrochemical composition of their neurons, producing new dendrites both in the frontal lobes of the brain and across the hemispheres. As these nerve fibers continue to grow through a constancy of effort and discipline, a connection is formed joining the right and left cerebral hemispheres resulting in a total integration of the brain-mind, what the Source refers to as the "Crown of Enlightenment":

> There is an ancient promise which says, "He who seeks will find," and "to him who knocks the door will be opened." Now these statements, promises, are made with certainty, without qualification, and as they are applied in such a manner, they do work for the establishment of a relationship with the Source of wisdom, the Source of life. With mathematical precision, they work to accomplish this.

> First, as you read the lives of the mystics, those who have had personal, experiential relationship with Source, do not compare yourself with those but rather use them as a source of inspiration. Comparison of self with them will always increase the gulf between your present experience of the knowledge of God and theirs, accomplished over the time of their life. Make not then comparison, but [take] rather inspiration from these lives. Then follow on in this manner: devotion and discipline are to a great extent two different paths, and yet they must be married, for they are the two serpents entwining the rod that is the carrier of the life force, the kundalini. And there is a need to release much of what becomes pent up or repressed drive, passion, as will allow you to more greatly recognize, and to enhance your desire for your need to know your Source.

> Now this is well established in your time, even outside what is called spiritual circles. In the disciplines of psychotherapy, it is now well established that there is an innate intelligence referred to by researchers as the "Inner Self Helper", referred to by teachers and mystics throughout the ages as the Higher Mind, the Higher Self, the Christ in you. We mention this that you might consider that God is neither outside you nor beyond you, but within you. And this Presence, the guiding light, the inner light, this living Presence within you, is described as non-assertive, non-judgemental, always loving and supportive and quite capable of healing.

> Now, we mention this that you might particularly understand that the first attribute of this inner self is that it is non-assertive. The importance of realizing that lies in this: because the Inner Self Helper, the Christ in you, is non-assertive, you must seek it with all your heart in order to find it, to

awaken it, or to build your connection with it. If there are any doubts or hesitation, if there is not a wholeness of absolute commitment to communicating with, experiencing this Inner Self Helper, if you do not want this more than anything else in life, then the door is not opened. To him who knocks, the door will be opened. The knocking at the door is what is sometimes referred to as the Abrahamic sacrifice, the willingness to set aside all other things for one single purpose: to open that door that is the gateway of the heart, to giving the life in devotion, to knowing, making a friend with, encountering and personally experiencing the Inner Self Helper who is the Comforter, the Holy Spirit, the Christ in you.

And if you will actually apply the principles of these teachings we speak of, of kundalini yoga, of tantra, of the Taoist secrets, literally arousing the passion in you to bring it from base to crown, we would have you understand this: that as your brain is structured in hemispheres, separated except at the base through the corpus callosum, there is an ability to know God experientially, to awaken to enlightenment, the Crown of Enlightenment. Understand that there is literally erectile tissue in the mind-brain, the master glands, the pineal and pituitary. There must be aroused with the energy that comes from absorbing within the self the arousal from erectile tissue of the gonads. For understand that this master gland, literally, when the vitality is brought to the crown, this gland will literally begin to vibrate, then will literally stand erect. And this experience, which has been called the crown orgasm, is also called the opening of the doorway.

When this gland of the endocrine system receives the spiritual vitality that is in the lower self, the vitality of creative energy and sexuality, when there is that stimulation to this organ at the top or the center of the brain, when this becomes erect, you will find that the fluids which are separated from one another in the two hemispheres through the opening of this doorway, the standing upright of this gland will allow that these fluids meet one another. They combine. It is this that we have described as achieving the Crown of Enlightenment. For the reason that as the opening of this doorway allows vitality to flow from one side to the other of the brain, then you have overcome the experience of being a cleft-brain species.

The importance of this is simply that the cleft brain of man is that which prevents man from being all that God is. God consciousness occurs when these two hemispheres are allowed to build neurons and synapses across the crown rather than at the base, rather than through the corpus callosum, rather than from neocortex to neocortex. As the fluids allow for the exchange of electricity and vitality, there is first the integration of the brain. But more importantly from the opening of the crown chakra, which is the standing upright of the master gland, you will experience not only brain synchronization or brain integration, but more importantly, brain transcendance.

It is this, overcoming the cleft brain and making it one again in the experience of the Crown of Enlightenment, that was described in kundalini teaching: that the heads of the serpents are as two electrodes. And when the electricity is brought from the tail to the crown of these cobras, then there is the spark, the lightning flash, a literal spark which flashes from one pole to the other across the top of the brain creating the Crown of Enlightenment, creating there a pool of light which opens the doorway. And it is for that reason that this gland is called the doorway, opening the doorway to communication with the Divine, the Higher Mind, and this is the description of the creation of the Crown of Enlightenment.

Now how will you begin it in you? You begin it first by accepting yourself as you are, including the nature of your sexuality, being willing to experience the stimulation of that vital force, which is a drive to create and maintain life. It is this vital energy that can heal and remake the human body. But it must be brought from the expression of the appetites and the emotions which are the nature of the lower three seals, then from there through the gateway, the door that is the heart. As this is opened, then the vitality which has been aroused and which has been turned to passion, passion reawakened within you, will be allowed to pass through the heart into what is called the supernals, the higher three chakra centers, and eventually to the crown orgasm or the breakthrough to light.

Now this is the purpose, to transmute that energy, that vitality, to achieve what may be achieved in transcending the brain, the body temple, that is man. It is there for those who seek that diligently, with that combination of discipline and devotion brought together to create and experience the Crown of Enlightenment (Solomon Reading No. 1478, 5/10/91).

THE "META-HUMAN"

In truth, the act of transcendence or union with the Divine Nature may express itself in many different forms. It may occur with or without loss of personal self. In the latter case, self may come gradually to a state of transfigured awareness as from the growth of a seed. Within every seed there hides a genetic blueprint, the finished form waiting to be unfolded. Through a conscious and disciplined effort, the self may unfold naturally and harmoniously, every feature and facet, into the dynamic of the higher Intrinsic Order. Roots do not abnegate branches, though they grow in opposite directions. While the self still remains, it evolves as something wholly and marvelously different from what it once was. Nature is as consistent in the realm of mind as she is in the physical world. In this manner wisdom is incorporated gradually. It becomes, first, part and parcel of the personality and then, at last, one's whole essence and only state of being. The unconditional self becomes elevated to, and established in, a pure Causal realm of universal omnipotence.

Gradual enlightenment, therefore, the more common experience, is easily understood in terms of ordinary neural mechanisms. A committed effort conditions the individual to suppress negativity and to express love and acceptance such that synaptogenetic changes on the smallest levels of brain activity over time alter and elevate brain wave patterns to frequencies commensurate with those of the Causal Mind.

In the case of the awakening of the chi or prana or universal energy of the kundalini, the experience of enlightenment may come suddenly, though for some, perhaps, after long and arduous training. The kundalini, described in the Tantric systems of Buddhism and Hinduism as the 'serpent power' and metaphorically represented by the uroboros, the serpent of Eden, lies asleep coiled in the depths of the *muladhara*, the "root base" of the human spine which is associated with the unconscious or instinctive energies of nature. Once aroused, either by some happening in life or by application of a technique designed to awaken it, it begins its ascent through the *sushumna*, the channel piercing the spinal cord, and rises progressively upward opening and illuminating the higher chakras or centers of consciousness. The progressive stages of consciousness are symbolized by seven major chakras, each representing a center of consciousness corresponding to a specific region of the spinal cord and the bodily areas related to them. The energy released by the opening of each chakra rises to the next higher level, potentiating the central symbol of that chakra, until in the highest, the crown or *sahasrara*, nothing is left but the ineffable center, all else having been absorbed.

When this, then, might be opened in that manner so that there is revealed just beyond it the Will of the Source and your own Divine Will for yourself, you will have moved your life force, your very life itself will have moved from the earth to the supernals, the understanding of the very much higher nature of the purpose of your being on the planet. So that a separate will, a personal will, gives way to the Divine Will as the rising of this energy goes beyond the heart gate into the supernals and you begin to see the world simply as it is, not in terms of judgement or good, bad, right and wrong, but accepting what is, as it is, so that it gives the power of the saint or the mystic to accept what is, however tragic it might seem to others, to accept what is as it is without fighting against.

Building for that you believe in, yes, but not through antagonism to that which should not be, for this again will drain away that positive, enlightening force that can move just that one more seal to the erection of the master gland and the bringing together of the two hemispheres of the brain which is in itself. As this occurs within you, this is literally the ending of duality at all levels. Good and evil no longer exist, nor do life and death. Only life will exist. Neither light and darkness, only light will exist. And neither love and fear, for love only will exist, and you will have overcome what seems to be the very basic nature of duality, of living in the physical where it seems that there are limitations to your human body. Even the perimeters of the body, the shape of the body as you now know it, seems to be a container which makes a statement: "This is what I am, and that outside the container is what I am not." But as the master gland opens and the mind becomes unified, the body is no longer a container, but an instrument, a tool, a vehicle to be used. But you will understand, you will even see for yourself, quite literally see, that the physical container is so much smaller than what you are and that a much larger container, if you will, though it is not that, a much larger vehicle or instrument will be revealed before your eyes, which is an instrument not limited to time and space and therefore not dualistic in nature, but singular and at-one-ment in nature with the Source of it all.

You will find yourself able to overcome that which you had thought of as the

limitation of the physical, and entering into the Kingdom of Heaven so that you can eliminate the thoughts or perception of duality and experience the reality of unity instead (Solomon Reading No. 1483, 6/22/91).

The crown is exteriorized in the pineal gland in the upper half of the brain. When activated, the pineal gland becomes the radio receiver in a sense with the higher realities of pure spirit. It is through the crown that the power of Logos directs its energy downwards, causing an ecstatic tingling sensation to be felt throughout the physical brain and body. This indicates that the Universal Christ Energy has stimulated the neo-cortex causing neurons to fire. By means of this surge, these activated neurons send electrical energy to the rest of the cerebrum converting the higher dimensional light into new channels of perception wherein the deathless and boundless universe is opened to the vision of the meta-human mind. "In this state, that is the last state of love," states St. John of the Cross. "The soul is like the crystal that is clear and pure; the more degrees of light it receives, the greater concentration of light there is in it. This enlightenment continues to such a degree that at last it attains a point at which the light is centered in it with such copiousness that it comes to appear to be wholly light and cannot be distinguished from the light... for it is enlightened to the greatest possible extent, and thus appears to be light itself."

There is a power, an inexhaustible strength and light in this awakened state which simply cannot be verbalized, and which tends to weaken by reflection. In this God-conscious awareness is stored, as in the power of birth, the joyous infinity which knows nothing --- which knows of no thing --- and which sustains the departure of self with no thought to its loss. The expression of this awareness begins where the thought of it ends. It is born of the mind's refusal to accept, to repudiate, to prize, to consider, to reason the concrete. It sacrifices the desire to judge and the stubborn hope that there is anything to be known. It is impartial to the world and, in all its purity and original formlessness, it is the eternal life of which all wisdom speaks.

In the past, it was believed that such experiences occurred only to a few divinely chosen masters. Priests and religious hierarchies who had a vested worldly interest in protecting their privileged status taught that it was heretical to think otherwise. But legions of men and women, many of whom have undergone no spiritual discipline and some of whom had not even a belief in God, have had this singular experience thrust upon them in grateful amazement. While meditating, listening to music, walking through a woods, or even working, the doorway is suddenly flung open allowing them to peer beyond the veil and to experience that for which there is no parallel on earth: a living, conscious and boundless ocean of divine beauty, peace, and inexpressible love. As the Source describes, it is the inherent "first breath" of spiritual life within each of us:

The veil of separation between the perfect soul of your enlightenment is only a cloud of unknowing. The separation from perfect enlightenment is a veil so thin, so fragile, that in moments of perfect asking --- without wanting, without wishing, in moments of willingness to be as enlightened as you truly are, by nature --- that contact with knowing can come.

The perfectly enlightened one is one who knows love without fear, one who

is Christ-consciousness, one who is God-conscious. One who lives with the consciousness of God is simply one who has attained the ability to recognize good without evil as a point of reference. This is one who can experience and express perfect love that casts out fear. A Christed or enlightened being is one who experiences absolutely no fear, who can live without the expression of fear in the heart, the mind, the life.

Perfect love without fear is the way of life of one who is joined with God and has no concern for whether he was enlightened one moment ago or whether he will be enlightened one moment from now. In this present moment, he knows, "I am God. I am no one else. And any voice from within me that expresses separation from God is a creative voice of imagination, a false voice. It is a voice of fear. It is a voice of doubt. It is the voice of the veil."

There has never been a time when you were not. You have existed as a soul from the dawn of the consciousness of God, when God breathed the first breath and from that breath came the universe. In that first breath of God, you breathed as well.

There are souls who yearn for at-one-ment with the Father. There are also souls who yearn to experience and express themselves as independent individuals, separate from God. Those souls who are prepared for the experience of enlightenment are those who no longer fear loss of individual identity. If one is afraid that losing identity of self, that merging with God, will cause him to lose consciousness of self, this fear will keep him separate from God. It was expressed by the Master Jesus in this manner, for he said, "He that findeth his life shall not lose it, and he that loseth his life for my sake, shall find it." He who sets life aside for the sake of being one with God will gain his life.

If you are willing to be perfectly God, without being self-separate-from-God, you can be enlightened. That is the experience of enlightenment --- to know self to be only God, and not man, nor self, nor separate. Who you are is God projecting Himself into this world through a body. You are not the body. You have a body for the expression of God in the world. You are not your personality. You have a personality as an instrument to express God in the world. But if you are afraid of the loss of that body or that personality, if you are afraid of not being you, that fear will maintain the veil of separation between who you are as God and who you have believed yourself to be as separate from God (Solomon Reading No. 1163, 6/25/90).

Philip Kapleau records the case of a Canadian housewife who in a flash of awareness was spontaneously awakened to just such a state. As she herself describes it:

One spring day as I was working in the garden the air seemed to shiver in a strange way, as though the usual sequence of time had opened into a new dimension, and I became aware that something untoward was about to happen, if not that day, then soon.... The next morning, just after breakfast, I suddenly felt as though I were being struck by lightning, and I began to tremble. All at once the whole trauma of my difficult birth flashed into my mind. Like a key, this opened dark rooms of secret resentments and hidden fears, which flowed out of me like poisons. Tears gushed out and so weakened me I had to lie down. Yet a deep happiness was there…. Slowly my focus changed: "I'm dead! There's nothing to call *me*! There never was a *me*! It's an allegory, a mental image, a pattern upon which nothing was ever modeled." I grew dizzy with delight. Solid objects appeared as shadows, and everything my eyes fell upon was radiantly beautiful.

These words can only hint at what was vividly revealed to me in the days that followed:

1. The world as apprehended by the senses is the least true (in the sense of complete), the least dynamic (in the sense of the eternal movement), and the least important in a vast "geometry of existence" of unspeakable profundity, whose rate of vibration, whose intensity and subtlety are beyond verbal description.

2. Words are cumbersome and primitive --- almost useless in trying to suggest the true multi-dimensional workings of an indescribably vast complex of dynamic force, to contact which one must abandon one's normal level of consciousness.

3. The least act, such as eating or scratching an arm is not at all simple. It is merely a visible moment in a network of causes and effects reaching forward into Unknowingness and back into an infinity of Silence, where individual consciousness cannot even enter. There is truly nothing to know, nothing that can be known.

4. The physical world is an infinity of movement, of Time-Existence. But simultaneously it is an infinity of Silence and Voidness. Each object is thus transparent. Everything has its own special inner character, its own karma or "life in time", but at the same time there is no place where there is emptiness, where one object does not flow into another.

5. The least expression of weather variation, a soft rain or a gentle breeze, touches me as a --- what can I say? --- miracle of unmatched wonder, beauty, and goodness. There is nothing to do: just to be is a supremely total act.

6. Looking into faces, I see something of the long chain of their past existence, and sometimes something of the future. The past ones recede behind the outer face like ever-finer tissues, yet are at the same time impregnated in it.

7. When I am in solitude I can hear a "song" coming forth from everything. Each and every thing has its own song; even moods, thoughts, and feelings have their finer songs. Yet beneath this variety they intermingle in one inexpressibly vast unity.

8. I feel a love which, without object, is best called lovingness. But my old emotional reactions still coarsely interfere with the expressions of this supremely gentle and effortless lovingness.

9. I feel a consciousness which is neither myself nor not myself…. It is like a stream into which I have flowed and, joyously, is carrying me beyond myself.[39]

As much as this represents merely one among the myriads of forms that enlightenment may take, it is nevertheless an acquaintance with the hidden essence of a "reality" which is said to lie behind all ordinary and illusory experience. It is a reality in which all opposites and contradictions are united and harmonized into a dynamic and organic whole. Likewise, it is the pearl of great price that lies at the core of all great religions. This, in fact, according to the Source, was the original purpose and true intent of religion, for the word "religion" in its original form from the Greek would be "re", the syllable meaning to repeat or to return, and "ligious", meaning to your Source. Returning to Source. Thus religion originally was understood as that combination of all arts and sciences which can lift the human mind closer again to merge with its Source:

> Thus, if there be a new religion, it will be a universal religion, meaning that it will not replace or destroy any current religion or religious practices. It will rather be a holy celebration and worship which honors God in all forms, all names, all languages, all understandings, all cultural settings. That is to say, an inter-faith religion which condemns no other person's experience of God, but honors all those who seek to return to their Source. In the greatest possible sense, it is not a new religion. It is rather the restoration of the original, the roots and foundation of all religions.

> Religions in this day and time differ only because they were born under different cultures and reflect the cultural roots. The essential portion of every religion is the realization of love --- love for self, Source, and others. And to take the words of the Lord Buddha, three simple instructions refrain from all forms of evil, evil meaning any act which decreases life or liveliness in self or others. First, refrain from doing harm. Secondly, do all good that you can find to do. Whatever is set before you which will be of help and assistance to self and others, including healing, assisting others in any way, giving to others, teaching. This was his second command. And third, be of a joyous, joyful spirit. Thus the Lord Buddha has commanded that those who follow his philosophy should be joyous and peaceful people. Enjoy life, refrain from harm, do all good, and be filled with joy, light, laughter, and truth. Thus as stated by the Lord Buddha, one who practices these simple tenants will find that enlightenment itself is quite natural. It is the normal state of any human. It is unnatural to be unenlightened. It is simply natural --- the nature of man --- to be enlightened.

> And all would be enlightened were it not for the forces of influence in early childhood which separate all parts of the world into categories --- good and bad, right and wrong, good and evil. This duality has caused the consciousness to divide itself into a cleft-brain of the species. Each half or hemisphere of such a brain works against the other by virtue of one simple fact. The left hemisphere of the brain, observing any activity or image, will see in one particular way. Now deprived of the senses which feed to the left brain, if the same object or activity is observed by the opposite eye, a completely different reality will be seen and experienced. Thus, the mind of man has

come to the point of argument with itself, confusion, and what has been called wandering through the wilderness in darkness searching for a light. That light comes when an individual is taught to recreate the wholeness of the brain and the mind so that there is no separation into duality (Solomon Reading No. 1721, 7/3/93).

To Saint Paul, this wholeness was "the peace that passeth understanding." Zen Buddhists know it as *satori* or *kensho*. The Sufis speak of it as *fana*, and the Hindus call it *samadhi* or *moksha*. In Taiwan it is the "Absolute Tao". All in their essence are the result not of adding anything of intrinsic value *to* consciousness, but of the lifting of all veils and the removal of all barriers to a true awareness of the One. The greater the degree of one's awakening, then, the more universal and more permanent the "suchness" of this confluent reality becomes.

If everyone physically on earth were to be so enlightened, then every one of us would have our own unique story to tell, for as the Source points out, **there are as many ways of understanding, of revealing God, as there are stars in the heavens** (Solomon Reading No. 186, 6/15/73). It's as if the entire universe is conspiring to awaken us to its Source, and as we are all expressions of itself, it doesn't give a damn how we get there as long as we complete the journey.

The Long Journey Home

A PARABLE

While there are as many ways to God as there are individual temperaments in the world, still, like streams winding to the same ocean, eventually all lead to the one Source. Meanwhile we struggle through that cosmic interval where through matter, through its spectral terrors and wonders, we are molded and refined and taught to stretch ourselves toward the undivided and imperishable life of the spirit. To image forth the visionary reality of our sojourn through flesh and time, Paul Solomon gives is this parable:

> In the beginning there was a creative being whose nature, whose very essence, even His name was Love. So complete was the absolute expression of this infinite being of love that He sought nothing, for love is sufficient unto love. And yet a love so great is selfless. Seeking only to give of Itself, It longs for union with a lover. So it was that the creative being resolved to make a perfect creature to be His mate.
>
> Because love re-creates itself, He reached beneath His rib and from the most vulnerable part of Himself, from the bottom of His heart, He brought forth His beloved. He joined love with life and produced the light of pure mind. Dearer to Him than the heavens themselves was she to His own heart, for He so loved her with all the immensity of His being that His every effort was to fill her life with joy. And she, her heart's blood flowing with devotion, affirmed to Him, "I am only happy where you are."
>
> You might think that she would have found in her cherished companion all of life's fulfillment. For the creative being bodied forth for her enchantment creations one after the other in harmonious diversity --- suns, moons, worlds without end, star streams sprinkling the heavens like luminous snowflakes in the night. He fashioned for her a garden paradise conceived of the same perfect essence of eternal love. But as she wandered into its far distant mountains she gradually became lost in wonder. With each new vision and experience she sank more deeply into herself. Little by little, as the spirit of the world seduced her, she closed her mind's eye to the spirit of her creation.
>
> In time she discovered sensuality and found pleasures to be exhilarating and feverishly addictive. What began as simply a casual attraction steadily overpowered her until it grew to become the whole of her conscious desire. Now the passionate mistress of sensuality, she insisted on living only in the erotic delight of her immediate present and blocking out all remembrance of her eternal origin. In a mad cycle of promiscuity and lust, and a growing hatred born of its dependency, she sought over and over again for a fulfillment impossible of attainment. Her abortive attempts to satisfy sensuality shadowed forth only her blindness to a love that was profoundly real. Her life had become pathetic, a delirious, suffocating dream, and with it came the

realization that sensuality's charms no longer moved her and the vulgarity of his demands appalled her. Having finally wearied of her slavish dependency, she broke free and courted yet another lover.

Striving to fill the void which her life had become, she transferred all her hope for happiness to wealth. So she pursued him and made love to him and gave birth to his children. But as with sensuality before it, wealth became a rigid and resolute master, and her life soon deteriorated into a sad sequence of bitterness and enslavement. Only too late did she recognize wealth as nothing more than a self-exalting fantasy, counterfeit in the realm of real value.

So she embraced yet another lover, this time fame, and she became god-like in her own self-infatuation. Countless admirers ministered to her vanity and gratified her lust for approval until, finally, she became poisoned by the bane of her own self-importance. For she had become an imposter to herself and a slave in her subservient need for praise from others. Forced to play her role always and everywhere, she again grew weary, and the clamor of her admirers eventually grew hollow.

So she moved on, from lover to lover, growing older and more wretched with the years. But somewhere, in the far-distant twilight of her memory, she dimly recalled the primordial love she had once known and all the bliss that had been the true gift of her heart. And with it came an increased loneliness, a feeling of severance from the only source of love and complete fulfillment she had ever truly experienced. Now she could only hobble with the help of a stick, but with the thought of that first glorious love she summoned all her strength and took to the streets asking everyone, "Have you heard of His name? Have you seen Him? Do you know where He can be found?" She thought to herself, "I'm old and tired, used and wasted. I know He wouldn't want me. But if only I could find him … maybe I could just be His servant, a maid in his Kingdom." She searched in vain, only to return in despair. Utterly exhausted, she fell fast asleep.

She slept for what seemed like ages when, in the stillest hour of the night, she suddenly awoke out of a dream --- a grotesque, nightmarish dream. In the dream she was old and ugly and wasted. She had prostituted herself to a multitude of lovers, each as tormenting, defiling, and degrading as the next. But it was all merely a dream. As waxen images consumed before a fire, the ghostly terrors that gave fashion to her fears now gave way to an inexpressible sense of relief. That which lay sleeping in the depths of her being was not a shriveled hag but a beautiful young girl.

As she came more fully to consciousness she was startled by a light coming from the corner of the room. Looking more intently, there appeared the form of a glowing being. And it spoke to her and said, "Don't be afraid. I'm not here to harm you. I'm an angel. My name is Gabriel and I come to you with a message. God has found you fair and beautiful. He is in love with you and wants you to be the mother of His child. Know who you are and prepare to receive Him. Your son will be called Emmanuel, "God within", and he will be a king. He will lead all people out of bondage and will bring heaven to earth." Finally departing, he said to her, "Hail Mary. Know thyself and thy commission." With that he disappeared.

As was spoken, a child was born. Kings and shepherds alike came to pay homage to him. Others, fearful for their power and privilege, sought to destroy him. Many came to be healed and yet others to find the kingdom of God that was within them. For all those who found him to be a threat, there were multitudes who saw in him a world of intelligible light transcendent to their consciousness. And when they stripped him of his flesh and crucified the one who loved them most, they found that not even the inexorable laws of nature could block the infinite power of God's sovereign love.

And she? She went to sleep again, and when she awoke her feet were resting on the earth as her footstool. Wrapped in a robe of light with a crown of twelve stars above her head, she was now as she had always been, the queen of heaven and earth.

This, Solomon tells us, is the only story in the Bible. In fact, the entire meaning of the message delivered by the Source is contained in this parable. Everything else is simply a variation of this single theme. Beginning with the Book of Genesis which contains the codes for spiritual life, to the Song of Songs which is a compendium for spiritual growth, and finally to the Book of Revelation which with its opening of the seven seals holds the key to spiritual transformation, the whole of the human journey is revealed. In it, from the primordial fall or 'exile' to the New Jerusalem, from spiritual crisis to resolution, the entire history of consciousness is mirrored and given understanding.

Just the same, the story is not simply about the personage of the mother of Jesus who lived some two thousand years in the past. It's about each of us, here and now. **You can see it this way,** relates the Source. **You are as Mary was, a container, a stable, a manger, a womb, a place in which that expression of God that is His child can find a receptacle, can be nurtured and warmed, can be given birth, can grow within you. Understand this, you are a potential mother of the Christ in this time. What greater need is there in your society, your culture than for Christ to live again incarnate and walk among you? There is not one of you lacking the potential for being that incarnation of the Christ by providing your body, your mind, your thoughts, your actions, your purpose as an instrument, a tool, through which that that is the mind of consciousness, the child, the expression of God to express.**

Then if you would accept ultimate responsibility become the Christ by providing that house, that instrument, that you are as a place for that consciousness to live. And to so perfectly live that all that is within you that is not the expression of the Christ will die or be finished. And there is within you, then, a transformation, a transmutation of both consciousness and structure that will reflect and express that presence of the Christ among men (Solomon Reading No. 1069, 1/24/81).

"The most important thing for you to know," Solomon reminds us, "is that God is absolutely fascinated with you. He is in love with you and wants you to have His child. And if you allow that to happen, if you allow Him to plant His love in you so it grows, then you'll experience having this child living inside you that you will call Emmanuel ('God within'). And when he is born people will respond in peculiar ways. Wise people will recognize him. People will want to take advantage of your love and your power. Those who have a vested interest in controlling you will try to take his life and stamp it out. There are both the threats and the beauty. But when he grows, he will become a ruler over your consciousness and he will create heaven on earth. And when you awaken again, you'll know who you are --- the bride of Christ, the queen of heaven, the lover of the original Divine Lover. And you will have completed your relationship with the Source. You will have found your heritage, which is what you came here for. *That's* the end of the story. It's your story and it's personal. Take it personally, and respond to it personally."

Yes, but respond how? Simply responding in an emotional way to the wishes and dreams, longings and aspirations of all that Solomon lays before us, we merely succumb to the most childish of illusions. All the Source's teachings become nothing more than the hollow sound of a voice in an empty hall if they cannot awaken us from the degraded and fallen condition of our drugged sleep. How, then, do we translate it all into the life-directing elements of a higher and more universal self, one that transcends the drunken ego to which we have unthinkingly committed ourselves? Paul Solomon tells us that it's really quite simple:

You have created a wondrous body, which is a singularly impressive feat. You need to direct those same creative energies into building beautiful, effective, joyous experiences and relationships. Your mind is the builder, and you need to channel your life energy, through your thoughts, into masterful living.

Step into heaven. Live there now. It is a matter of living where your Source lives.

If you go in search of your source, and your source responds to you by saying, "What do you want?" you are really a poor, dumb creature if you say, "I want to be rich. I want to have a good reputation. I want to be well educated. I want to be famous. I want to amount to something." If on the other hand you say, "I want to live where you live," your source is going to say, "Come and see. Come into my world with me. Step out of that place where you have been living, where you have been struggling and fighting and scraping. Step out of what feels like hell by realizing that the experience of living in hell is nothing other than walking around in heaven while looking for it. Come home with me to a place of joy and confidence. And live here."

That is what life is all about. Live where your creator lives. Live where the creator in you, where the highest that is within you, thinks the thoughts and makes the decisions and generates the actions. Marry the highest and the best within you and the child of that union will be effective, joyous life. By living in the name of the Father, you will live in the nature of the Father.

The choice is whether to be joyous or oppressed by life. To live joyously and fearlessly even in the face of life's relentless everyday challenges requires a shift of thinking for most of us. The place to start is in adopting the theory that choosing joy as a regular response to life is possible, reasonable and beneficial. It is important to embrace the idea completely and to consider no other possibility. Over time, theory changes to knowing through daily practice, as you reaffirm the decision minute by minute. Joy becomes a way of life.

Replace the negative diatribe of your mind with the statement, "I am loved." Say it to yourself over and over. "I'm not going to be afraid anymore. I'm not going to feel alone anymore. I'm not going to feel powerless anymore. It's my decision. And even if it isn't true, I'm going to live as if it is, because it serves me to do so. Let the rest of the world believe as it wants. Let it even try to convince me of what it will, because I have made my decision and I can't be swayed. It works for me to assume that I am a very loved child of a very loving Creator, even when I make mistakes, even when I forget what really matters. It makes me happy and it makes me a better person, to believe and to know that I am the apple of God's eye."

Then live as the apple of God's eye.[40]

THE AGE OF TRANSITION

Like the journey of the prodigal son who strayed "into a far country, and there wasted his substance with riotous living," then, remorseful, returned to the house of his father who joyously received him, so as the Source observes, we who have strayed from unity into self-dividedness are about to embark on a return to our enduring reunion with the One. All the collective achievements, all that we have seen and experienced in our long wanderings in the wilderness of oppositions and distinctions is infinitesimally insignificant in the light of our reintegration with our eternal Source. As Anisie, the old sage who is the embodiment of homo religiosus in *The Forbidden Forest*, declares: "All the other rights that history struggles to gain definitely --- liberty, for instance, or respect for the individual --- are just a preamble to the only right that is truly inviolable, the right to immortality.... We have to hope that someday, here, we shall discover the primordial Adamic condition, that we shall live not only in Time but also in Eternity."[41] According to the Source, that "someday" has now arrived. Primordial man, a cosmic androgyny who "fell" into the material and bisexual world of differentiation and conflict, is now about to recover his lost integrity. In the words of the Source, **we've reached a time, the dawning of the day when man will be lifted beyond the separation of the sexes, the separation of polarity, [when] the very expression of polarity will be ended and all shall become one. The duality from good to evil will be ended; [it] will not exist. The planet Adam will rule and men will be lifted beyond Adam into God, the return of consciousness. The dawning of that day is upon us...** (Solomon Reading No. 685, 8/14/75)

This is the teaching, then, that needs to be brought in this day... that that which has been moral training, that which has been rules for the sake of rules, must be abandoned in this time. There must be ignored that polarity that has existed between sexes, just as there must be eliminated that polarity

that exists between man and God. This is the ending of the age of duality; this is the purpose of the age: to ignore that which was conventional rules concerning the duality of man, not only between man and God, but between the sexes. (Solomon Reading No. 94, 12/10/72).

However one may conceive of the Absolute, clearly It must be regarded as beyond polarity and opposition. If Solomon is correct in his vision that we will come to know within ourselves the undifferentiated Totality of All, then we must re-enter the womb of things, the matrix of unknowing where, severed from all distinctions and limitations, we can rediscover the perfection of the Beginning and join once more with the Infinite. This, as the Source observes, is the very purpose of the age now before us: to complete ourselves in the form of the spirit of the cosmic tree which bears us.

We exist at the end of an epoch, in a time of transition. Standing on a ridge of history from which through the eyes of the Source the contours of the whole are visible, our impending future will be, we are told, as different from anything we have known as the twentieth century was from Neolithic civilization. We are given the promise of an ultimate liberation, a liberation that will not simply reform but will wholly transform all that we immediately and naturally are. Indeed, the self is inherently unified with the world. When one awakens and perceives that the apparently objective and extrinsic are a result of the brain-mind's undisciplined thinking, one understands the tragic confinement of this freedom.

Such awakenings, however, do not occur without disciplined effort. That is why the Source teaches that we must retrain our minds to see and to express holistically, beyond the disjunction of opposites, beyond all metaphysical polarity. We must clear away the cobwebs of duality and distinction and, quite literally, **create new circuits, as it were, of electrical passageways between the hemispheres of the brain.**

> And in the doing so, understand that as there is the passageway built between the two hemispheres over them, there is a layer, as it were, there is a building of a magnetic field, an electromagnetic field which crosses from hemisphere to hemisphere.

> ... each movement from the conscious thinking process through the depths of relaxation to still the mind [allows for] the ascension through the power centers of body and mind to climb to the peak of the mountain --- we would call this the cleft mountain, the cleft volcanic mountain with reference to the cleft between the hemispheres. And the secret of ascending ... into the holy temple is the building and building and building and rebuilding of electromagnetic pathways between the hemispheres until that forms a kind of dome, a helmet, a crown. [I]n the times of meditation, and particularly in the times of invocation of vital force [Chi, Ki, Prana] down into the base wheel and pumped, stimulated by the breath and lifted to the . . . top until there is brought a force of high vitality to add greater and greater electromagnetic/biomagnetic, neuro-electrical biomagnetic transfers of energy between these hemispheres, there is built a crown which grows with each application until its radiance pierces the armor of the cave [the skull] and

rises to sit like a halo of light on the crown of the head.

And so is created that field, so is invoked and evoked that field of consciousness called the opening of the crown, for the cleft mountain erupts. And in
its eruption is the opening of the thousand petaled lotus. And there in that
radiance rests the instrument that is the Ark (Rev. 11:19), and there radiates
from the dome two pillars, Jachin and Boaz, as depicted as the horns on
the statue of Moses (I Kings 7:21). And between these two pillars which are
the Seraphim guarding the Mercy Seat (Exod. 25:19), there sits the Child of
God, the Light at the base of the Shekinah. And in those times of ecstasy the
Shekinah ascends as a golden umbilicus to the Great White Throne.

And so the master of the seven golden steps, the master of the temple, ascends into the limit of his own Higher Mind, and encounters there a holy
instrument with power unimaginable to the human mind. There [he] encounters that sacred pillar that is called Jacob's Ladder, upon which angels
ascend and descend, bringing messages to and from the Throne of Grace
(Gen. 28:12) (Solomon Reading No. 1339, 4/7/88).

For those who have become so awakened, they will have emerged finally from
the mist of their finitude to be confronted by the Light itself that not only illu-
mines but gives life to all. For it is the miracle of the awakened Self that when
it expands into the boundlessness of Divine Love, it evokes in the world the
extraordinary "Light" of the Logos Itself.

PARAVRITTI

That sublime, beautiful, and transcendent reality calls to the visionary
depths within each of us and to which each of us must, sooner or later, respond. Not by building towers out of one's own ideas and thoughts will we
reach to the highest levels of that "new Heaven", however, for a higher level
simply cannot be apprehended or reached from a lower level. Only, as the
Psalmist says, "in Thy light shall we see the light" (Ps xxxvi. 9) and thereby
attain to the light. There is nothing we can do of ourselves but to be still and,
as the Source puts it, **to allow the light to illuminate the hidden corners, the
false pretense of all that is unlike itself both as light and as love, and indeed
as life as well, and in so doing cast away, banish and abandon all fear with
an unconditional willingness that all of the past, all that has been hidden
will be brought into view by the light** (Solomon Reading No. 1696, 7/13/92).

How many, however, are so willing to face honestly the dark shadows mirrored by their own fears? It's a fairly daunting thought for any of us. Victor Hugo writes: "Every man has within him his own Patmos. He is free to
venture, or not to venture, upon that terrifying promontory of thought from
which one can see into the shadows. If he refrains from doing so, he continues to live an ordinary life, with ordinary thoughts, ordinary virtues, ordinary beliefs and ordinary doubts --- and it is well that he should. It is clearly
best for his internal peace of mind. For if he ventures on to this summit, he
is lost. He will have glimpsed the mighty waves of the Marvelous --- and no
one can look upon that ocean with impunity.... He persists in contemplat-

ing this alluring abyss, in exploring the unexplored, in remaining detached from life on the Earth, and in his efforts to penetrate a forbidden world, to touch the untouchable, to gaze on the invisible he returns again and again to the edge of the precipice, leans over, takes one step down and then another --- and that is how one penetrates the impenetrable and loses oneself in a limitless extension of infinity."[42] Losing one's self ... like a drop of rain water falling into an ocean. The Buddha called it "Paravritti": the turning about in the deepest seat of consciousness, becoming one with the infinite Presence.

Most of us, however, have never dared to mount the climactic summit of our higher selves. Outlandish tales of God-intoxicated saints and madmen merely signify for us the vagaries of transcendental insanity that go hand-in-hand with the direct experience of God. Oblivious to the pathological insanity of the world around us, we merely content ourselves with the most superficial prepackaged, consumer-oriented versions of substitutional faith that modern religion for the most part has to offer. We purchase our Sunday-sermon drive-thru salvation just as we order a Big Mac and fries at McDonald's. It's ready-made, it's safe, and it requires no effort. But the palliatives offered by such religion do little to satisfy the human yearning for the sacred or divine. For there is simply no substitute for enlightenment, for the direct experience of one's own Source. It cannot be passed on by the institutionalized teachings of any religion or by any authority outside the individual. As the Source puts it:

> You are the only God of your incarnation. There is none other that can instruct, or give doctrine, rules, dogma, or laws. If you be the perfect manifestation of the perfect God, then His perfect laws apply in your life, your heart, and yours only, so that truth, as individual truth, knowing the truth inside the heart would make you free. Knowing the truth of another, whether a perfect master, or one fallen by the wayside, would not lift your heart. It is not from the words of another's lips that you learn of God, for all knowledge of God is already hidden within thine own heart. And in the turning backward to creation, to the Prime Central Stillness, will you find the words of God, the personality, the nature of God, revealed. And having known Him, seen Him, felt Him, becoming Him, you would express Him in your world. And if you would seek a perfect master, then be one! (Solomon Reading No. 82, 11/27/72).

NOTE

"Being one" entails, before all else, becoming conscious of being "One". Self-mastery implies self-abandonment. Put in other terms, one must first "wake up" from that sleep which is induced and maintained by thousands of sleep compelling habits and by one's surrounding life and conditions in order to be whole. This must be taken literally. We must be consciously in control of the rambling stream of our anarchic thoughts and imagination before the multiplicity of small egoic "I's" by which our lives are passively and mechanically determined can be unified into a coherent and undivided mind capable of penetrating the impenetrable barrier of the Source-mind Itself. Hidden from us behind this barrier lies the real world, the "Kingdom of Heaven that is within you," to quote the phrase used by Jesus himself. That is why the Source states: **Nothing can be done greater than complet-**

ing yourself, than integrating yourself, than making the Christ, the Source, Life, Love, Harmony, that that is the Christ, the ruler of your thoughts and your life. For the acceptance of that light is enlightenment and does far more to perfect the mind, the body, than any form of training or initiation that can be taken. This one thing, the acceptance of that presence as the Lord, Ruler, Controller, Source of mind and thought, the integration of your being --- this is the key to enlightenment..." (Solomon Reading No. 1368, 1/2/90).

MIRRORING THE INFINITE

Whereas in the past such awakenings have occurred only in the lives of a few misunderstood mystics, saints, and prophets who not infrequently incurred the fatal wrath of their less enlightened brothers, the Source tells us that in the age now before us such awakenings will be common. The time is already upon us, we are told, when many will "wake up", and will be set apart from the sleepers who cannot understand what it means to be "awake" to the immortal "I". This is the age of Emmanuel, of the reintegration of God and mankind: That you now see as human or limited to human consciousness and that as soul memory ... will drop the limitations that you call the conscious mind ... becoming integrated with all the memory that is and the laws of God, so that these souls attuned to the law of God [Law of One] will be able to apply the whole law. And when you see and read in wonder of the activities of Rau or Hermes or the others so aware of relationship with God and able to speak with Him as it were, conversing with the Father, [you] will find these abilities common among you because so much of the density of the atmosphere will drop away, you see, and so much less separation between that of the spiritual human and the presence of Spirit or God. Far easier the communication, then, of man with God in those times, as the atmosphere is shaken and loses that of the density from the pressing about (Solomon Reading No. 375, 6/74).

While every age signifies a step --- from the sensory-based awareness of a beast to a conscious awareness of self --- in the long chain of our biological evolution, the coming age portends a "quantum leap" of consciousness more significantly profound than any before it. A grand influx of sacred energies, we are told, is now beginning to flood the earth bringing to actualization new forms of being. As has been given, this level of existence, or this plane, will [then] be transmuted, will be changed to a different level, a different vibration of all that is. Then that which is the present strain of evolvement, or life on this plane, will not be life as is presently known, but will change, as it were, dimension, or feeling, nature of evolvement. Those now incarnate on this plane will likely have gone to other things, though there may be the many who will return for more and more training, more evolvement, more opportunity in that new dimension, that new system, that new order of things... (Solomon Reading No. 175, 6/8/73).

Hence in the age now before us, we are being necessitated and compelled to move beyond the boundaries of antiquity and modernity to a world aflame with unconditional life, with Logoic Love, and with a tacit surrender to the eternal One. Understand in this manner, explains the Source: that one would seek within the self to encompass the universe, and to feel all therein. Then see that it is the nature of the beginning, or the first step of the zodiac, or the procession of the equinoxes that one becomes aware of self. And in the ending, or the Piscean understanding, one sees no longer the self but only the others, for the self has become transparent. It is given only as a mirror or reflection that others may come to know themselves as God, for in such a way will God within all be revealed. In such a way will all be opened that you might see that there is no existence in a single soul or as a single body, but only as described, as a reflection of all that is (Solomon Reading No. 1219, 6/16/90).

In previous ages, such a mirror would perhaps reflect only the limited and fragmented image of a separate psychological "I", the infinite shrunken to the stature of the finite self. Only for the few --- a Jesus, a Lao Tsu, a Sidhartha or Bodhidharma --- would it reflect the true face of the universal spirit. But with the coming "second genesis" of this new age of Mankind it is humanity that is to awaken to mirror the All. It is in a sense a circular way of reaffirming the Divine Imperative that through the all-inclusive force of Logoic Love life be again made One.

That is why the Source tells us that enlightenment simply for the sake of enlightenment is a logical impossibility, just as losing one's self for the sake of exalting the self is an inherent contradiction:

Do be aware as you grow together that there need always be a purpose to your growth, a purpose beyond spiritual growth in itself. It was said by the prophet Edgar Cayce that each man, woman, will enter into heaven on the arm of someone he has helped. He spoke thus to say, enlightenment for its own purpose, for self, is, in a sense, a selfish goal. Enlightenment sought for the purpose of serving, serving the world, mankind, this planet and your Source is always a purpose for coming together. Thus as you meet together, discuss a point of focus knowing your minds are creators. Your mind, as you think, produces electrical discharge which causes the energies in the air about you to begin to take form, the form of your image or vision that you hold. Such thought form is quite real, and given sufficient power by the strength, will, the determination of the person creating such a thought form [it] can [be] sent forth to be an agent of healing, of assistance, guidance, direction for any of those who need it. Now, do be extremely careful with this precious gift, careful that you never use it in any harmful or judgemental manner. For used in such a manner, it is mirrored back to you and can cause harm.

Then learn the power of creativity within you, and if you can, keep your minds always empty of negative thought, thoughts of fear, worry, all negative emotions. These thoughts, conflicting thoughts, self limiting thoughts, these are very much like holes in the bottom of a container. In this instance, the container which is your temple, your body, containing an energy, life force which some refer to as kundalini energy. Negative thoughts, worries, anger, hurt, jealousies, all of these are as perforations in the container which holds this energy, the power force. If such holes or leaks were completely covered and the mind filled, mind and heart, only with thoughts of love, or caring, of optimism, of the positive use of energy, positive expectations of self and others, absence of self criticism and judgement, absence of judgement of others, mind and heart so filled with positive energy and with right movement, breath and right action, action applying love, real caring to the needs of others, these will cause that energy to rise through the center, the Middle Pillar as it is called, and rise to the level of the Crown of Enlightenment, which is quite natural. Would do so automatically if it were not stopped by learning to worry, learning to feel guilt, condemnation, lack of self worth and such --- all of these which come to be as leaks or holes which cause the loss of the life force that would naturally bring enlightenment.

To the extent that it is possible for you, study these things. Not that study in books or knowledge itself will enlighten anyone. It is rather the attitude of the mind, the commitment of the life, the single-minded purpose of being a perfect servant, this is the energy which brings life force to enlightenment, purpose (Solomon Reading No. 1723, 8/1/93).

Universal purpose, then, demands a universal attitude. Anything less become a wholly self-centered form of psychic athleticism. Its pursuit leads only to the edification of the ego and, ultimately, to spiritual self-annihilation. One achieves such liberation from the chains of the ego not through an avoidance or an escape or a negation of life, but only by service to one's fellow beings and through a mindfulness toward life in all its forms. Like the sun which gives its light impartially and without restriction to all who have eyes to see, so, too, the goal of our own awakening must not tolerate any form of exclusivity, but must bear with it the torch of liberation for all transient life if it is to at all succeed. In this message, then, is the beginning of cosmic consciousness, insists the Source:

Would you begin to understand, [then], that one on your plane who would come seeking to be a master, one who would come seeking to be more illuminated than my brother, has eliminated himself in so doing from the possibility of such illumination. It might be of benefit for you to realize that as there is the approaching the mystic brotherhoods, the secret brotherhoods, for the opportunity of initiation, that never has there been taken or accepted one who applied; that is, those who became the initiates were sought out by the master who was his guide in the initiation. The importance of this lesson, then, would be that humility is an essential asset for the beginning of wisdom.

Now that you might understand this lesson, we would have you consider that instrument of light on your plane and see it in this manner: that if a light bulb sought to enclose its light within self and become totally illuminated, all would remain in darkness, particularly the interior of the bulb. And if it were lit, it would be lit from the outside. If [on the other hand] the bulb would seek to illuminate all that were in the room, that light would come from the very central part of self and illuminate all. But how, then, would attention be attracted to the self? For does not the bulb itself cease to exist to the physical eye as it gives forth light? Is not the light that is shed abroad greater than the source of the light?

The lesson here, then, would be: as the light you shed abroad become so great, so intense that self fades from sight, you have begun the work of the

Master. If self, then, become the center of attention and would appear to give forth light, is it not illumined by those who gather around? Seek, then, that the message, the illumination, the light, would be more important than self. That which you would seek to illuminate is that [that] would be seen rather than self (Solomon Reading No. 101, 12/21/72).

The purpose of our awakening, then, and the very purpose of this age, is to raise in ourselves a spiritual body which, through the transcendent impulse of Love, will enable us once more to realize our undifferentiated unity with the All and thereby to take upon ourselves the common fate of all. Once we come to the recognition, the understanding and acceptance of the fact that enlightenment cannot be attained without identifying with all living and suffering beings, then we will have returned to the Source of creation, and through a holy marriage of mind and spirit, body and Christ, we truly will become, as we were intended, a creator in the image of God.

LIFE-RENEWAL OF THE SPIRIT

From the beginning ours has been an arduously long and seemingly formidable journey from the harmonious complexity of form and towards the awakening of spirit into unity, immortality, and limitless self-expression. This is the goal of all living being, that the Supreme Creator may be known, and that Its creation may be crowned with a return to the homeland of its origin, to the unknown oceanic Source of all energies. Our difficult passage from adolescence to maturity has, the Source tells us, only just now begun. Where up to now our mind-like receptivity, reflected in the steadily increasing power to analyze, perceive, discriminate, and make meaningful use of the world roundabout, has moved horizontally within levels, we are now about to move vertically to change levels. The long experience of the inhabited beast may soon enter into imaginative sympathy with a mind of a higher order. This, according to the Source, is the very purpose of this age and generation: **to lift the mental body to the higher plane. Just as the Atlanteans perfected the physical body on your plane, so it is the purpose of this generation, of this subrace that now exists, to perfect the mental body that would be the higher manifestation of the physical body, just as the new subrace being prepared even in this day would perfect the spiritual body and the bodies in which the manifestations come on this plane or on this sphere of earth will become less dense and more of the ethers.** This is seen in the heart of this one [individual reading] even at this moment that there is coming the understanding of these higher levels of existence and that which has been taught as the Second Coming, that [which] has been taught as the catastrophe of this planet and the ending of this age, is coming into manifestation within this heart (Solomon Reading No. 94, 12/10/72).

For the time draws near and there need be built in this day those light bodies that will prepare for those new expressions of heaven and earth. For the time of this vibration of the physical has passed and is no longer adequate for the development of man in his journey toward God, you see. There is time, there is need that these things be repaired, that there be the wiping clean of those things that are in this universe, this atmosphere, in this time, that there might be the preparation for that new light that will dawn and will spin and will form itself into the New Heaven, that New Earth, that new manifestation that should be populated by those who have gone beyond the need to return again and again to this plane of existence. For these lessons have been learned and should be given to all those ready and able to receive (Solomon Reading No. 285, 12/1/73).

That humanity as it now exists lacks the strength and awareness to see beyond its egoistic shell and thus rejects any possibility of its own causal nature is hardly surprising. We are, after all, still creatures of a Fall that is a continual and present process, a process that has become identical with the very reality of existence itself. And the forbidden tree still beckons us. What it forbids is idolatry, the taking of the visible object to be the source of creative power. It is only this that separates us from the causal Source. It is a caesura cutting across everything by which we might otherwise identify ourselves with the Logos of our being: love and fear; life and death; good and evil; the disjunction of all opposites.

There is still even in this day the attitudes, the tendencies of being caught up in the desires of the flesh even as that first day when those sons of God became sons of man and sons of beasts, and were caught up even in those bodies that were not perfected for the use of man. And they were intrigued even in that day with the pleasure that might be felt through those Divine senses that were given as they took on the use of those mechanical instruments, those things that you know as nerves, those things that you know as sensory devices that even in this day you have, and how much they are a curse to man, how much you are bound in chains as you walk upon this plane of earth. And even in this day you consider those things that you have been advised to overcome and understand the operations of, and as you are given opportunities to operate these and to subject them to your will rather than being subjected to them, you cry out as if you were being asked to give up this or that, or being punished or being deprived of something worthwhile. And can you not understand that you are Children of God and not children of man, and you are caught up in the bodies of beasts? And can you not understand that that was what was given even in that day by the one John the Beloved as he tried to help you understand the vibrations of man or the vibrations of the beast? And would you not understand the symbology that it was given even then, and cannot you understand and even conquer these bodies for a short period of time that there might be the conquering of those centers, those centers of energy, those seals that cause the Child of God to be caught up in the temple of flesh? And if those seals were opened, would you not be loose; would you not be made free? And do you not know that those seals are truth, and if you would understand the truth, each of these truths, and put them into operation, would you not be made free? And if you were not caught up in self, would you not understand these truths, and even loose them then that you might be turned away from the human body and see it as an instrument, as a mechanical device that might be given for the operation of God, even Jesus Christ in the earth? And would you not understand His Second Coming? (Solomon Reading No. 116, 1/27/73)

The world cries out for the magical life-renewal of "spirit".

But as the Source points out, this very condition of our fallen nature contains the seeds of its impending apocalyptic transfiguration. Beyond our played-out world of fragments a world of Totality awaits us, a world wherein mankind may soon renew contact with a spiritual world that has long since been forgotten. All the channels of communication between this world and the realms of the spirit will be opened wide, to let in a powerful draft. And when that moment arrives, we will lose our 'selves' in a limitless extension of infinity.

The path from ignorance to insight, from complexity to simplicity, from incohesiveness to synthesis, from somnambulence to enlightenment so clearly visible to the Source now stands before us. The entire sum of human history is unfolding as a total epiphany of the sacred. And yet, the Source advises that the precise terms for the unfolding of events are not inevitable. While the immutable working of Divine Purpose is seen as providential, and while the hidden order of that Providence may eventually manifest for human inspection, the causal relations of events themselves are determined ultimately by free will. For if the patterning of future events were to unfold as smoothly and effortlessly as all that has been given, the whole scope and audacious novelty of mankind's historical, intellectual, and spiritual journey to self-knowledge would be trivialized. It is we who, in the transparent darkness of our trance, must choose the light. Even though the world revives around us, it is for each of us, individually, to struggle with pride, to accept within ourselves those life-affirming values that give purpose to our hope. Time and history, past and future, will continue jointly to support the aspiring human spirit in the upwardly winding path toward Infinite Being, but it is we who must appropriate the vision to ourselves. Even though drawn inexorably by the prospect of the height it is each of us who individually must cross the ever wilder and more terrifying terrain to reach it.

> ... you would see those phenomenon that are referred to as the stellar events, as if the stars have fallen, the moon turned to dripping blood, the earth renewed and wrapped in a robe of light, shining to rejoin the [Universal Light]. These things may be difficult to visualize or even to understand, and even frightening if you knew their implications. But it will come that ... this planet earth will be so destabilized that virtually every mountain and valley, every sea will be changed in its geological nature quite literally. Earthquakes as have been prophesied since the beginning of time will change the face of the earth. But all this is the labor pains for the birth of a new Eden on earth. And then you will know that mankind would never have appeared on this planet were not the planet sufficient to his every need to live, to survive.

> And so it shall be again, when all that is false, all that is manipulated and denatured about the face of the earth, be broken down and returned to the earth ... then shall Eden bloom again, and man live in harmony and there shall be no more war. And there will not be a dark side and light side of earth, even in the literal sense. For light will shine on every side. There will be no more night, nor need of sleep. Sleep is not needed when the brain is not bicameral. Then when these things are heeded, man becomes whole, then shall we find a new heaven and a new earth established (Solomon Reading No. 1466, 1/21/91).

Part Five

New Earth/New Eden

Chapter 18

Standing On The Brink

A TIME OF LABOR

We stand at the very threshold of a time of universal transformation unparalleled in the ages of the earth. **You stand on the brink, now, of the passing of the [Piscean] Age into the dawning of the day you've called Aquarius, the day having been described by the ancients, the teachers, as a period of time and peace, the heavenly peaceful kingdom in which the lion will lie down with the lamb and there will be no more war. All men shall know peace, a peace that passeth understanding** (Solomon Reading No. 854, 7/23/76). Calculating from God's creation of Adam to the birth of Christ the orthodox time span of five millennia, the 16th century prophet Michel de Nostradamus foresaw in the distant future the transformation of mankind into a higher state of universal consciousness and a thousand years of peace when the seventh millennium, "the revolution of the great number seven," shall have arrived.[1] It would be an age wherein the spiritual descendants of mankind would, in the words of Pauwels and Bergier, "*see* the Light, *see* Eternity, comprehend the Laws of Energy, integrate within [themselves] the rhythm of the destiny of the Universe, consciously apprehend the ultimate concentration of forces and, like Teilhard de Chardin, live the incomprehensible life that starts from 'Point Omega', in which the whole creation ...will find its accomplishment, consummation and exaltation."[1]

The "seventh millennium" has at length arrived. The new Age of the Spirit is upon us. "The emergence of the future fifth world has begun," say Hopi Elders of their ancient prophecies. "You can read this in the earth itself. Plant-forms from previous worlds have begun to spring up as seeds ... the same kinds of seeds are being planted in the sky as stars. The same kinds of seeds are being planted in our hearts. All these are the same, depending on how you look at them. This is what makes the emergence to the next, fifth world."[2] As the imperishable seeds of Love planted by Christ two thousand years ago come finally to fruition in the womb of planetary consciousness, so the universal incarnation of Divine Being is becoming manifest in Its totality as the embryonic anatomy of the human spirit takes form:

> Hear ye children, and know, that as surely as the men of God having completed their trials and come through great tribulation --- in the dark night of the soul and the period of crucifixion --- so this ball of earth, herself a living being in relation to God, enters now into her travail. The time of labor in the womb has begun. The process of birth has begun. Blessed are ye who live through these times of the groaning of this earth in bringing forth her seed, for she is a Magdalene --- soiled, but on her knees, serving. The Divine Plan for the period, just before you, is written, is given, as the rebellious woman who has become a harlot but now bows the knee to wash the feet of the Master. Then bow ye your heads in service, that that which has been Magdalene becomes now in her travail the Virgin who had given birth to

the Christ Child. Don't you know, can you not realize, that these changes of
which you have spoken, the ripping asunder of the surface of the earth, will
give birth? Did He not say, "I will come again, as you've seen Me go"? And
He came in the womb of a virgin, but this time the macrocosm becomes
the giver of the birth, as did in that day the microcosm, or, that is, Mother
Mary brought forth her firstborn child, laid Him in a manger, so this earth
on which you live will bring forth that Presence that is Christ Consciousness
as a result of the period of labor; and you shall see what you've been looking
for, that men have talked about, His light in the sky, His Coming. It will be
a birth, the birth resulting from the humility of the woman who was soiled
(Solomon Reading No. 854, 7/23/76).

And as the fiery prolific of human energy is linked once more with the infinite energy of Creation, humanity is destined to arise literally out of itself, to
abandon its present form for the luminous body of its primal origin:

... there will be those among you, and those present, who in that time will
be changed in a moment, in the twinkling of an eye. Not that you would
drop the physical body here, but suddenly you will understand that physical
body and the light body, and transmute that deep, denser material into light.
You will lose nothing of the physical, nor will you leave the dead physical
body behind, but transfer that which is dead into that which is alive. So will
you then be more alive than ever has been before. Those not understanding, then, unable to relate in the heart to the presence of such goodness, will
remain encapsulated and reborn for those periods of destruction (Solomon
Reading No. 185, 6/15/73).

Commensurately, as the inauguration of a new earthly Eden approaches, the
whole cosmos must be delivered by a great harvest and vintage, as in the Revelation of John, till all realms of universal existence are as we are, that we may
be as they are, released from every limitation and therefore re-integrated into
the all-encompassing reality of the Absolute.

And so it shall be again, when all that is false, all that is manipulated and
denatured about the face of the earth, be broken down and returned to
earth ... then shall Eden bloom again, and man live in harmony and there
shall be no more war. And there will not be a dark side and light side of
earth, even in the literal sense. For light will shine on every side. There will
be no more night, nor need of sleep. Sleep is not needed when the brain is not
bicameral. Then when these things are heeded, man becomes whole, then
shall we find a new heaven and a new earth established (Solomon Reading
No. 1466, 1/21/91).

Then, as the new Age of the Spirit nears its apocalyptic completion, a regenerated mankind will regain its proper place in the cosmos of Eternity: **The
planet Adam will rule,** declares the Source, **and men will be lifted beyond
Adam into God, the return of consciousness. The dawning of that day is upon
us...** (Solomon Reading No. 685, 8/14/75).

But we must first reach beyond midnight to get to the dawn. For the new age

cannot be consummated until the old age has been either completely recon-
ciled to the work of creation or utterly destroyed. The brute actuality of a
history which has lost all its roots in the sacred, that is a wholly isolated expression of mankind's autonomous will, self-deification and egotistic advancement must first be either radically transformed or obliterated. That is why the
Source warns of the impending destruction of this world from whose ruins a
New Creation will rise and the universal Law of One be restored. **This ball
of earth will be smashed flat and reformed into the birth of a new age. It is in
that time you'll find a new government, a new heaven and a new earth, and a
reign of peace** (Solomon Reading No. 646, 7/4/75).

This is a perilous moment, we are told, both for the human and its earthly
habitat. The multitude of unprecedented crises that now confront us --- the
world food crisis; the imbalance in global economies and international systems of exchange; worldwide deforestation, depletion of natural resources,
and industrial pollution; global warming and climate change; the growing
trend toward national separatism and power; nuclear proliferation, global terrorism, and the threat of all-out thermonuclear war, which we might regard
as instantaneous and total environmental collapse, to name just a few --- are
simultaneous and dynamically interrelated. Together they constitute a single
crisis of planetary proportions --- an obvious indication that humanity is at a
turning point in its historical evolution.

More than that, declares the Source, **you would see the cycle of the present as
the culmination of a period of history, the ending of an age --- more than an
age. [It] might well be described as the ending, the dispensation. You have no
word for that we attempt to express, except that you [would] call it the ending
of a life-wave. So that there is a period upon you of refreshment, of refinement,
of reformation of the earth, of building a New Heaven and a New Earth.**

> **Now, understand in this time there will be changes in all things --- land-
> mass, economies, the direction of the soul growth --- all these things come
> to a peak of intensity as a result of that peak and strain and tension, distress
> that would be felt upon the physical as well [as] upon the soul, the spirit.
> [You] will come to the ending of one time, the beginning another, ... a new
> direction for entering a whole new understanding of life and the develop-
> ment if it. The new earth will not be much like that you presently experience**
> (Solomon Reading No. 719, 11/14/75).

REMEMBER YOUR CAUSE

In our pride over our present accomplishments, it is perhaps natural for us
to think that such a vast release of physical energy and human potentiality
has never taken place before. But, according to the Source, this proves too
flattering an illusion. Time and again, as the Source sees it, races of humanity had climbed to the same social, material and technological height as ourselves, only to be undone by some hidden consequence of their own nature and
achievement:

> **Now we understand this repetition of that which occurred in the sinking**

of those lands [of Atlantis] when there was the drawing in of the Sons of Belial from the environs and vibrations of that red or roaring planet [Mars], wherein those of the Divine forces, or that that was given of God for Divine purposes, began to be misused and turned against one another for purposes of war. It was in that day, in that time, that the Sons of the Law of One were among the soldiers, as might be called, who were used for the protection of those lands and were aware of the focusing of the crystal by those of the Sons of Belial in that day.

Now it might be noted historically that there were the factions, the turning of brother against brother, of father against son, some generation or so ago in the past beginning with that time of the Civil War in this country [U.S.], reaching the peak, then, in those periods of the World Wars, then slackening. The same would be said to occur this time with the coming of the warring factions --- those souls exchanging when this [red] planet grew so near --- coming into incarnation on the [earthly] plane and bringing with them the war, the fighting. There was, as well, a coming in of a great number from the realms and influences of Venus, and particularly in this day, in this generation, there are found great numbers of these coming that might be called peace-loving --- those gentle, those bringing the doctrines of passive resistance and the applications of the Laws of Love.

Understand that which happens in coming into the dense planes [of Earth] from those other levels of vibrations, for it might be understood that life as is expressed on those planes, in those realms, would not be third-dimensional, would not be heavy, would not be the physical body, for there is not human life as you know it in those realms, in those areas. Then those projecting the self from the vibrational influences of Venus into this dimension, taking on the heavy, cumbersome bodies and the thoughts that detract from the inner ideals or the higher ideals, that which was their purpose in entering this plane, become distorted.

Now understand it is natural in coming into the denser solar rates of vibration that this would occur, so that that which is the purpose is hidden from the mind. Then it would be the purpose of these Readings to awaken within [the self] that which was the original intent. Now understand this well, that in coming into these levels, these planes, for such intent, there is the building of that which you would bring into manifestation on this plane. Understand those descriptions of the Second Coming and the purpose thereof. As you would wonder concerning the building, concerning the preparations for those times, understand that which you build here is that which would make possible the Second Coming, the Day of our Lord, the changing of all to high rates of vibrations. And it is the purpose of those coming from other realms, from other levels or the inner planes, for the building in such ways.

Now understand in those times of the life in Atlantis when these came there, that there was given a great deal of power, understanding, and those things that you would seek in this day. Now, children, carefully see the comparison here, for the message we would attempt to bring this day is vital, and the message is this: that even in those last days of Atlantis, those who were the Children of God gathered and sought from God understanding and asked often, even as you would come and ask in this day, "Where are those methods, those tools that we might use for the healing of our land? And how may we prepare for those calamities that are to come?" For in that day they knew, even as you in this day know, that there are the calamities, the catastrophes, the changes in the surface of the Earth to come. Understand, children, you repeat that which was done in that day. And history never more so closely repeated itself than is happening, that is coming in this place in this time. Understand your purpose, then, for repeating that which was the life [then].

Then know that God poured forth his blessing in that day and gave power, gave understanding, gave those tools, that pyramid energy, that focusing of the terrible crystal, and it was given in that time for Divine purposes. Now understand that power is power, and that which makes for good or for evil is the manner in which same would be directed. Then know even in this day as in that there will be given, there will be taught, these methods for focusing energy, for bringing power. And in that time as in this there were the Sons of Belial, and recognizing power, they knew that these could be used for the selfish purposes, and would steal, would drain in this way and direct energies in other ways. Now, understand as well that that occurred within the Lord's people in that time, in that day, for even these were in those bodies that were susceptible to the drawing of pleasure, the temptation to do this or that, the partaking of self. And there was seen here "that we can gain for the self" by focusing energy in such a way. "I can build for myself those things that will bring pleasure to the self." Then as there was the partaking of self, there was the taking of the bite from the apple in the garden. Now understand the symbology here. Then there was the separating from the knowledge, "We are of God," and there was the identification of that which was the apple, or the physical. That which was taken into the body, into the system, is that which was identified with. Then man, thinking himself man, lost his identity as God.

Even as in that day, so in this. Now know that you have drives, appetites, interests in those things of this earth plane, and you were attracted from those finer planes, those subtler levels of vibration to this planet even as a magnet. You came to change that which was foreign to God. That which could have been and was a Garden of Eden, you came in this day to restore. And in great bands and droves, in great ships of great numbers you came, to change this planet, its nature, bringing your love of beauty and peace that again this planet might become Eden. Now remember your cause (Solomon Reading No. 176, 6/9/74).

If history repeats itself, it is because the essential energy of history remains unchanged. It is the same bestial impulses and unassuageable cravings that continue to goad us over and over into the inhuman conduct which stubbornly perpetuates for us the story of our race. For as long as history records, it is the energies of darkness and fear that have, for the most part, given shape to the world. And it is repeating once again with the same character strains as before: those deceived by egoism and blinded by materialistic power, greed, and passion; those desensitized masses whose energies they command and on whose treadmills they find themselves sweating; and those fully awakened to the principles of unity, life, and love.

What is so distressing is that an earlier race had long ago possessed and spent the vitality and other-conscious energy of love that we ourselves now need merely to survive. They, too, had forgotten their cause. As, little by little, they came to think of the terrestrial factor of mind as truly 'themselves', the unity of their paradisiacal innocence was gradually torn asunder. As for the proverbial Tree of Good and Evil, we have been bowing under the weight of its fruits ever since. Had our antediluvian predecessors not become addicted, perhaps we ourselves would by every measure be far in advance of where we are. Such speculation, however, is pointless, for in every heart there still rages the old conflict between the beast and its higher creative Cause. The evidence, as the Source points out, is plain to see: **Look about you in this time and see the destruction of consciousness. See the minds of men destroyed by the conditions under which they have lived, by the lack of beauty, and peace, and serenity about them. See the result of wars. Not the wars of the battlefield, but the wars of daily life, of battling one another, the conditions** (Solomon Reading No. 694, 8/21/75). Indeed, subjective conflicts and wars are no less imperious than global ones, and so long as we as a race identify with and give authority to our animal reflexes and their external compulsions, the forces that are driving us to destruction will continue to be uncontrollable.

Will we, like those of an ancient race, succumb to the mania of power? Are we, asks the Source, among those who will face the destruction of our world without any agony of compassion, but only regret at the loss of the social and technological machinery which brought our civilization to a close? While each of us bears the imprint of our biological DNA along with the correlates of our social, class, and cultural conditioning, so, too, we each bear the imprint of the universal: that which is translatable into all tongues and which carries with it our common destiny. Will we, therefore, find within ourselves the spiritual strength and wisdom to resist the powers of fear and aggression, to seek in the communal bond of mutual insight that universal energy of Love that would spare our world it's devastating fate? If the latter, the Source tells us only that the inveterate conflict between Arabs and Jews must first come finally to an end. For it is these "two separate nations", these "two kinds of people," which archetypically represent the underlying conflict within us all.

The ancient rivalry, divisiveness, and warring hatred between Arabs and Jews has contributed in part to the reigning diagnosis of our own age of conflict and anxiety: the claim made nowadays that humans are by heredity creatures of perpetual war and aggression. We may, in fact, come to find that fear and aggression are the genetically inherited properties of a bicameral brain. But it is just as likely that we have by memory and habitude *made* ourselves creatures of aggression. Hatred and fear are learned, and where there is fear from an unforgotten and unforgiven past, no peace can exist. The inevitable consequence, forewarns the Source, will lead not only to the devastation of our terrestrial home but to an unprecedentedly fateful Armageddon destined to end without any victors in a final global holocaust. In fact, many of the more sanguinary, truly apocalyptic events foreseen earlier by the Source would already have occurred were it not for the deep insight and moral courage of one man who, through a direct personal relationship with his own Intrinsic source, "remembered his cause", thereby altering the fate of the entire world.

I AM ESAU RETURNING TO JACOB

"If God as some now say is dead," writes author I.F. Stone, "He no doubt died of trying to find an equitable solution to the Arab-Jewish problem."[3] Indeed, the conflict between Arabs and Jews is not only intractable; it is the concentration of five thousand years of bitter memories, resentments, and rivalry into a single seventy year interval of open and unmitigated hostility.

Dating from the initial moment of Israel's statehood, the Middle East has endured a series of crises whose shadows have darkened the world. Only eleven minutes after David Ben-Gurion formally proclaimed the establishment of Israel as an independent state on May 14, 1948, the armies of Egypt, Iraq, Syria, Transjordan, and Lebanon descended on the fledgling State of Israel claiming the Land of Palestine as part of the Arab-Islamic world. After all, they reasoned, while the Jews had been going in and out of Palestine for three thousand years, had the Arabs not stayed put, rendering to their own claim to the land a greater superiority? Underscoring their claim was the argument that Jews (and Christians) had always lived among the mainly Arab Muslim population in peace and dignity. Why, then, the need of an independent Jewish state in Palestine? The fighting, which brought all of Galilee under Israeli control, raged for eight bloody months until finally, on January 7, 1949, the first Arab-Israeli war ended in Jewish victory.

From that time on, the history of the entire region has been marked by turbulence, unremitting bloodshed, and fratricidal strife over lands, borders, and political/cultural rights. In fact, for over a half-century the world has at times held its breath as the Arab-Israeli rivalry periodically exploded into armed conflict drawing cold war adversaries to the brink of nuclear confrontation. During the 1973 Yom Kippur War, for instance, American forces were placed on full worldwide alert in case of Soviet intervention, bringing the two superpowers closer to a nuclear showdown than they had been since the 1962 Cuban missile crisis.

Only a little over a month before the Yom Kippur War broke out, the Solomon Source warned:

> Now we see yet two more battles, two more wars for this nation [Israel]. Then there will be the destroying again by earthquake [or nuclear explosion] of that place that has been set upon the Mount here. And ... immediately following, there will be the attempts, then, to bring that of the Temple of God. So will Solomon's Temple be rebuilt in its own place. Yet, this will be taken as a direct affront to those other nations, for that holy place of the Muslims will be destroyed in such rebuilding, and will bring that war of wars [Armageddon] (Solomon Reading No. 219, 8/21/73).

By the time of the 1978 Camp David accords, it is fair to say that Solomon's prophetic warning seemed well on its way to fulfillment. The hope for any kind of Mideast peace was going down like a sea turned slowly into a giant maelstrom. There was simply no benefic vision to integrate a lost brotherhood or to facilitate an escape from the past.

Then, on March 26, 1979, there occurred an event that was to significantly alter Solomon's prophetic forecast. In a White House ceremony marking the event, Prime Minister Menachem Begin of Israel and Egyptian President Anwar Sadat signed an historic treaty formally ending the state of war between their two countries. Thus, obliged to amend its earlier prediction, the Source stated:

> ... know that much of your world ... still stands today because the latter expression, the most recent expression of Esau as President Sadat went, attempted to go to Jacob and make peace. So was forestalled some of the events predicted by the Prophet Cayce that would have caused great destruction in the Mideast at that time and, in effect, that would have triggered destruction even in these islands of Japan.
>
> That event, then, was delayed or stalled by the coming of Esau to Jacob ... (Solomon Reading No. 1285, 3/8/88).

In 1978, the third day of his stay in Cairo, Paul Solomon met Anwar Sadat. It was the first of several significant encounters between these two men. As Paul Solomon tells it, "A few of us were visiting the plateau of Giza. We were there to see the Great Pyramid, and as we walked across from the pyramid to the home of the man who restored the sun boat of Egypt, we went to visit his little cabin. As we did, he pointed out that the house just a few yards from us was the summer house of President Anwar Sadat.

"So we were taking pictures of that little cottage. It's not a big impressive thing. It's not a mansion. It has a little fence around it. And as we're taking pictures, we walked over for a closer look and wondered when the security guard was going to stop us, but we were going to go as close as we could just to see his villa. And the security guards didn't appear, but Anwar Sadat came walking out of the house to the fence, waved at us and called us over. So we went over to the fence to talk with him."

"Do I know you?" President Sadat seemed to have proportioned his greeting more to the indelible features of the face than to the unfamiliarity of the man. ("I think I have one of those faces that everyone thinks they've seen before," explains Solomon. "It usually comes to them when they see the Santa picture on the Christmas card.")

"No, but I know you," replied Solomon. The words came easy enough to merit a playful response from the President.

"Oh, you do. And just who do you think I am?"

With unassuming candor, Solomon answered simply, "You are Esau." The words flowed almost in spite of himself.

Sadat was caught entirely off guard. Realities stronger than themselves had suddenly intervened. He must have had the feeling of being laid bare for, accustomed as he was to the easy domination of groups, Sadat now found himself dazed by this stranger who could unmask the deepest measure of his soul. Finally, he relaxed noticeably, took a deep breath, and said, "I am Esau, and I will return to Jacob."

As Solomon comments, "when he said that, it was important to what was about to happen. Because it was only a year later that he flew to Jerusalem and when he stepped off the plane, he said to Israeli Prime Minister Menachem Begin, "I am Esau returning to Jacob. But then later, he told us, "I returned and Jacob wasn't there." So, Anwar Sadat clearly believed that he was the reincarnation of Esau."

Jacob and Esau, the biblical sons of Isaac and Rebekah, were born twins, Esau the elder by little more than seconds. It was these precious few seconds which entitled first born Esau to the birthright, meaning that Esau not only would inherit a double portion of whatever considerable holdings his wealthy father left, but that he would become patriarch of the family with all the rights, responsibilities, priestly privileges and duties which were entailed.

Before the birth of the two boys, however, the Lord spoke to Rebekah, saying: "Two nations are within you, and two kinds of people. The one shall be stronger than the other, and the elder shall serve the younger." The prophecy was puzzling to Rebekah. But, indeed, as time passed and as the boys grew, Esau displayed a marked indifference to his birthright, preferring instead the rough and hearty life of a hunter. And true to the words spoken by the Lord, Jacob came to be the weaker and more domestic of the two. And encouraged by the favoritism of his mother Rebekah, Jacob came more and more to resent the misfortune of being second born.

One day, after a hard and unproductive hunt, Esau returned faint with hunger and begged his brother Jacob for food that he had prepared. "Feed me," he pleaded, "I pray you!" "I will," returned Jacob thoughtfully, "if you sell me your birthright this day." "What good will a birthright do me if I die of hunger?" thought Esau. "Swear it to me!" demanded Jacob. "Swear that you will sell it to me if I give you food this day." Thus Esau ate and drank in exchange for all the power and privilege of his birthright.

It came finally to pass that, when Isaac was old and nearly blind, he felt the time had come to confirm the birthright and grant the requisite rights and riches to his firstborn son before he died. So he sent Esau into the wilderness to hunt venison in order to prepare a festive dish for the occasion. In the meantime, Rebekah ordered Jacob to go before his father disguised in the skins and clothes of Esau and to receive the blessing before Esau's return. Goat was prepared with the taste of venison, Jacob played sufficiently well the part of Esau, and the ceremony was completed. When Esau returned finally, Isaac realized the duplicity, but it was too late. For such a blessing has both social and legal significance, both a sanctity and a power of will that cannot be revoked.

Esau let out a bitter cry. "My brother! Is he not rightly named Jacob, 'the supplanter'? Twice he has taken my place; twice he has used trickery to take something that is mine. He took away my birthright; and now he has taken away my blessing. Oh, my father! Have you not saved any blessing for me?"

"How can that be?" Isaac replied with dismay, "I have made him lord over you…. What can be left that I may do for you, my son?"

Esau, his voice heavy with grief and despair, begged of Isaac: "Have you only the one blessing to give? Oh, bless me, too, my father!"

Sorely troubled, Isaac obliged with a blessing upon Esau, "but it cannot be what I have already given Jacob of my own," he said woefully. "Your dwelling shall be the richness of the earth and of the woods and the fields you love, and of the dew of heaven from above. You will live by toil and by the sword, and you will serve your brother. But the day will come when power shall be yours, and then you will break his yoke from off your neck." Isaac's words were meant more as a judgment upon Jacob than a blessing upon Esau.

Thus, the prophecy of God, that the "the elder shall serve the younger," was fulfilled even in the day of Isaac. And the greater prophecy, that "two nations are within you," came to pass after many generations as the twelve sons of Jacob, each of whom fathered a tribe of Israel, and the children of Esau split into separate nations and "two kinds of people," Jews and Arabs, as the Lord foretold. And Isaac's judgment that one day Esau would break his brother's yoke from his neck came finally to be realized, according to the Solomon Source, when Esau, in the expression of Anwar Sadat, returned to Jacob (Menachem Begin) to make peace. For the yoke represented not so much the power Jacob had over him because of his father's ill-fated blessing; rather, it represented the bondage of his own soul to the effects of a past injustice which could be absolved only by the sacrifice of self, by the willful resignation of personal and self-centered forms of fulfillment to a power beyond self. Thus, his was a peace that came from the act of forgiveness. And with it came a peace shared and shouldered by two nations, by "two kinds of people" sired many generations before by the two sons of Isaac.

Thus, it was emphatically the strength and spiritual character of Anwar Sadat that turned the relentless tide of confrontation and war to the wisdom of mutual security and international civility between two ancient peoples. For, "Why should we bequeath to the coming generations the plight of bloodshed, yes, orphans, widowhood, family disintegration, and the wailing of victims?" asked Sadat in an address given before the Israeli Knesset on November 20, 1977. "Why don't we believe in the wisdom of God conveyed to us by the wisdom of the proverbs of Solomon: 'Deceit is in the heart of them that imagine evil: but to the counsellors of peace is joy.' 'Better is a dry morsel, and quietness therewith than an house full of sacrifices with strife.'"[4] Thus was the drama of generations of conflict altered to the contours of peace by a man many regard as a spiritual brother of Gandhi.

Commenting on the spiritual stature of Sadat in a talk given in January 1981, just months before his assassination, Paul Solomon stated:

We happen to be blessed by knowing one of the great spiritual people of our time. The President of Egypt is presently one of the highest spiritual adepts on earth, and is having an effect on the world, not just in Egypt. But an effect on the world that will make an enormous difference in the future of the planet. He is actively and knowingly participating in the fulfillment of ancient prophecy. He knows that he's doing that. He's doing it very deliberately. And he spends a great deal of time, every day of his life renewing his understanding of that, asking for direction, listening to it, and acting on that direction. He and his wife, both, are dedicated to using meditation and prayer, spiritual guidance for what they do. And I don't think that I have ever been more impressed with the work of any spiritual adept in all of history than I am with Anwar Sadat.

Because of the spiritual efforts and political triumph of one man, therefore, the configurations of world destiny were changed. Indeed, from the time of the 1973 reading when the Source foretold the coming of only two more wars before nuclear destruction of the Temple Mount in Jerusalem, the world has been witness to the Yom Kippur War of 1973, the 1982 Israeli invasion of Lebanon, and the uprising, beginning in 1987, among the Arab population of the occupied West Bank and Gaza, known as the Intifada. Additionally, the battlefields of the Mideast have played a grim host to the protracted Iran-Iraq War (1980-1988) in which more than a million people lost their lives, the Persian Gulf War of 1991 in which Saddam Hussein threatened the annihilation of the State of Israel with chemical weapons, and the numbers of civil wars that have now spread across the Middle East, from Libya to Yemen, creating a power vacuum for militant Islamic Jihadists such as ISIS, Al-Qaeda, and their clones to seize the advantage. "Turkey, Israel, and Iran are the only strong states left in the region," as one Arab leader put it. "The Arabs are hell's firewood." Above all, it is the chaos in Syria, where foreign jihadis, now numbering over 50,000, have overwhelmed the Western strategy of support for the moderate opposition, that has already driven both the West and Russia toward greater involvement. Sectarian cultural, ideological, and theological divisions are only becoming more implacable, and there's little sign that tensions in the region will abate before they explode into all-out war.

AN EARTHQUAKE IN JERUSALEM

If Sadat brought a new hope and vision to the prospect of a Mideast peace, therefore, it can only be seen as the opening processional in the march of a thousand miles. For while certain apocalyptic events may have been "delayed" or "forestalled" through such courageous efforts, the Source clearly states that such events have not in any sense been prevented from occurring. For, indeed, the single most important issue in the Arab-Israeli dispute has yet to be resolved.

The conflict over the political fate of Jerusalem traditionally has been intractable and remains the ultimate hurdle toward a lasting settlement between Arabs and Israelis. Regarded as holy to both Muslims and Jews, Jerusalem is not a rational subject for either. "Jerusalem must be under Palestinian sovereignty," states Sari Nusseibeh, a Palestinian leader who worked closely with

PLO Chairman Yasser Arafat. "Personally, I'm prepared to recognize (Jewish) West Jerusalem as part of Israel. But I need in return East Jerusalem as part of Palestine. If not, peace is not worthwhile. The future is not worthwhile." Statements to the same effect have been made by Arafat himself. Israeli Foreign Minister Shimon Peres, on the other hand, reflecting the official view of the Israeli government, states "This [Jerusalem] is our only capital, and for them [Palestinians] it is their never-never capitol. They can dream --- we deny no one his dreams --- but united Jerusalem is and will remain Israel's eternal capital."[5]

Equally emphatic are the thousands of voices of teachers, writers, philosophers, and clerics heard from both sides. "I tell my Israeli cousins, 'Deal with us, the Palestinians, on Jerusalem for it is just one of many issues between our peoples, and we will be reasonable,'" declares Palestinian writer Nasser Eddin Nashashibi. "If we do not find a just solution for Jerusalem, however, the whole Arab world will become involved, and then the whole Muslim world, more than a billion people, and they will not rest without Muslim sovereignty over Jerusalem, I tell you, they will not rest." Rabbi David Hartman, a leading Israeli philosopher, predicts that the conflict over Jerusalem will be "enormous, earth-shaking, cultural, primordial." In the words of Rabbi Jonathan Blass, head of a rabbinical training program, "Peace means a lot, but Jerusalem is worth more." As if in response, Adnan Husseini, director of the Islamic trust that maintains the Al Aqsa mosque and other Muslim holy sites in and around Jerusalem, states, "OK, the Jews have their promises (from God), and we have our promises. But this is a childish quarrel, and if it is carried to the extreme as Israelis are ready to do, then it will bring a religious war, nothing less than that, because Jerusalem is holy to all Muslims."[6] To this unfortunate end, the Source states:

> For that which has been spoken of as an earthquake in Jerusalem is likely to be the mystic's interpretation of a great explosion of nuclear force in the Holy War which has its seeds already in the antagonism between those of the Hebrew and the Palestinian or the Arabs, the sons of Jacob against the sons of Esau (Solomon Reading No. 1285, 3/8/88).

In fact, despite the best efforts of Anwar Sadat, the same spirit of enmity and discord that has endured from the time of Jacob and Esau has in our day stiffened to where it is by now far more probable that ancient animosities rather than sincere efforts toward reconciliation over the issue of Jerusalem will rule over the birthrights of today's generation of children. Moreover, it is no mere Holy War that the Solomon Source envisions, but the final great war of all nations, one whose formidable power and dynamics has already been unleashed in the heavens.

THE FORCES OF LIGHT AND THE FORCES OF DARKNESS

Following the old Hermetic doctrine, "as above, so below," that man is the mirror of the spirit, the Source tells us that **the physical manifestation of that which occurs in the spiritual or in the heavens is out-manifesting as a war between men.** The greater war of Armageddon, then, far greater than any individual could possibly imagine, is that being waged now, in the subtler dimensions of the spirit. As the Source points out:

> In the sense that you ask the question, "Is this Persian Gulf War the literal battle of Armageddon?"--- the war of Armageddon --- then the answer is: what you see before you being played out between the forces of nations with armies in the physical is a physical reflection of the spiritual war which is already begun, and has been for the time since the prophecy was given. And specifically since the time of the appearance of Christ as Jesus of Nazareth as He ascended the earth and left to every man responsibility to become the Christ as He is the Christ ... in the moment. When he ascended, the war began (Solomon Reading No. 1466, 1/21/91).

The war marked by earthly contingence, therefore, is merely a shadow, a reverberation, of the deeper significance of that heavenly war fought from the time of Christ's ascendance. Spirit prefigures matter. Thus, do be careful to remember the words of the Master as he spoke and said, 'what you see in the physical is like seeing the movement of leaves on trees. But what you do not see is the wind that moves the leaves.' And so when you see the tanks and armor and guns you are seeing the movement of the leaves. But the real battle is in the air, not among missiles but in the air in the sense of being in the subtler dimension of heaven within you and between you/about you (Solomon Reading No. 1466, 1/21/91).

So then, the full gravity of this great war of Armageddon comes finally to light. As the Source puts it, the great battle to which you refer, the battle of Armageddon, is a battle between Light and Darkness, not confined even to this planet, but to the entire system which you would refer to as your solar system in which the site itself is the cathedral of light and this planet a manger. And in that perspective, know that the spiritual forces of Light battling Darkness are far greater than you can see, and more meaningful than the gathering of armies, however powerful, and however disposed against one another in the flesh (Solomon Reading No. 1466, 1/21/91).

We live in a time of relative and conflicting values, when we have lost our certainty about what good and evil, Light and Darkness, truly are. The Source tells us that the forces of Light and Darkness that surround and are interior to us are boundless, inconceivable to any finite mind. Human language and even human thought itself are by their very nature incapable of embracing the endless potentiality of their power and influence. To their veiled and incomparably greater presence, we are, as W. I. Thompson puts it, "like flies crawling across the ceiling of the Sistine Chapel: we cannot see what angels and gods lie underneath the threshold of our perceptions."[7]

When, in the Beginning, the dissentient powers of a newly awakened universe divorced themselves from the Divine context in which they had previously existed, they established themselves as a rival Absolute, an alternative repository of meaning. The more progressively they dissociated themselves from the Logos, the creative matrix from which they were conceived, the more they wove themselves inextricably into the tissue of separate and rival worlds of their own. From that time before time began to our own period of history, relates the Source, that apotheosis born of rebellion has stood opposed to the Divine purpose occasioned by God at the moment of Creation.

But it was not until Christ ascended into the heavens (into the spiritual realms within) that the great battle between these worlds began. It was a battle fought on every level, individual and cosmic, human and divine, to restore to the creative spirit its primal and undifferentiated unity with God. Thus, for two thousand years, these vast living energies, broadly construed as Angelic and Demonic, have been engaged in the ultimate struggle of Armageddon. The wild and ruthless power of absolute Darkness against the searing and irresistible powers of infinite Light. And from the vast reach of these inner worlds which permeate and influence our own, mankind sifting about for meaning has been forced to choose between the megatheric powers of Darkness and the penetrating spirit of Light.

Now this great cosmic struggle is upon us as well, warns the Source, it having at length objectified itself from an implicate reality beyond / within the horizons of our own physical world. And following the same Hermetic Law, the inexhaustible powers of Light and Darkness around which the inner battle rages have their incarnations in our world as well. As seen from the prophetic standpoint of the Solomon Source:

> And it comes; even in this time, in this day, shall it be revealed and should you understand those spiritual laws governing it, that it should be such, that there was gathered upon His shoulder and about Him, that He absorbed, that He took in, as He described it Himself, all the sin of the world. Those vibrations of sinfulness, then, were called to come in and surround Him. And in that moment that there was taken the sword and put into His side, His soul was all released. And those vibrations even of hell, as might be described, were given to that sword. And that which committed that most infamous act ever has been given on your plane, became a storehouse for such vibration, such evil, and has been passed, even as that Holy Grail was kept by those of the right hand or the servants of the Christ, so was that spear kept as a sacred relic by those of the left and used by that infamous one, that leader of Germany [Hitler], even in the most recent times, so came his power. So then does it still exist in the world today.

> As one will pick up that [Holy] Grail, so will there be taken up as well, in that land called Italy, one who would be a ruler over this land, one so infamous that those deeds committed in that time in Germany will pale by comparison. As he takes up that spear [of destiny] and begins to take up the cause of the poor and of the church, so will many be attracted to him and think this is the return of the Christ, and so will he be proclaimed.... Even those who are the students of metaphysics and those who are in those studies of spiritual growth shall cast themselves at his feet and say: "It has happened; that one has returned that would unite all and proclaim the Law of One." So many will be attracted to him, and he would be called the Antichrist.

> So will one come, little known, and his works shall not be so dramatic; but he is the Beloved of Christ. Quietly will he gather the faithful, not look-

ing for new converts, not seeking to reveal himself by the miracles, by the crowds; yet will there be comfort in his touch, and a feeling of Christ in his walk, and the look of compassion in his eyes. So will you who have known him and been the faithful be attracted to his camp, to his following.

But wait for that day and serve one another until that moment comes when he shall be the conqueror. For he will destroy the other and set in motion that new system, that new order of all that is to be. It will be his finger, his hand, that will point toward the clouds, as you will see His light, as the skies will open --- and our Master will appear to make this ball of clay His footstool and set up His kingdom on this earth. (Solomon Reading No. 1016, 6/24/73)

Thus, on the one hand, declares the Source, there is that one who, as the very embodiment of depravity and evil power, would beguile men into believing in him and would, for power's sake, bend all to his demonic will:

The Antichrist who is the absolute embodiment of darkness will appear: but he will appear as an angel of light. And many among you will be confused for he will first seem to be a savior in the arena of the Middle East. But having gained power and favor, will become then power mad, drunk with power.

And take a lesson, if you will, from the approach of the prophet Edgar Cayce when he saw in earlier days of Hitler's rise to power. He saw him as a positive force. And it is not that the prophet Cayce was incorrect at that moment, but power quickly corrupted and paranoia set in. And a man who intended to be a savior was led by his ego into the embodiment of the antiChrist. And so it will occur again. (Solomon Reading No. 1466, 1/21/91).

Again and again throughout the centuries such warnings have been sounded by visionaries, mystics, and prophets who have identified the period of time in which we now live as the "end times" or "latter days", and who specifically refer to this "man of perdition". Writing in the 12th Century, Saint Hildegard, renowned for her prophetic ability, perceived that "the Son of Corruption and Ruin" would appear "towards the end of the days of the world's duration.... He shall come in the last days of the world."[8] Nearly two centuries later, Saint Bridget of Sweden foresaw the birth of the Antichrist at the end of this age. "The time of this Antichrist, well known to me, will come when iniquity and impiety shall above measure abound, when injustice shall have filled the measure to overflowing, and wickedness shall have grown to immeasurable proportions."[9] Writing in the 14th century, St. John of the Cleft Rock forewarned that "twenty centuries after the Incarnation of the Word, the Beast in its turn shall become man. About the year 2000 A.D., Antichrist will reveal himself to the world."[10] Sister Bouquillon, writing in the 19th century, observed: "The beginning of the end shall not come in the 19th century, but in the 20th for sure."[11] In the reported 1846 Secret of La Salette, the Marian apparition revealed of the last days that "there will be bloody wars and famines and plagues and infectious diseases. It will rain with a fearful hail.... There will be thunderstorms which will shake cities, earthquakes which will swallow up countries.... Here is the king of kings of darkness, here is the Beast with his subjects, calling himself savior of the world."[12] Then in 1982, reflecting the witness of the Source, the acclaimed visionary Eileen George made reference to the Antichrist as living "under a cloak of secrecy."[13] Finally, on June 7, 1986, the Mother of Jesus announced to Father Gobbi of the Marian Order of Priests: "The hour is in preparation when the man of iniquity, who wants to put himself in the place of God to have himself adored as God, is about to manifest himself in all his power."[14]

If indeed the arrival of the "man of perdition" is herald to the last days of the world, then the beginning of the end is now irrevocably upon us. For as the Source affirms, there is **already living among you... that force of power of darkness** (Solomon Reading No. 1068, 1/23/81), that one who, exalting himself as God, would bring in his train the horror of war, plague, famine and devastation as prophesied by John of Patmos; the devouring monster of chaos who, bending the power of One to his demonic will, would evoke the desolating sacrilege as foreseen by Daniel:

> ... we would have you seek to understand that the Antichrist already has come. Yet, there will be those who will personify this force, this spirit, for if there would be the returning of the Christ, and if there would be the establishment of His Kingdom upon this plane, then would there first be the expression of that opposite power in such definite way as to produce that point of reference. For would you appreciate His Power, His Force, His Kingdom of peace if set upon now? Yet, would there not be the greater appreciation, would there not be the greater understanding of His force, would there not be the greater revelation of His nature if there first is given him who is the ruler of this plane?

> Now, as has been given, this plane was created for the purpose of allowing such a one, such an Antichrist to rule that there be given free choice to those who are the creations of God, those who are the Sons of God that you might choose to love good or evil. Then in such a way was evil given opportunity to manifest, or to rule upon this plane. Then there will come that time before the destruction, before the lifting of this plane, that such kingdom be set up by the Antichrist, or that he would be allowed to rule, or that those forces of the higher spirit will be withdrawn. Then there will be, and is offered even now, that Spirit of the Christ, that Greater Spirit, that Ruling Spirit, that Personality. All that He is surrounds even now this planet, this sphere, this atmosphere. And wherever there is one here or there who recognizes his relationship with the Father and sees himself to be of the Father, then it is as though a call would be sent up, or a line from His Presence above that atmosphere, tapping in, then, to all that love, that heat that would surround this plane. So will he be drawn from earth upward, then, to the Presence of the Father, and becoming less and less of the physical, would he be attracted to that which he is like, separating, then, the self from the earth. So will that Kingdom be established.

> So then in enveloping this earth with His love will all that is the opposite nature of earth, or the nature of God then, will He begin to rule. And how would it be that if there be the rulership of God upon this plane, that which is opposite God would endure then? Or would it not create such intense

heat, such intense change that all that is upon this plane would be transmuted to higher nature? Then would it be the fearsome, awesome spectacle for those given to the Father? Would these have aught to fear? Yet, they would be of that vibration and not contrary thereto and would not suffer.

Then understand all that are of the Father and have recognized their being, their relationship, these then would be changed, would be caught up in the twinkling of an eye, would be given to the Father (Solomon Reading No. 190, 7/1/73).

Exactly when this final chapter in the human story will begin to manifest is nowhere given with any exact measure of certainty, for to reiterate, the actual timing of such events is never firmly fixed. Rather, it is dependent on the free will and determination, on **the actions, the reactions, the thoughts, the purposes of man** insofar as they are in accord with the eternal Law of Love. Hence, the Source cautions that we be vigilant: **watch not for those who swagger and boast, and are too obviously forces of evil. For the Antichrist is far too clever, and will appear first as a savior. Be not swayed by everyone who comes in robes of light** (Solomon Reading No. 1466, 1/21/91)

On the other hand, states the Source, there is [one] who carries with him the Light of Christ and who even now **prepares himself for the task at hand and becomes to your time a prophet, a leader...** (Solomon Reading No. 1068, 1/23/81).

[This one] already plays a greater role than you might guess. He is an influence behind the diplomacy that exists, and which has kept Israel from responding thus far [1991 Persian Gulf War]. Single handedly, he has stayed the hand of Israel to this point.

He will, however, become a leader of light only when that one to whom we have referred who appears as a savior (Antichrist), when he appears, [the other] will appear as his adversary. But it will be difficult for you to know at first the one from the other. But perhaps the greatest test of which is [the emissary of Christ] will be his opening of the Hall of Records and revealing to you the ages past, the earth before this earth, the time that gave birth to this civilization. [He is] that one who came from Amelius to Adam, and whose son was John who returned to be the beloved, was Benjamin with Joseph; this one has returned and becomes one who will help the establishment of a kingdom of peace over which the Christ will reign.

As to when he shall appear, understand that reading from these records does not allow us to dictate when Israel will act, when Jordan or Syria or Iraq will act. We can only read the disposition of these toward action, and tell you what we see in the records of the result of the action. We do not attempt to orchestrate these events, rather only to read them. And [he] will make himself known sometime after the second battle has begun to rage.... And he will be seven years in making himself known about the earth to the extent that he will be considered a figure of international import (Solomon Reading No. 1466, 1/21/91).

In the cosmogony of the Source, the powers of Light and darkness have now fully manifested in the separate identities of this prophet of God and his antagonist. Very shortly, we are told, these two will make themselves known in all places and among all people. And between the earthly polarities of these two there exist the spiritually unanchored and ambivalent masses of humanity, disillusioned by the failures of materialism and profoundly willing to follow en masse any genuine leader able to confer meaning on seemingly empty and meaningless lives. Just as iron filings are drawn toward a magnet, the Source tells us, so too many will be attracted by that one who has usurped the divine dignity, that one who claims the power to shape the destiny of the world. Others will be guided by the works and compelled by the all-gentle figure of this servant of the divine. Then shall legions of support constellate around these two; then shall the great earthly battle of Armageddon begin.

KING DAVID'S RETURN

All that Sadat had ever hoped for in his struggle to restore peace to a broken world will be achieved, promises the Source, through the quiet dignity and unifying spirit of this one who in fact will herald the restoration of Eden. That one... will become involved in the political arena somewhat, declares the Source, but as a spiritual figure, particularly involving himself in the relationship of Israel to the other nations of the Middle East and the world, but particularly Egypt.

> And in this relationship with Egypt, the restoration of peace will be at his hand, and the merging of those nations ... Egypt and Israel, to common cause at a time when the both of them will be surrounded by hostility from without, and will cause the necessity for a melding together.

> [T]his one... [will be] a prophet with such indications of accuracy of that that he will show and teach that he will cause the nations to listen, particularly Egypt and Israel, and those who [will] listen throughout the world --- especially those who become aware that even those not attuned to the philosophies, words, teachings of the spiritual ones, even others are becoming frightened of the times, of the changes, the geological changes of the earth and other instability (Solomon Reading No. 1068, 1/23/81).

Prior to the Source readings of Paul Solomon we are provided only one glimpse of this mysterious individual. In a 1934 reading Edgar Cayce heralded his arrival by stating that the Apostle John "would soon enter the earth." Referred to by the Cayce readings as "John Peniel," he "would be beloved of all men in all places when the universality of God in the earth has been proclaimed." It is he, we were told, who, as a "messenger" of God, would bring to the Earth "a new order of things." The age of the spirit would not dawn before John Peniel had brought a new light to the world. Such was he announced and as such was he awaited by millions the world over as the forerunner of Christ's reappearance.

As the years passed, however, the spotlight passed on, leaving in mysterious darkness the figure proclaimed by Cayce as that one who would inaugurate the coming age of universal peace. And the darkness remained for over forty years until finally, in 1976, there came a startling disclosure from the Solomon Source. **That great one who comes and will bring the new order of things does live and is among you [now].**

> Now, the one of whom it is spoken, "He will come," is already on your plane and in the East. [He] has attracted some attention to himself by proclaiming, as a child, that he was and is the return of David, once king of Israel. [He is] the son of a teacher, and has spoken of the poetry of the ancients. [He] has astounded those who have seen him already with his proclamation of self as a teacher. In that sense [he has] already [been] discovered; [he] has not attracted attention for sometime now, but will again soon (Solomon Reading No. 850, 7/4/76).

In fact, legend already attended him, for in 1968 a Fate magazine article[15] recounted the amazing story of a young Israeli boy who in 1964 at the age of 3, possessed not only a remarkable grasp of ancient Hebrew but also specific knowledge of the first Temple's architecture as well as the military tactics employed in ancient Israeli victories. Having captured the attention of biblical scholars, the young boy led a team of archaeologists to the site of a secret tunnel that ran under the fortress of King Hezekiah. The astonishing find concurred precisely with the biblical account of King David's successful attack. Additionally, the boy was frequently observed lapsing into trance, speaking prophecies concerning the future of the Israeli state and the rebuilding of the Temple on Mount Moriah. With reference to the young prophet, Rabbi Yedidia Cohen of Israel's Supreme Religious Council stated in 1968: "We cannot admit anything openly, because the Jewish faith is based on the theory that King David is the Messiah, and when he returns to earth, the Kingdom of God will prevail. This means the resurrection of the dead and other things, such as eternal justice, immortality, and the like. I don't think the world, mankind, or even we Israelis are ripe for it yet. But if the boy is not Messiah, he cannot be King David --- provided one believes in reincarnation."[16]

In 1976, the Solomon Source affirmed that not only is the boy the most recent expression of the biblical King David, but of John the Beloved, the apostle of Christ, as well. By extension, the Source had wedded ancient Jewish prophecy and Christian prophecy with the coming of a great world leader in "the latter end of days." The name accorded him by the Source --- John Peniel.

> You'll hear of his work first in the East, not speaking so much of the work of the Christian, for [he] is a Hebrew of the Hebrews at the time, but [he] will lead the work to the understanding that has been given. For it is said among the prophets, "I will send one for the remnant of Israel, for those who have not believed, that in the latter day they might be brought." And so he will appear among them as one of their own, but will establish an understanding of the ministry of the Son of God in a new and acceptable manner to those; not that there is a new word or message, but a greater understanding might be brought.

> He will come, then, to this land [United States] as a teacher, one having acclaim, and men will marvel at his words. He will be called John. The last

name is not, by birth, Peniel, but that name adopted for its meaning, "where I met Him face to face." And [he] will use, then, that name in the ministry and will be known of men not because of his use of the name, but because of his teaching and his work among men.

... Then he is known already among you. His work will be established. And let those of you who have specific interest, and can be about the search, find. For already in the popular press have been stories of his entry: in the earlier time, in your generation, the story of a child spouting words of ancient wisdom and quoting ancient signs, declaring to his elders that he is the return of David.

Look unto him, for this is the one of whom it was written, "He will come." (Solomon Reading No. 850, 7/4/76).

And whereas we are told that the world will have to wait until sometime after the next war involving Israel has begun to rage to know publicly of his presence, in the extraordinary events of Paul Solomon's life John Peniel had already come. In ways that would be utterly disconcerting to the rational minds of most people, this great leader of light had appeared time and again, meeting with Paul Solomon under the most unaccountably mysterious circumstances. During his 1982 Israel tour, a headlong pace interrupted sporadically by stretches of exhaustion forced Paul Solomon to select all his hotels entirely at random. Despite the fact that not even he knew where or when he would settle in for a moment of rest, he found that all his rooms were paid for in advance with a broad bouquet of flowers waiting for him when he arrived. For weeks, the mystery continued at every stop. Not until he boarded his plane for the flight home did his mysterious benefactor finally appear. Seated next to him was a young, brown-eyed, middle-eastern man who offered his hand and said: "Dr. Schlomo (Solomon), I am John. It's nice to see you." Following a genial exchange in which the young middle-easterner acknowledged his involvement in the hotel room mystery, the two of them proceeded to discuss the unfolding of events in the Middle East as well as the young man's role in the far-reaching future of that region. Unfortunately, nothing more is ascertainable from this initial meeting. Given John's obvious need for anonymity, Paul himself remained, for the most part, elusive when asked for any comment regarding John's identity. Paul's silence on the matter extended even to those closest to him. In December 1983, for instance, Paul, along with his adopted son David Solomon and a few close Fellowship aides, departed Washington Dulles Airport for Israel to speak at the "Forecast 1984" conference in Jerusalem. As David explains, "When we boarded the plane, I discovered that we did not have the window seats that I had asked for at the reservation desk, but instead we were given aisle seats. I thought it strange at the time. One of the last passengers to board sat in the empty aisle seat opposite Paul. He was a solidly built man about 5'10" tall, thick mustache, short curly black hair, brown eyes, light brown skin, Jewish, and wore cowboy boots and a suit.

"Out of the corner of my eye, I saw Paul chuckling to himself, as if the incident of the man sitting across the aisle was funny. Suspiciously, I thought to myself, 'Who is that man? Is it John Peniel?' It seemed ridiculous, but Paul had told me that John had a peculiar talent for arranging meetings like this.

"Sometime during the first hour of the flight, Paul noticed that the man was reading a Jewish newspaper. In turn, the middle-easterner noticed the pamphlet Paul had pulled out and began to strike a conversation with him. Paul mentioned that he was going to Jerusalem to the Forecast 1984 conference. The man knew about the conference, but played down its real importance, indicating that he thought it was something of a circus sideshow. The most interesting comment he made concerned the meaning attributed by Jewish religious scholars to the year 1984. Letters and numbers in Hebrew are interchangeable and have specific meaning. Accordingly, 1984 meant destruction, and he wrote the Hebrew letters on paper. But then, he added that he disagreed with the scholars regarding the 1984 prophecy.

"When we finally stopped in Paris to pick up more passengers, we had an hour break to get off the plane and tour the duty-free shops. While there, I spied the man sitting on a bench in a rest area. I noticed that he had shaved off his moustache. Why would he do that? When we again boarded the plane leaving for Jerusalem, he had disappeared.

"I looked for this man again in Jerusalem, but to no avail. Was it John Peniel? I think so. But when I asked Paul about it, he simply shrugged his shoulders and acted innocent. He would neither confirm nor deny the incident."[17]

There appears to be something in the spiritual energy of both John Peniel and Paul Solomon that periodically brought them together and gave strength to them both in what the Source calls a time of great urgency. Both, in a sense, are witnesses to the coming reappearance of Christ on Earth. And, as indicated by the Source, there is a third witness, one now living upon this plane, who has yet to make himself known:

> There is... one who will act in a role similar to John the Baptist, a harbinger who will work together with John the Apostle (John Peniel), Paul the Apostle who is before you (Paul Solomon), and Peter who is incarnate on your plane in this time. Understand that these three will come from three distant corners of the world, and their coming together with one from these environs of Japan will be three witnesses who will usher in the dawning of a new day, particularly through the establishment of the Order of Initiation allowing the Crown of Enlightenment. Thus will be fulfilled the dream of restoring the Temples of Initiation, and this must come within the present generation (Solomon Reading No. 1560,9/91).

Thus, as John Peniel is revealed to be John the Apostle, so Paul Solomon himself was clearly identified by the Source as the most recent expression of Paul the Apostle. Together with Peter who has yet to make himself publicly known, these three constitute the three witnesses to the sacred mystery of Christ's manifestation of Divinity in this time. As in that former time when they served the cause of humanity, the Source tells us that these three have been reunited in our own day for the purpose of bringing to light the inner forms of our liberation which lie beneath the veil --- in that Living Source within. As given by the Source, **it is essential in that work that the three apostles, John, Paul, and Peter together will establish the foundation of the New Age. Paul will then pass from the work (pass from the physical), and the entering in of** the New Age will be accomplished by those who remain (Solomon Reading No. 1567, 10/7/91). Thus the Source in fact prophesied the passing on of Paul Solomon. Like Paul himself, however, the remaining two witnesses are possessed of the same determined and single-minded purpose of bringing about the transformation necessary for an age of enlightenment. But preeminently, the Source maintains, it is for John of Peniel now to live the very revelation that he witnessed nearly two thousand years ago in the apocalyptic vision of the Apostle John.

THE GREAT SHIP IN THE HEAVENS

That vision would most probably mean the end of the world --- the sum of cultural achievements and human relationships which constitutes what we mean when we speak of "civilization". But even with a diagnosis so grave and prognosis so unfavorable, it is a minor vicissitude beside the vaster mystery which it unveils and which only faith can accept. For we are told to expect the unexpected, the unpredictable, the all-but-impossible. Following the most miraculous of all signs and portents, the final great conflict of all nations will culminate in that event toward which it has been destined from the beginning --- the long-awaited Advent of Christ:

> During the time of this bloodshed or confusion, look for another event which will distract the attention of the entire world. This is a celestial event, the coming of a light from the sky. This event will be so great in magnitude as to distract the attention of the world from war and fighting. It will give to all men common cause, greater than that which is the concern of the war. For it will seem to every man that the very existence of the earth will be endangered. His light as it comes in the sky will be brighter than that of the sun. Because of the magnitude, the sun will appear to turn black. It will be as if it had collapsed, giving its power to that which comes.

> Then two will stand, one drawing attention to himself as if he were a savior of the world. He will seem to have answers and means of protection. His approach will be one which will attempt to destroy the incoming object. Then you will know the savior by the fact that his attention is turned to the individual. It will seem foolish to most that man will be invited to accept and to welcome the incoming light. But keep in mind the ancient prophecy of His coming. You are warned that when others say, "Lo, He is here, He is there," you will then know it is not correct. For to point here or there is to point without yourself, outside the self. As the true savior comes, He comes within you.

> This does not mean that there will be no presence among you which can be identified. It means rather that your identification of Him will come from inner recognition rather than looking without to some other man. For He is the embodiment of the light which will come, and He will establish a new manner of living a New Order of the ages. And His manner will be one of living together in peace, harmony, not only with one another, but with the heavenly body on which you stand.

It would do well that you understand the nature of a space vehicle or space ship. For many will interpret the incoming light in that manner. It has been seen by some as standing as a great ship over Jerusalem. For your better understanding of that you might call a spaceship, think of the planet itself as a great ship. For that celestial body which comes will be similar in that manner. Not as if it were a craft, but as it were a celestial object, having more similarity to a meteor than that you think of as a UFO.

This will be the coming of His light in the sky, and will bring the dawning of a new age, a new Eden. The earth will be renewed.

Look toward the building of the Temple as your most important sign of the coming of these events (Solomon Reading No. 1560, 9/16/91).

Although perceived by many as threatening to the Earth itself, the Source tells us that this great globe of light in fact belongs to an entirely different contextual plane. Descending from the very highest spiritual regions, it will shine into the depths of matter and quite literally transfigure the world. So dazzling will its light be that it will cast a splendor grander even than that of the sun. To many it will be taken as a sign of terror and of doom. But this heavenly light, we are told, is the principle annunciatory sign of the physical appearance of Christ. It is the final sign of fulfillment. "For as the lightning flashes across the sky from east to west, so shall my coming be, when I, the Messiah, return," Jesus tells his Disciples. "And then at last the signal of my coming will appear in the heavens and there will be deep mourning all around the earth. And the nations of the world will see me arrive in the clouds of heaven, with power and great glory" (Matthew 24:27, 30). Indeed, affirms the Source, it comes at a time when there will be the excitement about the earth, an atmosphere of expectancy, but much fear. There will be the bowing of the knee before God in such numbers as have never occurred before on this plane. And those who have predicted and those who have lived and taught and made the self to be like the servants of Him will be respected, honored, revered in that day. But their purpose will be to understand the awesomeness of that occasion when the skies will light up with a light like never before has been seen on this planet, and it will be known that this is His light (Solomon Reading No. 176, 6/9/73).

We are told further that each of us will discover in this light what we are spiritually prepared to discover. For many it will be panic and alarm. For others, an overpowering sense of reverence and awe. Yet there are a few who will experience a complete convergence with this light. Caught up in the transcendent Otherness of this luminous manifestation of Christ, they will be transfigured, even as Christ Himself was transfigured on the Holy Mount. From this instantaneous initiation (mystical marriage of the Lamb) accompanied by sudden illumination, they will acquire another mode of being. They will undergo a physical change of substance, becoming less dense. It will be as though if the earth were crumbling beneath you; you would still walk on solid ground into a new kingdom, not affected by the crumbling of the earth (Solomon Reading No. 1173, 8/14/84). Quite literally, we are told, they will be born of the Light and consist of Light, giving them access to the subtler realms of the spirit. And those who are prepared would be drawn by that light as it would appear in the clouds, and will leave these bodies. And lifting themselves, it will be as if they have become light and will be attracted like magnets to that light that is a part of themselves. They will see and recognize that that is their Father, their home, and attracted to that light, so they will be caught up to meet Him in the clouds. And those unprepared will be left looking up and crying toward the heavens that He accept them even on that day, but those are not prepared and it would be too late (Solomon Reading No. 176, 6/9/73).

Just as Jesus spoke and said, "two men will be working together in the fields, and one will be taken, the other left. Two women will be going about their household tasks; one will be taken, the other left" (Matthew 24:40-41), so the Source declares:

> Now understand this: there has been spoken and written in that Book, of a time when the two shall be standing together and suddenly one taken and the other left. There have been spoken those times of the changes of the plane about you --- of the physical structure of the earth. There have been the warnings of the times of hunger and famine, and of confusion, and the crying out. Now all these things come; and would it not be for this reason that we have accelerated attempts to find, here and there, those who would prepare for the changes and for the lifting? And if you would understand how it could be that one should be suddenly taken and the other left, how would you see it?

> Know that as the dimension is prepared and the calling up to the Great Ship that is the Christ would occur, those who are prepared to step into the dimension, then, will leave that of the denser and enter into the lighter plane. It is this you prepare for, and the preparations are not of the physical, but of the heart. For those of the Master will recognize the Voice. Those belonging to that Ship will be called to that Ship, as it would leave or traverse itself to another plane. You may understand, in that sense, the Christ Presence in the re-entering that it could be described as a Great Ship that would carry those who have prepared themselves, and belong with that Vessel, to the new state of being that will be (Solomon Reading No. 307, 3/13/74).

And these things which have been met with incredulity and ridicule by many will very shortly and quite literally come to pass, promises the Source:

> Then if you would wonder concerning that that is preached about, or that Rapture of the Church that is called, is described in this manner, we would have you see that these are not so far off that that you have considered superstition. And those that have been ridiculed among the Bible preachers, you would see in this manner: that it is simply necessary that this plane be altered to a higher state of all that is. And if one, then, would change the dimension suddenly, so would he be caught up, to be with the Christ in the air, as is described as the Rapture of the Church (Solomon Reading No. 241, 1973).

These, then, are the "elect" who, through their perfect devotion of mind to spirit, are exalted above all others. Referring to these same "chosen" few, the

Source states:

> There is an Order from the Throne of Grace which has already been issued
> which says to the Angel of Destruction: "Let not these forces loose upon the
> earth until My Beloved ones are brought before Me into a New Heaven and
> a New Earth." There shall not be harmed one hair on the heads of those
> who have committed themselves as instruments through which that new
> day will dawn. To those who have become the New Essenes, the Pregnant
> Ones, through their commitment, through their new birth, through their
> attunement to living Love, will be added the ability to keep that which they
> have committed to. So shall they give birth as the Bride of the Christ to
> usher in the dawning of a new day, and then shall there be chained that
> dragon, death; fear shall be led away into that place of darkness. And as it
> has been described, the sun will go out, and yet, there shall be no need for
> that light, in a new way, having overcome fear, and so Love will provide and
> light the way. And there shall be no pain, no tear, or disharmony among
> you as a result of having stepped into Life. To those who have overcome,
> who have overcome fear and death, He shall give a crown of Life (Solomon
> Reading No. 1147, 9/3/83).

It is these few who, along with John of Peniel, will herald the restoration of
Eden:

> These, then, shall not only step into a new life, a new day for themselves, but
> become ushers of those who have been left behind to step into a new place
> and a new way themselves. So might you understand that in these months,
> years, that are upon you, you will find a continuation of war and pain and
> disease and death; changes in the earth and in the weather, in economy, in
> disease and such. And yet shall you discover that as these teachers, proph-
> ets, those who have made great commitment to a new way, a new order of
> things, begin to awaken one and another until integrity becomes important
> and love becomes a power perceived, recognized as stronger than fear, and
> life stronger than death --- as this spark shall reach that critical mass for
> change, so shall you see suddenly the dawning of a new day, His face seen
> in the clouds, and every man, every man who is committed to Life shall see
> Him. And those with whom there is a bond of commitment, these shall be
> led into peace and new life. And to those committed to the beast, the anti-
> Christ, these shall experience much pain and hurt, and destruction. (Solo-
> mon Reading No. 1147, 9/3/83).

Then skyward, from this radiantly awesome Light, the nature of which is written
into the very structure of the Divine Cosmos, the Source tells us that the physical
form of Christ Himself will emerge. And from that light He will form and become
a physical being, returning even in this day as in that. And why would those attempt to explain away His coming in a physical manner? Did He not live upon this
earth and create His kingdom in the physical? And will He not return to conquer
that which was taken away in that day? Now understand these are His purposes
upon the earth and there will be the rule, the reign, upon this physical earth for
that period of time (Solomon Reading No. 176, 6/9/73).

Whatever stubborn hope for peace may yet be left in the human heart will find a passionate fulfillment in the day of Christ's return. For as foretold by the prophet Zechariah, "Then shall the lord go forth, and fight against those nations [of the world], as when he fought in the day of battle. And his feet shall stand in that day upon the mount of Olives, which is before Jerusalem on the east, and the mount of Olives shall cleave in the midst thereof toward the east and toward the west, and there shall be a very great valley; and half of the mountain shall remove toward the north, and half of it toward the south." (Zechariah 14:3-4) Indeed, states the Source, it will be fulfilled precisely as prophesied:

> And it will be toward the climax of that battle that the Mount of Olives will be split into two parts creating a valley, a valley leading to that ancient place of the Golden Gate (of the Old City in Jerusalem), where it is prophesied that the Messiah will enter Jerusalem, where clever men have created a cemetery knowing that the Messiah, according to ancient tradition, would be soiled by approaching through a cemetery. And yet as that mount is split and the valley is created, the cemetery is separated and a path made to the entrance. And so it is taught in your Scriptures. And you may read it there (Solomon Reading No. 1173, 8/14/84).

From this point forward, Israel's seemingly hopeless fortunes will have turned in its favor. Strengthened and encouraged by those superior forces of Light, Israel, as we are told, **will not only survive but be victorious. That itself will be miraculous among men, for this tiny nation shall have stood against the whole world, even this nation** (Solomon Reading No. 1466, 1/21/91). And the greater war, that fought between those forces of Light and Darkness, will finally end **when the Christ is born in the hearts of those who are able to receive him,** states the Source. Then, finally, that fatal storm of Armageddon shall have passed, and the dark night of humanity's soul will have ended. Then will we see **a dawning of a new day.**

> So then shall the Beloved of God introduce the New Order as is being introduced now by the prophets among you, those who have prepared for this purpose. So then shall He, the Lamb of God, the Christ, rule over that New Heaven and New Earth (Solomon Reading No. 1147, 9/3/83).

THE GIFTS OF THE PROPHET

This, then, becomes the real work and true purpose of John of Peniel. The Source promises that he will bring a new dimension of experiential truth, one which links Self once more with the cosmos. By restoring a lost unity between Arabs and Jews, John of Peniel comes to restore our lost integrity --- with God, with Self. As the Source observes:

> The work of John of Peniel is to end duality and separation. It is the work of this enlightened one to build the capstone of the Mystery School, the re-establishment, as it were, of the capstone, the crown stone of Giza. And the return of the capstone is also the returning of the Crown of Enlightenment to the mind of man.

Thus, the work of John of Peniel and those who work with him ... is the work of making available to every man the Crown of Enlightenment, brain transcendence, the mending of that which is rend in twain, the rending of the veil.

We would have you understand that the tablets ... to be brought together again from the prophecies of the Hopi, the tablets can well be said to be the left and the right hemispheres of the brain, which when brought together again by an enlightened initiate, can be made one tablet of wisdom. These are the same tablets brought by Moses from the crown of Sinai. They are the same tablets spoken of by Joseph Smith as Golden Tablets.

Now in the physical dimension, you will also find such tablets of wisdom written, engraved, Smaragdine tablets in the chamber of Records at Giza. Understand that Smaragdine refers to emeralds. The emerald tablets are the tablets of the heart of emerald green.

As the chambers of the heart are one, the hemispheres of the brain are one, a change in the nature of the species to androgynous. Much of these occurrences are beyond imagination at the moment. But understand that all refer to the end of appearance of duality and the establishment of the Law of One (Solomon Reading No. 1560, 9/91).

By its very nature, our logical, dualistic, fact-accumulating mind is simply barred from an understanding of a life utterly free of all duality and distinction. Only when in the fullness of time the power of creative, or thaumaturgic, vision is restored shall we finally see and experience through the whole spectrum of consciousness the underlying unity of life.

Second, any transcendent shift in human consciousness of the magnitude described by the Source would necessarily reflect itself in a corresponding shift away from an energy-intensive and dissipative technology and toward the life-affirming values of a nature-based science. It is the work of John of Peniel to restore a healthy ecological balance between ourselves and the Earth and to bring a "New Order of things" in our ability to access the unified forces of an integrated cosmos. What is meant by a 'New Order of things'? challenges the Source. Let us attempt to describe it in this manner:

... all of your science of this day is based upon the principle of destroying matter to release its energy with the idea in mind of supporting life. Now listen to that philosophy carefully. Your science is based upon a belief that that which lives must die in order to release living energy to support life. It doesn't even sound reasonable, does it? It is a technology of death and destruction. All of your energies, all of your energy sources that you use for fuel, all these are produced by the breakdown of matter --- taking life out in order to attempt to support life, producing death to support life. We speak of a very, very basic violation of law, built solidly into the infrastructure of your science and technology, the way you live in your day and time.

When we say that one will come who will bring the New Order of things, what we speak of is simply this: that there is one to come among you [John of Peniel] who will introduce a very simple vital formula for a new technology, a technology of a new age. This is, in reality, a reinstituting of an ancient technology, for there was a time on this planet when it was possible to move about the planet in ships, ships that flew by a principle, the principle which allows stone to float in the air. Now the idea of floating stones in the air seems rather odd to your thinking in this time, but let us point out these things.

The monument you call the Great Pyramid of Giza was built by floating stones in the air. Now that sounded strange when it was spoken from these records many years ago. Yet, recently, it has been discovered that baked ceramic material, being a superconductor, when lowered in temperature to near freezing, these pieces of stones or slate or ceramic are caused to float by the magnetic field produced within them. This is observable in your laboratories in this day and time, right now, today. The qualities of superconductor ceramics begin to demonstrate the principle we speak of, of stones floating in the air.

Now, we speak of that in this way, that discovering these materials, these new relationships between materials, will allow your technology to discover that ships may fly not only through the air, but through the earth and water as easily. You are beginning to realize in your technology that your body is not so solid as it has seemed, that the spaces between the molecules and the atoms should easily accommodate the spaces between the molecules of the earth. And so, as your understanding of physics is just slightly altered to see the earth as it is, to see the relationships between the bodies as they are, so your new technology will allow for the communication of lines of force, not around the earth in satellites and such, in such a ridiculous system as circling the globe for communication with the opposite side. When through the use of the superconductivity of the inner mantle of the earth, communication can be passed from this side of the earth to the other without time lapse, by using the mantle of superconductivity. The energies that are now passed in the atmosphere around the earth from one side to the other can be passed through it, and so can travel be accomplished in a similar manner by moving through.

Now, the establishment of the New Order of things depends upon a simple formula for the introduction of the principle of accessing energy at its point of entry, rather than accessing energy by the breakdown of matter to force it to release the energy that gave it life. This simple formula for the revolution of science will make energy available in such a way as to make all current science obsolete overnight.

All of the current means of production of energy become obsolete in the moment that it is discovered that energy is so available about you on the surface of the earth that it can be accessed without the destruction of natural resources, and so the atmosphere of the earth can be made to provide electricity freely, without the breakdown of matter, without the enormous cost and with the availability to each individual of the freedom of energy about him.

Such instruments as a great negative ion generator that could gather from the city about you the destructive materials that you call smog to be attracted to such a generator and this material collected and recycled to the earth. Such instruments as anti-gravity devices, as instruments for moving into what has been termed hyperspace, all these instruments which sound like advanced technology, but which are simple understandings of the blending of the interests of life with life, living in a natural manner on the planet. These formulas for a new science are the establishment of a New Order of things.

Let us attempt to say it in very simple words ... by the prophets who have come before you: live simply and in harmony with the earth, and that which is needed as the basis of life will be provided.

... How will John [of Peniel] access this understanding of a new science and technology? The instruments we speak of, instruments for renewing the earth, for repairing the ozone layer, for building ships which might be described as that which makes stones to float, that which can, as it were, almost vacuum smog and acid and the destructive elements from your environment --- these instruments exist and are set aside in a tomb near that monument you call the Pyramid at Giza. If the initiate [John of Peniel] who has prepared himself, an initiate of the Law of One, shall enter into this Hall of Records, these instruments might there be found with the living formula of a new basis for technology and science (Solomon Reading No. 1282, 3/5/88).

The Source tells us that the ancient records were not, as many have believed, **sealed until the evolution of consciousness ... arrived at that point of attunement deserving of the information contained there**; rather, **they were stored against a time when they were needed. Simply put, they were preserved not as a judgment against a consciousness of a race, but particularly to serve a race in a time of its need** (Solomon Reading No. 1068, 1/23/81).

Fifty years earlier, the Edgar Cayce Readings had likewise disclosed the existence of what they called a "time capsule" or "storehouse of records," "that holy mount not yet uncovered," and found it lying entombed, situated somewhere between the right paw of the Sphinx and the Nile River. Sealed within, said Cayce, are the records of Atlantis "from the beginnings of those periods when the Spirit took form or began the encasements in that land, and the developments of the peoples throughout their sojourn..." to "the final destruction of Atlantis and the buildings of the pyramid of initiation, with who, what, where, would come the opening of the records that are as copies from the sunken Atlantis; for with the change it must rise again." Thus, contained in this "pyramid of unknown origin," according to Cayce, are works "for the interpreting of the earth as it was, as it is, and as it is to be."[18]

But the works themselves constitute not so much a history of the technological, moral, political, spiritual successes of a race as a history of its failures. They were intended not to aid in the further advance of a future technology, but to assist a future race in escaping that fate which befell an earlier civilization. See it this way, explains the Solomon Source:

These instruments, words, teachings, ideas, understandings were preserved by a group of people that you might call a dying race or a finishing of their time. And these instruments and records relate as much to their own mistakes as to their discoveries. And they were hidden in such a way, or preserved in such a way, [as] to be awakened at a time when the needs of the earth were similar to the time of their creation. As if these Masters, Teachers, were saying: in the evolution of mankind and the development of his technology and such he will again arrive at the point we have arrived at and will make some of those mistakes that we have made and could well destroy his earth, his land, his race, as we have destroyed so much. But let that that we've discovered through our own mistakes, and our growths as well, be made available to that next race that should reach such a point (Solomon Reading No. 1068, 1/23/81).

Given our present capacity for self-destruction, it would be suicidal indeed to assume that we are not that next race, that there is yet time to spare in despoiling our global environment, in the ruination of our global economics, in the gross inequality of resources shared by rich nations and poor, in treating the causes of famine that have left tens of millions starving each year, in the further proliferation of nuclear arms, in the overshadowing threat of nuclear war ...

Pride goeth before a fall, it is said, and just as pride served as the conditioning factor of the Atlantean fall, so now it has delivered our own time to the precipice as well. **For so similar are the thoughts of these, these entering from the same period and the same time, [that] there is [a] repetition of history. And if there would be [a] repetition of history..., if history would repeat, it will repeat with those same souls incarnate in that corresponding period of history, you see, that might lift the cycle a little higher, producing a spiral to the Godhead.** Therefore, **the choice is thine whether it be cycle or spiral,** warns the Source.

The question forms itself; when will the tomb be opened and the records found? How long before we are prepared? Cayce himself had prophesied many years before that it would not be opened until the fulfillment of that time when the "nature of selfish motives in the world" is beginning to break up.

Now, on the eve of those great events foretold by Cayce, the Solomon Source proclaims that **The time is now, the time has come for the opening of the records, and the initiate John of Peniel is being prepared** (Solomon Reading No. 1068, 1/23/81). Not that the selfish motives of the world are as yet breaking up. Rather, according to Solomon, that the cataclysmic changes that are nearly upon us will shortly and out of necessity serve to render those selfish motives subservient to a new consciousness of trust, to mutual reliance, and to the assisting of others if human survival on this planet is to be at all possible. All shall act as one when the common enemy is found to be ourselves --- our fear, our self-indulgent pride, and the consequences of our own self-motivated behavior. Then will this great Prophet of God, John of Peniel, reveal himself in deed by opening the Hall of Records where, according to the Source, we will find:

... formulas, descriptions of methods, very simple methods in truth, for har-

nessing, for using the power of nature itself. It is not necessary to take fossil remains from the earth and burn it to produce energy on this planet. For the planet itself is designed in such a way that holding its balance, its relationship through magnetic forces and through the forces of gravity and movement in relation to other bodies in the system, produces enormous free energy. And it is simple when working in harmony with nature to use the energy nature produces and provides both through the movements of water on the planet and the influx of energy from the sun, not just the energy of heat, not just that you see as solar energy, but rather magnetic and gravitational forces; and these may be harnessed in a number of ways, that most available through the use of crystals. It is no secret that crystals easily can accept the rays of the sun, focus and magnify them to produce a greater source of energy than that it receives. This taken, then, and converted to other purposes. [It] does not require a great deal of machinery and structure as your current technology thinks of energy production and use. As you see these devices and formulae of a past time, you'll see them appearing to you as somewhat primitive and yet in the application of them far superior to that you have. For all that exists now is dependent upon mechanical manipulation of matter without the understanding of subtler energies resulting in matter. And the harnessing of these does not require machinery as you think of it. Then some of the importance of what is stored there would be for the resolution of your energy requirements and your tendency toward the destruction of the planet.

... this is a part of the importance of the discovery, but beyond that, a better understanding of the relationship of the result to its cause, or the relationship of mankind, the human form, to the Source, to [the] Source of thought and action, the Creator. Now these understandings are recorded not as a religion, but rather as that [that] can be demonstrated and used in practical terms. [They] will clarify much of the confusion you know as religion in this time.

Then there are those records of instruction in matters both of a technical nature and in the evolution of consciousness itself, and the teachings of these (Solomon Reading No. 1068, 1/23/81).

The Source cautions that the harnessing of such energies as are contained in these instruments and formulas could as easily be applied to destructive technologies, weaponry and such, as to their intended purpose for the cleansing and restoring of the atmosphere and the natural balance of the Earth. Should this be the case, there will be **an ending of the earth as you know it,** warns the Source. If they are used appropriately, however, **you will find a restoration of the earth to a green place, a balanced planet....** (Solomon Reading No. 1068, 1/23/81). The choice is ours.

THE SYMBOLS OF ASCENDANCE

If there is to be uncovered a providential design in the physical expression of John of Pineal, it is necessary to integrate the existing form and moment in which he has appeared with the eternal symbolism by which his life is given meaning. His worldly life as a man holds a sacred meaning for us all. As expressed by the Source,

John of Peniel as a physical individual is an incarnation of the one who was called the Beloved, the Apostle of the Christ. The Peniel experience is the experience of each man in his encounter with his Source, with God. Thus, we give you interpretation on two levels --- an experience and an incarnation of an individual (Solomon Reading No. 1560, 9/91). It is in that interior dimension of the sacred, therefore, that the experience of John of Peniel the man overflows into the life of everyone. Just as the name "Peniel" signifies "where I met God face to face," so it is in the very essence of being that each must come face to face with God. For it is only here that the sacred manifests itself in its totality, and that each becomes fully awakened to a unity with the cosmos.

And yet, the Source tells us that the symbols of revelation need not be limited to the words of prophets or confined by reference to the fate of individuals. They are present even in the origin and destiny of nations. Just as John of Peniel is a living symbol of our gateway to the Divine Source of being, so too Israel becomes for us a living symbol of our birth into the highest state of Christ consciousness. It is in this spirit that the Source refers to the nation of Israel, the birthplace of John of Peniel, as representing **the cradle, the umbilicus, the place of entry for the birth of consciousness** for all (Solomon Reading No. 850, 7/4/76).

> It is as if you might see that nation as being the crown, for that as will express the crown of the body of Adam Kadmon. Other nations, other peoples of the earth might best be seen as hands, feet, organs of expression while this, then, becomes Adam among the people.
>
> Not that in any way you would worship such a nation, or make it separate or apart. It is a part of the body, and as the Apostle has said, "Can a hand say to an eye: 'I am more important than you? Or, you than me? Or any other such part of the body?'" Yet look to the ambition of that nation and her belief of herself in regard to world affairs. See her as attempting to function as the breadbasket of the world, the mother of the nations. See her belief in that, you see. And what you see in that manner, the point of focus, self-image of Israel --- let that be that image, that consciousness of your community. Be Israel in that same sense --- the place of redemption, the chosen people. For that you are.
>
> Then this is an outer manifestation of that which will occur in the people, for what will happen? The opening of the crown chakra of the earth will bring to the entire body the sight of the Christ; that is, the Second Coming (Solomon Reading No. 966, 7/8/77).

Properly understood, Israel becomes for us an instrument of knowledge. It represents not only the point at which consciousness entered into a physical world, but also the highest spiritual state to which consciousness aspires. It symbolizes the crowning of spiritual enlightenment. Not least, it represents that power which exists within each of us, within our own minds, to search for and establish those transcendent correspondences that stand between us and the mysteries of the world. As a point of focus between the human and the Divine, the Source states as well that Israel holds the key to understanding of our final destiny:

> ... realize... that Israel is the group of believers, those baptized into the Body

of God, and not a nation as you know it in this plane, in this time. The karmic destiny of Israel has followed, with the group soul, the development of the consciousness in relation to the Father; then Israel is scattered abroad in this time and that occurring, then, in that you know as the nation [of Israel], a point of focus. Then love. Love Israel, in particular, as that point of focus that she is. . . .

And the Master will return there, even as you saw Him leave. And the herald [John of Peniel] will appear there, and his work will be centered there. It will be the reflection of the confusion of the masses, and a gathering place of the saints in this time. Then let it be a cause for prayer among you, as the tensions build again . . .

And look for the preaching, the teaching, among the people there, saying, "Let us rebuild this temple. Let us build a shrine that will be a focus of our national interest, the establishment of our national identity," as come the destruction of the shrine of one people for the erection of the shrine of another. Come the sign, then, of the ending of the Earth as you know it. Let it be a focus for prayer, then. Identify with Israel, not saying that it is another part of the world nor another people, for it is your birthplace. You are the seed of Israel, having grown from her; and [you] should see that nation, that karmic destiny, as a focal point of your own, a barometer of your consciousness (Solomon Reading No. 850, 7/4/76).

If Israel is a "barometer" of human consciousness, then it must somehow hold the key to human conflict as well. The obsession with war that inwardly stems from conflicts buried deep within the human soul, stems as well, the Source reminds us, from endlessly generative seeds of jealousy, fear, and hatred which may have been planted as far back as the time of Genesis, in the lives of Cain and Abel. For it is this initial conflict in the human drama which, the Source maintains, has its final reenactment in the last great war of nations:

Let us look at . . . the struggle within mankind that comes not only between the sons of Ishmael and Israel, but even as early as the sons of Adam, of Cain and Abel, being the side of the will or the logic [Cain], and the side of the inspiration [Abel], or the connectedness with the Source, for was not Abel born first? And was not first thought always the result of inspiration, of listening to the Source of Light? Is this not where thinking came into the mind?

But the jealous second son [Cain] was the slayer of this receptor of the knowledge of its Source [Abel], jealous of its right to bring forth from the earth its own knowledge and discovery, the need for independence, for separation from God, and even from self. The opportunity to be separate, distinct, brought into self, into mankind --- brought controversy, brought conflict. And so created an evolution of the literal thinking organ, or the brain, into two parts, so that it has fought with self against its own interests for the centuries. And it is so symbolized by these two peoples [Israel and the Arab Nations], who live in a land in which you have that lake [Galilee], the river [Jordan], and the Dead Sea, which are the inscription on the earth of the pattern, the form of the lowest point in man and the highest, the flow of the river of life, the Jordan, [which represents] the Kundalini [force], lying on the one side. And on the other [side] these two hemispheres of self have not come to understand the oneness, the unity of self as yet. And until this occurs in the consciousness of the individual, it will not occur between these two nations. And until these two nations become one, so individual mankind will remain separated within the self. One aside from the other. One process of thought from the other, conflicting with one another --- separation from self, separate from Source (Solomon Reading No. 1390, 11/7/88).

As beheld by the Source, the world itself is an instrument of prophetic awakening. God employs signs and symbols to speak to us not merely through cultures and the historical destiny of nations, but even through the topographical features of the Earth itself. The physical geography of Israel --- the river Jordan, lake Galilee, the Dead Sea --- has itself become an instrument of the Divine revelation through which the energies of the universe express themselves in vast, abstract magnitudes; where ciphers and symbolic idioms are charged with myriad forms of spiritual meaning that densify into facts of a physical universe and that express even the dimensions of human conflict through the divisions of our nature.

As symbolized in the experience of Cain and Abel, the very land itself serves to indicate that the lethal propensities that catastrophically drive Arabs and Jews to war with each other are the same which make for conflict and disorder in the bicameral brain of the individual. We see it expressed everywhere. Human violence, once confined more or less to the battlefield, is today murderously rampant on city streets. And a riot in south-central Los Angeles is fed by the same unconscious disposition for violence that is found between Arabs and Jews. Oblivious to the liberating and self-reflective language of life, man is quite literally destroying himself.

Yet, it need not be. For the teeming abundance of visible signatures in the world about us find their invisible analogies within us as well. According to the Source, the ascent of the river Jordan from the Dead Sea, which is the lowest point of land on Earth, to the headwaters flowing from lake Galilee at its summit is equivalent to the ecstatic journey from identification with matter to the nirvanic consciousness associated with the highest of spiritual realms. Were we to explore the ways in which the forces of the universe move in and through us, were we to relearn the language that God has distributed through the symbolic fate of peoples and nations, the Source assures us that we would reestablish our kinship with divinatio --- the Divine. Once we are permanently able to awaken in ourselves the deeper mind, the many interlacing forms of meaning that communicate the link between ourselves and the planet will be fully capable of being revealed. Then, if we have not destroyed ourselves, we will have entered a new age of peace:

All these factors relate to one another in the evolution, the step of mankind into the Age of Enlightenment or destruction, for both of these paths lie before you. The step into the Age of Enlightenment, the step into the destruction of the planet, either could occur in this critical time, and in fact, both can occur in the sense that many may be caught up, and the others left. And yet, out of it all will be produced a new Eden, a new blooming of a new planet after the time of transition (Solomon Reading No. 1390, 11/7/88)

Chapter 19

Apocatastasis: The Restoration

AN EVIL CHEMISTRY

When the rabbi of Rizhyn was a child, he was once walking up and down in the yard on a Friday toward evening time, when the hasidim had already gone off to pray. A hasid went up to him and said: "Why don't you go in? The sabbath has already begun."

"The sabbath hasn't begun yet," he replied.

"How do you know that?" asked the hasid?

"On the sabbath," he answered, "there always appears a new Heaven, and I can't see any sign of it yet,"[19]

So it is with ourselves. Looking at the grim state of the world that surrounds us, we can only nod sadly in agreement with the young hasid. Even though the Source assures us that **this is the dawning of a time of a new Earth, a new Heaven, such as you have not known and the mind of man cannot imagine**, its empowered worldly presence is not yet remotely visible, even on the horizon of our hopes.

But as Paul Solomon points out, so long as we remain locked into orthodox patterns of social and cultural conditioning, even if a new Heaven were to appear in our midst, its presence would remain a hidden mystery. For unless we're willing to open ourselves to the power of the Word, the vision, the presence of what lies beyond the surface of our consciousness, we'll never know anything of the greater realms of inexhaustible wonder that envelop us. That, then, is the challenge that Solomon lays before us: to release from within our own minds and hearts the illimitable energies of change, to confront them with the fears, hostilities, and limitations that betray those very energies, and from that common source to begin laying the foundations of a new world ourselves:

The sacred texts of many civilizations predict a time on this planet when there will be no fear, no pain, no hunger, no disease, no crime, no war, no death, no longer any reason for tears. A utopian world of peace and plenty will manifest.

People generally consider the concept of a peaceful, plentiful world to be a fantasy, a pretense, a metaphor, a myth, a joke, not real-life, religious folly, something that may occur in some elusive place called heaven. Almost no one takes personal responsibility to see that it absolutely occurs within our generation.

Sacred texts also predict that this new earth will come because of specific conditions. There will be a group of people present on this planet who have already begun to live in the consciousness of that new world. At some point, those people will catch the rest of the population up with them. They will cause other people to join them in that consciousness, and the new world will manifest.

According to these texts, at any given moment, we are presented with two options. We can choose to live in a world with so much pain, anger, fear, disease, sadness, cruelty, crime and war that it has become the norm --- a world where people believe it is impossible to make a difference, and that self-interest and self-protection are the only answer. The alternative is to choose not to live there. Should you choose this option, you will be glad to know what may look difficult to accomplish turns outs to be less troublesome than what you are already experiencing.

There are two ways to go. We can continue on our present path perpetuating actions that have become habitual since birth, destroying the earth and ourselves in the process. Or right now within our lifetime, we can make a commitment to become the parents of a new world where the children yet to be born will not know sickness. They will wonder what it means when people speak of something that used to exist on earth called death. They will be unable to understand such concepts as war, competition, limitations or hurting one another. That option is available to us.

Perhaps that sounds far-fetched. It is more far-fetched that humankind is considered the most evolved of the living beings and yet purposefully hurts and kills members of its own species for no useful reason and is systematically destroying its home planet. Which world sounds more far-fetched, and which sounds more feasible?

If you are tired of living in a world where pain, starvation and war are considered normal and expected, there is an alternative. If you are willing to take responsibility for creating that alternative, it is possible to produce a new world. The knowledge necessary for accomplishing a new world has always been present. The wisdom to do it must be achieved.[20]

Even if in principle we were to agree with what Solomon says, practically speaking, a conscious universe plainly represents a bridge too far. For evil is a constant presence, not only in the world but in the human soul. Ivan Karamazov's bitter diabology speaks to the point: "If the devil doesn't exist, but man has created him, he has created him in his own image and likeness." Indeed, humanity is all too often vicious, violent, corrupt, atrocious. Even those who don't believe in the existence of evil must face the horrors of the world.

While some parts of the earth glow with a bright transparency of peace, harmony, and benevolence, clouded by storm systems of massacre or famine, murders, genocide, black snows, much of the world has grown simultaneously darker. Nor are any of us immune from those evils that breathe the same air --- the drugs, crime, child abuse, global pollution, biospheric destruction and atmospheric depletion that now inclusively and uniformly threaten us all.

While the fear of nuclear holocaust, which not long ago was the nightmare at the center of the imagination, seems to have receded, the Source tells us that even that evil will again resurrect itself through the elemental ethnic hatred that fuels the blood-soaked conflicts in the heart of the Middle East. Just two years prior to Paul Solomon's passing in 1994, the Source reaffirmed: **Do not, *do not,* misunderstand. We change *not* our assessment of the recent war in the Middle East, and we do warn you that nuclear and other devices *are being gathered* and still will soil the earth at the Temple Mount and destroy the Dome of the Rock, upon which occasion Israel will begin erection of the Third Temple.** (Solomon Reading No. 1699, 10/15/92). Continuing, the Source adds: **To those who have faith in evil..., "faith in evil" we use as a definition for the word fear. Fear is faith in evil. Fear can only be practiced by individuals who have more confidence in evil than in good. Faith in evil has brought the world to the brink of economic ruin. There is no turning back. The systems of economy are, in these years approaching, completely discarded, and a new system shall arise phoenix-like. But in the interim [there comes] the most dangerous period of the more literal marking of the beast. Not to say that the interpretation of the beast is not already upon you. You carry already the mark of the beast, but there will also be added a mark on the hands and the forehead in the place one might say of what is issued now as credit cards. No longer cards to carry, but a number on the individual. Look to these times for these are the times of the reign of terror of the mark of the beast. And John of Pineal stands in the wings waiting to attack the antiChrist from those conditions.**

As we begin sorting through the different forms of evil, among its cast of characters there stands head and shoulders above all others that of the Dark Lord, of the "dark side of Sinai" in the words of Dante, one who according to the Source has already assumed flesh. Do we foolishly empower its darkness? How, we might ask, can we do otherwise? The demonic ethos of power, privilege, and profit that dominates our world controls us as well. Its field of play is the individual soul. And given the opacity of our jaded and corrupt senses, we have neither the resourcefulness nor the courage to challenge the paralyzing official consensus that shapes our societies in order to apply, even in our own individual lives, the one greater Law that can free us all. An evil chemistry seems to be turning Solomon's dream of salvation into damnation.

HEADING TOWARD THE PRECIPICE

The age, long ago predicted in the Pali Buddhist texts, of "the men who are ten years old" has, it seems, at length arrived. Of them it is written, "violent hatred against each other will predominate, with violent enmity, violent malevolence, violent lust for wholesale killing." If this past century has taught us anything, it has taught us that the freedom of the beast, like that of a willful and disobedient child, is not easily brought under the sway of reason. Unable to circumvent the snare of its own unripened ego, however, it is easily manipulated by every conceit that feeds its pride and arrogance to the dehumanizing inferiority of the Other. Thus, an "Aryan" could kill a Jew; white men could slaughter red men or drag a black man out of his own home and hang him. But as Bertrand Russell observed, "adding together even large numbers of individual evils does not explain an Auschwitz...". Or the Khmer Rouge, for that matter, who sent to the killing fields all who spoke French or wore glasses or had soft hands. The indiscriminate torture, slavery, and slaughter now taking place on two continents should leave us in no doubt. We are now faced with a wholly new incarnation of savagery, a new apocalyptic order of fanaticism and hatred which as the Source foresees, if left to its own pathological resolution, will surely and very shortly consume us all.

Before us, however, awaits the Maitreyan Age, the age of wisdom, compassion, and a return to the center of our origin. In the Kabbalah, the Sefer ha-Temunah (The Book of the Image) tells that we are entering the third Schemata under the sign of Rachamim (Compassion). Our present age under the sign of Gevurah (power) or Din (Law) represents the most divisive and depraved of all possible worlds. Never before has mankind been so totally immersed in a profane consciousness. The coming age of Compassion, however, will witness a return to wholeness of all things. The age of Law will pass to an age of Love, and from that to an age of the Spirit. There will be no families, only "one great family", no death until the end of the Schemata and then "death with a kiss." We will lead bright and translucent lives, like the angels.

We are in the very midst of a time when, to paraphrase Arthur Clark in *The Children of Icarus*, history is holding its breath, and the present is detaching itself from the past like a wandering caravel that has broken from its moorings to sail across the boundless ocean. As we drift aimlessly between two shores, it is we alone who must awaken within ourselves the wisdom to navigate our way across. And as the Source cautions us, if we do not soon learn to navigate, we will with certainty wind up on the rocks.

We now find ourselves in an age overshadowed and swayed by titanic forces, when grave choices must be made in crisis after crisis, and no simple or familiar principles are adequate. And because our ancient wisdom has either been lost or discredited by the outer knowledge that science has provided us with, mass, energy, and photonic light, rather than the light of human consciousness, has become the overriding factor in our understanding of the world and of ourselves. The formidable powers that we've fashioned and developed have now run away with us, and by all indicators it seems that we no longer possess the wisdom, ability, or wherewithal to overcome them.

Lurching from one crisis to the next, it's hard to imagine that even the most militant of rationalists any longer seriously believes that the critical problems of today's world can be solved within the confines of empirical science alone. Collecting massive gigabytes of data, we research all the world as if our very salvation depended on the results, but without even the shadow of a sustaining wisdom to guide us, our crises continue to mount. The point is neither trite nor trivial. Solutions based only on objective facts cannot account for the subjective influences that to begin with brought about the very crises that we as a civilization now face. The terrors that now afflict us are of our own making. So accustomed have we become to accept that "reality" is ultimately determined by nothing else than a strict and precise description of the world as perceived through our senses and instruments, however, that we sometimes overlook what a purely scientific rationality can neither quantify nor measure nor fully comprehend --- ourselves. And it is here, within our very nature as humans, that the whole drama of our existence as a species and our world will play itself out.

But rather than changing ourselves, most of us do nothing. Overwhelmed, we feel helpless and look away. We are silent. Prostrate, our heads in the sand, we face the future. So habitually are we committed to a life of distracting, self-absorbed particulars, and so rare is the habit of viewing life as a dynamic interrelated system, that we cannot from our nearsighted perspective recognize when civilization as a whole is in danger. In our willful detachment we cannot see or even choose to understand that no part of it can be safe until the whole itself is made secure. Far easier, perhaps, to deny the truth that is all around us or simply "leave it to the experts". Given our current trajectory on this basis, the Source forewarns that only through blind, universal violence --- a worldwide Armageddon, say --- will we eventually be delivered from the trance of self. On this basis alone, it is perhaps not an exaggeration to say that we are now living through the most perilous and unpredictable period in the entire chronicled history of our race.

For the most part, changes in human civilization have been incredibly slow. Were we to look at the whole of human history as the image of a river, we would no doubt see it from its earliest stages wandering sluggishly for perhaps tens of thousands of years. Throughout all this epochally vast stretch of time, of course, from the Neolithic Age to the age of industrialism, the storied experience of many civilizations has sunk into oblivion. Knowledge gained is knowledge lost, only to be "rediscovered." Nevertheless, the whole unfolding drama is experienced over the protracted course of millennia. Then abruptly, with the advent of modern science and mastery of physical nature, the slowly fluctuating stream becomes boisterously accelerated. For nearly two and a half centuries the waters rush forward as rapids at which point we make a terrifying and ominous leap into the nuclear age.

The deliberate systematic application of science to technology, has, indeed, transformed our world, conferring upon it godlike benefits unknown to any civilization in recorded memory. But like the djinn of Aladdin's lamp, it is morally neutral. It is a slave which serves its master with unlimited power, whether the orders given to it are wise or foolish. It cannot decide for itself what it ought to do; it can only provide. It must be guided by a wisdom that can discern and manage those same powers we have learned to conjure if it is not to become --- as it is rapidly becoming --- an end as well as a means. And judging from the current state of the world, wisdom is in short supply.

As seen from the Mind of the Source, the design of history, of the outcome of the great narrative plot, can no longer be an innocent vision. Left in the hands of sovereign governments which have conscripted such power for their own self-interest and for the further development of their military-industrial might, the choices we make can only be dictated by the existing schemata. In what the Source calls a "time of labor" while we yet stand on this benighted side of rebirth, it is clear that the historical forces and pressures of cultural conditioning that shape our consciousness along with cumulative prejudices, fears, and animosities of our world will continue to drive us down the same ill-fated path. Against these, not all the prophetic warnings in the world can count for much. Our world and way of life, we are told, cannot be sufficiently transformed to escape the coming Fall by forces of technology and politics and religion that now actively prevail.

The crushing dynamism and colossalism of modern technological/industrial society is too radically flawed, and the rigidity and inertia of its institutions simply perpetuate the values and premises that have been built into them. Moreover, the classes and sectors of society which, based only on short-term needs, have made the nearsighted, politically expedient, and self-serving decisions that have shaped our unsustainable present persist in the same mode of thinking that will betray all our hope for the future.

Traditional institutions of religion, which could offer the greatest alternative and perhaps the sole hope of salvation for our world, have lost touch with the experiential basis of their teachings and so have lost themselves in a fog of doctrine and dogma. While the doctrines that they profess outwardly still contain the latent possibilities of their deeper meanings, because of the want of these more profound truths even on the part of those whose role is to keep open the bridges of direct experience and whose function would be to guide the rest, they are all too often no more that the blind leading the blind. While faith provides the archetypical wisdom of trust and acceptance that forms the core of any doctrinal system of belief, it's nonetheless a poor substitute for sacramental experience in the most universal sense: the vision born of ecstatic harmony with the universal Source of all being. Deprived of any semblance of intellectuality and divorced from the transcendent potentiality that lies at the the very heart of human consciousness, their effective influence amounts to very little. They simply fail to go deep enough to touch what is most fundamental in human nature.

In short, no system of ideology, creed, or belief, no institution of state, no social movement has yet or ever will, even with the best of intentions under the most favorable of circumstances, be able to resolve the grimmest of crises we as a civilization now face. While at times they may provide a temporary amelioration of frustrated needs --- the sense of fellowship provided by a community of worshipers, say, or the redistribution of social benefits --- they simply cannot offer anything fundamental by way of change beyond that which their ordinary capacities for adaptation will allow. None can bring us the fulfillment of a higher order of life than has yet appeared, let alone the kind of "new world" as spoken of by the Source. We may stand on the threshold of a grand transformation, but in the complex interplay between the promethean powers of modern technological society and the evolution of individual and social character there is simply no guarantee that we'll make our way across. Meanwhile, the river of human history continues to surge toward the precipice of a cataract.

THE AGE SHALL BE ROUSED

We are like helpless drifters on a rudderless dinghy headed for an abyss. How, given the sheer enormity of their force and power, can we possibly navigate the raging currents of the social, political, and economic engines and pressures that shape and control our destiny and that of the entire world? Is it even possible? Or, perhaps, as the Source would ask, between our growing insularity, indifference, and intolerance on one hand, and our potential for awakening to the full consciousness of a love undistorted by dogmatism, ideology, or creed on the other, can we, or rather will we summon forth the collective wisdom and consensus necessary to make all people, nations, tribes, and religions the beneficiaries of that love, freeing them of hatred as well as fear? That, according to the Source, is the supreme test of our time. For only in a world where fear ceases to rule the minds and hearts of the peoples of the earth can we, in the words of the Apocalypse, come within speaking distance of each other. Only then will the opportunities for an ever-widening partnership with life --- a life universal --- become possible.

Our lives and our world, however, are saturated with fear. It enters the door with the daily newspaper; it's broadest 24 hours a day on network news stations; it's omnipresent in the digital world of the internet. As we hover on the anxious edge of the ultimate destruction that fear itself precipitates, the thanatic fears harbored by nearly all religions of the world only grow more fervent. Fear and terror have never stalked through the world on such a scale, sparing no people, nation, or religion. The world as seen through the lens of the media locks us into cycles of fear which slip unnoticed even into the specters of sleep. It's dark influence overshadows our best efforts to live wisely, to think deeply, to awaken ourselves and to love generously. It preempts any future hope for either reconciliation or redemption. Fear has become the father of our fate.

And yet, as the Source points out, **there is no cause in real-ity, in real-ization, there is no cause for fear,** for the visible portents of our dark future do indeed conceal a light. And it is from this light, from that divine influx that raises us to a higher level of conscious awareness, that the energies of a new creation will be released. So it is written, "the age which is not yet awake shall be roused, and that which is corruptible shall perish" (II Esd. 7.31, cf. II Bar. 44.9, 12). As seen through the all-pervading mind of the Source, that day and age is now upon us: **Do understand that systems you have depended upon are coming to an end, and a new order is beginning to be established. Now, that new order might rather be looked upon with anticipation for the establishment is the order spoken of through these Records, as we have said, that the Beloved of God will bring a new order of things, will establish a New Order. And so it has begun --- it _has_ begun** (Solomon Reading No. 1147, 9/3/83).

And it is first and foremost with those who _have_ awakened that the restorative dynamics of a collective emergence is now beginning. For as the Source informs us, **that which is set in motion as a Divine Plan for this period is not necessarily that which will be realized, or which will occur; but the Plan itself, the purpose, the ideal is set. Nothing about the Divine comes but through the servants of the Divine** (Solomon Reading No. 853, 7/22/76). In other words, the Divine Plan is in its essence to be understood not in terms of any particular sequence of historical events or even in the occurrence of events themselves, but rather in relation to its final goal or _telos_ which concerns the progressive awakening in the direction of mankind's root and source. That is, toward the embodiment and final establishment of the Law of One in the collective consciousness of our race. How that awakening --- to the richness, delicacy, depth, and harmoniousness of all being --- ultimately manifests is given into the hands of those who are themselves aligned with the Law and who thereby have become the instruments of that awakening in others. **Might best be expressed by relating to that period in which Israel came from bondage into the Promised Land, for you stand in the wilderness and there is before you a land of promise (the New Eden). But in the consciousness there are giants in the land needing to be overcome for the moving into the consciousness. The battles you fight in this time will be battles of consciousness revealing the nature of God. Might do well among you in this time to set aside appearances of strangeness or difficulties for others to accept. It might do well in this time that you concern yourself with presenting truth in a manner that is acceptable as nearly as possible to all men. For it is of concern that men recognize truth --- not so much that they be emotionally stirred nor convinced of extraordinary things, but rather [that they] recognize real, universal, Divine Law** (Solomon Reading No. 853, 7/22/76). In a world increasingly callous to violence, corruption, and catastrophe and everwilling to suspend the principle of truth, it is through the mental alertness, inner receptivity, and ethical depth of these "servants of the Divine" that the truth will find its fearless heart.

THE NEW ESSENES
the Unvaccinated (?)

Casting It's other-dimensional gaze over our sphere of time and space, the Source perceives what we in the blindness of the flesh can only imagine --- the scattering of the seeds of enlightened consciousness strewn amid the darkness of a world lost in night:

If we could cause you to see an image of the energies that occur about your plane in this time, you might see first of all a pinpoint of light about the Earth in areas here and there where consciousnesses have been awakened to the destiny of man and his movement toward his intended state. The points of light in many are individuals who have come through great tribulation and training and are washing in the blood of the Lamb, and striving individually and in many groups brought here and there to form a light. These have been in some instances separated one from the other, that they might better grow and impregnate the area where they are found.

Now, in every place that you might look down and see a place of light, you would further see for every one a thousand, ten thousand angels, with drawn swords that fill the atmosphere, if you would, about this place with potency; a hushed waiting, a feeling, a sense of preparation. And beyond that, those [spirits] who have lived through experiences here, a million or more of the brethren, who have learned from time to time in your plane and have risen above it, and, as it were, hold almost the breath each time a soul enters your plane in this time; a feeling almost of counting those who enter for the purpose of lifting the consciousness, and those of the Sons of Darkness who find their way as a counterbalance.

There is [a] delicate equilibrium that is maintained, and as there is a moving toward those changes as will come, a great anticipation fills the universe with electricity. Those looking down then on [the] Divine Plan pour their vials of incense, the prayers, before the Throne of Grace; and their care, their pleading, the prayer of the saints, enters in this time as a wave of love lifting. And especially are those born in this day and this time impregnated with that intent and purpose (Solomon Reading No. 645, 7/6/75).

Here and there, in the most seemingly nondescript corners of the world, we see through the eyes of the Source these gems of enlightenment appearing who prefigure, in their lives and actions, the collective transformations that must take place. Not so many, not so many in this moment as can maintain that integrity to which they aspire. But the thought, the aspiration is becoming [a] motivational force, building in increments so that the building becomes a living movement. And when with that commitment to integrity, and with the increasing understanding of the peoples and the nations that there are interactions [and] relationships which work, which are supportive, which are preferable because of the harmonious results they bring, when love is introduced by the Beloved as is being taught even now, when that power begins to replace fear, when that thought of commitment to integrity shall reach a critical mass, then shall those who have made that commitment find themselves able even to keep that commitment, to maintain it. And so, as recognition of love, security, confidence as a power, a force, a support of life, reaches as well a critical mass, then we have these forces of change which allow the Christ for His own... (Solomon Reading No. 1147, 9/3/83).

The Source refers to these as the "New Essenes" or, just as the Essenes of antiquity were known, the "Expectant Ones". Now we will mention to you here [that] the word itself, the name 'Essene', meant expectant, or more to the point, the word meant pregnant. And the group was called that because they considered themselves to be pregnant people, both men and women, pregnant with the seed of God inside, capable of being nourished and nurtured, to give birth in the life to the indwelling child of God. And so in their life and teachings they prepared themselves as a community for the arrival of what had been spoken of by prophets of many religions, not only Judaism, [but] many religions. But it is especially recorded in the history of Judaism that there was the expectancy of a Messiah, and few people know that such expectation was also held by the Greeks in their mystery schools, their worship. It was held in Egypt, and all other lands expected the coming of a leader, a living incarnate presence of God to lead the people. And yet, the Essenes knew that the most important birth is that which occurs in each individual. However, as a result of their preparation there was born the One whom later the Greeks chose to call the Christ, but who in His lifetime, in His birth and expression among the Jews, was called Yehoshua or Jesus. (Solomon Reading No. 1662, 5/22/92). And just as the Essenes, the Therapeutae, the mystery cults, that heralded the coming of a Messiah in that day, so too in this there are those "New Essenes" who are working deliberately and assiduously to prepare for the physical return of Christ Himself and to carry forward into a new order and dispensation the seeds and principles of a New Eden. They are the custodians of this garden, and the energies that they bring to it are preparing the field. Study the Essenes and what they did for the preparation of the Christ in that time, instructs the Source. **You're in a similar period here. If you're looking for the return of the Christ, then prepare for His return by preparing a fertile field as did the Essenes in that period.** They were busy about preparing a field, a force-field in which He might enter. **Now, these groups that are dedicated and understand His call and His cause and the periods of history, these have the opportunity, and because of the opportunity they have the responsibility for repeating that greatest advancement that man has made to the creation of the force field in which the Christ might enter. Look to this, study those opportunities, see what they did and see what you might do in this time to prepare for His coming** (Solomon Reading No. 551, 4/4/75).

The so-called "force-field" referred to by the Source is no mere sophistry, but in fact an ancient Vedic principle. Thousands of years ago the Vedic tradition held that consciousness, which was seen as an infinite, all-pervasive unified field of pure intelligence, is the primary source of all energy, force, and physical phenomena. But the energy possessed by this illimitable and eternal ocean of consciousness is likewise infinite. It is force without limit, without dimension, without the limits of form, and is therefore outside the dimensions of time and space. Energy in infinity means energy uniformly extended without limit. It has no beginning, no end, no location. It is conscious force, the fundamental, primary power of existence, a state of infinite being that, until acted upon by some intervening specific resonant intent, remains utterly inactive and completely at rest. It is what the Source refers to as the Christ Energy which bears within Itself the power of creation.

Science now knows that both the electrons which spin in the energy field located around the nucleus of the atom and the nucleus itself are made up of nothing more than oscillating energy grids. Solid matter, strictly speaking, simply does not exist. Hence, the entirety of what we call human --- brain, consciousness, and all --- is, like the universe which surrounds it, nothing more or less than an extraordinary complex system of energy fields that respond to and holographically reflect the limitless field of "the Absolute".

The Vedanta teaches that the human mind at its source is identical with this limitless field. Once the frequency and amplitude of the human brain are rendered coherent through deep meditative peace or prayer, it is possible to begin accelerating both so that the human mind is soon resonating at higher vibrational levels. The mind can then bring itself into synchronization with the more sophisticated and rarified levels of unconditional love spoken of by the Source. Put plainly, **as you give the heart in love and as you would seek to serve here or there so would you create thought forms. And as you see yourself or another as a perfected vehicle or vessel or Christ, so will that thought form or that person created in thought, such perfection, such idealism, rise above you and join in a group as it were or a collection of such thoughts. Then would such thoughts form a force field through which those whose intentions were in keeping with that vibration or the vibration of that thought field, that force field, so would those whose intentions and purposes be diverted toward this thought field or force field, so would they be able to tap its energy and direct it toward its purposes or obtain the understanding therefrom. Now see the importance of this, for one need not be a high initiate, an occult adept, to tap that force field of wisdom, of understanding, even of energy and force,** from that Great White Brotherhood. Yet he only need attune himself to that purpose so that he would become, then, a channel for the emptying out of the understanding, the power, the energy, for the creation, for the channeling of such purpose (Solomon Reading No. 192, 7/4/73). Hence, by invoking the infinite organizing power of this field of pure consciousness through the heightened frequencies of love and volitional intent, a force-field of such amplitude and power can be generated that, as the Source puts it, the expression of "the Christ may enter."

Given the corrupted state of the collective consciousness of our world, however, the Source tells us likewise that it will take an army of this new breed of Essenes, working openly and steadily but quietly and unpretentiously from all points of the globe, to bring about the awakenings necessary for even the briefest incarnation of divinity. And would you believe that it has been an accident that throughout the centuries, those works of the Essenes and the discipline of their community were hidden, and in your lifetime have become unfolded and revealed, asks the Source? Would you not accept this as a sign that as in that day there was preparation for the coming of the Master, so in this day there must be made similar preparations? (Solomon Reading No. 99, 12/19/72).

Just as in that earlier time, so in this, preparations, though for the most part unrecognized, are being made, but not with lofty words or proselytizing rhetoric, not through ethical precepts, religious insights, or knowledge taken at third hand from books, but with humility, through simple acts of love and kindness that give hope and encouragement to those of the greatest need.

Mother Teresa with her Indian Mission for the Destitute and dying is a case in point, but her's is only one example among many thousands scattered through every country, all equally modest and yet heroic. Of far lesser notoriety is Narayanan Krishnan. An award winning chef on his way to a very highly successful career, his life was put on a different path with the sight of an old and destitute man eating his own human waste out of hunger. He abruptly quit his job and within a year he had founded the Akshaya Trust which feeds and takes care of the destitute and mentally disabled people in Madurai, Tamil Nadu. He prepares and serves three warm and fresh vegetarian meals every day, which he often hand feeds to the people that he seeks out under bridges and other desolate and abandoned spots. He also carries with him a comb, scissors and razor to provide extra dignity to those he cares for. Today, Krishnan sleeps in Akshaya's kitchen along with his co-workers. He has no income and scrapes by with the support of his parents. To date he has served more than 1.5 million meals to India's destitute.

Aki Ra was a very young boy when he was conscripted by the Khmer Rouge to become a child soldier. He laid thousands of mines for the Khmer until, after having himself seen the horrific effects in the thousands of maimed and slaughtered Cambodian children, he started to illegally clear and defuse mines and UXOs with nothing but a knife, leatherman and a stick in the areas where he had once fought. As word of his self-sacrifice spread, tourists flocked to his home to see for themselves the collection of defused artillery Aki Ra had risked his life to disarm. Charging a dollar per person, the Cambodian Landmine Museum was established, the proceeds of which provided Aki the means to adopt hundreds of the injured and abandoned children he found in the surrounding villages. Today, 29 children live at the Cambodian Landmine Relief Center.

Jorge Muñoz came to America as an illegal immigrant in the early 80's. One evening as he left a bar in Queens, NY he could not help but notice all the destitute and illegal laborers, most of whom slept under a bridge or in Elmhurst Hospital's emergency room and who skimped on meals in order to send money to their loved ones at home. The flame of his heart was awakened. From that very moment on he has been cooking enough warm, nourishing meals to feed dozens of day laborers each day. Estimates are that he has served over 100,000 people since 2004, all financed from the $600 he receives weekly for driving a school bus along with donations.

Thousands of such examples could be cited of entirely humble people who, either by a single act or effort, demonstrate through their selfless love the radical shift in attitude that is needed if we are to lay the foundations of a new world. But it must be built, not structurally, institutionally, or bureaucratically from the top down, but from the bottom up, through direct contact and living experience. Beginning from the innermost recesses of the Source, the energy, love, and insight gained must express itself at every level of society --- in the family, neighborhood and village on one end, and in world affairs, embracing the whole of humanity as John of Pineal at the other. But for the transformations that must take place on whatever level, the Source tells us that we must first make the love in our souls visible to others, moving them by way of example into a closer union with their source:

> Understand, then, that service, that work to be performed on this plane in this way: there is often heard those instructions of witnessing of big events and the telling of the story or the teaching of this or that, the assisting to unfold others upon the planes and upon the path. Now it could be understood in this manner: that it is not always for the teaching or the great teachers or masters or instructors who would do the greatest work on your plane. But if you would understand that it very often takes some lifetime or more that one even should understand and the interest is cultivated concerning those things of the spiritual development or awakening that self within, that spark of God that would lie within each soul. Then [for] those that would awake that kinship in others, understand the many methods of which these are awakened. And if it would take some two or some three lifetimes that such an interest would be cultivated in some, the beginners, then it would be for some to set about that work, that task of awakening those on this plane to that which they are.

> Then it would not come that one would unfold the great and the deep doctrines, but by the living of the life and by the communication by that manner in which the shoulder is rubbed with the stranger. So will there be a spark awakened and an interest brought about from the magnetic, the vibratory fields about this one.... And how often would it occur that there would be the compelling to go here or there simply to meet this one, to shake the hand, and how often there is not the mention of this or that of the spiritual..., but only the shaking of the hand and wondering afterward, "Why did I meet

this one? Why was he or she brought into the life? For what purpose has there been the crossing of our paths?" Yet that contact was made as directed from inner planes, for there are the hosts gathered about one at all times for such direction, bringing together those that are interested.

Now understand that ... when there is the glow, the spark of interest, the opening of one on this plane, then there would begin the manipulation of the ways in which these would walk their steps during the day [such] that another with such a glow, another with compatible auric field about and with [an] interest with the levels on the path, would meet one another or would cross. And from the simple meeting, the speaking, the nodding of the head, the passing within the auric field of vibration, one, then, on lower step might be lifted. And without a realization that would come to the one, he would be led to this or that situation or a book here, a book there, without knowing the contact that has been made, and such instruction will come. Then there has been one who was the catalyst, never speaking of this or that, but only being that which would cause the change.

Now understand that one given to the purposes of God might never be given such a ministry that would be dramatic in nature or that would bring praise or recognition. But never would it be possible that a soul on your plane could say to the Master, "Use me, make me productive," that it does not become so. Then understand that you will not always know the good that you have accomplished and where your feet have taken you nor the purpose for this. And those steps taken on inner planes and the contact made may never be realized, for even as the Master has spoken, "If the reward be recognized, then you have your reward, but how much greater that the reward be laid up in heaven where then you may grow and pride cannot become the stumbling block, for you were not aware of the accomplishment." But make the self accessible to those on inner planes who would communicate, not only by the word of mouth, but by the touch of the hand, by the attitude, by the interest, by the love that would come forth. And will not the students be led and others prevented from coming? And will not those be chosen that will come into the life? What challenge would there be that you would take the seeker already high on the path, but him with the problem will be brought to that one who cares and has the strength to meet the need? Then one in service will attract those who have the greater needs and would be healed. Observe those attracted to the Master and those He attempted to help and serve, and know that one who is in service on this path will not attract those already accomplished in His ways, but those with needs, those crippled, lame, ill. And in the spiritual as well, so will He bring those that are sick that you might be the physician.

Then understand in the difficult situations, whether within the family or within these others that would be brought, that there is assistance here and guidance for those who wait. And where there is the sparrow with the broken wing or the child fallen by the wayside, would you make the self available. For there are those here on inner planes whose heart would go out to one stumbling, faltering, and would look for a strong one, a light in the darkness. And if there would be the willingness within thy heart, then those on inner planes will guide their steps to you. Though it may cause grief in your life and some pain, so will he be lifted. And if you are not able to help, then pray. Release him, then, to the Highest Good. And know that those same guardians, those directors, those guides, those angels on inner planes will cause him, then, to be turned to another who can take the next step in his growth, and one by one each may be able to contribute some spark of himself that a soul might be led to that Light.

And as the greater awareness comes and as the feeling of being used in such a way, so many more will be attracted. And feel it not necessary in the purpose that you speak to them of Christ or of religion, of spiritual things, but show in the attitude the caring and that which is in the heart. Understand that the thoughts will have more effect than that which is spoken through the lips. Then be of concern, yet not worry, but knowing that that caring in your heart sends perfect energy for the building block, for the repairing of these thoughts, these vibrations to those who are attracted and would seek to learn. Then understand this. And as there is the arising daily, ask that your feet be directed to one who would need your service this day. Then when a face appears, whoever that one might be, and the faces in succession throughout the day, assume that here is one who needs my touch and I am [the] direct connection between this one and the Father, that energy of the Divine that will awaken that kindred spark in him and send, then, his own connection to the Divine that he might understand and spread that word, that light. (Solomon Reading No. 180, 6/12/73).

REACHING CRITICAL MASS

While it's hard to imagine that anything so quiet, so modest in dimensions, so personal, could help bring about a profound change, the Source tells us that the seeming insignificance of this original step is an important part of the discipline of lifting the consciousness, one individual at a time, into awareness of the energy of their source. It is the power of the awakened consciousness of even one individual attuned with his or her own source that is the starting point of new effects. Just as it takes only one spark to kindle a great forest, so the power of unconditional love embodied in even one is sufficient to produce the necessary effect on the whole of civilization. As the Source points out, **thinking, attuned people can affect on a wide scale the consciousness of less conscious people, those who are not in control of their thought processes and whose thoughts consist of whatever feelings, ideas, images or whims come through the mind. Consciously attuned people have a superior power, except in the face of one who is consciously attuned to a dark force.** (Solomon Reading No. 1386, 8/27/88).

The Source teaches that a consciously awakened human mind acts after a fashion of a laser beam which produces a disciplined stream of light. Since consciousness is the source of all reality, the thoughts of any individual in an expanded state of awareness have the power to influence the development of reality in space-time as it applies to a desired objective if those thoughts can be projected with adequate intensity. **The power of love itself in the form of what you call 'chi' may be thrown, projected, for it has field properties and can travel from one individual to another.** (Solomon Reading No. 1455, 11/7/90). The stream of energy is projected with total coherence of both frequency and amplitude such that the concentrated energy can create an indomitable influence over the fear-based collective consciousness of less awakened segments of populations. **You must understand better the vitality, the energy, the living one that is love**, instructs the Source, **and know how to apply it. If you can fire love as directly aimed at the heart of a man as can a missile be directed, then you have understood the force that is on your side. Not a force of anger and resistance, not a force that is intended to hurt or destroy. But a force that gives birth to the giant sequoia tree is the force that can defeat any army of earth.... If you can understand all this, then you can overcome** (Solomon Reading No. 1466, 1/21/91). The more complicated the objective sought, however, and the more radically it departs from the current reality, the more time the universal energies will need to repattern and reorient one's reality sphere to accommodate the specific intent.

> Then, understand the ability that you have as conscious, loving, attuned people to sway the consciousness of the masses, done carefully, without fear, and through attunement, through the use of the tools of prayer and meditation. Do not feel limited, but know the strength of those abilities.

> Now we've said that to say this further. There is a further need among you and purpose for your being among people in [whatever] place where you are. It is on many levels to meet the practical needs as you seek to do. This is a part of the task. Broader than that, a part of the task is to demonstrate the power of love among the people in your personal lives and your relationship with them. To be a source of inspiration, to be an example of love, that is a part of the purpose (Solomon Reading No. 1386, 8/27/88).

The more that the unlimited energy of the Source of life itself is manifest in even one among our species, therefore, the more that same energy is liberated in others, collectively. Beginning, then, in just one in whom the springs of conscious life are flowing. When life is no longer reduced to the mechanical regimen of uncontrolled thoughts wandering aimlessly through the mind, the inherent love in that one becomes visible to others, courting the potentiality of their own yet marginal state of self-awareness. These awakened personalities then begin to multiply, and from a hundred similar sources other springs will pour their waters forming together into a mighty stream that will carve new channels through the lands below. When at length a number sufficient to constitute a critical mass is reached, a collective shift in the field of consciousness occurs changing the entire landscape. Scientists at the Social Cognitive Network Academic Research Center (SCNARC) at Rensselaer found that when just 10 percent of the population holds an unshakable belief, their belief will always be adopted by the majority of the society. Factoring in the resonant powers of our awakened mind to shape the conscience and consciousness of millions who, in T. S. Eliot's words, are "distracted from distraction by distraction", the Source tells us that the percentage required drops emphatically. This, according the Source, is how a new order will arise.

MORPHOGENESIS

Theoretically speaking, it is what the biologist Rupert Sheldrake refers to as a "morphogenetic field." In his book, *A new Science of Life*, Sheldrake proposes that organisms are capable of selecting morphologies from energetically equivalent forms, such that an additional causal principle of organization is required. He calls this "formative causation", and the vehicle of this principle he calls a "morphogenetic field". Much like the quantum potential as defined by physicist David Bohm, a morphogenetic field is a nonmaterial (nonphysical) organizing collective memory field that affects all biological systems. This field can be envisioned as a hyperspatial information reservoir that brims and spills over into a much larger region of influence when critical mass is reached --- a point referred to as "morphic resonance". Furthermore, this field acts without attenuation over both space and time such that organisms can influence the morphology of other organisms despite separation in space and time. This has been demonstrated in a considerable number of independent studies.

In a series of experiments conducted in the 1920's, Harvard psychologist William McDougall studied the behavior of rats to determine how quickly they could learn to escape from a maze filled with water. He found to his amazement that successive generations learned the task much more rapidly. Contrary to accepted genetic science, and lacking any reasonable alternative explanation, he concluded that such acquired knowledge could only be inherited. He was quite mistaken, however, for in later experiments to duplicate McDougall's work, researchers in Scotland and Australia found that their first generation of rats, bred from a completely separate strain, started at the same level of proficiency as McDougall's last generation. Some even "learned" the task immediately without making a single error. Somehow they already "knew". The skill was being learned by other rats, both in the laboratory and across the world. In commenting on these experiments, Sheldrake said: "If rats are taught a new trick in Manchester, then rats of the same breed all over the world should show a tendency to learn the same trick more rapidly, even in the absence of any known type of physical connection or communication. The greater number of rats that learn it, the easier it should become for their successors."[21] In other words, once a critical mass is arrived at, the whole species (plant, insect, human, etc.) is changed.

Morphogenetic fields can be used to describe not only how conceptual consciousness is shared, but as the Source points out how states of benevolence and compassion can be shared as well. Dr. J.T. Greene[22] of Georgia University trained ten white rats to obtain food pellets by pressing one of two levers in their cage. One lever produced fewer pellets and was hard to depress, and the rats soon found this out and ignored it, concentrating on the other. Now Greene wired the levers so that when the one which yielded food was pressed, a rat in the next cage received an electric shock. What did the food seeking rats do? First they recognized that their actions were giving their neighbor pain; then no less than eight out of ten of them went over to the other lever, even though it was hard to work, and concentrated on it, saving their fellow creatures from further harm.

If we can observe as much in the behavior of a rat, can we not extend to ourselves the same inclusive feelings toward fellow members of our own species and then some? Applying Sheldrake's theory to the development of those "higher" states of human consciousness whose rhythms resonate to the subtler energies of impersonal and universal love, we can reasonably infer that the more individuals begin to raise their own levels of consciousness and compassion, the stronger the morphogenetic field for higher states would become, and the easier it would be for others to "learn", follow, and be induced into these states. A little leaven will leaven the whole loaf. Society would, then, through an influx of vitality from the source of each of its members, exponentially gather momentum toward a conscious awakening to its own spiritual depth and maturity.

But that such a change cannot be effected so easily goes without saying. For if it were as simple as all this, all the hostilities that now undermine our civilization would have vanished long ago into the light of a new Heaven. Nevertheless, the assurances that the Source sets before us are not an unapproachable ideal. It's just that any awakening of consciousness with the potential of remaking the world at large must be framed in a world picture that stretches far beyond our common daily horizons.

Beginning, then, as something profoundly personal and esoteric in its earliest manifestation, the energies of an awakened consciousness must find their entry and outlet into a more spacious world from and through the transpersonal expression of inner light. **We draw the analogy of the relationship of a light bulb and light,** explains the Source, **from the words of the master of masters, the Christ Himself, who said, Let your light so shine that those about will see the light that is in you.' Let your light shine so that men may see the results and glorify the Source of those results from within you. Fill yourself, so fill yourself with light, life, love and truth that what was thought to be you, the illusion, the personality, the separateness from God, will and must disappear. And in its place, those who see, those who have eyes to see, not those in darkness but those who have opened their eyes to the light, will not see a you that is a separate being from God, but will see only that which is real. Real-ization** (Solomon Reading No. 1696, 7/13/92). Once having awakened ourselves to the light, then, says the Source, **express yourself effectively to one another, to the community and to the expression within the community, then to the nation. See, then, that you begin at home and expand your horizons only as you meet one challenge reaching to the greater challenge. Do not begin attempting to change the nation until you have changed your household and its relation to other households among your family. Then, when you have been effective as a family in changing the consciousness of your community, then spread that thought and that word until it affects the nation.** (Solomon Reading No. 966, 7/7/77). Given that the impetus for such change in the great mass of humanity is limited by inertia, it is only by a repetition of the original experience, from oneself to others, then from those to yet others, that the experience does not lapse into a stereotype and that a true rebirth of consciousness begins to occur. And as it takes root in one's native soil, so then it becomes possible to reach out beyond what is exclusively indigenous to begin the task of creating a true world community.

The stimulus for such fusions and blendings on a worldwide scale, however, must be based on common purpose and common need. Not by offering, but by *asking* for help, advises the Source, will people even from the ends of the earth respond and be drawn to the opportunity for first-hand contact and cooperation. By turning the unmotivating abstraction of world cooperation into a working reality, a touch of the universal society of which they can form an active part becomes a practical reality. **Let us say that in this way,** explains the Source:

> There are many on the planet who are concerned with the condition of the planet and wish to participate, particularly concerned with trouble areas as they are called about the world, but feel there is nothing that one can do to assist, to help. When these learn of that you are doing in that area, [it] gives opportunity for their participation, their identification, their feeling, "I am contributing to a change in this part of the world." Allow that participation. Begin to communicate by whatever means. They have, in turn, participation and effectiveness and know they are contributing to a difference in a critical area and to the balance of the planet. Then see that as a two-fold objective: to re-educate a people in an area where you are, and to allow an outreach into the world.

> And understand a principle here. When you and other people of other nations feel in a positive way that you are making a contribution to correcting a situation, to assisting the situation in a troubled spot, there is a change in consciousness, a change in consciousness in any individual who feels, "I can make a difference," rather than feeling simple frustration, concern and fear. When these about the world read of challenges, of riots, of government collapse, of suppression and difficulty in a particular area of the world, there is, then, stewing and fretting and worrying. That individual who has learned of it becomes affected by it and the planet is carried further into dis-ease. When an individual feels victimized, the disease is spread. When that victim feels that he is making a valid application of a therapy, a treatment to his situation, a healing process begins. This is why an individual taking a therapy which he deeply believes has great opportunity to overcome the disease or symptom, because of the belief, the expectancy, because of the sense, "I am doing something about it," he will then heal. Then this is a part of the responsibility, to give those outside your local community or nation a sense of doing something about it rather than watching a situation collapse and deteriorate.

> Then become an anchor for the concerns and the participation of those outside and know that this too is part of the mission. Not only the local work that you do in the community, but becoming a lifeline, a point of communication with the rest of the world, allowing those local to know that others care, and allowing others in other parts of the world to know that there is something being done in the local area. And to re-educate a people, to create a family and a community, to communicate with a people an ability to lift themselves up with dignity and to prepare a unit that will survive a time of trouble because of communication between individuals, the building of a new sense of family, a global family (Solomon Reading No. 1383, 8/17/88).

Civilization has an especial need for such direct action. For what emerges in any serious therapeutic exploration of one's cultural identity shapes the course of social change. Through it, the walls of hateful egoism and aggressive pride which keep people apart can be broken down, and the complex activities of a higher society will begin to form. It is thus that civilization will gain the upper hand over the forces that threaten it.

Yet the pressure of a secularized culture and the imperious demands of the national state will at first limit the full scope of this integrating movement such that not more than a few groups of individuals will be affected. But like the wildflowers that continue to promulgate and force their way up through every crack in the solid pavement, the resourcefulness of ordinary people who have been awakened and put in touch with the real problems of their global community on every level can indeed profoundly alter every institution and transfigure every possibility. **As this realization, then, is introduced into the political world and the social world far beyond the religious world,** states the Source, **nations will begin to think in a new way. Nations are but collections of individuals and it cannot be experience expressed from the government down to the people, as it were, but rather from the people to the government. That is to say that as a nation of individuals feeling good about themselves, fulfilled, worthy, loving themselves, confident in that love, begin to relate to one another without blaming one another for my feelings, my hurts and pains, then the result of people living in that manner would be a government expressing in that manner and so will integrity be built with the government, the nation, the people. So will politics become an expression of cooperation instead of competition** (Solomon Reading No. 119, 3/15/83). The Source in fact tells us that in the hands of a small but sufficient number if the Readings of the Source Itself were to be faithfully employed, a total change in the otherwise irrational and unconsciously motivated self-destructive tendencies of the great mass of humanity could be effected within the span of a single generation, sufficient to lift the consciousness of the entire race as far beyond our present condition as we are now from our anthropoid ancestors.

Unmaking the whole culture of exploitation along with the entire military-industrial enterprise that feeds it, however, still cannot help but to seem a mind-boggling process. It's simply hard to imagine that a proposition as intrinsically and individually unique as that posited by the Source could in the faintest way lay the foundation for the worldwide transformation of consciousness needed. But for those whose awakenings have occurred, even if their acts do not take the heroic form of a Gandhi or a Martin Luther King or an Anwar Sadat, still they can remove debris that others have allowed to block their vision and restore to them the power of love and awareness that contains all the endlessly ramified potentialities that belong to the meta-human. When these, then, begin to multiply, the load of fear and anxiety that hangs over all of humanity gradually begins to lift.

Commensurately, like so many rivulets of water eroding the imperious heights of the old citadels of power, weakening them at critical points, hollowing them out, opening cavities for larger cascades, all the structures of human separation would henceforth collapse under the inexorable force of the rising tide. In the ensuing miracle of a world integrated by a harmony of purpose and illuminated by the consciousness of a single reality, all the sweat and rubble and brutality of the world left behind, even among the war-torn peoples of the Middle East, would seem like a nightmare that had vanished with the morning light. **You will have won a war without bloodshed,** declares the Source, **a war fought by love and by peace for the first time of all of history. You will have overcome darkness with light and you will have proved that love is stronger than fear** (Solomon Reading No. 1114, 2/7/83).

A RISING CONSCIOUSNESS

We are rapidly approaching the last and most difficult phase of our historical existence as a species. Without the unlimited universal insight and guidance of the Source, we simply cannot know the extent to which this heightening of energies has begun to penetrate into the depths of the collective psyche and permeate the world around us. Clearly, a minority have felt this need of human unity and, indeed, have a vague though perhaps unformulated loyalty to the Law of Love, the supreme law of life. Still, it remains to be seen whether mankind's blundering search for wisdom and for love will at last culminate in that critical mass necessary to meet the crying needs of our time.

Dr. David R. Hawkins, MD, PhD, is a psychiatrist who has conducted extensive research into the fields of consciousness, or morphogenetic fields, that form the essence not only of each and every individual's experience but that of entire civilizations. Following several life-altering changes in his own state of consciousness from an ego-based mind focus to a constant, steady connection with the Source, or the "Presence" as he calls it, Hawkins' attention was drawn to "address the causes of the endless stream of spiritual distress and human suffering." To do so, he created a heuristic tool that he calls the Map of Consciousness. As he puts it, "in a world full of sleepers lost from their source, here was a tool to recover that lost connection with the higher reality and demonstrate it for all to see."[23]

Using applied kinesiology as a method for determining the different frequencies at which consciousness resonates, Hawkins devised a scale from 1 to 1000 to record these different levels of frequency, each level coinciding with determinable human behaviors and perceptions about life. The numbers themselves are purely arbitrary, the significance of each lying in the relationship of one number or level to another. Hawkins describes the lower levels of consciousness as ego dominated where one thrives on the emotions of animal survival. These are aligned with pleasure, predation and gain. Below the 200 level, an individual is left-brain dominant, which means that input goes directly to the amygdala, so emotional response is triggered before intelligence and cognition. Shame, guilt/hate, apathy, grief, fear, desire, anger and pride characterize the responses of these levels. On the other end of the scales lies pure selfless enlightenment.

Although Hawkins goes into great detail about the various levels of consciousness, he distinguishes two turning points as transitionally crucial. There is first a huge transition at the level of 200 wherein right brain dominance reflects the increasing influence of spiritual energy and where "the willingness to stop blaming and accept responsibility for one's own actions, feelings, and beliefs arises." At this point, input is fast-tracked directly to the prefrontal cortex and the emotional center. This influence brings progressive awareness and openness to the energy of love and to the state or condition to which that level of energy is endemic. The second major transitional level, from 500-599, represents a state of consciousness wherein love and nonjudgmental forgiveness become a way of living and where "exercising unconditional kindness to all persons, things, and events *without exception*" becomes the motivating factor in one's awareness. This level denotes a shift from the linear, provable domain (classical physics or Newtonian physics) to the nonlinear, formless, spiritual realm. Only 4 percent of the world's population reach this level according to Hawkins.

Currently, he states, approximately 78% of the world's population calibrate at below the level of 200. The destructive capacity of this majority would drag down all of humanity without the counterbalancing effect of the 22 percent above 200. But because the scale of consciousness is logarithmic, each incremental point represents a giant leap in power. As such, one person calibrated at 600 counterbalances the negativity of ten million people below 200. Although according to Hawkins and his researchers only 4 percent of people alive today have reached the critical energy field of 500, individuals in these states have an extremely powerful morphogenetic influence on the well being of society as a whole, each counterbalancing 750,000 individuals calibrating below level 200. As a result of their influence, the whole of humanity has for the first time just recently passed above the 200 threshold. Now calibrating at around 207, humanity's collective consciousness has, according to Hawkins and his team, moved from an overall destructive force to an overall creative force on the planet.

Whether it will be enough to bring to our race the wisdom, intelligence, justice and social will to cope with the problems we now face and to further the establishment of a unified global family remains to be seen. But if true, it's certainly an encouraging sign that we are beginning once more to recover our humanity: our capacity for rational conduct, free from compulsive fears and pathological hatreds, and our capacity for love and confidence and cooperation in our dealings with the rest of the human race. Perhaps those servants of the divine are having their effect after all. **For there is a rising consciousness in mankind, adds the Source, a conscience of people who can no longer support the concept of hostility for the working out of the interface of wills and egos among men:**

> **And those of you who would change the face of this war [Armageddon] must learn that love is not simply passive. Not in the manner of those who protest against war, for protesting itself is a negative activity. But those activists against war who build bonds between men in a meaningful way, one helping the other ... this is love in action. And love passive and afraid, quiet as a lamb, and withdrawn, will not win a battle. But love alive, in action, healing, this will win a war. You must learn to make your love alive and active. Understand it to be as great a force as it is, for there is no force of darkness which can stand before light.**

> **Thus, you must shine your light in dark places. Shining the light in dark**

places will first mean the dark places within you. Seeing yourself as you are that you might become what you can be, without fearing what you have contained within you, to reveal it. So that you might be cleansed and be a vessel for the manifestation of the Christ. This is the concern of the battle of **Armageddon** (Solomon Reading No. 1466, 1/21/91).

While both Hawkins and the Solomon Source affirm that it is formatively happening even now, concomitantly, the energy yield of the world's weapons grows year by year, without ever declining, only to be lessened when the warheads are consumed in use. Practically speaking, it's simply naive to imagine that all the tragic decisions and colossal failures of unaided wisdom throughout human history would, even with the most herculean efforts of these "servants", experience a sudden transformation. The botulism of fear and hatred that has seeped into the soils of nearly every nation on earth undermines our faith and hopes for any dramatic change in levels from the human to the divine, at least in our perilous and foreseeable future. We must at some point come face-to-face with the palpable realities that surround us: a new Heaven is nowhere within reach. Catastrophe is perhaps nearer to us than salvation and, judging from all the psychotic violence and destructive forces currently being unleashed in so many areas of the globe, a war of unbridled extermination is perhaps nearer to us than the benign dream of universal peace.

Although as Hawkins points out, the higher spiritual energies of some of us may already have lifted us all to where many of the events foreseen by the Source have been mitigated, they have not as yet been averted. People simply cannot heal a sick world unless they have a sounder, richer, and more independently fearless one inside themselves. The vicious demand for conformity with the collective continues to subject most of us, and where conformity to the sickness of fear --- of other people, nations, races, religions --- is taken by society as a sign of normality, the metamorphosis of a world rising out of darkness will remain as nothing more than an imaginative hope. What the world so desperately needs is even a small number of superior beings, those who, having abandoned all worldly passions and all illusions, possess extraordinary powers of vision to lift the consciousness of the sleeping masses from their earthbound egos into the awakened light of an intrinsic love for all things. For it is no longer a question of pessimism or optimism: it is a question of love.

THE RETURN OF THE AWAKENED ONES

There are, in fact, a growing number who, according to the Solomon Source, **remember their cause** and who from their own awakened source carry within them the memory of that eternity around which the great cycles of time slowly turn. And from an eternity that seeks its reflection in the mirrors of history, our impending fall is as nothing more than a brief interval of perdition, of the traumas of liberation, out of which forms the apocatastasis, the Great Restoration. It is precisely for this mighty and majestic event that, as the Source informs us, these "awakened ones" are now entering: **Study the nature of the expansiveness here and the influence of these on the destiny, the purpose of the Earth at this time. You find those entering in in this day who are here for no other purpose than to assist in the transition of the nature of this plane. There are changes to come, a birth of a new** time, a greater realization of purpose of all on this plane. And those who feel in the heart, and have known the changes in earlier days, have returned here to assist (Solomon Reading No. 604, 5/14/75).

Having fully awakened to their source, they are, to again use Solomon's term, "Meta-human", those with the power to redefine our beliefs about what is humanly possible. Their virtues are not the same as those embodied in the rest. They are not driven to triumph over others. They know love without a craving to possess. They worship without any thought of salvation. And they are possessed of an impracticable wisdom that is perhaps too rich for the provisional tastes of the majority of their fellow beings, one which seems to combine selfless love and self-disregard with a discernment that penetrates right down to the buried chrysalis of the spirit even in those evidently seamed with evil. By their exquisite contrast, the golden thread which their living presence weaves into the dark tapestry of our world reveals to us all a light hitherto obscure.

For those few, then, who *have* fully awakened and in whom the seed of full and redemptive identity with the One has unfolded itself, mere belief becomes a trivialization of the most fundamental and indispensable need in human nature --- the need for an epiphany of the infinite and awakened spirit. Having advanced beyond the barrier behind which lies hidden the eternally awakened "I", their minds opened by a direct revelation from the Source, all else is merely a dream. Only the immortal "I" is truly awake. It abides in the direct presence of that living Truth which is Love Itself. All inferior loyalties to state and religion vanish into the effulgence of Its divine light.

Indeed, the otherworldliness of the creeds and doctrines of the world's major religions has proven too remote and specious for these few who want a heaven closer at hand. Disaffiliated from the mainstream assumptions of their society and possessed of a vigorous and lucid loyalty toward the phoenix birth of a new humanity, they are 'cut from a different cloth' from those around them. They refuse absolutely to have any part in the great madness that stigmatizes the human race.

Filled with the very Source of life itself, so they are emptied of all unworthy distractions of the physical. The evidence is unconcealable. It is reflected in their tone and conduct, in their wisdom and personal depth, in the power of their very presence, and above all in their unyielding devotion to an undivided Truth. For they alone can affirm that through and through the entire universe is celestial, and that all things within it work together for the perfect expression of that energy of love that abides in that eternal consciousness at the heart of its Source. As Solomon explains:

These are the rare individuals who know their source first hand. They speak with God daily, hourly, moment to moment. They are never *not* communicating with God. They have a relationship that is experiential, personal and constant. Individuals who truly know God have had an experience so personal that it was different from any experience that anyone else has written about or talked about in history. The experiences are unique and personal because they belong to individuals. They are like fingerprints. A personal encounter with God is what these individuals share in common, yet no two encounters or relationships are alike.

So it is difficult to describe a specific means to this personal encounter with God. There is no guidebook or road map. The Biblical prophet, Elijah, described his search in this way. "I went to the mountains to find him, and he was not there. I looked on the great cliffs and the high seas, and he was not there. I sought him in the whirlwind and the hurricane, and he was not there. I sought him in every powerful place in which I could look for him, and he was not there. And then, in a moment of quiet, a still, small voice came and spoke --- and he was there." (I Kings 19:11-13)

When he stopped doing everything that he was so desperately doing, what he had sought revealed itself in a non-dramatic moment. He had looked in every powerful place imaginable. And in a desperate, hopeless, helpless moment, he stopped *doing*. In the vacuum created by his stillness, God spoke, and Elijah heard him and was made a prophet by the experience.

There is not a specific technique for knowing God. However, there is an attitude or an environment or a vibration for knowing God. You must want to know God more than you want anything else in the world, including life itself. You must want to know God more than you want your family, more than you want prosperity, more than you want good health, more than you want world peace, more than you want to make a contribution, more than anything. When knowing God personally has become more important to you than life, family, health, success, possessions, knowledge, beliefs, religious doctrine, even enlightenment, and you are willing to set those aside for a personal, experiential relationship with who God truly is, whatever that is, you have provided the conditions in which the still, small voice can speak. And you can listen.

... An individual who is in a personal, experiential relationship with his or her divine source will be easily recognized, because that person will look for a way to serve, which will also introduce the source to others. That individual may be a healer, a psychic, or a teacher. Or he may be none of these. What will be obvious is that that individual is in love.... When an individual encounters his source face-to-face, he immediately falls in love. It is like coming home. It is everything perfect and wonderful in life. That individual is so full of his newfound love that he cannot contain it. He wants to share what he has found, not so that others will believe as he does, but because he knows that everyone deserves to know God personally, and directly, and to reap the blessings of the creator's love.

You will recognize an individual who has met his source face-to-face because his life will illustrate that there is more to God than belief. He will encourage others to seek a personal relationship. He will not attempt to describe the path or define the parameters of the relationship. He will only point the way, with a joyous enthusiasm that is irresistible.

For individuals full of the experience of God, things that used to be interesting may seem unimportant now. The focus will change. They may never use the term God, but they will devote their lives, their time, their energy, their attention and their money to helping other people make a similar discovery. They will want others to have a personal, unique experience of the divine nature that lives within, and they will devote the rest of their lives to that goal.

Such people may never be known as psychics. However, they will have a unique way of saying just the right thing at the right moment --- just what others need to hear. God will speak through them to other people. They may never acknowledge that, or even be aware of it, but the listener will be moved unexplainably and wonder, "What made her say that? How did she know I was thinking about that?"

Miracles are natural and commonplace for a person in an interactive relationship with the source of the universe and everything in it. Others may not even notice what is happening. However, to the individual, it will seem as though a guardian angel is handling things, helping situations to work out, causing problems to resolve and relationships to improve. An element of magic is present in the individual's life.

People who have a direct relationship with God have a unique kind of wisdom. It may not be revealed through doctorate degrees or even good communication skills. These people will just be in the right place at the right moment to say just the right word. They will be there to provide an arm to lean on at just the right time. They are the people that save others' relationships, well-being, even lives, by saying or doing just what is needed, often without any knowledge of what they are doing. They have the wisdom to be there because they have become tools of the living presence of the divine. Situations and circumstances are created so that these individuals can be used to make a difference in other people's lives.[23]

Having risen far above the endless hate-warped and mind-crippling conflicts and crises of history and society, therefore, they are now obedient to a different order of necessity. Their purpose, in the words of Dionysius: to "guide us [all] to that topmost height of mystic lore which exceedeth light and more than exceedeth knowledge, where simple, absolute, and unchangeable mysteries of heavenly Truth lie hidden in the dazzling obscurity of the secret Silence, outshining all brilliance with the intensity of their darkness, and surcharging our blinded intellects with the utterly impalpable and invisible fairness of glories which exceed all beauty."[24] In somewhat less rhapsodic terms, perhaps, their purpose is as a sherpa, to guide others to the "topmost height" of the New Kingdom where they themselves already abide. Paul Solomon himself was one of these, as is John of Pineal, and as was Edgar Cayce and Mohandas Gandhi before them. Manifest in even a small confederacy of such fully awakened beings, it is this single organic force of conscious Love that will ultimately bring about that critical mass needed to transform the global vision of all humanity. As David Hawkins has indicated, only one individual calibrating at level 700 counterbalances 70 million individuals calibrating below level 200. In the Talmud it is written that "the world must not contain fewer than thirty-six Just Men who have been allowed to contemplate the Divine Presence." Described as leading obscure and hidden lives, their powers are revealed only in cases of need, when the survival of the people or the world is at stake. Even one fully awakened individual, according to the Source, can shift the equation of consciousness for an entire nation. Throughout time, the idea of a group of enlightened beings working behind the scenes to guide our planet has been conveyed in spiritual teachings, in literature, and in myth. This group, known by various designations such as the spiritual hierarchy, the Elder Brothers, or as referred to by the Source, the "Great White Brotherhood", has ever come forth in times of crisis and, as Paul Solomon himself tells us, today's needs have never been greater. The society of the Brotherhood are among us now:

Over the eons, the Great White Brotherhood have used whatever methods necessary to reunite individuals with their true identity. They have influenced the history of humanity's existence on earth to affect its evolution.... These souls who make up the Great White Brotherhood have entered from time to time in physical bodies, as with Jesus Christ. Their students, the ones awakened in the healing temples of ancient Lemuria, Atlantis and Egypt, have also lived as leaders and saviors of particular races and cultures. Each of these great race-leaders taught at-one-ment. The Law of One --- that all are one with God and that there is only one God --- has been the message and the teaching of this Brotherhood throughout time.

The purpose of the Great White Brotherhood has been to illustrate the Law of One, to show humankind that we are one, that we are not separate. Its members have entered throughout history and have brought understandings as yet unreached. Some have attempted to develop the concrete, thinking mind to the point that it could absorb the concepts of higher consciousness. Others have initiated brotherhoods of the arts, or what has been called the Schools of the Divine. Others have affected humanity through discoveries and developments in health, science and government. Others have appeared as great spiritual leaders bringing new understandings, which have too often become buried in dogma. Others have appeared as great philosophers, even political leaders....

We begin to understand that the Brotherhood is far greater than a fraternity formed on this earth. The movements of the stars in their paths are affected by its influence. Yet the importance of its scope should not take away from its personal nature. As this consciousness generates influences that affect humanity as a whole, simultaneously it affects the individual mind of each person on earth.

Chapters of the Brotherhood exist on earth today... The Brotherhood is not a visible body, labeled as such. Groups that claim to be the Great White Brotherhood are not necessarily the result of that work. Essentially, you can recognize that a group is being influenced by the Brotherhood when the focus and central purpose of its work is the lifting of humanity's consciousness back to at-one-ment with God. In such a group, the members will not teach or advocate separatism, differentiation, hierarchies, etc. Teaching at-one-ment with God is an explicit stamp of the Great White Brotherhood. In addition, all who teach that concept, whether as individuals or within groups, are being influenced by the Brotherhood even if they do not know it....

It is every individual's certain destiny to grow in the knowledge of his true nature and to rediscover his source and origin. The Great White Brotherhood was born of a purpose linked closely with that destiny. And in time, the Brotherhood and all humankind will succeed as One.[25]

THE BURDEN OF OUR AWAKENING

The cold fact of the matter, however, is that not even these enlightened beings can carry the entire weight of the world. While their task may be to awaken others, it will take many others who through their own disciplined effort have ascended to that height of suprasensory awareness to do the job. And if together we are to succeed, then we must not sit and fatalistically await the arrival of any prophet, master or messiah to reveal to us the truth that is buried beneath our own flesh. **Now you have heard it said that there is one who comes,** instructs the Source, **one who is and has been called John, and that he would take that mantle and preach the Word and teach that story and establish the new order of things. But let it be known among you as well that those who sit and wait for John will die and their bones will be bleached before he comes --- if ye sit. For the Christ should be born now and should live as surely in your heart as in the heart of the Master** (Solomon Reading No. 894, 10/21/76).

Enlightenment is not, nor has it ever been exclusive to the 'chosen few'. The Source reveals its presence to all of us alike, **for all that anyone of you ever may know of the Father is written already in the tablet of your own heart** (Solomon Reading No. 894, 10/21/76). It is as available to any of us to the same wide margin and unlimited parity as for any of those whose egos and memories no longer form the basis of their identity. Just as those enlightened already among us emphatically affirm love as the foundation of all life, so too we, with a gaining insight into the very heart of existence, can likewise discover in our own hearts the simple truth that is rooted in our nature. It is the power of life, the very Source of our every breath:

> To the extent that any of you has life, it is because God is expressing in you, for life is of no other nature. God is life. Life is God. God is light, and Light is God. God is Love, and Love is God. God is Truth, and Truth is God. Thus you have a single being, the Absolute, which expresses in a triad of force, form, and in reaction, yield. As a physics formula, this is the Holy Trinity: the three, the four, then the four square, the foundation of the sacred mount, the foundation of the pyramid with the capstone of purest crystal magnifying and shining abroad the light.

> The foundation, then: light, life, love, and truth. Those who experience and accept this without fear, without reservation and without condition, these are the enlightened. The gift of God to those who are enlightened is ... knowing themselves to be sons and daughters of the Most High, and in so being, there is the recognition and, more importantly, there is the "realization". We use that word in a specific manner, for real-ization is to make real, to be real without falsehood, without keeping something under cover.

Thus the real-ization is that those who stand in the light know themselves to be sons and daughters of God and become real expressions of God and only of God, of no other nature (Solomon Reading No. 1696, 7/13/92).

This, to again use the term, is Paravritti, "the Awakening" that can be ours only after we have ceased the war within ourselves, only after we have stripped away all the layers and levels of conditioning that separate us from the unconditioned and unlimited Source of all power, meaning and purpose. It is, as referred to by the Source, the "Power of One":

Then as to the building of discernment and cooperation with the forces of the Law of One, there is no substitute and never will be for attuning within yourself to the source of self. There is too great a willingness among you to depend upon others for guidance, thus giving up the responsibility within yourself for discovering the truth. There is no way to substitute your own responsibility for knowing the source of self that is ever, always within you.

You will only recognize the harmony in another's words and in their teachings by developing that ability to listen to [the] harmony within the source of yourself through turning within, through meditation, through taking responsibility for making discoveries within the self rather than fanciful entertainments with images and ideas and the worship of a guru or teacher or such. Go beyond that to the discovery of inspiration within yourself, and then when you hear, recognize, feel the harmony of another speaking from that source, so the spirit within you will recognize the spirit in that one. You build, then, cooperation and support for that you recognize. [There is] no substitute for recognition, but recognition comes only when you separate those impulses of the senses and the appetites, the appeal to ego, the appeal to drama and such. Look for that within you, that [which] makes a demand upon you, that you order your life, your thoughts, in harmony with those about. Look to that force within you that causes an impulse to love and accept and support, that impulse within you that causes a love without requirement on others that they change or meet your expectations or belief system, that within you that gives an ability to discover an element which can be loved in the heart of others, however dark they may be in their actions or expressions. Look for the source of harmony and love within yourself. Develop that as if it were a tiny spark at first and then [a] glowing light so that you can depend upon that in yourself which causes change ever within you --- change toward harmony, change toward understanding of the self. That in you which constantly points out to you disharmony in your actions and thoughts and appetites, that which points out to you inconsistency between your ideal and the expression of your life, that within you that makes demand upon you that you grow ever and change, expressing not judgement, not condemnation to others, not disapproval and correction of others, but rather that within you that causes you to see wrong action and thought in others as a symptom and causes a welling up within you of love, acceptance, and support for them which will cause the light in them to be exaggerated or built, rather than focusing condemnation upon their mistakes. Learning to discern that within you will give you discernment of those who act upon such harmony and will allow you to support and to accept.

There is no other way than the discovery, the evolution of consciousness within yourself to serve the source. It is not through serving others, not through becoming a part of a band or a cult or a group, but rather through the highest development of your own consciousness that you lift the evolution of consciousness of the entire planet. One person on this planet attuning perfectly to the source will lift the consciousness of all others on this planet a little closer to the Source.

Then make that your responsibility. You can see it this way: you are as Mary was, a container, a stable, a manger, a womb, a place in which the expression of God that is His child can find a receptacle, can be nurtured and warmed, can be given birth, can grow within you. Understand this: you are a potential mother of the Christ at this time. What greater need is there in your society, your culture than for Christ to live again incarnate and walk among you? There is not one of you lacking the potential for being that incarnation of the Christ by providing your body, your mind, your thoughts, your actions, your purpose as an instrument, a tool, through which that that that is the mind, the consciousness, the child, the expression of God to express.

Then if you would accept ultimate responsibility become the Christ by providing that house, that instrument that you are as a place for that consciousness to live and to so perfectly live that all that is within you that is not the expression of the Christ will die or be finished. Then there is within you a transformation, a transformation of both consciousness and structure that will reflect and express that presence of the Christ among men.

So then that is the challenge. And if you would speak of these things to others, speak not so much of superstitions, ideas, mysteries, but of the practicalities of using those energies that are natural about the surface of the earth, discovering ways to channel them in natural directions, rising above the conflicts of emotion and interaction. Speak of practicalities of improving the manners of communication and relationships among you and so bringing that harmony that is the life of Christ.

Then, accept that. Become initiates even of the highest order for they are desperately needed among you in this time. And becoming aware of that possibility you become candidates for that initiation. Then be about it (Solomon Reading No. 1069, 1/24/81).

As preposterous as it may sound to our ego-ridden and socially-conditioned minds, nevertheless, the Source emphatically tells us that it is true: any one of us, properly attuned with his or her own source, may lift the consciousness of all others on this planet. While every individual's thought contributes for better or worse some infinitesimal trace to the world's store, it is only the power of a fully conscious mind that can free a collective mass of semi-conscious individuals from their perpetual confinement to the fetters of brutal ignorance and fear. Given that the amount of power and freedom of will one possesses is directly proportional to the depth of one's consciousness and connection to one's source, so one's scale of influence is thereby limited only to that same extent. We simply need to understand the power that we have as awakened beings. **Can you understand that if you can heal a single human body that you** can also heal a nation, a land, masses of people, asks the Source? The power that you have, an attunement with God is greater than the power of millions of people in darkness. For darkness has no real power. Only the creativity of the human mind which is a gift from God can empower darkness. So that all darkness and evil is the creative power of God being misapplied by co-creator Man. But that power that is channeled to the dark is never as great a force, can never stand against the waves of love and light directed toward it. Do, by all means, magnify. And never magnify and magnify more greatly your own ability to hold visual image in your mind and empower it by the creativity given you by the Father to command all elements on this planet, all elements of all kinds, to move in ways harmonious to the purpose of love ruling and reigning on this planet (Solomon Reading No. 1499, 8/5/91). No one can measure such a power and no one can weigh it. No one can touch it with his hands or see it with his eyes. Yet something that emanates from any individual that embodies it mysteriously takes form in the consciousness and experience of all living things.

This, then, is the summons that is put before us. If we want a new world, we can get it only by striving for it. But the real struggle lies within ourselves, that we must first awaken ourselves from the miasma of our sleeping consciousness. We must free from our hearts and our thoughts all that makes for war, hate, envy, greed, pride, force, fear, and material ambition. But it is only when a sufficient number of others awaken to the visionary energies that enable them to likewise transcend such tribal and transitory rancor that we'll be able to cultivate the creative power necessary to transform our world into a New Eden. To that extent, through the subtle powers of spiritual discernment and the coalescing from every corner of the earth of the vitally active force of love, will the burden of our salvation be lifted and the stimulus for a "new Heaven, new Earth" be at all possible. For love is now a question of human survival, not a question of human luxury.

The Source tells us, then, that the age of reclusive mysticism and personal salvation that gave rise to it is now past. We have all been born during the darkest period of our long history, and given the scope and scale of our current needs Paravritti has become a social responsibility:

> For in this time of global consciousness, when these who develop the superconscious, the Source mind, or the spirit within, the higher mind, God consciousness, there is a growth, an evolution beyond the tribal unit to the good of the planet. And only when the thoughts of man's mind reach beyond boundaries, and when there is the breakdown of the separation between countries, and the evolution of thought knowing that one country alone cannot curtail the atmospheric and environmental changes that can destroy their people, as it becomes realized that only through a global cooperation can the planet and the life of mankind be saved, then thinking will go beyond individualized containment. And a few, only a few enlightened beings will take on a Cause mind capable of comprehending the challenges of the planet, the world, the earth. And such enlightened beings, then, must be those who take these problems in hand and bring the planet beyond the earth changes into a new world, a new Heaven and a new Earth (Solomon Reading No. 1378, 7/16/88).

When enough fully enlightened people, a mere one percent of the earth's human population, create that field of force, the consciousness of the world will change. This is not to say that a few awakened individuals will change the world, but the Source tells us that they can if they will it, and we simply cannot face the future without this hope. The civilization of the age calls for it.

"ONLY TWELVE CHRISTS"

Were we to recognize the unlimited energy of the ultimate Source of life as manifest in even one of us, we would thereby liberate in ourselves that same energy, both individually and collectively. For once transformation is seen to be incarnated in the world, others can readily recognize the same hidden potential within themselves, awakening thereby the god who sleeps at the roots of their own being. And like rivulets forming into a stream, gradually the energy awakens in yet others, allowing each to carry more and more of its light into the world's dark corners. This, to reiterate, is how a new world will arise. In the words of Paul Solomon:

> What the world needs is a nucleus of people who have taken responsibility for living consciously, without fear. It matters that the course of history is changed. How many magicians does it take to change the course of history? If you have billions of unconscious people and one conscious person, can that one conscious person change the course of history for the billions who are unconscious? Yes. And this is the reason that it is possible. Unconscious people are like sheep. They follow in whatever direction the current trend takes them. If the current trend takes them toward hate and war, and the politicians and priests instruct that it is patriotic and in the service of God to fight, those sheep will even go to battle and kill each other.

> However, one man or woman who knows God personally can anchor the consciousness of humanity and become a voice that will cause the underlying knowledge of God contained within each of us to be awakened.

> How can one person make a difference in the lives of billions? One conscious person is more powerful than a billion unconscious people because one conscious person can cause the thought forms that the unconscious people will pick up and act upon. If a person is consciously evil, they can produce disasters of planetary proportions. If one person is consciously, positively effective, the planet can be changed on a global scale, in a way that will make a positive difference in history.

> Do not discount the possibilities. It is possible to heal our nations. It is possible to change the course of history. It is possible to create a new world. And it is time for that to happen.

> Consider the possibility that you can create a bond of love so strong that it can awaken the consciousness and anchor the knowledge of God in the hearts of all humankind.[26]

And yet, as the Source points out, **if the challenge of enlightening all of mankind seems too overwhelming, then consider the challenge of producing just** twelve. Twelve, who simultaneously on earth express utter confidence in life, in God, in harmony, and in truth. And so you can change even the manifestation of destruction on earth. Twelve men can stop an earthquake. Twelve men can stop a war, a World War. Twelve righteous men can bring Armageddon to a close without another shot being fired. For twelve among you represent the consciousness of the earth, and that percentage of consciousness is sufficient to affect consciousness of all others on the globe, and to enlighten mankind (Solomon Reading No. 1352, 4/27/88).

One of the reasons for the power of the twelve to change the direction of the planet, explains the Source, is that the twelve were splintered and sent out in what has been called the Diaspora into all parts of the world.

> And twelve men, women, twelve individual souls about the globe agreeing in common on one thing have the ability to bring about that thing. Then world peace can be established literally by the presence of twelve beings, only twelve, about the world, who agree in common to lay down their differences and know themselves to be one --- one with self, one with one another, one with the Source of life and one with the planet.

> Such beings are by nature enlightened beings. And what is required of them that they become so enlightened? It could be said that they need only to know the Christ, but the word has been made sectarian, though it was not in origin. And to know the Christ one must come to the awareness of who or what the Christ is. For what made Jesus the Christ? Or what would make any man the Christ but to be that one energy, the one power, that is the expression of God. It is the power that gave life, that is life, and is not divided against itself, therefore it has no expression within itself that seeks to take away or destroy or to diminish life. This is the force that is love, that is light (Solomon Reading No. 1368, 1/2/90).

In the language of the Christian Aramaeans, the word for savior was MAH-HeIANA, "he who causes to live." "I am the way, the truth, and the life," proclaims Jesus, meaning that the way to God, the way of liberation from all death, the way to manifesting the power of the Source of eternal Life itself, is through the universal Christ Spirit, that same energy that made Jesus the Christ. And if the power over all life is given to but **one body in which the Christ might manifest alive and complete,** declares the Source, **that body would have no identity of its own, would only be a vessel, a vehicle of the Christ. And so would that man be as much the Christ as Jesus Himself.** And if that could be accomplished in two of you, then there would be two on earth as powerful as the Christ has ever been, whether in Jesus or other manifestation. And if there be two Christs on earth, then it would change the consciousness of the planet. If there be three, you will join the greatest portion of this planet to its source. And if there be four, then you will have joined the four cardinal directions into one single point in the center of this solar system. And if it be five or six or finally twelve, only twelve are required to lift the consciousness of man beyond even the nature of this planet so that the imbalanced movement of the planet would be corrected, its relationship to other bodies in the celestial systems would be changed (Solomon Reading No. 1466, 1/21/91).

Twelve individuals, then, having unfolded from within themselves the mystery of the Christ, only twelve having become entirely one with their Source, would be necessary to liberate the infinite potentiality that the human spirit sacrificed in its initial descent into matter. Only twelve would be needed to raise the physical nature of the Earth itself to the level of divinity:

> Then feed upon this that you might become one of twelve, just twelve required to alter the coming changes, including war. But the requirement upon each one of those twelve is that he be one who lives with utter and absolute confidence in God, believing in God more than believing in the power of destruction. When one is afraid of the power of destruction then one's knees are bent before the altar of destruction. You are empowered by who you believe in.

> Then worry is the worship of destruction, because it is the manifestation of believing in it; but confidence is the fruit of worshipping love and life and that which is, and this is why the truth will set you free. Knowing the truth that life is greater than death and overcomes it, that light is greater than darkness and overcomes it, believing in that so much that you know with confidence that it is true. That is knowing truth. That makes you free, free of worry, so that where your footsteps walk the earth feels confident, for here is one who knows God, knows truth, that life is greater than death and overcomes it. Nature where you walk will spring to life and be encouraged, for it is written: "How blessed upon mountains are the feet of those who speak of Him, who speak with Him, who walk with Him." For the very footsteps of those who know God bless nature and bless life so that the earth herself is encouraged by the feet of one who walks as a manifestation of such utter confidence that God is alive and well, that life lives and cannot be stamped out, that all the forces of hell and darkness, of destruction, of evil and fear have no power to stand before the living One.

> You know the truth when you know the truth is alive, living truth. And when you live with truth as a friend, truth reveals himself to you that he lives and is the living one, and thus knowing the Law of One, that there is but one God, one Truth, one Life, one Power of Love, of Creativity, and it is greater than all of the forces that appear to work against it. Let not your heart be troubled, neither let it be afraid, but instead let absolute confidence reign within you, and this is believing in truth, believing in God. This is the truth given by all religions in their intent, and this is the salvation of the self, and the earth.

> Become one of the twelve, then, knowing that you walk beside two or more others who also have such confidence ... that life is in control and ... will continue to live and thrive and grow and manifest in spite of all powers and darkness (Solomon Reading No. 1352, 4/27/88).

The Source challenges us, therefore to become one of those, one of those so few in all of history, who can live the remainder of your life with never so much as a hint of fear or worry or even stressful thoughts as would deplete your energy:

If you may live as one whose heart, mind and life are so filled with the power of love, then you may also claim the promise of the Master who promises only to the wisest of the wise. He has made the promise that, should you claim it through His nature, you may so, and so it will be true: "All power is given unto me both in Heaven and in Earth." And this is not for the reason that you become a powerful force in world affairs or such particularly, but only that in your creativity, in your loving communication with the Source of life, you might always make petition for all beings on this entire planet and for this living Earth herself; that you might claim all power in Heaven and in Earth to empower the healing of both the planet and her people; that the people of the Earth gain knowledge and experience and the wisdom of knowing finally, that the power, the force of love as an energy, a vitality, is far greater than that force related to fear, power, destruction, death, darkness (Solomon Reading No. 1642, 5/4/92).

Then, if we can break the chrysalis of the conscious ego by casting out all that is not of the Christ nature, the Source tells us that we will awaken fully to a consciousness of our responsibilities in the cosmic struggle between life and death, light and darkness. Then, we are told, will a new Eden bloom, when the tower of Babel falls, when the walls between nations crumble, when man learns ... of the life and light, [of] understanding that is love, that is Christ, the expression of God. And will you fight the final battle in that war, Armageddon, then will you have completed, and you will see the beginning of a new Heaven and a new Earth (Solomon Reading No. 1154, 10/83).

If, on the other hand, we have not first gained the initiative for self-transformation, we can offer no plausible relief to the world. In that case, we can only brace ourselves for the imminent approach of unprecedented worldwide disaster. As the Source declares, only a few short years remain before our epic journey may come finally to an end:

... that is to say... you will either find that the earth is beyond salvation, or you will find that because there has been a change in the consciousness of man, a change in science and technology, that you have begun through the re-establishment of plant life, the trees, to re-establish your oxygen and . . . make of the deserts a place that blooms, and of your earth a planet of wholeness again. It will be a day when there will be a dismantling of unnatural structures about the earth, and a time of man entering a period of time of living, as it were in Eden again.

Now this can be done deliberately at the hand of man, making a commitment to live in harmony, or it will be done with the disruption of life, and there will remain after that date only a scattered few of your race upon the earth who will find about them the earth having shaken off an old age, beginning, as it were again, primeval and growing ... into a dawn of a new history, only sparsely populated. History will be lost and will begin again as if it were from the roots, from the founda-

tion. It will be recorded in future generations as a beginning of time, and the world that existed before that day will for a time be lost to history (Solomon Reading No. 1282, 3/5/88).*

Given the ever-increasing speed at which we are advancing toward our final destiny, therefore, we can ill-afford to defy or ignore the mighty dimensions of the storm now visible on the horizon.

---

* The date originally assigned by the Source for needing to have reached a critical mass for change was May 5 of the year 2000. A number of factors have since intervened to alter that forecast, not the least of which was the 1992 United Nations Framework Convention on Climate Change (UNFCCC), the 1997 Kyoto Protocol Treaty on Global Warming, and more recently the 2015 adoption of the Paris Agreement on Climate Change signed by 195 nations. Altogether, their effect has been to mitigate somewhat, though not to halt, let alone to reverse the problem. Given the ever-increasing yearly rate of atmospheric greenhouse gases, it is safe to assume that, while the Source's timetable may have been delayed, Its prevision of impending effects remains in every respect wholly and unimpeachably valid.

Chapter 20

The Light Of A Single Truth

A FAR HORIZON

Is it absurd to imagine that a just and peaceful world, meaning a world without poverty, fear, or human conflict, might be attainable at this very moment? Is it impractical to consider seriously the proposition that a world in which the most generous dreams of universal community and human fulfillment have become the most ordinary conditions of living, one in which all the immense energies and vast knowledge of mankind are concentrated wholly on the up-building and regenerative functions of life, might be perfectly possible right now? **It is unbelievable to the mind of man that there could be an age without war, without crime, and even disease,"** states the Solomon Source. **But let us declare to you that there was such a time on Earth and can be again** (Solomon Reading No. 1332, 4/3/88). The Source in fact tells us that we are at the very dawning of such an age: **This is the dawning of a time of a new Earth, a new Heaven, such as you have not known and the mind of man cannot imagine. There are no words to describe that new day, that new life, except to say that it is and will be a new Heaven and a new Earth, and it is a time for entering that there can be nothing of greater import than opening the consciousness of the masses to the possibility of the change from this to a new Heaven and a new Earth** (Solomon Reading No. 831, 4/14/76).

new age now (handwritten margin note)

The Source assures us that were we to become suddenly responsive to the Law of Life, to the supreme Law of Logoic Love, were we to realize all at once that our whole way of life is alien to the essential source of our lives, an age of universal peace and fellowship, which seems now like so much utopian gibberish, would be entirely possible at this very moment. For at that moment when the two become one, when all human fears melt away in the fullness of love and an ever-widening partnership with life, at that very moment the unseen will become visible, all that had been unattainable will be surpassed, obstacles that once seemed insurmountable will crumble away, and a new world will indeed emerge. **Do you not know that the loving hearts of the loving people of this planet,** declares the Source, **if they were joined together without lines separating one organization or faith from another but through creating that disc that sits just above the crown of this head, that shining disc, [that they] could be that whole representation of the light of love of those who are related to one another by bonds greater than the bonds of blood families? The bonds of those who are bound together as loving families for the purpose of peace on Earth, overcoming duality and separation; the establishment of what has been called a new Heaven and a new Earth where there will be new and greater beauty** (Solomon Reading No. 1642, 5/4/92).

Seen through the eyes of the Source, such is our long-awaited destiny, for as creatures of an eternal spirit it is our birthright. The seed of our full and destined identity with the One lives within each and every one of us. We need only awaken from our present state of "conscious sleep" for a new Heaven and a new Earth to break through the clouds of our unknowing and be made visible. Every one of us, in fact, if not narrowed and corrupted by fear and if not burdened by limitations, by unworthy distractions, and by mechanically habituated thoughts, feelings, and behavior, is fully capable of that mind-like receptivity and awareness that opens us to an Eden already close at hand.

While the visionary truth of it all may call out to us like a far, inviting horizon, seen merely through human eyes the path back to our full unity is as torturous as it could possibly be, full of pain and suffering, failures, barbarism and grave malevolence. Although the Source tells us, **God may be revealed in what He Himself created,** the infallible truth if the One is daily repudiated by the events of our lives. Their de facto diversities, not their de jure onenesses, are what shape our awareness and understanding, both of ourselves and of our world. Moreover, as prisoners of bias and self-induced repetitiveness, the unity we long for continues to be a hidden unity, ever a deus absconditus, ever believed in, never encountered --- an article of faith, not a fact of life. Even though the Source tells us, **You have the ability and opportunity to introduce reality from behind a glass darkly to face to face,** very many of us are so strictly dominated by our own desires, fears and prejudices that any thought or valuation even worth suggesting is at once summarily rejected. And one primitive mind's awareness of another is often so erroneous and biased that the perceptions which would make for true consensual understanding of the other fail to occur.

If the prospects of our journey together toward the great goal of human unity seem impossibly remote, it is because even within ourselves we are incapable of integration or change. Many of us who may hunger for a degree of community which our condition demands but our cowardly and selfish egoic personalities can by no means attain take refuge in the herd-life where the trials, difficulties and suffering of others becomes simply a matter of shared indifference. And in that indifference lurks the demon of our disunity and despair. The gods of our fathers, who once possessed the power to pierce the veil of that sorry demon, have all now been swept away in the great running tide of our scientific scepticism. All that we're left with is a godless universe, a spontaneous salutation that offers no comfort, no common meaning, or hope beyond that which only science can provide. Many others, however, who perhaps in a benign simplification of their faith refuse to abandon hope, continue to scan that far horizon for a return of a savior who bears in his wake the promise of a peaceable New Kingdom.

THE PULSE OF A MILLION HEARTBEATS

In the science fiction classic *Childhood's End*, Arthur C. Clarke conceives an earth governed by the benevolent forces of alien Overlords. The supremely rational and scientific Overlords are sent to save humanity from self-destruction until its impending metamorphosis into a new evolutionary form. Acting as "midwives" for the birthing of a new humanity, the Overlords must first reform and improve the human race. Because the human potential for transcendence necessitates a heightened sensitivity to the suffering of all living creatures, the Overlords warn that such cruelties as bullfighting must come to an end. The people refuse to end the sport and the following Sunday a huge spaceship appears over the biggest bullring in Madrid. When the first pic penetrates the bull's flesh, an agonizing scream is let forth from the crowd, for the Overlords had caused every spectator precisely the same pain as that felt by the bull. The bullfighting abruptly ceased.

What would happen if such a thing were possible? What would it be like if the sorrows and sufferings of all others were suddenly to strike at our being becoming consciously interfused with our own? What if, all at once, the walls of human separateness were to crumble away and in the flash of a single instant the collective sum of humanity's pain, the whole epiphenomenal flow of mankind's sorrow and sadness were to flood in upon each of us individually from all parts of the world?

What if...?

The initial shock of an agony so palpable and violent would have an overwhelming --- no doubt murderous --- effect on us all. Of the 7.5 billion or so members of the human race, conceivably many could not endure a physical and emotional trauma of such magnitude. Of those that survived, it would act upon them like an ordeal by fire, searing the deepest and most impregnable regions of the soul.

Then, under the vast weight of the world's sorrow would come the increasing awareness of the littleness of the individual. Vanity, conceit, arrogance would be swept away in a deluge of pain, grief and despair. Haughtiness and pride would be irresistibly overwhelmed by sympathy and by profound sentiment for the welfare of all others. The narcissistic self would be dwarfed to the point of insignificance. The principle of tolerance would be broadened to the utmost extreme. Individuals formerly tormented by mutual animosity and by violent propensities for self-gratification would find themselves suddenly responsive to the plight of millions. Knowing that we would destroy the most vital part of ourselves more surely than any enemy would destroy us through warfare, human conflict at every level would abruptly cease.

The whole energy of mankind would at length be transformed bringing with it a power of self-knowledge and mutual insight far beyond anything ever before experienced on earth. Like a single, mentally continuous body of consciousness, we would come to see with a million eyes at once; the pulse of a million heartbeats would be felt as one; we would become as close-knit as the integrated constituents of a nervous system. And with such insight, writes George Leonard, there would come tears:

> After the scream of pain, after the shock of recognition, all the world would weep, not just for the needless torture, but for the moments squandered, the beauty overlooked, the potential unrealized. The world would weep for the words unspoken, the painful confrontations eternally postponed, the fathers fallen with their secrets locked in their dying hearts; for all the walls between us that we have not pulled down. Feeling this and far more for which no words exist, all the world would weep (for a week? for a month?) until the last tears had soaked into the earth. And in this flow humanity would know

at last the true meaning of the Flood, the universal and saving catastrophe which is not the end but the beginning of the world.

And after the flood of tears --- we know this too --- there is joy, the simple, matter-of-fact joy of existence. The tears of loss would turn to tears of joy. For beyond the pain, beyond all the man-made walls, there is always the elemental vibrancy. To attain contact with it, pure and clean, seems a miracle. Once attained, as Suzuki Roshi tells his students, it is nothing special. It is existence. It is the sheerest, most miraculous ecstasy. It is nothing special.[27]

In the long and seemingly perennial human quest for the original, undifferentiated state of solidarity with life --- all life --- the same but dormant core of each individual would finally awaken to its imperishable unity with the great realm of Universal Being. The deep within each of us would answer to the deepest part of the All. The world and "I" would become eternally one.

Then, from that boundless dimension of experiential truth that lies beyond the reach of the questing speculative mind would come the understanding that there at the very heart of life, at the very center of our own existence, is the generative force of all creation --- the infinite power of divine love. From out of the stillness of endless ages the long-buried chrysalis of the spirit would at last emerge and disclose to us the simple truth that life without love is not worth living, and that the severance of love is the deadliest sin against life. By the light of this single truth all the gossamer nonsense of metaphysics, the miasma of ideology, the opiate of demagoguery and dogma, would be cast into an eternal forgetfulness.

The only categorical imperative that reason would accept would be that which dictates that whatsoever a man does to another he also does to himself. The only inescapable obligation that we would feel would be to that life-enhancing principle which holds that if a man lifts the burden of another he rises a little bit above himself and so lightens the entire world. The only remaining law that we would be compelled to honor and serve would be the law of love which includes every other law since "love is the fulfilling of the law." Life thus devoting itself to life, the division of life against itself would come finally to an end.

THE DIVINE IMPERATIVE

It is precisely this to which the Source refers when It speaks to us of the "Law of One." Just as it is written, "God is One," so God's Law is the expression of His own Nature and Being and of His Divine Will as It is manifest in the world. It is the unity of the eternal and the temporal, the one power of life, the one and only true basis of the relation between God and mankind. See it this way, explains the Source: There is one power that is the power of life. All forces which take away life are literally powerless. Only creativity, which is the force of life itself, may be misused. Understand this Law of One --- that there is only one power, there is not an opposite power [as in] light and darkness, life and death, good and evil, love and fear. There is only one force and one force only. Yet mankind has been created as co-creators with God, as partners with God, which has allowed that men and women have been able to

(marginal handwritten notes: "Liberated from duality thru the Law of One")

use that creative power of life in any manner or form that they choose. When there is confusion in life and when fear enters, depression and other such, [then] there is the use of the creative energy which is life itself to apply it as if it were in reverse, giving strength to such things as pain and difficulty, of hurt and emotional suffering and such. All of this comes from creativity. Now, the soul is finally liberated from duality when there is the realization, the absolute realization of this Law of One (Solomon Reading No. 1569, 10/9/91).

Without relevance to human deeds, however, the Principle remains merely an abstraction. Just as the thoughts of God must speak to us in the language of men, so therefore the Source translates for us the theoretical One into a practical rule of living:

(marginal handwritten note: "bringing all together is the understanding of self")

> ...until my brother is raised to a higher plane, I cannot manifest on higher planes. Therefore, there is a universal law that requires that we raise our brothers around us. Then when we are healed, we share our healing. Those vibrations that are raised within us we share with others. We seek not to be more spiritual or the more enlightened one, but we seek to be that channel of enlightenment that would raise our entire race a little closer to the Godhead. For without the evolvement of the entire universe, or this world, or this level of manifestation, there cannot be the evolvement of a single soul, not an atom of the universe --- you are the universe! This is the Law of One. In the understanding of the bringing all together there is the understanding of self (Solomon Reading No. 42, 10/19/72).

Just as every person is a microcosm, so, we are told, each of us, in that endless interior sea of our being, carries within us the soul of all humanity. There is nothing in nature in fact, nothing in another, nothing in God's creation that is not self, explains the Source. That is, see not self as a separate entity, but see all that is about us as an extension of yourself. Those who are suffering are part of you. Therefore you suffer through their suffering, and through the empathy there is realization of the suffering. And then one would seek to raise to high level that which is causing the suffering, thereby producing healing in the other, whether plant or animal, another human being. There would be the empathy, the sharing within. See not self as separate individuals but bring others together with one's self in love. Realize that there are reasons for all that manifest on this plane and attempt to see that which is behind that which would cause suffering. Seek, then, that each person would realize their greatest good from those situations he or she comes in contact with, and realize that self cannot be the highest emanation of God until self is attuned with others. If I would reach a higher plateau in spirit life, I would bring another along with me, for we all must reach a higher plane before there can be the perfect expression of the Law of One (Solomon Reading No. 45, 10/23/72).

While perhaps a noble sentiment in principle, in reality it remains purely conjectural. For rather than elevating ourselves to a higher level of conscious truth, out of our obsessive fantasies of fear, power and retaliation we've managed to lower ourselves to the level of beasts. In a world that no longer has any absolutes to anchor it to a meaning that may be clearly understood, almost any behavior, any devaluation of the "Other," can in some twisted way be justified with reference to the "laws of Nature." If animal behavior justifies sodomy, why not the murder of rival males in courtship? Why not the slaughter of rival tribes for territorial dominance? Why not the systematic torture and wholesale extermination of Jews or the ruthless repression of Blacks on the basis of "genetic superiority"? Why not simply nuke our enemies and be done with it? While as Solomon points out fear and violence are natural responses, indeed psychological accessories to the survival of the beast, the beast has ruled this planet nearly to the point of its own extinction. Taken now to its extreme, the beast may very well wipe out the larger part of humanity and perhaps make entire regions of the planet permanently unfit for life.

There are no Overlords to forcibly compel our social will. Even if there were, what would it tell us about ourselves that the responsibilities which should have been ours and ours alone to bear --- for being our brother's keeper or as faithful stewards of a living Earth --- would, with however much benevolent intent, have to be implanted in us or imposed upon us by some greater power beyond that of ourselves?

Granted, there are many who would welcome the arrival of a Messiah figure or some great leader to guide our ways and fix what's broken. There are many others who've simply lost the intrinsic power to act who might find the utopian imagery of it all downright appealing and worth whatever the sacrifice, even if it meant the submission of their own autonomy and individual will to the "greater good". After all, having not yet removed the beam from their own eye, how can they fail to judge others as anything but separate and competitive? All the moral antipathies and equivalencies --- of good and evil, right and wrong, friend and foe, them and us --- that shape our reflections about the world simply blind us to the unity of our common Source and heritage. The degree to which we've shriveled ourselves through jealousy, vengefulness and insensitivity in our own personal lives and the unmitigated abuse of power and resources among nations collectively reveals unambiguously the extent to which we've compromised and corrupted the power of life. The very thought of a peaceful and compassionate world by whatever means might find a grateful retinue.

Nevertheless, what would it say about our ability to achieve personal self-integration or to attain mutual harmony among ourselves by our own hard-won efforts? Or about our propensity for making adventurous leaps of self-discovery and self-transformation on our own? That we are incapable creatures governed by nothing more than our own conditioned reflexes, impulses and appetites? If so, human life in all its dimensions, in its manifoldness and purposefulness, would by definition be shrunken to insignificance. What does a good deal of hard growing count for? Solomon's answer: "Everything". This, in fact, is the very purpose of the soul's entry into time and flesh.

GOD IS NOT MOCKED

Though we be Princes of this world, we are likewise prisoners in this world. Through our incarnation the eternal has become enmeshed and suffused in the temporal, the dark prison of the luminous soul. But through the decisions we make and the actions we take --- in other words, through the freedom of our individual will and intent --- we are provided every opportunity to rise on the ladder of visionary awareness and to raise the temporal once again to the status of the eternal. Although the Source assures us that human affairs are observed and swayed by invisible but mighty presences, so even they must yield before the God-given autonomy of every individual soul that has yet to awaken. **The angels themselves weep, for they are not allowed to interfere with the wills of men until called upon, and when called, there is the promise that there will be the thousand at your right hand to fight the crucial battle** (Solomon Reading No. 1696, 7/13/92). We are therefore not forced onto this battlefield, but go of our own free will to gain wisdom and experience and ultimately return triumphant to the Source of our origin.

From the moment when we accepted the serpent's gift of knowledge, we were free to sin and prone to sin. The angels in the Koran foresaw that man, once he reached self-consciousness, 'would work corruption and shed blood.' From that time to this, the serpent's yoke has been on our shoulders. Human history has been soaked in blood. But for each moment lived we are given the chance to lift from ourselves the yoke of the serpent and to again become the perfect mirror of living Truth. By every act that we perform we leave a legacy that only God fully understands. Every word uttered reverberates in higher spheres. Every thought committed to memory contains the unpredictable capacity for either perpetuating the errors of the flesh or for bringing to light the full consciousness of the spirit in its identity with the One. **Each act, each breath you take is a lesson in spiritual growth, declares the Source. Not that you need growth, but all the time belongs to thy God. That which you fail to face this day thou will face on the morrow. Now as it was given of Him and has oft been repeated, 'God is not mocked. Whatsoever a man soweth, that shall he also reap.' If you would take the time, then, that is given so precious in this existence and cast it then to the swine, so will you reap. And as you feed the body on that food of the swine, so shall it become. Then in meeting that which has been given on this plane, in facing the situations that you are given to meet in this body, would you then make a choice or strike a balance between the good and the evil, or between the growth periods and that which would be pleasure, or that that would be cast aside or thrown aside** (Solomon Reading No. 115, 5/30/73).

To understand the events and circumstances, troubles and burdens, fortunes and misfortunes of our lives individually as well as humankind collectively, we need simply to understand that what we have wrought in the lives of others will ultimately be wrought in our own, perhaps not in this lifetime but in God's time. We need no Overlords to lift us from our earthly sorrows into a super-earthly self. Any salvation into which we're forced, in which our free will has no part to play and with which it did not cooperate, would be vicarious and, so, meaningless. Our actions are predetermined and our fortunes predestined by no other power than ourselves. By applying the power of life, either in behalf of life or for our own selfish gain to the detriment of others, we chart our own destiny. For any who out of self-righteous hypocrisy would judge or condemn another, so by that same measure would they lay judgement upon themselves. **We would see it in this manner,** instructs the Source. **In the** manner of the Christ teaching on this plane, we would offer you a parable:

> There was a southern farmer, a very wealthy man, who had living on his land, in a shack, a very poor black man. Now this farmer attended church every Sunday, and to outward appearances was of God. The black man knelt in a glen daily and worshipped God. Now the farmer came across the black man one day as he worshipped and, in seeing him worship when the sun was up and fields could be worked, he abused him and said, "God doesn't look on your kind anyway. Forget your praying, you'll never get to heaven." Now we would find that there came a pestilence in that land, and both became ill and died. They were caught up, then, to meet their Maker. And as this white man was caught up past the clouds, he caught a glimpse of his black neighbor resting in the arms of a form clothed in white, and the head and the face of the glorious form was wreathed in white, and he passed through the clouds expecting his judgement when the light cleared and faded, and he looked into the face of a black God. Knowing his own judgement, he walked away sorrowing.
>
> Now how would you look upon your black neighbor? Look upon him as you would look if you knew God himself was black, for He is. God lives in the heart of the black man as He lives in you.
>
> As to the future of the black race as a race, that will depend, then, upon how you, as a white man, look upon him. "For as you do it to the least of these my brethren, you do it unto me." God seeks out and takes care of His own. The future of the black race, and your race, is in your hands and as you would treat those, so shall you be treated (Solomon Reading No.9, 3/22/72)

The parable is of protean significance, for enfolded within its meaning is not only the absolute principle of 'justice', but 'righteousness', 'truth', 'love', and 'law'. "Judge not, that ye be not judged," states Matthew. "For with what judgement ye judge, ye shall be judged: and with what measure ye mete, it shall be measured to you again." (Matthew 7:1-3) Although the parable dramatically illuminates the highest truth of this scripture, nonetheless, it's purely allegorical. The Source goes on to give us some perspective of the symbolism:

> There should be an understanding that as individuals build karma, so do nations, so do areas or particular segments of population build karma. This was [an] indication of the figurative return of the karma that was built in this area [of the Southern U.S.]. It should be noticed that as well in the parable there was referred to "in this land." This also was inserted for this particular purpose: that it should be realized that not only the South, but any land and all land which would build for itself a karma of abusing one particular segment, ethnic group, or race, builds for itself a karma that will return as karmic visitation in the future of that particular part of a country, or that segment of nationality.

It should be noted, as well, that all of this being parable, was symbolic. It might be misleading to some to think of the idea of these two coming to physical death and immediately being judged by a higher being above the clouds. Realize that as these things are given symbolically in Scripture, they are given symbolically through this Source. Understand the evolvement of man; understand [that] he who judges is within us. And as we come to realize those things of our karmic pattern, we judge these things and adjust to them. We build our own karma; we build our own judgement. It was given, "He then knew his judgement." Within himself came the awareness of his judgement, of his karma, that which he had built and that which he must meet. He went his way to meet that debt (Solomon Reading No. 24, 5/9/72).

From the eternal lessons that lie hidden within the finite and ephemeral experiences of our daily lives, therefore, we are provided a heightened opportunity to control our bestial prejudices, fears, and impulses and a heightening capacity to understand them. From this, comprehension will begin to form and in time, out of that comprehension, a conscious awakening to the impersonal truth of our existence. **Then understand spirit and spiritual laws in this way,** explains the Source: **that there is not [the] opportunity to accept or reject that which is truth, for truth is. That which is spiritual law is universal law, and governs every step. Then there is not the choice of whether I would apply self for spiritual growth, but every step, every moment that is lived is a lesson in spiritual growth. The manner in which we handle these relationships are those lessons that we would learn and that [comprises that] book that is being written concerning the self. This is not given that there might be the feeling of guilt or condemnation, but there might be the understanding that you would not worship or serve a God who would delight in punishment, for realize that your success is His success; your failure would be the failure of thy God, for thou are created in His image and are his daughter, a spark of Himself. Then He will do all within the framework of the universal laws to provide those lessons, those opportunities that you would need for ultimate growth in this lifetime or any other** (Solomon Reading No. 167, 5/25/73). This, then, is the spiritual law that guides and informs us both individually and as a race from our first fumbling and bruising steps towards the full maturity of a humanity broadened to a consciousness of our common Source and destiny. It is the way back to that Truth that the serpent has wrested from our grasp.

THE BROTHERHOOD OF ONE

Given the all-pervasive significance and purpose of this universal law, it is inevitable that mankind should grow from the darkness of its animal heritage into the full light of a consciousness immeasurably greater than itself. Not by following any doctrine, ritual, or mandate, however, **not by given a set of rules that you may say this is right, that is wrong,** will we transmute our ignorance into wisdom or our blindness into the illumination of a higher awareness, **but only [by] that new commandment which**

He gave that thou shalt love one another. Having said this, then is not all said? For the only sin, then, is self, and that selfishness that would deprive others of that growth. For no man alone can grow into the Kingdom. It is only in assisting others that you would make your way into His arms (Solomon Reading No. 115, 5/30/73). As written in the *Aquarian Gospel of Jesus the Christ*, "There is no lonely pilgrim on the way to the light. Men only gain the heights by helping others gain the heights..."

The real necessity, then, of faithfully observing the law and thereby overcoming the law is, in practical terms, derived from the need to identify with the individual concerns of others and with humanity as a whole. But simply saying that in principle we identify with the cosmic fellowship of all beings is fatuously devoid of any real meaning unless we are able to translate that abstract unity into the immediate problems of living. Here the rule, relates the Source, begins with what lies nearest at hand:

Who must you help? It must be all those who come into your sphere of existence. You must look toward all those you become aware of without limitation. Whoever comes in your sphere of existence, these are to be influenced by you, and you influenced by them, and yet you must see yourself as a column, cornerstone, a pillar for all others, not dependent upon them but only your source of prosperity. With this assurance, this concrete awareness of the Source of life and prosperity, your actions, your security, your joy of life, your peace, this will help and will teach those you have come here to help and to serve.

Thus, it is ever true in the ageless wisdom, seek first in your life the establishment of His kingdom of peace and all these other things will be added to you. That is to say, seek first healing, wisdom, right thinking and living within yourself. Heal yourself. Heal yourself first. Depend upon yourself and your source first. Then those who need be helped by you will come to you. They will be drawn as to a magnet, and those who are there, those who you see need help, these there you must help.

[handwritten note in right margin: heal yourself first]

[Then] will you enter the higher kingdom. The kingdom some call heaven will enter your own highest consciousness and awaken on the arm of one you have helped. See it as spoken by the prophet Cayce. Those you help will open the door for you. You may help one who is of lesser understanding than yourself, yet that one awakened before you to the Crown of Enlightenment even can prevent your being able to follow one you have helped. Turn to the law of higher wisdom. Encourage them to go even beyond yourself. Then you find them opening the door.

Help those who come, those who seek, with no limitation. Don't decide this segment or another of the world or only they are those I will help. Help those who come into your sphere of influence. If you become aware, offer them your hand, your guidance, your light. More than all this, help all the people of this plane in this period of time by taking the Light Bearer and making this light available to [all] (Solomon Reading No. 1703, 4/93).

Rather than simply surrendering ourselves to an indiscriminately allusive spirit of the whole, we are called upon and challenged to regard from the visceral depths of our hearts any man, woman, or child as if he or she were all of humanity. That is, [if people] could see each other as they were in past incarnations and see again that new relationship on this incarnation and respect each other as being equal, they would learn the Universal Love, the Brotherhood of Mankind. If they would see each other as being one, if they would see self and the world, this Brotherhood of Mankind, as being parts of the same creature, parts of the same body, each with his own function, with that mutual respect and admiration between each, this would be seen as the developing of the Universal Love that would heal the sick, that would cause the blind to see, that would develop that perfect Law of God, for this is the Law of One. This is that Force that brings all healing; it is the [Logoic] Force that brings all love. It is the green force of balance that would see the world lifted a little closer to the Godhead (Solomon Reading No. 34, 10/13/72).

It is this single force of Creative Fiat from which the eternal Law of One --- one people, one undivided Truth, one divine unity of purpose --- will ultimately and inevitably be restored. But how much more pain and suffering must we endure before this Law comes to rule in our parliaments and in our hearts? While there are no doubt many who would scoff at this "higher law", in their own hearts they already know that it's the only damn thing that makes any sense. All the passions --- of socialism, communism, capitalism, of liberalism or conservatism, of nationalistic pride or this creed or that --- by which people deliver themselves over to half-truths and idiocies should make us realize what this force could bring to all humanity the world over if there were but a handful of enlightened individuals in every nation who could demonstrate to those who still had open hearts that it is possible to struggle and sacrifice in the name of love without turning the world into a vast slaughterhouse.

Were we to be given the chance to change the course of human history, to redirect mankind's tendency toward separation, hatred and fear so as to avert the global conflicts which as the Source foresees almost certainly lay in wait for us, how would we begin? Were we to set forth to constructively change the tragic course of relations which the Source tells us we shall have with our own descendents in the next one hundred years, where would we start? Were we to initiate just one inviolable principle which, if faithfully observed, would unify mankind's fragmented and warring inner nature and, as a direct result, open our hearts to accept fearlessly and without prejudice or preconception whatever of the truth might fall within our comprehension, what would it be? Were we to introduce to the world but one precept, one single postulate which would awaken in us all the wisdom, benevolence, and consciousness necessary to free us of time's squirrel-cage of perpetual eye-for-an-eye justice and bring about a unified one-world family, a veritable 'city of God' on this earth, what manner of truth would it be?

The answer given by a Jewish Rabbi, a Muslim Imam, and a Christian cleric, all of whom intentionally built their houses of worship side by side on the same 35 acre plot of ground in Omaha, Nebraska, is that it must embrace the fundamental spirit of unification, universalism, and mutual respect. As Rabbi Azriel, one of the three explains, "We didn't create this [project] to tolerate each other. We didn't create this just to have a dialogue. We have done all this stuff already. It's about what we are going to do together. What are we going to do for the betterment of humanity?" The project, called the Tri-Faith Center, is being built on the grounds of an old golf course developed by a "Jewish Club" in the 1920's when Jews were excluded from other clubs in the city and around the country. A land once formed out of division has now become a symbol of love and brotherhood. A bridge running over "hell creek" will connect the entire campus. Appropriately, it is to be called "heaven's bridge."

The idea was born out of the tragedies of 9/11, when fear was at its highest level and the Rabbi and some of his congregants went to defend a local mosque from vandalism. Friendships were formed and a dialogue between members of the two faith communities ensued. Even now there is still some apprehension and suspicion about the mixing of faiths among congregants, parishioners, and others in the outside community. The Rabbi tells of one man who asked, "What if there's a live hand grenade rolled in the middle of the aisle during holy days?" The Rabbi answered there were two options. "One is to run away. But as a polio survivor, I can't run far away, he said with a mix of sarcasm. "The other one is for me to fall on it." The answer, recounts the Rabbi, brought tears to the man's eyes. The man later became a donor for the project.

Indeed, as the Imam, a Syrian native, expressed it, "Our mission is not about compromising anybody's faith. We are here to learn about each other and to live as neighbors with each other." After all, he added, the conflict between Jews and Muslims in the Mideast should not be an impediment in making peace in the Midwest. It's a sentiment that the Rev. John Dorhauer, general minister and president of the United Church of Christ, shared during ceremonial groundbreaking for the new church. "Let this be the story we tell our children," he proclaimed, "that once upon a time in a land called Omaha, the Jew, the Muslim and the Christian started a movement that changed the world."[28]

This is the quintessence of the Law of One. It is precisely with this spirit and attitude and in such a community that we find the experiential base for a morality of love, truth, brotherhood, and justice. And this, according to the Source, is the very purpose of this age and time --- to bring humanity into direct contact with the eternal process of reconciliation and renewal both in the cosmos and within itself:

> ...the great prophets speak of the end of the cycle of evolution as we have known it, or the earth as we have known it, and speak of the New Age not only as the precession around the zodiac to the Age of Aquarius, but this particular entry into the Age of Aquarius [must] be also a lifting above the spiral on which the plane of earth has

spun in its karmic axis over these periods of history, into an Age of Redemption, or that which is called a New Heaven and a New Earth. That is to say that the many prophets have spoken of this particular transitional age is having greater significance than the movement from age to age throughout the precession of the equinoxes in an ever continuing spiral of growth. They speak, then, of a quantum leap of the ending of a cycle of ages, an Age of ages, so that the movement from this Piscean to Aquarian Age has greater significance than the movement from the preceding age to this one, or even that [age] preceeding, for the reason that this period of change manifests in two major ways: the changing of the earth geologically as we know it, and the changing of the consciousness of mankind. Both of these are conditional in this sense (Solomon Reading No. 1390, 11/7/88).

Conditional, that is to say, based on our ability to bridge the chasm that has widened between ourselves and the planet that gives us life; conditional on re-establishing our link of creative relatedness with the underlying and primordial web of all life. Above all, it is conditional based on our renewal and acceptance of the ancient understanding that there is but one foundation, one eternal Law, one Divine Imperative to which we are all held accountable. It is the implicit truth which binds all life with the Source of life and which proscribes the unity and reconciliation of all races, religions, nations, and creeds.

Now let us attempt to say it in this manner, states the Source:

In your heart you know God. In your heart you know that love is greater than fear and yet you have been led to believe that fear is a powerful influence, and men have bowed their knees to worship at the altar of fear. This is the source of all weaponry on your planet. Now when even one among you believes that which he knows (understand that one can know and believe differently than the knowledge of the heart), you know that the Law of Love is stronger, that the power of Love is stronger, and yet fear has an ability to cause you to bend the knee and worship at its altar. When you fear one another, when you fear anything, even the powers of the dark forces themselves, when there is the slightest inclination to fear to the extent that you entertain that fear, you worship at the altar of evil or destruction or death or fear. This can only be overcome by invoking the Law of Love, the Law that sees no need to protect itself, knowing the power that is in me is greater than the power that is in the world. Hear the words of Christ: "The power that is in me, the Law of Love which is the Law of Life, that which sustains life, that which overcomes death, that which rules over every dis-ease, that which is the law of harmony, is greater than the law of fear, destruction, and death."

Become the Apostle of Love, the teacher of the Law of Love, and so introduce healing and harmony and the Law of One to your people. Speak to Love. Be aware of the source of your thoughts, for the conversation that is your thinking either comes from the love and light that is the kingdom of heaven, is sourced out of heaven, or comes out of hell, hell being the kingdom of fear. As long as thoughts of love rule your thinking, your thoughts come from the kingdom of heaven and you live in that kingdom. The kingdom of heaven is within you. For as long as that kingdom that is love, that is light, that [that] is the kingdom of heaven rules over your thoughts, your emotions, your body, your consciousness, to that extent you become a body of light, an influence of light, an initiate of light, and so give that light and love again to the world. Let yourself be a channel for the reintroduction of the simple formula of energy from love and light as ruling over the energy which comes from the destructive forces. Save this planet.

Now, the only step which can prevent the coming slaughter [of Armageddon] in this time is the reintroduction of the Law of Love. The challenge is that men must be made to see that the power of love is greater than the power of fear. This is a practical step to be taken and can be taken by the focus, the intense focus of prayer which is the basis of support for John [of Pineal] to discover the simple formula of the access of energy without destruction, the Law of Love as opposed to the law of fear. Otherwise, it can be possible to invoke a cooperation of brotherhood from beyond this planet that would cause you to see, if you could visualize it, a cluster of great light as if it were the great spiral of the Milky Way, the galaxy, coming down, descending upon Jerusalem, where the ships of that spiral then will be allowed to communicate their influence. Again, this being the influence of the knowledge of this energy of which we speak, the energy of construction as opposed to destruction, that which would be as the interaction of an extraterrestrial brotherhood, an involvement in the affairs of man.

Now this involvement has been forestalled to this point because of the Law of Divine Will. That is, these forces have not imposed themselves from without this planet because of the reluctance to interface with the will of the people of this planet. That reluctance can be overcome by the invocation, or the invitation, of the forces of the Laws of Light and Love into the affairs of man by those enlightened ones of earth inviting, asking for this participation from the Universal Brotherhood of Light that is the Force of Light and Love existing in your planetary spheres, your solar system, your universe. Invite the forces of harmony to work through you and so you may have opportunity to avert destruction and to introduce the New Jerusalem without the fiery annihilation of the planet.

Reintroduce, then, the Law of One, the Law of Love to the people. Overcome the destructive forces and build the New Jerusalem, the Holy City. Build a new Heaven and a new Earth. The new Heaven and the new Earth do come. They do descend, even now are descending upon you. There is only one question, the question being: Must Armageddon be a destructive experience? Must the forces of fear and destruction destroy the planet before the establishment of the Holy City? Or can you in peace cause the Holy City to descend by becoming instruments of love on earth?

You see, there are many prophecies of destruction before the introduction of the New Age, the age of peace and wholeness. But these look at one of two possible scenarios, the first being of a great battle fought in the air, fought about the environs of earth which will cause what has been described variously as earthquakes or nuclear explosions, or what have you. They are in essence the same. They are seen as the same in the eyes of the prophets who look, seeing these forces of explosion from volcanic activity, from earthquake, from nuclear explosion. One cannot be discerned from another. When seen through the eyes of the mystic they simply are seen as a rain of fire. [It has] been described as the sea burning like tar, the moon turning to dripping blood, the stars falling like cinders. All of these descriptive phrases refer essentially to the same thing, to the possibility that man's commitment to fear can destroy life on this planet. Or, [the second possible scenario] being there can be brought down, descended upon earth, the Laws of Love and Harmony which bring the New Jerusalem through prayer, through attunement to the force of the Divine.

Those among you who are becoming aware of the Law of Love have the responsibility for attempting to communicate the truth that the greater force is the force of Love and can overcome fear. This is your challenge. This is the purpose that is set before you. Can you build a network of cooperation and harmony among you so that you may more perfectly say that which we have attempted to say to you, that it may be broadcast to the world, that it may come to the consciousness of the people? (Solomon Reading No. 1285, 6/25/90).

Into the hands of each of us, therefore, has been placed the future of the entire race. If we are to awaken sufficiently and in time to avoid the wholesale disasters that our own fear and arrogance will soon inflict upon us, then we must first awaken to the truth of One; that is, that the destiny of all of us is at stake in the destiny of every one of us. Contracting our infinite senses, thoughts and feelings, we behold as an isolated multitude, but like those of the Tri-Faith Initiative, expanding we behold as one. "This is what lets this planet come together as one family living on one small planet," remarked Paul Solomon, "but only if we live together in love." For as the Source asks, who is your sister and brother, your daughter, your son? He who has no father or mother is your daughter and son. He who has a need is your brother, your sister..."

Thy purpose, then, is to shed abroad that light, that love that was the Christ; to see as Christ said upon the Cross, "these are my mothers, these are my sisters, my brothers." Realize that as close as a family might be as a unit and as much love as might be shared between members of this family, this should be no different from the feeling toward these in the world. With every creature with whom you come in contact, realize that there is a karmic tie. See it this way. This one has asked, "Are there karmic ties between myself and my family?" Realize that there are karmic ties between self and every individual you will meet upon this plane [in the world]. Realize that there is not a single individual that you would meet on this plane who is not and has not been a part of your family. See these as immediate family. Realize that not one can make a mistake on this plane, that he is not thy brother. And you are responsible toward him as a brother. See people in this manner. This is your purpose. This is the perfecting of the Law of God (Solomon Reading No. 34, 10/13/72).

Our belonging in the world therefore entails our love of all humanity as a single family and our unconditional dedication, faith and loyalty to the Law of One which makes us one. Out of the divisions of nations and races, not only by Divine Imperative but by the exigencies of sheer animal survival that now confront us, we. like Anwar Sadat, *must* forge unity. Out of the separations of religions and cultures we must create common goals, based not on doctrines, ideologies, or creeds, but on values, purposes and ideals that will unite us as responsible agents for and guardians of all life. We must come to the realization and understanding that we are all, from every nation, ethnicity, and religion, however isolated geographically or in appearance, brothers and sisters, part of an infinitely complicated and interdependent ecological partnership of planetary dimensions.

The whole course and burden of our destiny, therefore, significantly depends on our will to collaborate in the transcendent task of reestablishing through the world --- in every nation, religion, and tongue, in every human heart and intellect --- the eternal Law of One. Then, from these germinal beginnings, the Source tells us, the reintegration of spirit and substance, the world and God, will take seed in a New Eden. For just as each of us is the totality of the sum of us all, so is the New Eden the total epiphany of "One Man". He or she who rejects this truth betrays the ultimate destiny of humanity and of the world.

A QUICKENING

We have now arrived at a crossroad where our own immediate choices will determine whether Solomon's prophetic warnings become our cataclysmic past. The solution, of course, is wakefulness, that the preponderant balance of humanity may come to a more realistic approach to responsibility, toward not only the cosmic powers that are now in our possession, but for meaning in life and to the Source of life itself. Only through a wholesale quickening of many minds, the Source tells us, might we restore the collective balance necessary to avert the global catastrophes that now threaten us all.

In fact, a quickening had begun. Even now, the luminous dawn a new earthly Eden is breaking. "A new world is born", declares the seeress Mira Alfassa. Known as the Mother to thousands of devotees and spiritual successor of the celebrated Indian saint Sri Aurobindo, Mira Alfassa asserts that "It is not the old world that is changing. It is the new world which is born. And we are right in the middle of the transition period, when the two overlap, when the old is still all-powerful and entirely controlling the ordinary consciousness. But the new slips in, still very modest and unnoticed --- so unnoticed that externally it disturbs hardly anything ... for the moment, and is even absolutely imperceptible in the consciousness of most people. But it is working, it is growing."[29]

The transition *is* underway. Its morphology is unfolding with the emergence of what Eckhart Tolle, the author of *The Power of Now*, refers to as "space consciousness" which he sees as the next step in the evolution of humanity. "If there is only object consciousness in our lives," states Tolle, "we remain trapped in the conditioned, trapped in form, which creates an appearance of separation. We are always trying to change the form or are resisting it in some way. We are looking to the world of form for salvation. But when we are aware of space consciousness, aware of being aware, we are freed from identification with form, which is ego, and there arises within us a sense of oneness with the whole and with our Source."[30]

Space consciousness recognizes the universe as fundamentally not materialistic but relational, not an edifice of hard, inert building blocks but rather a delicate fabric of meaningful and vital interrelationships. As Tolle points out, no amount of forcible tinkering with or overturning and altering the visible and tangible features of a culture will ever be enough to transform separateness, cutthroat competition and "individuality for its own sake" into the holistic qualities of unitedness, mutuality, conscious inter-reliance, and cooperation. There has to be a fundamental change in awareness. Such an awareness shatters the old habitual patterns in the mind and cuts new neural pathways across the brain, shifting the webs of connection and meaning in the world such that separate things are perceived as part of each other and in which everything is always fresh, uninhibited, and unique. It is precisely this to which the Source refers when It speaks of the "formless" in which everything flows within one and the same rhythm, effortlessly:

> You come [now] to a point in time in which time itself has so accelerated in the furious activity of man attempting to reach his final initiation on this planet that as it exists now it is obsolete, you see. For you will have gone beyond the movement of matter with matter. That was an initiatory phase in the entering of man into this material planet, and exiting from it will require the re-learning of the movement of matter with that which is not matter, the formless.

> Then your study is the impression of the form from the formless, from the formless into form and from form into the formless, returning [again] to the form. That is the triangle, the apex, that is the purpose, to lift mankind and the planet through its initiation, the thirteenth path into a new state, a new expression, a new dimension, a new Heaven and Earth in a very literal sense. For the character and nature of the Earth itself will change in its healing and in the final step of initiation of mankind as humankind now exists. That is

the summons to the high crusade that is before you (Solomon Reading No. 1216, 7/2/90).

For many who are now awakening to this "space/formless consciousness" there is the experience of utter freedom --- of breaking through the outmoded forms and into the pure light of the formless. When one perceives that the apparently objective and accidental is a result of the ego's creation, one understands the tragic confinement of this freedom --- the freedom from an overwhelming and claustrophobic absurdity.

We at this moment stand at the evolutionary intersection of two worlds and the change now occurring is that of consciousness itself. From the "Source" of Al Miner, one of the only other authentic Source channels currently on this planet, we are told that "the consciousness of those who are seeking is collectively rising to the point where the Loving Neutrality within many of you as individuals, but all of you, collectively as a greater grouping, again, is rising. This will give you the impression that the veils are thinning, but in truth, you are "rising" (using that term to create understanding). Your consciousness is accelerating so that the higher frequencies (using these terms, now, for understanding)... the higher vibrations or frequencies can be discerned while yet sustaining life in the lower vibrational frequencies. In other words, a simultaneity of consciousness.... You are growing in your consciousness because you are choosing. The more so you grant yourself the opportunity to experience, the more frequent and clearer your experiences will be."[31]

Additionally, the Solomon Source tells us, a tremendous influx of Logic energy and divine grace is flooding the earth with multidimensional forms of a new order of being beyond our reach, or at least beyond such comprehension as we now have. This is all a part of what the Source means when It speaks of the "lifting above the spiral" into an "Age of Redemption." The Lama Sing Readings from the Source of Al Miner are in complete accord: "With these rising energies, it is, as the saying goes, *God's rain falls on all peoples*. This energy is impacting all souls expressed in spirit form in a lifetime in the Earth, and elsewhere to be sure. The heightened energies bring forth those qualities which might otherwise lie latent for long periods of time; the energies, as they raise the hidden and the beautiful and ugly alike (as you would define it), this is the purification process that has been prophesied."[32]

Given that such a grandiloquent assertion can neither be proven nor falsified, nor consciously felt or experienced within the "normal" human parameters of sensory awareness, skepticism if not outright cynicism on the part of some would come as no surprise. But in spite of all appearances, the Source tells us that a new world *is* being born. Like the tips of icebergs whose real significance --- and connection --- extends deep beneath the surface waters of the ocean, so beneath the superficial turbulence of our conscious lives move dynamic forces of cosmic change that are inconceivable to any finite imagination. It spills out first from the interior world, entering only through the minds and consciousness of those who are intrinsically open to its effects and those willing and choosing to receive it. The Lama Sing Readings from Al Miner describe it in the following manner:

For those who bear the light and have been faithful will know Him. And those who are in opposition will know His light and will, in that moment of decision, need to choose which path they shall follow: whether it be to continue on a path of illusion... or whether they would choose to release these intentions and find their own peace within. So doing is the only pathway that can truly set those who are in dis-ease and dis-harmony free, for all the attempts that are force-meeting-force will only produce a prolonged reaction of same. The meeting of force with the Peace and Love of the Christ gives the force nothing to oppose, no substance against which it can apply its hostilities. If anger is met with peacefulness it will pass the peaceful by and they will rise into the Kingdoms of God and into that land which reflects the beauty of who and what they are.

It is good that all in the Earth recognize in these times that the energies are continuing to heighten, and the apex (if you might like to call it such) is just ahead and will be sustained for a period of your time measure. During this, there will be continued shifts in consciousness and there will be the continued conflict between the forces that seek to dominate and those which are seeking freedom..., and then shall the Promise appear and the choices will be made. ...These are energies that are eternal; they will not fade. They will rise up, and those who wish to be free may rise up upon them. And they will rise up in a manner that is difficult to describe, but let us (humorously) attempt to do so, nonetheless: As you have a heat energy rising up from an asphalt highway, it rises up visibly from certain angles. And if you are in a lighter-than-air aircraft, or you are a creature of the air, a bird, you can ride these heightened energy centers higher and higher. It is likened unto that. The Earth is the reflecting level of consciousness where these energies are coming into focus in the present. And the 'reflection' (so to say)... the heightened reflection of these energies bursting forth from the Earth will lift up others who are willing. And this is, in part, how the two realms were vacated (so to say); they were and are risen and set free due to their previous position.

Those who are in the Earth have the same opportunity. Those individuals who were lifted up and set free who were in finite form were and are (so to say) riding these energies, as you would see a bird circling and soaring higher and higher.[33]

The uncovering of reality goes forward, then, as these first emanations of the Divine succeed in awakening in themselves the first passionate stirrings of an eternal consciousness in a wholly new ontology of the spirit. It is through their presence and activity that this resonating field of energy expresses itself, triggering a transformation in others who may be tottering on the brink. A chain reaction could, as the Solomon Source points out, tip the balance of humanity into a wholly new evolutionary threshold of consciousness.

For these, then, shall not only step into a new life, a new day for themselves,

but become ushers of those who have been left behind to step into a new place and a new way themselves. So might you understand that in these months, years, that are upon you, you will find a continuation of war and pain and disease and death; changes in the earth and in the weather, in economy, in disease and such. And yet shall you discover that as these teachers, prophets, those who have made great commitment to a new way, a new order of things, begin to awaken one and another until integrity becomes important and love becomes a power perceived, recognized as stronger than fear, and life stronger than death, as this spark shall reach that critical mass for change, so shall you see suddenly the dawning of a new day, His face seen in the clouds, and every man, every man who is committed to Life, shall see Him. And those with whom there is a bond of commitment, these shall be led into peace and new life (Solomon Reading No. 1147, 9/3/83).

I see signs that it is already happening," affirms Eckhart Tolle:

For the first time there is a large scale awakening on our planet. Why now? Because if there is no change in human consciousness now, we will destroy ourselves and perhaps the planet. The insanity of the collective egoic mind, amplified by science and technology, is rapidly taking our species to the brink of disaster. Evolve or die: that is our only choice now. Without considering the Eastern world, my estimate is that at this time about ten percent of people in North America are already awakening. That makes thirty million Americans alone, and in addition to those people in other North American countries, about ten percent of the population of Western European countries are also awakening. This is probably enough of a critical mass to bring about a new earth. So the transformation of consciousness is truly happening even though they won't be reporting it on tonight's news. Is it happening fast enough? I am hopeful about humanity's future, much more so than when I wrote *The Power of Now*. In fact that is why I wrote that book. I really wasn't sure that humanity was going to survive. Now I feel differently. I see many reasons to be hopeful.[34]

Indeed, as the awareness of our perilousness as a civilization and the precariousness of our planetary motherland begins to spread, people the world over have begun to respond. Thousands of books have been published championing the urgency for love and cooperation among nations and in the flourishing of life. Theologians and physicists have, in tens of thousands of conferences, each inspired by our human potentiality for effecting global change, collaborated on new cosmologies addressing the mad ontologies of our dysfunctional cultures and ways of awakening them to higher states of awareness from which our interconnected problems can be interpreted, explained, and ultimately resolved. Millions more have pledged their commitment to end world hunger and to promote a fair and equitable distribution of the world's resources. Social cohesion has grown up around the new change in consciousness regarding our dominance of nature and our concerns for a living Earth. We are beginning to at least think differently. "One of our fundamental teachings is that in all our actions we consider the impact it will have on seven generations," the Anishinaabe activist Winona LaDuke told an audience at the University of Ottawa in 2012. "Think about what it would mean to have a worldview that could last a thousand years, instead of the current corporate mindset that can't see beyond the next quarterly earnings statement."

But we do not have another seven generations. All we have is perhaps another 10 or 15 years to translate all our rhetoric and passion into political action capable of saving our technological-postindustrial society, indeed the entire world, from self-annihilation. **The choice is thine**, warns the Source: either cultivate a new world or be passively brutalized by the old; either lift this world into the firmness of Eternity or perish. **You are on the brink of death and destruction, but you stand at the same time at a precipice at which you have the power to change the forecast. The lifting of consciousness to a responsibility for the living Earth can change the current movement toward destruction, yet you stand on the brink and have not much time** (Solomon Reading No. 1389, 11/7/88).

THE SONS AND DAUGHTERS OF LIGHT

While the consciousness of the race is increasing as the Children of Light continue to multiply and advance, nevertheless, at this moment there is only a dove with an olive branch indicating the approach of a new dawn. It yet remains to be determined whether the morphological lineaments of our embryonic awakening are the mere flicker of a firefly in a dark forest or if they truly become part of a universal movement. Should the worst come to pass and the whole long effort of human history be brought to a catastrophic close, as the Source points out a new world will still be built from the ruins of the old: **Whether there come the Prince of Peace to establish His Kingdom and reign among you, or whether He not before that period [of destruction], there still will be restructuring of this planet --- the preparation for a new dawn, a new day, a new Heaven and a new Earth. You'll need to understand, as few have, that the two events do not necessarily coincide. For the Prince of Peace *will* establish His Kingdom. Will it be on your earth as you know it? Will it be on the new Earth? Dependent entirely on the receptivity of the people, and the preparation** (Solomon Reading No. 408, 8/20/74).

That is to say, before a new world can be built, the ground must first be cleared for it, either through a cataclysmic leveling of civilization or by a lifting of the consciousness of mankind beyond its egoic state of fear, isolation, and estrangement into an awareness of its inextricable connection with the web of all life. It all hinges, in other words, on the relationship between our destructive capacity as a species and our first glimpse of a form of human identity so inclusive that it embraces the whole of our race and our world. In the final analysis, love begets love as surely as fear begets fear and hatred begets more hate, and until can we master the lessons that fear and hate should already have taught us from the very beginning, given the destructive power now in our hands all life will be in danger. Merely recounting our sins will serve no purpose other than to leave ashes in our mouths and cinders in our eyes. Rather, we must awaken ourselves to the whole in which we live and move and have our being. But either way --- from the ashes or from the consciousness and activities of these Children of Light --- a New Kingdom, we are assured, will arise. Hence, the Source urges, **let yourselves be ruled by love, by light. Become the sons** and daughters of light in this time so completely that you are radically different from those out there who consider themselves to be average humans. Become something different. The Children of Light must establish themselves now --- the time is short. You do not have time to waste, but must be about this (Solomon Reading No. 1114. 2/7/83).

There are, in fact, a growing number who, from their own source, discern the signs and visible symptoms of impending collapse and who even now are working deliberately to carry forward into a new order and dispensation the seeds and principles of a new Eden. Even though they be tested, challenged, ridiculed and denounced by a new breed of pharisee, of them it is said, "wisdom is justified of her children." It is well that you understand as these changes come, informs the Source, as the hardships, the travail, the shortage of food, the concern for money, all these things, as they enter upon you (understand here that that we describe will come little by little, a bit at a time, so that men may scoff and scorn), as you begin to build your community, saying, we are building for a time of collapse, you will feel so much like the man described as Noah, Noah who stood building his ark as men laughed and jeered, pointed the finger, shooting out the tongue. And will you have the faith of him? For his faith would have been greater, perhaps, if great drops of water had been falling. Will it not be easier for you to build the temple, the tabernacle, in the wilderness after the troubles have started? But then how much will you accomplish? (Solomon Reading No. 854, 7/23/76).

In the face of the overwhelming trials and tribulations and tragic struggles that lie ahead, even before life reaches that downward curve, the Source tells us we need to establish firmly within ourselves and among ourselves an ethics befitting a world governed by one Law only, an ethics that will extend the domain of love beyond the hostile and self-serving world that now envelops us and into a New World ready to receive it. Then enter the Divine Plan in this manner, saying that without regard to shortage of food or money, without regard to the changes in the surface of the earth, with regard only to the choice for attunement to the Divine, we will remove ourselves from the places of false value and the expression of false value. And we will turn our time and attention to the things that are of great value, and we will love one another. And rather than accumulating that [that] we can draw to ourselves, and own, and spend, and be possessed by, we will rather give, give, give to one another (Solomon Reading No. 854, 7/23/76).

It is in this spirit, and through the awareness, foresight, and courage of such autonomous individuals as these, that a new world will take form, beginning from within. Whether there will be a number sufficient to outweigh our collusive madness and to avert the catastrophes that our irrational pursuit of power has prepared for us remains to be seen. Day by day, however, the issues become grimmer and the dangers more threatening. Not for one moment should we ever discount the possibilities of our committing mass suicide, either through the mindless destruction of our planet, through all-out war, or both. So as the Source warns us: Realize that the days are close, the time is at hand when the end is near, when the dawning of the New Age, the New Day, is upon us. Realize, therefore, that there is *much* to be accomplished in this lifetime and waste not a moment, not a day in perfecting those Laws of God, in realizing the love that must be shed abroad and the ties that must bring [all men] closer together; the time that there must be realized that all on this planet are part of the same family and as one is guilty so we are all guilty, and He will not hold one of us guiltless as long as there is not perfected on this plane the Law of God (Solomon Reading No. 34, 10/13/72).

Even supposing the likelihood of our collective failure to achieve a higher and more universal self in time to meet the contingencies of that larger purpose, nonetheless, the Source assures is that on the other side of this "time of labor" there awaits a new Eden for those able to enter. Those who are able to cross over into this other dimension of existence will find the entire world to be an incarnation of spirit. This, again referring to the message of the Lama Sing "Source" as given through Al Miner, is the "Promise":

"What does this mean? The Promise is...that Call that is the original beauty of the Christ Spirit. And, therefore, it is the Christ Spirit that brings the Promise back into the fullness of consciousness in the realm of Earth --- and elsewhere, to be sure --- once again.

So, how can we say that the Promise is there, it is upon the Earth even as we speak? We can say this because you are there. You (individual reading) are a part of the Promise, You have journeyed with the Christ in the past and have chosen to continue to journey with Him, and to answer the call with Him whenever it was appropriate and wherever it was possible for you to do so. You are among a number of many others who feel much the same, who have experienced much the same, and who are reaching out, just so as you.

Why, then, do not all the wars stop if the Promise is upon the Earth? Why does not dis-ease vanish? Why would there be anything similar to conflict, disagreement, emotional challenges such as anger or hatred and that sort? The simplistic answer is because it can be; the more complex answer is, because some are still choosing it. What we believe will happen does not make it so. To be very, very clear to you: this is not a prophecy from we here, but it is not the opposite either. It is what we see as probable; it still remains to be chosen. As the sum of those who choose to dwell in the glory of their choices and habits (and, to them, it is their glory) continue to sustain their position, then, as the Promise reaches its full manifestation and becomes visible to all who are willing to see, a point of transition will occur. And there will be the continuity of experiences that are the choices of those who prefer to continue on as they are. (Note that we are stating these in the briefest of terms.) And when those who are His, and who answer the Call, come to the forefront, they will stand and face one another. You may see this in some instances in a variety of different ways, but the most prevalent will be at the level of spirit, and of mind, heart. Some will bring this choice to a point of confrontation, and the confrontation may invoke an upheaval that will be felt from the Earth itself, first as it reflects the energies of the Children Of God who are dwelling upon it, within it. And there will be that which is the beauty of those who are dwelling in the same way but in a sense of peacefulness.

The movement, then, will be into a state of separateness. Not to imply that anything is separate from the Oneness of God, for all things are of God, and God is within all that is. But... there will be separation, and there will be a movement of a level of consciousness that will carry those who choose the Promise to a new realm of expression..., a realm wherein no one is bound to another; that each has the right of choice; and that all of the expressions therein have the fullness of freedom to be as they are intended to be by the Word of God.

What does this mean to be in this fashion? Does it mean that the color red will be the color red? Or that the tone Middle E will be the Middle E? Perhaps so. But greater than this will be the realization that you are greater than you have allowed yourself to believe in the level of Earth that you just came from. That you are a Child of God, just so the same as the Master. And as you come together in this new realm of expression, you will manifest after this. You will be free --- to explore, to create, to acknowledge. And that which is left behind ... not in the literal expression of those words by definition, but by the inference of the choices of those who stay in the energies of their habits within the choices that they have collected over perhaps lifetimes, if you will.

So you would have a realm (let us call it that, if you will) wherein many souls have (quote) "graduated" (end quote) (with some tongue-in-cheek, here) because they have set themselves free from that which they have been dependent upon for many, many lifetimes. They have graduated because they now accept that they and God are One, and in the acceptance of this Oneness, they can be where God is; straightforward, that means where they choose.[35]

There are myriads of individuals, as therefore indicated, who will not be able to enter into that vision. Doomed by their own embarrassing arrogance and living in the shadow of pain and death, they are not permitted that consolation. And if the actual joy of some has not preponderated over the grief of so many others, it is because, mercifully, the actual fulfillment that is wholly missed cannot be conceived. Nevertheless they will suffer, as the Solomon Source points out, for **such a change in consciousness for those not prepared would be as disaster, as destruction, for the mind is not prepared to see, to understand, to accept** (Solomon Reading No. 694, 8/21/75).

... and you will find that those poor souls, recognizing truth, finding it unbearable, as the prophet said will cry for the mountains, the rocks, to fall upon them, to hide them in their misery. For truth will be revealed, and truth must necessarily condemn that [which is] alien to truth.

How would you face it in this moment if all acts of crime and evil that ever you have committed in the cycles of times --- for some of you hundreds, for some thousands of returns to this plane -- if all these were revealed before you in this time, how would you face it?

...better you pray that you might be ready for the accounting when it comes, you see. Be men before God, and say "All of that effort [that] has been committed in the selfishness, in the reaping to self through these times, these cycles, I face and I see, and with the grace of the Christ may I be counted one of His; and claiming that redemption, that power of His, let me become, then, an image of Him, and see only His overcoming of the dread sins of the world that my record may be cleansed spotless white through the blood of the Lamb, that I will not have to face such."

Those, then, who have refused to face and account, and attempt to balance, will suddenly find [that] that which they have been condemning all this time, has condemned them. Those who are ready, then, will gladly accept and live it. Those who are not will see before them thousands more times of coming, and facing, and working. The truth will stand stark and white, condemning, fearful, awful, before them. There will be a time of greater polarity than has ever been, for there will be a dividing of the sheep from the goats, the one on the right hand and other on the left. Can you not see that it must be so? Revealing of truth would do it. Automatically it must do it according to Universal Laws (Solomon Reading No. 645, 7/4/75).

Yet eventually, even for these shall the way be clear, states the Source, and opportunity given that those who suffer may more clearly see the option of stepping into new life and a new way (Solomon Reading No. 1147, 9/3/83). Then, when the husks of empty creed, of fixed habits and conventions and of selfish pride that clings to well-established evils fall away, shall a new Heaven become visible to all. Become, then, the New Essenes, the Pregnant Ones, commends the Source, and with your expectation, create that power that will produce that critical mass for the transition. And as there is transformation among one and another of you, so will there be transformation of the earth. And that transformation will be, of course, a reversal of polarity. But we speak not of destruction; we speak rather of a heightening of power, the lifting of the earth into a new expression that is not one of polarity, the effect of that reversal, so that no longer will you encounter good and evil, life and death, but rather Life shall reign for that time, for that season (Solomon Reading No. 1147, 9/3/83).

SOULS ON FIRE

If the destiny of mankind, after its long preparatory period of separation and differentiation, is at last to become one, it will be so, then, not as a cumulative result of human "progress" in any purely technical sense; nor will the strange dialectic of the world's history mysteriously culminate in such a state. It will be so only when, in the words of Lewis Mumford. "A sufficient number of men and women in every land and culture take upon themselves the burden men once sought to transfer to an Emperor, a Messiah, a dictator, a single God-like man."[36] Unlike the unenlightened Emperors of the old guard, however, the fierce will required of this self-assertive effort must be wholly devoted to the universal, rather than to any individual benefit. Self-love is the diuturnal enemy of the self-less obedience to the Law of One which manifests itself always in loving service to every suffering, striving creature in the world.

Rebbe Hersch, son of the Baal Shem is depicted by legend as a shy, rather insignificant man. While his father lay dying, he was asleep. He had to be awakened and taken to the sick Master's bedside --- who spoke to him, but Rebbe Hersch did not understand. Called upon to take over the movement, he was found lacking in authority. He withdrew into himself, and in the end, spoke only to his dead father. In his dreams, he asked him: "How can I serve God?" The Baal Shem climbed a high mountain and threw himself into the abyss. "Like this," he answered. Another time the Baal Shem appeared to him as a mountain on fire, erupting into a thousand flaming fragments: "And like this as well."[37]

Baal Shem's words to the young Rebbe speak thunderously to any who ache for the comfort and salvation of the world. They speak not to any who desire a timid peace, but only those who embody a victorious spirit in the stern strife of actual life. Only through a bold and advertant living of life to the very limit, by sacrificing oneself wholeheartedly, in a spirit of humble courage and with a willingness to take a blind leap into the dark, can we ever hope to transform the discords of our world into a symphony of common dreams. **Love that is passive and afraid, quiet as a lamb, withdrawn, will not win a battle**, the Source insists. **But love that is alive in action, and healing, this will win a war. You must learn to make your love alive and active. Understand it to be as great a force as it is, for there is no force of darkness which can stand before light. Thus you must shine your light in dark places. ... This is the concern of the battle of Armageddon.** (Solomon Reading No. 1466, 1/21/91). The world cannot long endure if its foundations are not laid deep in such audacity and undaunted courage. Any reaction of shrinking back, of faintheartedness or complacency, merely confirms and hardens a mind yet shackled by fear to the chains of ego. Whenever knowing and doing have parted company, the freedom of the soul is lost. Hence the Source warns, **here there be dragons, and the dragons... come at times as complacency, that is in this sense:**

> **There is a sense of having dedicated the self to the Father, to the Light, to the purpose of the One to becoming one; then the assumption that such a dedication has been made and I am being guided and a tendency to become complacent, assuming that that is so. Do be aware that moment by moment, every moment requires its dedication of the heart and the life again, a singleness of purpose, a focus of the mind and the mind's eye, a dedication of the heart. There are so many distractions; even blessings sometimes become a curse, because in happiness with making progress, we make an assumption. This blessing means that I am attuned to the Lord and He blesses that [that] I do in His Name; and that is true, even the assumption is correct. But it does not mean that the next moment can be relaxed or turned by the way. To any other distraction or purpose make no assumption that yesterday's victories will guarantee tomorrow's dedication. To that cause seek ever, moment by moment, to be attuned to highest purpose. Do understand this --- do,**

that when there is one who should enter into any lifetime with a talent and a purpose, he is, because of his dedication to a purpose, exceptionally valuable to the Brotherhood, to the cause of the Christ; and so as well is he a threat to the darkness of men, and that darkness will lash out. Where there is great blessing, great opportunity, great talent there is great responsibility and great demand for strength and constant dedication. Understand that that is required of you is greater than that required of one who came not on such a mission, but rather for his own soul growth and knowing himself. Be careful for the appreciation of others chosen by the Master of Masters and set there carefully to participate in your mission and do not become the focus of that mission but see that as one serves in his way to fulfill the purpose of this mission, so you serve. And while the world will give you the glamor, the credit and the glory, by all means keep it ever in mind that another participated with his energy, his caring, and made it possible. Be ever humble as an instrument that He might use, never proud, never even assuming that you have made that complete dedication and always striving to do so. For one having found, no longer seeks, and then is in danger. One having become dedicated, no longer dedicates and thus is lost --- moment for moment, every moment, a living bond --- participation in life with the Master of Masters, with the closeness, walking at the side (Solomon Reading No. 981, 8/5/77).

Indeed, it was not weakness which made Christ hang from a cross, but obedience to the law of sacrifice, of love. It was not irresolution or complacency that inspired Gandhi to lead over 100,000 fellow Indians on a 241 mile salt march to the sea in defiance of British colonial domination. Nor was it a lack of vision or fortitude that moved Martin Luther King along with Roy Wilkins, Whitney Young, Philip Randolph, John Lewis, James Farmer, Jr., and others to lead more than a quarter of a million people to march on Washington D.C. in behalf of racial justice and social equality. Nor was it for lack of courage or compassion that Thich Quang Duc self-immolated himself on the streets of Saigon in 1963 in protest of the treatment of Buddhists, or the more than 100 Tibetans who have done likewise in just the past five years in protest of Chinese oppression. Such examples, although relatively scattered, are not framed in hatred or revenge, but in the spirit of love and sacrifice. If they have not been copious enough to fit a more inclusive and universal pattern, it is only because the majority of us either fail to acknowledge the moral insights and spiritual validity of their sacrificial acts or because of a tendency to turn prophets of merely human dimensions into gods. Preferring instead to bury ourselves in a state of constant inadequacy and guilt, even with mirrors we cannot see ourselves reflected in their image.

If, therefore, we now shrink from the hard contests where men and women must win at hazard of their lives and at the risk of all they hold dear, a new creation may never be born. **You are committed, or you are not,** the Source tells us. **You are Israel, the Prince, or you are contending with God.** As Christ said, **'You are either for me or against me.' There is no middle ground.** As John wrote, **'Would that you were either hot or cold, but because you are lukewarm I will spew you out of my mouth.' Until you become... a strong harbor for those who are troubled, you have not become the Prince, taking responsibility** (Solomon Reading No. 1114, 1/83).

Awakening to our responsibilities toward our fellow creatures and to all life on earth is our common duty, and it is only in the purifying fire of sacrifice that the dross of selfishness is consumed and the freedom of the human soul can take flight.

And if wakefulness is the solution, then it is those from every nation and corner of the earth who have themselves already awakened who must set the standard whereby so many others may be measured and appraised and perhaps become somewhat of the stuff that they are made of. That is not to say that one need set oneself on fire or suffer the fate of an assassin's bullet to, as Mumford says, "Make the sacrifices that would, if made in time, have saved our civilization from its corpse-strewn Fifth Act."[38] For when that New Day arrives, it will not have come from a single transforming agent. Rather it will have spread rapidly from a multitude of determined and high-hearted individual centers, millions in every walk of society, in every country, each and every one of them a pure channel of unity and love, each a reflection of all. **You have all that is needed,** declares the Source:

There are many facets of the world of preparing for John and for the Messiah. The facets of this work are so all-inclusive that they touch every institution that supports your civilization and culture, including education, justice, government, religion, and communication. All these areas that affect your life are areas to be touched by this work because there are so many tasks and challenges that are a part of this work. There is much to be done, and you have much to give.

Do not be ruled by those parts of self that are yours, but not you. When you are hurt, when you are caused to feel fear or resistance, examine it quickly and ask, "Where does this come from within me? Why am I harboring fear? Do I want my life to be ruled by fear? What fear is there in me that makes be vulnerable to this hurt and pain? Eliminate that and let yourselves be ruled by love. Become the Sons and Daughters of Light in this time. Become different from the rest of the world --- in it, but not of it. The Children of Light must establish themselves now, for the time is short. You do not have time to waste, but must be about this.

Build the new age first in the higher planes of consciousness. It must exist there in completeness before you bring it down to your level of Earth. Begin to create it there and see it at work. If two minds among you see the same model, operating in the same manner precisely, the same heaven on earth, it will occur on your plane. That is the law. Begin effectively seeing the same vision, for in that moment that any two of you agree perfectly, as touching any one thing, it shall be. This is your creative potential. Then be about it (Solomon Reading No. 1114, 1/83).

It is from the creative potentiality of the causative source of mind that, if it is to unfold peacefully and without friction, a new age will form. From the self-discipline born of a passion to achieve a widening purpose, those possibilities that give energy to a greater creation can be brought into manifestation. It is from just such a self-disciplined vision and challenge that the nation of Israel was conceived, and that our astronauts were finally carried beyond Earth to the moon itself. Now imagine what only a handful of fully awakened beings could achieve as creators of an interior universe so powerful as to galvanize the entire mindscape of ordinary humanity into a new key. What would this look like? **And we would ask you if, perhaps, you might be able to see it as such a day dawns, for in that day of that raising of consciousness, that initiation of mankind, darkness as we have known it will disappear completely and will never again be known. That on any corner of the planet or of the universe you will dwell only in light, and the sounds will be pleasant, the forms of beauty and the life experience one of joy and harmony, fulfillment. This is the ushering in of the new day, the new age, the day of the light of our Lord** (Solomon Reading No. 1642, 5/4/92).

While this may sound fanciful, nevertheless, as the Solomon Source, Hawkins, Tolle, Lama Sing, and many others tell us, it is happening. Though perhaps not to the extent yet needed to sustain a total shift in human awareness, an acceleration of consciousness is occurring. Although we are told that, relative to its own level and frequency of enlightenment, an awakened mind is capable of elevating the consciousness of tens of thousands of others, still, the day when reverence for all life comes to replace indifference toward life, when nations will no longer war against one another but join together in ways of peace, seems like an ultimate distant goal. Yet even that extra small degree of "space-consciousness", of freedom from fear thus far realized --- perhaps one percent --- is enough to transform the whole world and make life seem utterly different.

Altogether, then, there seems to be at least an a priori possibility of dodging the bullet of our own fear and insanity bringing about the day of our reckoning. But, **at the same time there brews in that part of the world where the Tabernacle was, the troubles that are the foundations of war and even the release of weapons such as the world has not seen since Sodom and Gomorrah,** warns the Source. **And as the fire consumes the Holy Temple Mount so must the Ark of the Covenant be established again, but in the body of a man.**

Such a "man" referred to is any man or woman who, possessed of a steel-like dedication to the eternal Law of One and having been passed through the purification of selfless sacrifice, has been transformed into the divine embodiment of the Ark of Truth. Untrammeled by convention, moving independently of the ordinary currents of human thought and action, they are to become, we are told, the very expression of God's mercy and love on this Earth. As the acclaimed author and philosopher Jacob Needleman writes, "It is only in and through people, inwardly developed men and women, that God can exist and act in the world of man on earth. Bluntly speaking, the proof for the existence of God is the existence of people who are inhabited by and who manifest God.... God needs not just man, but awakened man, in order to act as God in the human world. Without this conscious energy on the earth it may not be possible for divine justice, mercy, or compassion to enter the lives of human beings."[39] If, as it is said, Love is the key to the mystery of existence and points the way to the Divine, then in it is awakened individuals such as these who will point the way for many others.

However many are called, few will actually respond. While the seed of our reconciliation with God's Law of Love may be planted deep within each of us, how many will actually spare the effort to cultivate it? "The wind of God's grace is always blowing," the Indian saint Vivekananda used to say, "but you must raise your sail." The object now, given what the Source foresees as our present march to Armageddon, is to awaken in at least some the conscious energy needed to become a living temple of truth. For as the smoldering resentments of this far-spreading catastrophe erupt into the flames of active malice and all-out irrational violence, it will be for these apostles of God's Holy Ordinance, those who possess the audacity and courage, to lead a remnant through the conflagration and into the light of a new world. **For there is the building of the Temple of Solomon in the etheric and in the establishment of the School of Prophets of the dawning of a New Day,** declares the Source, **so shall there be built simultaneously a new temple on the Temple Mount:**

> And this will be a troubled time as men attempt to bring together materials of the earth to contain a consciousness so great that it cannot be contained in that temple. And the pillar of fire and smoke as was seen by the Ancients shall be seen as a mushroom cloud... which will reach into and beyond the heavens as man thinks of them. And you must be prepared in that day for the consciousness, and the body must be taken to the place of the dwelling of the body of light. You must lift yourselves to that place that you may live above it. For so many souls on this habitation, this Tabernacle that is this planet must be lifted to a life beyond what can be destroyed by the breaking of this atmosphere as you have known it. You must be ready as Daniel to live in the fire in the Form of the Fourth, and understand that the Form of the Fourth is the Ark of the Covenant, the Ark of the Promise. This you must embody. And in the lifting of the fire through yourself where it burns within you must the spine be made straight. And as you so stand, so shall you be a bearer of the flame of the torch that will lift the consciousness beyond the seven spirals of manifestation on this plane and be prepared for the ascension.

> You must become impassioned with the building of this lifting of knowledge and understanding, this establishment of the wisdom of the prophets, this lifting of Jacob's ladder into the path that is straight, the Thirteenth Path, the middle pillar of the Temple as it rises, and carry with it the fire that is from the bowels of the earth through man, the antennae into the heavenly place where man's consciousness must not be shielded anymore by the shroud of this planet, manifest as the clouds. But so must you be [so] opened to the light that you can stand in the light without that protection. You must move beyond this. [This] Temple [must] form until you are a beam of light that will carry you through the sun to discover its Source. So must this Holy Mother be crowned with the crown of the twelve stars. It must be complete. And the moon which has stood in the shadow must become the footstool of this Holy Planet that was prepared as the bride. And so as the demons have timed, so must the virgins be brought to the feast.

> Then you have a holy purpose, all of you. And it is to lift the consciousness beyond this horizontal plane of the wandering through the wilderness. You must be lifted above it in your thought. And so must the mind become one, not separated from itself. So must the Crown of Enlightenment be re-discovered and re-achieved and placed where it belongs, on the crown of man. And so must the consciousness [have] gone beyond

thinking, processes of comparison, requiring evil to know good, darkness to know light. So must these things become unnecessary so that consciousness is lifted beyond that separation, the veil. So must the veil be rent for all, and Isis unveiled.

It is the moving of this light, the fire through that rod that will lift your consciousness to what it must be, so that all that you discover, all that you see with discrimination, will be joined together with the oath that is the Shema, "the Lord is One." Then may you put on the whole armor of God that you might fight that good fight and finish the race.

[With this] then, the prophets must go out, and healing must occur on all levels throughout this plane until this earth is an altar, and the sacrifice is made and accepted, and the moon will disappear having been absorbed as it were as the footstool, as the mastery of emotion has occurred, the mastery of the body and finally the mastery of the consciousness with its source. This, then, becomes the establishment of the Thirteenth Path, reflecting the lower face of man into the mirror of the lower face of God, reflecting the higher face and carrying man from Foundation through Tiphareth to Kether.

Thus may you prepare a new Twelve, those Twelve who will be hierophants, and the new Twelve who will go forth. And each of them ordaining the Seventy who will go out from them. And these, the five thousand, each. So will you reach around the world. And so then will the stars change in their path and this solar system meet its destiny and go on tobe only a jewel in a crown (Solomon Reading No. 1422, 8/5/90).

"ONE STEP AWAY..."

"The cultural era is past," writes the novelist Henry Miller:

> The new civilization... will not be another civilization --- it will be the open stretch of realization which all the past civilizations have pointed to. The city, which was the birth-place of civilization, such as we know it to be, will exist no more. There will be nuclei of course, but they will be mobile and fluid. The peoples of earth will no longer be shut off from one another within states but will flow freely over the surface of the earth and intermingle. There will be no fixed constellations of human aggregates. Governments will give way to management, using the word in a broad sense. The politician will become as superannuated as the dodo bird. The machine will never be dominated, as some imagine; it will be scrapped, eventually, but not before men have understood the nature of the mystery which binds them to their creation. The worship, investigation and subjugation of the machine will give way to the lure of all that is truly occult. This problem is bound up with the larger one of power --- and of possession. Man will be forced to realize that power must be kept open, fluid and free. His aim will be not to possess power but to radiate it.[40]

We are the bearers of this vision for all mankind. We are the shapers of a new tomorrow. Making a commitment to live in harmony, the Source tells us, an air of quiet inevitability will usher in an age of peace and universal fellowship. Were the creative energies of life to take hold within each of us and join with the vitally active force of love in a holy marriage of will and spirit, then, perhaps, we would see the entire history of humanity, for all its diversity, as Pascal once saw it, as the biography of a single creature --- Man. Failing that, observes the Source, **it will be done with the disruption of life, and there will remain ... only a scattered few of your race upon the earth who will find about them the earth having shaken off an old age, beginning as it were again primeval and growing ... into a dawn of a new history, only sparsely populated. History will be lost and will begin again as if it were from the roots, from the foundation. It will be recorded in future generations as a beginning of time, and the world that existed before that day will for a time be lost to history** (Solomon Reading No. 1282, 3/5/88). Will we extinguish the vision?

If it is too early to ask all men and women to think "universally," to consider themselves as elements of humanity as a whole, to bring about a world finally liberated from the main institutional evils of poverty, war, injustice, and global environmental destruction, the nagging question remains: "Why?" What alternative futures do we face? The future may be beyond our knowing, but as William Irwin Thompson writes, "the present is beyond belief. We make so much noise with technology that we cannot discover that the stargate is in our foreheads. But the time has come; the revelation has already occurred, and the guardian seers have seen the lightning strike the darkness we call reality. And now we sleep in the brief interval between the lightning and the thunder."[41] When the storm has passed what shall we awaken to find? That, perhaps, all our dreams, all our legitimate hopes for a New Eden, a world transformed into a full community of life and love, have infallibly materialized? Or will we awaken to the ruin of the global ecosphere and to a new age of mindless savagery and primordial darkness? Our own critical choices now before us, warns the Source, will determine whether our prophetic future becomes our cataclysmic past:

> Man standing before God in judgment; man standing on the brink of Initiation; man standing as the candidate for becoming new and one with God. You stand one step away from the throne of righteousness. Yet standing one step away from the Judgment Bar of God, the throne of His Presence, man never stood so close to the steps of hell. For one choice, one selfish choice, will remove all that is the glory of God. The eye must be single. The purpose must not be for adventure, for self in any way, but singly focused upon becoming one with God. The purpose must be a single setting apart to become one with all that God is.... The Plan, then, is one of preparing in these last days to separate the self from all that is of lesser consciousness, focusing the mind and the eye on these qualities that will last through eternity, and wanting nothing else, accepting only that, until all become that (Solomon Reading No. 854, 7/23/76).

NOTES

Chapter 1

(This chapter contains ideas originally conceived by Huston Smith and presented as "The Incredible Truth" in *Beyond the Post-Modern Mind*, Wheaton, Ill: Theosophical Publishing House, 1989.)

1. Fred Hoyle, *The Nature of the Universe* (New York: New American Library, 1950), p. 120.
2. David Bohm, quoted in *The Holographic Paradigm*, ed. Ken Wilbur (Boulder CO: Shambala Publications, Inc., 1982), pp. 56-57.
3. Robert Zastrow, *God and the Astronomers* (New York: W.W. Norton and Co., 1978), p.116
4. Jacob Needleman, *A Sense of the Cosmos* (New York: E.P. Dutton and Co., 1965), pp 18-19.
5. Rig Veda, quoted in *Oriental Philosophies*, John M. Kolber, ed. (New York: Scribner's Sons, 1985).
6. *Parabola*, Vol. VI, No 1, p. 44.
7. Eckhart, quoted in Aldous Huxley, *The Perennial Philosophy* (Cleveland, Oh: The World Publishing Co., 1962).
8. Plotinus, quoted in *Ibid.*, p.5.
9. Pfeiffer, F., cap. Ix, (1855), pp. 32,33. Quoted in Agnes Arber, *The Manifold and the One* (Wheaton, Ill: The Theosophical Publishing House, 1967), p. 4.
10. Guillaumont, P. (trans.), *The Gospel According to Thomas* (New York: Harper and Row, 1959).
11. Mircea Eliade, quoted in Norman Friedman, *Bridging Science and Spirit* (St. Louis, MO: Living Lake Books, 1994), p. 167.

Chapter 2

12. Quoted in Alan Watts, *Cloud-Hidden* (New York: Vintage Books, 1974), pp. 91-92.
13. Fritjof Capra, *The Tao of Physics* (Berkeley, CA: Shambala, 1975), p. 11.
14. Edward Tyron, "Is the Universe a Vacuum Fluctuation?" *Nature*, no. 246, 1973, pp. 396-397.
15. Huston Smith, *Forgotten Truth* (New York: Harper and Row, 1976), p.49.
16. David Bohm and David F. Peat, *Science, Order, and Creativity* (New York: Bantam Books, 1987), p. 183.
17. David Bohm, quoted in Renee Weber, *Dialogues with Scientists and Sages* (London: Arkana, 1990), p. 41.
18. *Ibid.*, p. 51.
19. *Ibid.*, p. 48.
20. *Ibid.*, p. 46.
21. *Ibid.*, p. 45.
22. Chandogya Upanishad, vi., 13, Trans. Juan Mascaro.
23. Lama Govinda, quoted in Ken Wilbur, *The Spectrum of Consciousness* (Wheaton, Ill: Theosophical Publishing House, 1977), p. 16.
24. Walter Sullivan, "Smallest of the Small," *New York Times*, February 5, 1967.
25. Arthur Young, *Which Way Out?* (Berkeley: Robert Briggs Associates, 1980), p. 2.
26. David Bohm, *Wholeness and the Implicate Order* (New York: Routledge, 1980), pp. 190-191
27. Houston Smith, *Beyond the Post-Modern Mind*, op.cit., p. 60.
28. Bohm and Peat, *Science, Order, and Creativity*, op.cit., p. 183.
29. Ken Wilbur, quoted in *The Holographic Paradigm*, op.cit., p. 266.
30. Jack Sarfatti, "Implications of Meta-Physics for Psychoenergetic Systems," *Psychoenergetic Systems*, Vol. 1, 1974.

31. Max Planck, quoted in Brian O'Leary, *Miracle in the Void* (Kihei, Hawaii: Kamapua's Press, 1996), p. 141.

32. St. Thomas, *Summa Contra Gentiles*, I. xiv.

33. Excerpted from Paul Solomon Public Lecture.

34. June Singer, *Androgyny* (New York: Anchor Books, 1977), p. 239.

35. Fred Alan Wolf, *The Eagle's Quest* (New York: Simon and Schuster, 1991), p. 123.

36. William A. Tiller, quoted in Peter Thompkins and Christopher Bird, *The Secret Life of Plants* (New York: Avon Books, 1973), p. 223.

37. Peter Thompkins, *Ibid.*, p. 219.

38. David Bohm, quoted in Weber, op.cit., p. 32.

39. Steven Weinberg, *The First Three Minutes* (New York: Basic Books, 1977), p. 80.

40. Theodore Roszak, *The Voice of the Earth* (New York: Simon and Schuster, 1992), p. 116.

41. Jacques Monad, *Chance and Necessity*, trans. Austyn Wainhouse (New York: A.A. Knopf, 1971), pp. 170, 172.

42. Radhakrishnan, *An Idealist View of Life* (London: Unwin Books, 1961), pp. 272-273.

Chapter 3

43. Richard Maurice Bucke, *Cosmic Consciousness* (New York: E.P. Dutton, 1969), pp. 326-327.

44. R. M. Bucke, quoted in William James, *The Varieties of Religious Experience* (New York: New American Library, 1958), pp. 306-307.

45. Kenneth Ring, *Heading Toward Omega* (New York: William Morrow and Co., 1985), pp. 65-66.

46. *Ibid.*, p. 88.

47. *Ibid.*, p. 127.

48. *Ibid.*, pp. 265-266.

49. *Meister Eckhart: A Modern Translation*, R. B., Blakney (New York and London: 1941), Sermon 18 and Sermon 22.

50. David Bohm, quoted in Weber, op.cit., p. 41.

51. Erwin Schrodinger, *What is Life? And Mind and Matter* (London: Cambridge Univ. Press, 1969), p. 145.

52. *Ibid.*, pp. 31-34.

53. *Ibid.*

54. Alan Watts, *Beyond Theology* (New York: Vintage Books, 1964), p. 222.

55. James Dickey, Introduction to Stanley Burnshaw, *The Seamless Web* (New York: George Braziller, Inc., 1991), p. X.

56. "Paul Solomon Speaks," *Human Potential*, Autumn, 1991, p. 15.

57. Edgar Cayce Reading No. 5755-2. Quoted in Eula Allen, *You Are Forever* (Virginia Beach, VA: A.R.E. Press, 1966), p. ii.

58. Sir Arthur Eddington, quoted in Theodore Roszak, *Where the Wasteland Ends* (New York: Doubleday and Co., 1972), p. 164.

59. Teilhard de Chardin, quoted in Weber, op.cit., p. 127.

Chapter 4

1. Wilbur G. Burroughs, "Human-Like Footprints, 250 Million Years Old," in *The Berea Alumnus* (November, 1938), pp. 46-47. Quoted in Michael A. Cremo and Richard L. Thompson, *The Hidden History of the Human Race* (Los Angeles: Bhaktivendanta Publishing, Inc. 1996), pp. 150-151.

2. Quoted in Cremo, Ibid., pp. 45-46.

3. Ibid., p. 29.

4. Ibid., pp. 143-145.

5. Plato, *Timaeus and Critias*, Penguin Classics, 1977, p.36.

6. *American Journal of Science*, Vol. I, No. 19, p. 361.

7. Crèmo, op.cit., p. 109.

8. Ibid., pp. 110-112.

9. *Los Angeles News*, Dec. 17, 1869

Chapter 5

10. David Bohm and F. David Peat, *Science, Order, and Creativity* (New York: Bantam Books, 1987), p. 201.

11. Eula Allen, *Before the Beginning* (Virginia Beach, VA: A.R.E. Press, 1966), p.55

Chapter 6

12. Paul G. Zolbrod, *Dine Bahane: The Navajo Creation Story* (Albuquerque, N M,: University of New Mexico Press, 1984), p. 36.

13. Mircea Eliade, *The Two and The One* (New York: Harper and Row, 1965), p. 43.

14. Quoted in Arthur Lovejoy and George Boas, *Primitivism and Related Idea in Antiquity* (Baltimore: John Hopkins Press, 1935), p. 437.

15. Eliade, op.cit., p. 30.

16. Elizabeth Gould Davis, *The First Sex* (New York: G.P. Putnam's Sons, 1971), pp. 63-64.

17. *Mahabharata*, Santiparvan, Moksadharma, 231, 23ff., trans. in Donald A. MacKenzie, *Indian Myth and Legend* (London: Greshem, N. D.), pp. 107-108.

18. Venidad, Far. II, 3-41. Quoted in S.G.F. Brandon, *Creation Legends of the Ancient Near East* (London: Hodder and Stoughton, 1963), p. 48.

19. Chuang Tzu, in Wm. Theodore de Bary, et. al., eds., *Sources of Chinese Tradition* (New York: Columbia Univ. Press, 1960), p. 70.

20. Tao Te Ching, quoted in Alan Watts, *Psychotherapy East and West* (New York: Ballantine Books, Inc., 1961), p. 46.

21. Arthur Lovejoy and George Boas, *Primitivism and Related Ideas in Antiquity* (Baltimore: John Hopkins Press, 1935), pp. 148-149.

22. Abraham Joshua Heschel, *The Insecurity of Freedom* (New York: Farrar, Straus, Giroux, 1967), p. 165.

Chapter 7

23. From the apocryphal *Books of Adam and Eve* (c. 200 B.C.), quoted in Rutherford Platt, Jr., ed. *The Forgotten Books of Eden* (New York: Bell, 1980), pp. 6-7.

24. *The Gospel of Thomas* (II,2), quoted in *The Nag Hammadi Library*, ed. James M. Robinson (San Francisco: Harper and Row, 1977), p. 121.

25. Eckhart, quoted in Aldous Huxley, *The Perennial Philosophy* (New York: The World Publishing Co., 1945), p. 39.

26. Professor Arthur Posnansky, Tiahuanacu: *The Cradle of American Man*, Vol. II, p. 91, and Vol. I, p. 38. Referred to in Graham Hancock, *Fingerprints of the Gods* (New York: Crown Publishers, 1995), pp. 65-66.

27. Hesiod, *Theogony* (trans. Evelyn-White, 1914), 11.693 ff.

28. H. S. Bellamy, *Moons, Myths and Man* (1938), p. 227.

29. *The Shu King, the Canon of Yao* (trans. Legge, 1879).

30. Leonne de Cambrey, *Lapland Legends* (1926).

31. *The Egyptian Book of the Dead*, quoted in Wallis E. A. Budge, *From Fetish to God in Ancient Egypt* (Oxford University Press, 1934), p. 198.

32. Plato, *Timaeus* 256-d, trans. Benjamin Jowett. Quoted in *Plato, the Collected Dialogues*, ed.

Edith Hamilton and Huntington Cairns (Princeton Univ. Press, 1961), pp. 1159-1160.

33. Plato, *Timaeus*, trans. A.E. Taylor. Quoted in *Plato, the Collected Dialogues*, ed. Edith Hamilton and Huntington Cairns (Princeton Univ. Press, 1961), p. 1224.

34. *Shoo-King, The Canon of Yaou*, trans. James Legge, Vol. III, Pt I of *The Chinese Classics* (Hong Kong, 1865).

35. *Midrash Haggadol*, ed. Schechter (Cambridge: 1902), p. 19.

36. Abraham Joshua Heschel, *Man's Quest for God* (New York: Charles Scribner's Sons, 1954), p. 62.

37. *Midrash Haggadol*, op.cit.

Chapter 8

38. Raymond Bernard Blakney, *Meister Eckhart: A Modern Translation* (Harper Torchbooks, New York, 1957), pp. 203 ff.

39. Richard Maurice Bucke, *Cosmic Consciousness* (New York: E.P. Dutton and Co., Inc., 1969), p. 384.

40. Teilhard De Chardin, *The Phenomenon of Man* (New York:Harper and Row, 1965).

41. D. H. Lawrence, quoted in *Unknown Man*, Yatre (New York: Simon and Schuster, 1988), p. 242n.

42. Henry Miller, *The Wisdom of the Heart*, quoted in *The Aquarian Conspiracy* by Marilyn Ferguson (London: Paladin, 1982), p. 53.

43. De Principiis, I, vi. 1-4, in *The Writings of Origen*, trans. Frederick Crombie (Edinburgh, 1869), pp. 53-59.

Chapter 9

1. Hesiod incorporates a fifth age, the "Age of Heroes" in his account, which, because it is not included in any of the earlier Greek descriptions of the ages of the world from which he drew inspiration, is omitted here.

2. Juares. Quoted in Louis Pauwels and Jacques Bergier, *The Morning of the Magicians* (New York, Avon Books, 1960), p. 326.

3. Estimates provided by the UN Food and Agriculture Organization report, 2015.

Chapter 10

4. Paul Valery. Quoted in Richard A. Falk, *This Endangered Planet* (New York: Vintage Books, 1972), p. 37.

5. Philo, *Moses*, II, x, 53. Quoted in Immanuel Velikovsky, *Worlds in Collision* (New York: Pocket Books, Inc., 1977), pp. 49-50.

6. Censorinus, *Liber de die natali*, xviii.

7. Plato, Timaeus, Trans., Benjamin Jowett. Quoted in *The Collected Dialogues of Plato*, eds. Hamilton and Cairns (Princeton, New Jersey: Princeton Univ. Press, 1963), pp. 1157 - 1158.

8. C. E. Brasseur de Bourbourg, *Histoire des nations civilisees du Mexique* (1857-1859), I, p. 53

9. Nathan Koenig, Louis Acker, and Michael Cornett. Quoted in Mark A. Thurston, *Visions and Prophecies for a New Age* (Virginia Beach, VA: A.R.E. Press, 1981), p. 30.

10. Tom Tarbet, "The Essence of Hopi Prophecy", *East West Journal* (October, 1977), p. 37.

11. Rabbi Nahman of Bratslav, quoted in Abraham Joshua Heschel, *The Insecurity of Freedom* (New York: Noonday Press, 1967), p. 127.

Chapter 11

12. Thomas W. Petrisko, *Call of the Ages* (Santa Barbara, CA: Queenship Publishing Co., 1995), p. 109.

13. *The Final Hour*, op.cit., p. 196.

14. *Call of the Ages*, op.cit. P. 109

15. *Ibid.*, p. 68

16. *Ibid.*, p. 10.

17. *Ibid.*, p. 11.

18. *Ibid.*

19. *Ibid.*, p. 103.

20. Thomas W. Petrisko, *The Fatima Prophecies* (McKees Rocks, PA: St. Andrew's Productions, 1998), p. 258.

21. *The Final Hour*, op.cit., p. 176.

22. *The Thunder of Justice*, op.cit., p. 160.

23. *Ibid.*, p. 162.

24. *Call of the Ages*, op.cit., p. 416.

25. *The Thunder of Justice*, op.cit., p. 148.

26. Albert J. Hebert, S.M., *The Three Days of Darkness* (Pauline, LA: P.O. Box 309, 1996), p.

27. *The Thunder of Justice*, op.cit., p. 342.

28. *Ibid.*, p. 148-149

29. *Ibid.*, p. 104

30. *Ibid.*, p. 49.

31. *Call of the Ages,* op.cit., p. 366.

32. *The Thunder of Justice*, op.cit., p. 342.

33. *Call of the Ages,* op.cit., p. 462

34. *Ibid.*, pp. 466-467

Chapter 12

35. Lewis Mumford, *The Conduct of Life* (New York: Harcourt, Brace and Co., 1951), p. 18.

36. Lewis Mumford, *The Conduct of Life* (New York: Harcourt, Brace and Company, 1951), pp. 119-120.

37. Jonathan Schell, *The Fate of the Earth* (New York:Alfred A. Knopf., 1982), p.231.

38. Charlene Spretnak, *States of Grace* (New York: Harper Collins Publishers, 1991) p. 78.

Chapter 13

1. Paul Solomon, *The Wisdom of Solomon*, compiled and edited by Grace de Rond, (self-published, 2010), p. 199.

2. Jacob Bronowski. *The Ascent of Man* (Little, Brown and Company, Boston, 1973), p. 374.

3. Paul Solomon. *The Wisdom of Solomon*, compiled and edited by Grace de Rond, (self-published, 2010), p. 239-240.

4. *Ibid.*, pp. 265-266.

5. Theodore Roszak, *The Voice of the Earth* (Simon and Schuster, New York, 1992), p. 40.

6. *The Wisdom of Solomon*, op.cit., pp. 265-267.

7. Ephesian 6:12 (A.V.).

8. *The Wisdom of Solomon*, op.cit., pp. 264-265.

9. *Ibid.,* pp. 261-261.

10. *Ibid.,* p. 241.

11. *Ibid.,* p. 262.

12. *Ibid.,* p. 241.

13. *Ibid.,* p. 263.

14. *Ibid.,* p. 299.

15. *Ibid.,* p. 242.

16. *The Wisdom of Paul Solomon*, op.cit., pp. 255-259.

Chapter 14

17. Idres Shah, *Tales of the Dervishes* (New York: E. P. Dutton, 1970), pp. 23-24.
18. *Ibid.,* p. 169.
19. Joseph Chilton Pearce, *The Magical Child* (New York: Bantam, 1980), p. 148.
20. *Ibid.,* p. 151.
21. J. R. Smythies, *Analysis of Perception* (New York: Humanities Press, 1956).
22. Pearce, op.cit., pp. 158-159.
23. Benjamin Lee Whorf, *Language, Thought, and Reality* (New York: John Wiley and Sons, 1956), pp. 213-214.
24. David Bohm, Quoted in Renee Weber, "The Enfolding-Unfolding Universe: A conversation with David Bohm", in *The Holographic Paradigm*, ed. Ken Wilbur (Boston: Shambala, 1982), p. 68.
25. *The Wisdom of Solomon*, op.cit., p. 169.
26. *Ibid.,* pp. 242-245.
27. *Ibid.,* pp. 259-251.
28. *Ibid.,* pp. 253-254.
29. *Ibid.,* pp. 246-247.
30. *Ibid.,* pp. 258-259.
31. *Ibid.,* p. 329.
32. "An Interview with Paul Solomon", in *The Movement Newspaper*, February, 1982.

Chapter 15

33. Martin Buber, *Tales of the Hasidim, Later Masters* (New York: Schocken Books, 1948), p. 259.
34. *The Wisdom of Solomon*, op.cit., pp. 29-31.
35. Aldous Huxley, *Collected Essays* (New York: Bantam Books, Inc., 1960), pp. 380-381.

Chapter 16

36. Marcus Aurelius, *Meditations*, vii, 1,6.
37. Kabir, ii, 320 (Sikhism). Quoted in Aldous Huxley, *The Perennial Philosophy* (New York: Harper Colophon Books, 1945), p. 2.
38. Aldous Huxley, *The Doors of Perception,* in *Collected Essays* (New York: Bantam, 1960), p. 329.
39. Philip Kapleau, *The Three Pillars of Zen* (Boston: Beacon Press, 1967), pp. 267-268.

Chapter 17

40. *Ibid.,* pp. 174-175.
41. Mircea Eliade, *The Forbidden Forest*, trans. MacLinscott Ricketts and Mary Park Stevenson (Notre Dame, IN: University of Notre Dame Press, 1978), p. 304.
42. Victor Hugo, quoted in Pauwels and Bergier. *The Morning of the Magicians* (New York: Avon Books, 1960), p. 314.

Chapter 18

1. Louis Pauwels and Jacques Bergier, *The Morning of the Magicians* (New York: Avon Books, 1960). P. 341.
2. Frank Waters, *Book of the Hopi* (New York: Penguin Books, 1977).

3. I.F. Stone, *New York Review of Books*, Aug. 3, 1967.

4. Anwar El-Sadat, *In Search of Identity* (New York: Harper & Row, 1979), p. 337.

5. Sari Nusseibeh and Shimon Perez are quoted from Michael Parks, *Los Angeles Times*, in *Saint Paul Pioneer Press*, Sunday, October 10, 1993. P. 14A.

6. Nassar Eddin Nashashibi, Rabbi David Hartman, Rabbi Jonathan Blass, and Adnan Husseini, *Ibid.*

7. William Irwin Thompson, *The Time Falling Bodies Take to Light* (New York: St. Martin's Press, 1981), p. 15.

8. Quoted in Ted Flynn, *The Thunder of Justice* (Sterling, VA: Max Kol Communications, 1993), p. 260.

9. *Ibid*, p. 261.

10. Quoted in Yves Dupont, *Catholic Quarterly* (Rockford, Ill: TanBooks and Publishers, 1973) p. 23.

11. *Ibid.*

12. Quoted in Michael H. Brown, *The Final Hour* (Milford, OH:Faith Publishing Co., 1992) p. 156.

13. Flynn, *The Thunder of Justice*, op.cit., pp. 262-263.

14. Ibid. p. 111.

15. Leo Heiman, "A Boy 3,000 Years Old?" *Fate*, January, 1969, pp. 32-43.

16. Quoted in *Ibid.*

17. From an unpublished manuscript by David Solomon, and shared with the author.

18. Mary Ellen Carter, *Edgar Cayce on Prophecy* (New York: Warner Books, 1968), pp. 104-108.

Chapter 19

19. Martin Buber, *Tales of the Hasidism: The Later Masters* (New York: Schocken Books, Inc., 1948), p. 52.

20. *The Wisdom of Solomon*, op.cit., pp. 247-248

21. Rupert Sheldrake, *Morphic Resonance: The Nature of Formative Causation* (Rochester, Vermont: Park Street Press, 1995).

22. *Sunday Express*, (London) 7 September, 1969, p. 21.

23. *The Wisdom of Solomon*, op.cit., pp. 37-40.

24. Dionysius the Areopagite, *The Divine Names and the Mystical Theology* (London: S.P.C.K., 1971), p.191.

25. Paul Solomon, *The Wisdom of Paul Solomon*, ed. by Grace DeRond, op.cit., pp. 193-213.

26. *The Wisdom of Paul Solomon*, op.cit., pp. 42-43.

Chapter 20

27. George B. Leonard, *The Transformation* (New York: Delacorte Press, 1972), pp. 159-160.

28. Dan Simon, http://www.cnn.com/2017/06/19/us/tri-faith-initiative-omaha-nebraska/index.html

29. Quoted in: Yatri, *Unknown Man* (New York: Simon and Schuster, Inc., 1988), p. 11.

30. Https://www.eckharttolle.com/article/awakening-your-spiritual-lifes-purpose

31. http://www.lamasing.org/posted-may-19-16-not-the-thinning-of-the-veils/

32. www.lamasing.org/readings/

33. http://www.lamasing.org/posted-apr-2-16-2?

34. Eckhart Tolle, Ibid.

35. http://www/lamasing.org/message-from-Lama-Sing/?ct=t(New-world12-18-2016)

36. Lewis Mumford, *The Conduct of Life* (New York: Harcourt, Brace and Company, 1951), p.120.

37. Elie Wiesel, *Souls on Fire* (New York: Random House, Inc., 1972), pp. 51-52.

38. Lewis Mumford, op.cit., p.115.

39. http://thesunmagazine.org/issues/432/beyond-belief

40. Henry Miller, *Sunday After the War* (New York: New Directions, 1944), pp. 154-155.

41. William Irwin Thompson, *At the Edge of History* (New York: Harper and Row, Publishers, 1971), p. 230.

Made in the USA
Las Vegas, NV
25 November 2020